JEREMY MORRIS is an Anglica⌟ Hall, Cambridge, until 2021. In Award for Education and Sc Canterbury. Since 1992, he has published eight books and many articles on church history and modern theology.

A PEOPLE'S CHURCH

A History of the Church of England

JEREMY MORRIS

PROFILE BOOKS

This paperback edition first published in 2023

First published in Great Britain in 2022 by
Profile Books Ltd
29 Cloth Fair
London
ECIA 7JQ

www.profilebooks.com

1 3 5 7 9 10 8 6 4 2

Typeset in Dante by MacGuru Ltd
Printed and bound in Great Britain by
CPI Group (UK) Ltd, Croydon CRO 4YY

A CIP catalogue record for this book is available from the British Library.

ISBN 978 1 78125 250 5
eISBN 978 1 78283 053 5

Contents

PREFACE: THE REAL HISTORY OF
THE CHURCH OF ENGLAND

'Enormous simplifications were possibly necessary to carry
a deeper truth than lay on the surface of a mass of unsorted
detail. That was, after all, what happened when history was
written; many, if not most, of the true facts discarded.'
                    Anthony Powell, *Temporary Kings* (1973)[1]

The church of St Peter and St Paul, Chaldon, lies at the end
of a long lane snaking along a ridge of the North Downs, just
beyond the outer limits of the London suburbs. Begun some
time before the Norman Conquest, it is a small, concentrated
bundle of different spaces reflecting different periods of church
architecture. Even today, when on fine days the downs will be
teeming with people walking their dogs, playing with their children or simply out for a stroll, the church seems somehow a
step beyond settled human community. To enter it is to enter
a remote, silent world, and to be confronted by a shocking
reminder of a different age and different values. For Chaldon
is best known for its 'doom' painting, a sole survivor of what
was once a multi-coloured interior. Painted late in the twelfth
century, on the west wall rather than above the chancel arch, as
would have been typical of later, conventional doom pictures,
its vivid colours have faded to a muddy cream on a red brick
background. Like many medieval wall paintings it owes its survival now to overpainting with whitewash at the Reformation,
and the careful uncovering and retouching by a gifted amateur
in the nineteenth century.

It is not the very existence of this painting that is shocking, but the sharpness and brutality of its division between the saved and the damned, and the complexity of its theological vision. Covering most of the west wall, it is bisected vertically by the ladder of salvation, and horizontally by a thick line dividing the blessed above, and the damned below. Below the line, devils torment figures representing the seven deadly sins, as souls tumble from the ladder into the fires below. Above the line, the saved are ministered to by angels, as Christ is figured spearing a prostrate Satan. It is hard enough, in the twenty-first century, to imagine how anyone can have thought that such a vision of the human condition would not have stirred deep revulsion in the minds of those who saw it, entering the church all those centuries ago when it was first painted. It is harder still to conceive of a mental and spiritual world view so vivid and sharp in its contrast of light and darkness, of good and evil, which was yet almost universally accepted at the time as the world of meaning within which all important decisions in life had to be constructed.

It would be easy to think that somehow this world view was inflicted on an unwilling population, or manipulated as a mechanism of fear and control by a self-contained clerical elite, but that would be to adopt a thoroughly modern prejudice to analyse the beliefs of our ancestors. For those – and they are of course many now – who have little or no affiliation with formal religious belief, often their understanding of Christianity is shaped by a narrative that sees the Church as dedicated to promoting intolerance and sexual repression or control, with a dark history of covering up abuse and colluding in violence. That this has been the case at times in the past is undeniable. But the particular shape in which this narrative is cast today is a modern phenomenon, taking its lead from the assumption that religion, and the institutions which promote it, are at best simply one small subset of the whole spectrum of human ideas and activity, having little to do with knowledge of the material world, and badly placed if allowed to lay claim to anything outside the realm of private, 'inner' or individual spiritual thoughts.

For most of the history of Britain, this would have been a very peculiar way to see the world. Until perhaps the mid- or late-nineteenth century – though for many a good deal later – there was little sense in which religion was simply an additional or optional feature of life, a sort of 'and' tacked on to whatever account one might give of the material conditions in which lives were lived. This is not to say that you find, in the past, people doing nothing but talk about religion. But it was none the less so bound into their culture, values and beliefs that it would have made little sense for them to see it as anything other than the overarching framework in which they interpreted the world. It formed, then, something like a sort of 'common sense' that lurked in the background of all of the decisions they had to make, the experiences they had, and the encounters that one way or another affected their lives. Biblical scholars sometimes speak of the *Sitz im Leben* of particular Biblical texts, that is, the life context in which specific teachings are expounded, and on which they depend. In a sense, that is precisely how we have to see the history of religion: it is not separable from the rest of human society, but woven in and through it.

To understand the past, then, and the history of religion, a considerable leap of imagination is required. We cannot assume that the Church today is what it was in the eighteenth century, or in the sixteenth century, let alone in the eleventh. Trying to tell the history of a single institution, the Church of England, in the short compass of a single book is a very tall order, and it really requires a constant attention to broader historical themes and trends – the changing *Sitz im Leben* – that help to shape and give form to the particular modes in which religious ideas and practices are expressed.

So the history of the Church of England cannot be told as if it was a tale of attenuation – as if one can start from what the Church was say five centuries ago, and assume that it is simply much the same now, but reduced in following to a small minority of the population. What it was then, in itself, is not the same as it is now, just as people's expectations of it, and their ideas about it, have changed dramatically since then. It is important to emphasise this from the outset, because believers and non-believers alike often collude in seeing the Church as unchanging: believers, because they like to stress the continuity of tradition over time, and it is tempting then to gloss over the massive changes that have occurred not only in society as a whole, but also internally, in what the Church is and believes; and non-believers, because it is convenient and easy to suppose that the Church that burned heretics at the stake is really the same institution underneath as the Church that runs food banks in the inner city today. Both views are essentially historical nonsense.

But there are continuities, none the less. When Chaldon was built, the community it served was tiny, poor – these downland parishes were almost all poor right up until the arrival of the railways – and far from higher ecclesiastical jurisdiction, its bishop sixty miles away in Winchester and the roads dreadful. For centuries, then, this tiny church must have seemed remote from the centre of power. And yet here it is today, still used for worship. Every Sunday, a small congregation assembles here, twice in the morning. At the Reformation, the old Latin rite was discarded and the English rite of the *Book of Common Prayer* (*BCP*) adopted. Despite all the vicissitudes of English religious history, up until recent times Chaldon church simply reflected the standard worship expected in the Church of England. Then, like many parish churches, within the last half century it has had to face a difficult choice over the style and content of its worship, and so over whether or not it should hold to the traditional services of the *BCP* or adopt more modern alternatives. Like many churches, it has compromised – early morning *BCP*, with the traditional language addressing God as 'Thou', or, later in the morning, modern English language, with the hope that families will join in.

The change of language – from the sixteenth century to the twenty-first century – implies a change in theological perspective, at least on the part of the institution as a whole. And this is crucial. How the Church worships determines, or signals, what it actually believes. Those who adhere to the traditional language of the *BCP*, using the old forms of worship for communion, or perhaps for morning or evening prayer, are expressing their most fundamental beliefs about the world – its making, its purpose, its guidance under God – in terms our sixteenth-century forebears would have recognised. Those who abandon those forms for modern language services almost invariably are accepting intrinsically modern ways of seeing these things. Of course, individual believers do not necessarily see it that way themselves. They bring to every act of worship a whole bundle of values and preconceptions which may or may not find appropriate expression in the rite. But the rite itself captures and articulates certain ideas.

Let us take just one, simple example. In the *BCP* service of Holy Communion there are several points – not just one – at which the believer throws himself or herself on the mercy of God. The strongest of these is the confession, in which we affirm that the remembrance of our sins is 'grievous unto us' and the burden of them 'is intolerable'. This is strong, forthright language which, however, has almost completely disappeared from the modern rite, where we say (am I wrong to think this is couched in almost glib terms?), 'We are heartily sorry and repent of all our sins.' There is something perfunctory, transitory and lacking in weight about *that* formula. And what it expresses, arguably, is a thoroughly modern awareness of the relative lightness of sins which, as we now know, all too often are almost forced on us by our nature, our genetics, our biological destiny, our upbringing and our life situations. We can apologise for these things, but they are not catastrophic – intolerable – as they were for our forebears.

Chaldon is just one of well over 10,000 parish churches, dating back to the medieval period, which make up the Church of England. More than most, perhaps, thinking about it sharpens up the journey we have to make, in our imaginations, from the world view of the Middle Ages to now. And yet here this little parish church is, still just one tiny part of an institution that can, with some justification, claim to have tried to serve the English nation for over a thousand years.

The story of the Church of England as we know it now is the subject of this book. It is a story often told through great figures, mostly men: the archbishops and bishops who led it; the thinkers who shaped its worship and ideas; the monarchs and politicians who influenced, manipulated, controlled and abused it; the architects and artists who built and adorned its churches; and the nobles and gentry who promoted and funded it. The story cannot be told well without them. And yet there is so much more to be said. The history of the Church of England is in a sense the history of the people of England, women and men, who for generations attended its services and made use of its pastoral provision. And since its history is also a divided and divisive history, those people who were thrown out by it, or who rejected it themselves, are also part of its history. In that sense, to tell the story of the Church of England is to tell the story of a people's Church, a Church that, at its inception in the sixteenth century as a 'national Church' freed from Papal jurisdiction, was practically coterminous with all the people of England, and which for centuries afterwards, even as that vision failed, conceived of itself none the less as the Church for *all* the English people, whether they liked it or not.

That, I hope, will go some way to explaining the approach I have adopted here, which is not only to summarise and update what will be, for some readers, a relatively familiar story, but to try to explain – even if I can only do it through the briefest of hints at times – just what this Church of England meant to successive generations of inhabitants. This is, then, I hope, a history not just of monarchs, bishops, books and ideas, but of lived experience, of Christianity encountered, shared and criticised by the very people who were the mission objects of the great. In practical terms, with a focus on the Church as it is now, I have had to leave to one side the story of overseas and imperial Anglicanism. I am all too conscious of that omission, but to include them would have demanded an altogether different book – and anyway there are other books, including the recent 5-volume *Oxford History of Anglicanism*, which do that superbly. I have included Wales, since it was an intrinsic part of the Church of England until the early twentieth century; but, consistent with my overall approach, I have not written about the Church in Wales since 1920.

One other controversial point is worth noting here. When did the Church of England begin? For centuries, this is a question that has divided Catholics and Anglicans. The breach with Rome in 1534 set the Church of England apart from much of Western Christianity, and put it on a different theological trajectory from Rome. Not only theology, but also fundamental aspects of local ecclesial culture disappeared or were dramatically changed in the sixteenth century. Above all, those who resisted the changes – traditionalists – eventually came to the conviction that the Church of England was not part of the universal Church, but an apostate or schismatic church; real continuity lay with Rome.

As an Anglican priest, and a somewhat renegade Anglo-Catholic at that, my sympathies are with those who prize continuity with the medieval Church. But there are practical reasons for beginning the narrative in the sixteenth century. The international, integrated nature of medieval Christendom makes it difficult to give a good account of the English Church without keeping an eye constantly on Continental developments. A generous interpretation of the Middle Ages posits nearly a millennium from Augustine's mission in the sixth century to Cardinal Wolsey's fall on the eve of the English Reformation: that is a very long time to cover adequately in a single volume. Even though just the five hundred years from Henry VIII up to the present day have seen dramatic and far-reaching changes in the Church of England, aspects of its theology and practice established at the Reformation have remained consistent: tolerance of clerical marriage, and its corollary, non-compulsory celibacy; worship in the vernacular; aspects of the relationship with the monarch and with Parliament; other aspects of local parish law, to name but a few. These things do not by themselves define what it means to be the Anglican Church today, but they do point to the preservation over time of an ecclesial body that in important respects defines itself differently from the medieval Church. So I have taken that road, but with the addition of an outline chapter showing how important elements of the Church of England's identity and organisation were laid down in the medieval period, and persist up to the present. This will seem a fudge to some people, but I think it is defensible.

Finally, I am conscious that writing Church history almost inevitably invites speculation about the prejudices and commitments of the author. I do not want to hide mine, but I also do not want to give the impression that what I am presenting here is just another attempt at an Anglican apologetic. Above everything, I want to present a coherent narrative that explains how the Church of England has come to be as it is, whatever its weaknesses as well as its strengths. Calling it a 'people's church' is not meant to lay claim to a position of assumed superiority denied to other Christian traditions, but just to highlight how the assumption that the Church of England is the Church *for* England, and for the people of England, has been central to much of its history, and at the same time a measure of how it has changed and, to an extent, failed.

This history ought to be one that non-believers can enjoy as much as believers. That, at least, is my hope. If there is an underlying conviction, nevertheless, it is not specifically a religious one, but rather a conviction borne out of history itself, and the study of history, that the relative decline of mainstream Christianity, and Christian practice, in our own time should not blind us to the impossibility of understanding the history of England and its people aright without attending to the history of their religion.

There are many thanks I ought to record, and I cannot possibly include all those I should here. But I am particularly grateful to the late John Davey, the Profile commissioning editor who first approached me about this, and to Andrew Franklin for taking up the baton when John died. My thanks also go to the excellent team at Profile with whom I've worked, including Penny Daniel, for going above and beyond. I am also grateful to the Provost and Fellows of King's College, Cambridge, and the Fellows of Trinity Hall, Cambridge, for stimulation and appropriate goading over the years. Personal thanks must go to Andrew Arthur, the late James Atwell, Paul Avis, Franco Basso, Zoe Bennett, Stephen Conway, Adrian Daffern, David Erdos, Cally Hammond, Alex Hughes, Jamie Hawkey, Alison Hennegan, Tim Jenkins, Heather Kilpatrick, Alex Marr, Peter McEnhill, Charlotte Methuen, Rob Mackley, George Newlands, Bridget Nichols, John Pollard, Claire Potter (née Taylor), Richard Rex, Nick Sagovsky, Jan Schramm, Peter Sedgwick, Rowan Strong (and remembering Gill, too), Peter Waddell and Rowan Williams, for help with particular points or encouragement in difficult times. I owe a different kind of debt to the Friday congregation at St Edward's, and to Little St Mary's. And above all my family – Alex, Isobel, William and Ursula, and my father, without whom …

Biblical quotations are, as much as possible, taken from the English versions that were current at the time of use; that means, mostly, the Authorised Version, or King James Version, first published in 1611.

PRELUDE: CATHOLIC CENTURIES

When and how did the Church of England begin? Was it in the reign of Henry VIII, at his will and catalysed by his desire for a divorce from Catherine of Aragon? This book has conveniently followed that view. But Henry himself, and his advisers, were at pains to suggest nothing of the kind. The Act of Supremacy, passed by Parliament under heavy pressure from Henry's minister Thomas Cromwell in 1534, effectively prised the English Church away from the Papacy by declaring the royal supremacy of the Crown over the ordering of Church affairs, substituting monarch for Pope. No claim to ecclesiastical novelty was made here, however. Although the preamble could not conceal the fact that something new was being declared – 'be it enacted by authority of this present Parliament' – it implied complete continuity between the ancient English Church and the Church of England as it now was:

> the King's Majesty justly and rightfully is and ought to be the Supreme Head ... the King our Sovereign Lord, his heirs and successors kings of this realm, shall be taken, accepted, and reputed the only Supreme Head in earth of the Church of England called *Anglicana Ecclesia*.[1]

By repeating specifically the Latin formulation *Anglicana Ecclesia*, the text was binding the newly separated Church to the history of the Church in England over the preceding centuries. The phrase could be translated several other ways – Anglican Church, English Church, Church in England – but 'Church *of* England' signalled the refusal of any alternative, authoritative conception of the Christian Church for the realm. Henry's Church of England was to be taken as the Church in England as it had been from time immemorial.

That was a plausible view. Abrogation of the Roman communion did not imply, for Henry, the repudiation of the historic structures and order of the Church. The territorial system of the Church – local parishes, organised into deaneries, archdeaconries and then dioceses, over each of which a bishop presided, and finally into the two provinces of Canterbury and York, headed respectively by the archbishops of Canterbury and York – remained largely unchanged. Unlike the Reformation in northern Germany and Denmark, where the leadership of the churches had to be forced out of office, with the exception of a few malcontents (swiftly executed) the episcopate and other senior clergy accepted Henry's changes meekly enough. They had little choice. Churches and cathedrals remained largely untouched. At first, visible changes in parish churches and cathedrals were few. The Church of England in the early years after 1534 looked and felt much as it would have done to earlier generations of worshippers.

Reforming theologians were keen to emphasise continuity, too, partly for pragmatic reasons: even minor changes could be controversial, and so, given the goal of 'settling' religious disagreement in the wake of reform, it was wise to stress how much remained the same once reform had done its work. But, above all, theologians really did believe they were doing nothing new. They were not 'founding' a new church, for that was impossible. The Church had only one founder, Christ himself. The Church was Christ's body on earth, his children – the faithful – members of his body, not only in the merely instrumental or institutional sense of 'belonging' to the organisation, but because they were, through baptism, incorporated into Christ's visible body on earth. They were *literally* 'members' of Christ, his limbs on earth. After all, had not St Paul himself said, 'For as we have many members in one body, and all members have not the same office: So we, being many, are one body in Christ, and every one members one of another'; and again, 'ye are the body of Christ, and members in particular'?[2] In practice, the English reformers were ambivalent about the medieval Church. It was in theory part of the Church of Christ. But it had become corrupted. The reformers could adopt and glory in some of the saints of the medieval Church. But at the same time they could conveniently put its defects, its weaknesses, down to human sin, and even to the work of Satan himself.

But these practical and theological notions of continuity could not hide the fact that a sharp break in England's religious identity was engineered by the Tudor monarchs in the sixteenth century. The failure of the Protestant movement outside northern Europe – or, to put it another way, the sheer institutional durability of the Roman Catholic Church – ensured that the idea that there was only one possible way of conceiving of the Christian Church in England could never finally take hold. But in the early sixteenth century, this was far from clear. Especially on the ground, in the localities, as ordinary English people went about their business, even the really substantial changes in worship and practice that were under way did not altogether displace the sense that the local church continued to occupy much the same place in local life as it had in previous centuries. The English peasantry and yeomanry, plodding to church through the wind and rain in those long, damp winters, would have noticed the transformation of the church interior, the loss of shrines, changes in the services themselves, perhaps with bewilderment, but they were still going to the same building, week in, week out, under the direction of a priest who continued to see himself as their moral and spiritual overseer.

This apparent continuity of experience did not necessarily reflect a deep continuity of piety, or of the shape and content of religious experience. People and ideas, after all, change over time – that may be an obvious enough comment, but it bears repetition constantly as we try to sift through and compare the religious experiences of the people of England over the centuries. Even by the end of the sixteenth century, let alone the seventeenth or eighteenth or nineteenth centuries and even later, English popular religion was very different in its doctrinal content and its religious practice from the popular piety of the Middle Ages. None the less, what we might call the 'prehistory' of the Church of England left its mark on the Tudor Church, and continues to shape it to some extent even today. It is well beyond the scope of this book to do anything more than give a brief outline of leading processes and features of the first thousand years of Christianity in England, but something must be said to describe a number of features which subsequently affected the history of the Church of England.

We have to begin by reckoning with the gradual and piecemeal nature of the conversion of England to Christianity from the end of the sixth century. Until then, little probably survived of Christian Rome. Even with the enormous advances in archaeology of the last half century (particularly rescue archaeology), the real impact of the Christianisation of the Roman Empire on the province of Britannia remains elusive. We can assume that by the departure of the legions in the early fifth century there were churches – basilicas – in the major towns, and that the new faith was making headway in the population at large, gradually displacing other cults. But much, if not most, of this growth was depleted by the Anglo-Saxon invasions. Historians differ over whether we have to assume a catastrophic, conquest model of settlement by the Germanic peoples, or whether the likely process was gradual, characterised more by assimilation. The outcome for Christianity, however, was not much in doubt. By the sixth century, the Christian Church had been forced to the margins of the British Isles, and had virtually disappeared in the myriad kingdoms established by the invaders in the regions that would eventually become the kingdom of England.

So, when Augustine landed at Thanet in 597, with a mandate from Pope Gregory to bring the Gospel to the people apparently called the 'Angles', there was probably little of an active *cultus* of Christianity to be encountered on the ground in most areas. It is true that the single most important source we have for the conversion – the Venerable Bede's remarkable *Ecclesiastical History of the English People*, as it is usually titled (the Latin again is pertinent, because Bede really says 'of the people of the Angles') – probably exaggerated the challenges facing Augustine, and the corresponding success of his mission. Bede was writing over a century after Augustine's arrival, and in the northern kingdom of Northumbria, but he drew on documents and oral traditions which derived from the mission itself. The Germanic kingdoms traded with the continent of Europe, and thus Christian beliefs, Christian traders, and even some Christian books, almost certainly made their way across the Channel. Probably the power and authority of the Continental Church – Augustine's mission loosely coincided with the rise of the Frankish empire – was a significant incentive to Anglo-Saxon royalty and notables to convert. But Bede casts the process of conversion more dramatically in terms of a cosmological struggle between the truth and might of the Christian God, and the impotence of the Nordic deities: Augustine and his accompanying monks came, Bede says, 'not armed with the force of the devil but with the strength of God'.[3]

Looming large in Bede's account are saints and miracles, extraordinary men and women wielding divine power through their extraordinary actions. He never loses an opportunity to draw the widest possible conclusions from the stories he had heard of healing by the intercession of the saints. After the death in the late seventh century of Ethelburga, founding abbess of the double monastery at Barking, for example, her successor Hildilid received a blind woman who was the wife of an Anglo-Saxon noble; this woman, having been led into Ethelburga's burial ground by her maids and fallen on her knees and prayed, rose up to discover she had recovered her sight: 'she lost the light of this world only for this end, that she might shew by her healing how great the light and what grace of mighty working [it] is that Christ's saints have in heaven'.[4]

Christianity as Bede conceived it was not only a system of

belief and a moral philosophy, then: it was a wonder-working technology, a practice with experts, received knowledge and conditions of success or failure that could both replace pagan rituals and occult techniques and provide reassurance and relief from suffering for those who submitted to the Gospel. And so it remained for centuries. Christianity proved almost infinitely adaptable: its monotheism, its sacred scriptures, its ecclesiastical hierarchy, its monastic traditions and learning, gave it an almost unrivalled power of assimilation to the aims of early medieval rulers; but its local saints and their miraculous powers, and the monks, nuns and clergy who actually carried its message into the settlements of England, meant that it shaped itself also to the land and to the people who worked it.

Over a period of several centuries, despite the Danish incursions, and despite conflict between the Saxon kingdoms, and the death of Christian monarchs such as Oswald of Northumbria (in around 641) and Edmund of East Anglia (killed by the Danes in 869), Christianity fitfully but persistently came to dominate the kingdom finally united by the great Athelstan in 927. Paganism was gradually supplanted, not so much in a campaign of persecution and suppression as in a dual process of local mission and the conversion of the elites. Pope Gregory's instructions to Mellitus, the first bishop of London and companion of Augustine, preserved by Bede, point to a more subtle approach than simple suppression. He urged that

> the temples of the idols ... ought not to be broken; but the idols alone which be in them; that holy water be made and sprinkled about the same temples, altars builded, and relics placed: for if the said temples be well built, it is needful that they be altered from the worshiping of devils into the service of the true God.[5]

Thus the continuity of sacred sites ensured that in many places rhythms of worship retained some familiarity, despite the impact of the new faith. In the north, Midlands and east, under the impact of the Danish invasions, monasteries were destroyed, and much of the established diocesan structure of the Church severely attenuated, but on the ground, even here, the fitful, patchy nature of the Danish settlement meant that Christianity itself was not eradicated, and reasserted itself forcefully after the defeat and conversion of the Danes in the tenth and eleventh centuries.

By the time of the Norman Conquest, the Christianisation of England had long been completed. A residue of Nordic pagan beliefs remained in some place names – Wednesbury, or 'Woden's Hill', in Staffordshire, for example – and in language in common use, including the names of the days of the week, such as Wednesday. Examples of Scandinavian art and mythology survive in the stone crosses erected at various places in the north of England, though even here the very fact that these were crosses is testimony, as one authority has said, 'that those who set them up were in their own eyes Christians.'[6] There was no 'underground' pagan tradition surviving in any meaningful sense, contrary to what some writers were to claim centuries later, though an imprint of non-Christian practices and beliefs may have survived in popular or 'folk' traditions and magical practices, fused with overtly Christian ideas.[7]

If the shape of medieval Christianity was influenced by the very processes of interaction with pagan beliefs that characterised the conversion of England, the other key 'boundary' was with an alternative version of Christianity itself, the Celtic one. Today, this is all too often pictured as an ecologically aware, tolerant, anti-hierarchical alternative to the imperial Christianity of the Papacy. But that is a travesty of the truth. Celtic or 'Irish' Christianity professed allegiance to the Papacy, and it was a strenuous, ascetical form of the faith every bit as indebted to wonder-working as were Augustine's monks and their successors. Its seeming distinct identity from the mission of Augustine was as much as anything a product of historical accident: it was the form of the faith left in the more remote parts of Britain after the Germanic tribes settled in the fifth and sixth centuries.

But it preserved local traditions and structures of authority that set it apart from much of the rest of Christian Europe and, to those trying to establish a strong, united Church in England, it posed something of a complication.

Admittedly, at first glance, the differences do not seem such as to matter all that much. The most notorious of them – again here we are almost entirely dependent on Bede – was a disagreement between the Roman Church and the Irish over the dating of Easter, a far from trivial matter, since it meant that there were some years when Christians from different traditions in the same kingdoms could not celebrate together the most important festival of the Church's year; in this situation, as one historian has pointed out, 'What did the unity of Christians mean?'[8] According to Bede, from the very beginning of Augustine's mission, there were difficulties, as he records a bitter confrontation between Augustine and seven Irish bishops, in which they refused to celebrate Easter on the same date, to celebrate the sacrament of baptism according to the Roman practice, to preach the Gospel to the English, or to recognise his authority as archbishop.[9] But Bede may well have embellished this story, or at least unduly emphasised it, for in the next half century there is relatively little evidence of conflict, and plenty of evidence of cooperation and coexistence.[10] The Roman missionaries were more than happy to acknowledge, as Bede does himself, the learning and sanctity of the great Irish monasteries at Iona and Lindisfarne, and the importance of many of the Irish saints. Dynastic rivalries in the kingdom of Northumbria almost certainly had a key role in crystallising the conflict, which was brought to a close effectively by the great Synod of Whitby in 664, at which the Irish bishops agreed to end their separate custom of Easter, and to accept in full the Roman tradition and the Roman jurisdiction.

However complicated and protracted the conversion of early medieval England may have been, what features of the English medieval Church is it particularly important to emphasise, looking towards the Reformation? In an all too brief survey, I would pick out four points as especially important, if we leave to one side, that is, the one point effectively resolved at Whitby – the Roman communion. First was the institution of monasticism. This was central to both the Irish and Roman missions. Augustine's missionaries were all monks. It was the monasteries which, over the centuries, not only preserved and developed learning, but which supplied most of the leaders of the Church, and many of its best-known and best-loved saints. The monasteries of northern England and the Midlands suffered depredation and destruction during the Danish invasions, but in the wake of the unification of the kingdom of England monasticism once again thrived.

If it seems puzzling to us that monasticism was such an asset for early and medieval Christianity, it is worth reflecting on just why the three-fold oath of poverty, chastity and obedience should have proved so durable. Monks – and later nuns – were poor, living in community, working to support themselves, or (as in the later mendicant orders) dependent on the charity of others; they were, in other words, cheap. They did not have the ties or distractions of family and of a settled life; their lives were dedicated first and foremost to God. They were committed. And finally, they were utterly at the disposal of the hierarchy, or at least of the Pope, and bound to a disciplined way of life. They could be sent wherever they were needed. The religious orders were the shock troops of Christian mission in the early centuries.

Second was the very shape and content of popular piety. Texts played a considerable part in the world of medieval Christianity: the liturgies through which services were conducted and the sacraments celebrated, the chants sung as accompaniment, commentaries on the Scriptures, theological treatises and commentaries, were all preserved in monastic libraries, and later in the collections of the collegiate institutions of Oxford and Cambridge, all carefully copied out, generation after generation. Above all, at the heart of the faith was the book itself, the Bible.

But the world of the faithful was not really a religion of

written texts at all, but a world of the imagination, a world of intense and vivid pictures, of customs and sacred rituals, of local traditions, of action. Literacy was almost non-existent in many parishes, especially in rural communities. Sometimes even the parish clergy themselves were barely literate. The Christian world view was a narrative of creation, fall and redemption, pictured on the walls and windows of church interiors, and in the stories told by the clergy. Supremely it was a local, practical world, in which the central narrative of Jesus's birth, death and resurrection was filled out with an elaborate subculture of saints. Saints were an access point to the divine, bringing God's blessing into particular areas of life. There were saints for almost every conceivable form of misfortune, for every economic activity, for every stage of life. In pre-Conquest Cornwall, for example, local Celtic saints such as Endellion, Petroc and Winwaloe abounded in church dedications, though they were often later suppressed or marginalised in favour of more universal Catholic figures.[11]

Pivotal was Mary, Jesus's mother, celebrated in songs and poetry, in church dedications, and in popular myth. Dedications to Mary easily outpaced those to all other patron saints in much of medieval England. Some 235 monasteries founded after 1066 were dedicated to Mary; the next largest category was Peter and Paul, with 49.[12] In Devon there were 79 church dedications to Mary; again, the next largest group was Peter and Paul, with 40.[13] Elsewhere this was not always so – in the diocese of Carlisle, for example, it seems Mary came behind both Michael and Cuthbert.[14] Wells and shrines were often associated with particular saints, sacralising particular places but also marking the source of prayer and healing. Wayside crosses, especially in the bleak upland territories of northern England and Wales, could mark significant religious sites, or pilgrimage routes, or even – as in the land around Romaldkirk in the northern Pennines – a 'corpse route' along which bodies were taken for burial.[15] Pilgrimages, which became increasingly popular from the twelfth century, reinforced this sacralisation of place. In this world of popular devotion the boundary between the sacred and the secular was far less complete, less visible than it is today.

Third, we have to reckon with the evolution of the English State, and its sometimes tense and difficult relationship with Rome. It is easy to exaggerate the conflict of Crown and Papacy, as Protestant historians did for generations, so that they could cast England's medieval history as an inevitable precursor to Henry VIII's break from Rome. England was as faithful a member of the Papal communion as were any of the kingdoms, principalities, city states or empires of Europe. But there were none the less features of this relationship that bear some discussion. Almost uniquely in western Europe, England was, from the tenth century onwards, a consolidated realm under one monarch. Its relationships with its closest neighbours – the Scottish kingdoms, the principality of Wales and Ireland – were fraught with conflict for hundreds of years, and the English kings' general claim to overlordship perilous. And it would be premature to speak of England as a 'nation': government was not really centralised for centuries; there is little evidence English people thought of themselves as 'one people' until the sixteenth century. It would be easy to take John of Gaunt's speech in *Richard II* (written in the mid-1590s) as a sign of an ancient national consciousness – 'This royal throne of kings, this scepter'd isle, this earth of majesty ... this blessed plot, this earth, this realm, this England'[16] – but of course Shakespeare was simply appealing to an Elizabethan audience just a few years after the defeat of the Spanish Armada, and there is little evidence of anything like so complete and formed a sense of national destiny much earlier than that.

None the less, that England was one realm, under one monarch, for hundreds of years before the sixteenth century, and an island realm at that, arguably made it more persuasive for later generations to claim a long prehistory of Church–State tensions than would otherwise have been the case. Henry VIII's anti-Papal legislation could draw on a cumulative history of conflict between the English Crown and Rome over many centuries. Henry I resisted the attempts of Popes early in the twelfth century to claim the power to appoint bishops and abbots in England; a compromise allowed the king to demand homage and obedience for secular duties, the Papacy for spiritual. Henry II, notoriously, allowed the murder of Thomas Becket, archbishop of Canterbury and former Chancellor, after Becket had defended the autonomy of Church law. In the fourteenth century, successive monarchs, again attempting to curtail the rights and privileges of the Church, sponsored statutes of *Praemunire* which resisted the exercise of overseas jurisdictions, including the Papacy, in England. All of these events provided useful precedents for Henry VIII's lawyers and theologians. Moreover, it was easy to argue that the Papacy had claimed too much power and authority for itself. Protestant controversialists were able to point to significant moments in the evolution of the Papacy at which its authority and status were definitely being enhanced. The summit of this elevation of Papal authority was Boniface's assertion, in the Papal bull *Unam Sanctam* in 1302, that even temporal authority was exercised under the authority of the Pope, and that it 'it is altogether necessary to salvation for every human creature to be subject to the Roman pontiff'.[17]

These claims were never universally accepted in the Western Church. The conciliar movement of the fourteenth and fifteenth centuries set out an alternative vision of authority in the Church, in which jurisdiction was not centred on a single point in Rome but shared with the bishops of the whole Catholic Church.[18] The decisive defeat of the conciliar argument by Pius II in 1460 ended the possibility that the Western Church might reshape itself according to a vision of ecclesial authority that might just, possibly, have staved off even the Reformation itself. On the eve of the Reformation, then, there was not one idea of Papal authority throughout the Latin West, but several: a theoretically absolute concept, enshrined in certain texts, was challenged by various theologians who none the less accepted the concept of Papal primacy itself; secular rulers accepted the authority of Rome, but not without reservations.

Perhaps the final feature of medieval Christianity that is worth emphasising at this point is in some ways the most enduring of all – its local, territorial organisation. This has proved one of the most abiding features of the Church of England. By the eleventh century its main outlines were in place. The whole realm of England, and in time Wales, was covered by a hierarchy of three geographical units. At the very top were the two provinces of Canterbury and York, the former by far the larger of the two, and each headed by an archbishop or primate. The archbishops were powerful figures in medieval government, but the province as such was probably the least significant of the three levels, so far as the organisation and management of the Church in the localities was concerned.

Underneath the provinces were dioceses, by the early sixteenth century seventeen of them in the province of Canterbury and five in York's. The dioceses varied enormously in size and wealth: the huge northern diocese of York, which covered all of modern Yorkshire, contrasted with the relatively small area covered by London. But London was the seat of power, populous and rich, and the bishop of London came third in the hierarchy of the Church after the archbishops of Canterbury and York. The diocese was an ancient form. It reflected the central importance of the figure of the bishop in the evolution of Christianity in its early centuries. Bishops were the chief executive officers of the Church, its generals or commanders of divisions, if you like. They were akin to the great lords, wielding significant influence and trusted as royal advisers – hence their inclusion in the great councils that were the origin of our Parliament. It was the bishop of the diocese who oversaw, and was responsible for, all the local organisation of the church. Nothing captures this more forcefully than the tradition encapsulated even today in the Church of England's canon law. Canon C18, 'Of diocesan bishops', is cast in language that goes back to the first formulation of the English canons in the early seventeenth century, but its theological principles are older still: the bishop is 'the chief pastor of all that are within his diocese, as well laity as clergy, and their father in God'.

From this flows the common understanding, actively contested today by some Anglicans, that the bishop is the chief priest of the diocese, and that all clergy hold their ministries as from him (or her). But this is only to put in words that are theologically loaded – it is the word 'priest' that is particularly controversial here, as some Anglicans think it an inappropriate adoption of the sacrificial, Aaronic idea of the priesthood of Judaism – something the canon proceeds to lay out a few clauses further on: 'Every bishop is, within his diocese, the principal minister, and to him belongs the right … of conducting, ordering, controlling, and authorising all services in churches, chapels …'[19]

At the heart of the diocese was the cathedral, which was the principal church of the diocese because it contained the seat of the bishop, the *cathedra* – the place, in other words, where the bishop would sit during the liturgy, and where his authority as principal minister was therefore symbolised. From the bishop, with his various assistants, and from the cathedral, with its clergy, flowed the jurisdiction through which the affairs of the diocese were governed. Clergy were licensed, corrected, encouraged, inspected, and their churches regulated, by the bishop and his staff.

But it was the parish, the most basic local level of territorial organisation, which represented the horizon of most ordinary worshippers. Some Anglicans like to parade the myth that the parish system is the heart of the Church of England, and that it represents a distinct, almost uniquely Anglican concept of pastoral ministry. But there is nothing uniquely Anglican about the parish. Scots Presbyterians have parishes. So do Continental Lutherans, as do Catholics in Spain, Italy and France. The parish is simply the local unit of ecclesiastical administration reflecting the settled condition Western Christianity achieved in the early Middle Ages. The powers and responsibilities of parishes vary from country to country, but the basic idea of an area for which a priest with a church is pastorally responsible is practically universal in Europe.

In England and Wales the parish system largely came into

being almost a thousand years ago, after several centuries of development.[20] By the later Saxon period the earlier practice of establishing 'minster' churches in or near larger local communities, with smaller satellite churches (the *parochiae* of the 'mother' church) in outlying localities – a practice never universally implemented in England anyway – was giving way to the almost inevitable pressure from specific communities to support their own church building under the direct authority of the bishop.[21] The geography of parishes – their size, distribution and shape – was influenced by many factors, including population density, terrain and the local economy. Village communities defined themselves over time through their parish boundaries. Civic and religious responsibilities overlapped; clergy and parish officers were often the only local government officials people might encounter in person.

At the Reformation, as we shall see, little of this was to change, despite radical changes in doctrine and worship. The local pattern of parish organisation was mostly complete in England by the eleventh century; we know this from the picture presented by the *Domesday Book*, that great survey of English society commissioned by William I in the wake of the Conquest. Chaldon, in the county of Surrey, is listed as simply having one church to go with its two 'ploughlands', or land for two ploughs, for example.[22] That pattern has remained largely in place right up to the present. Its greatest challenge came with the industrialisation and rapid urbanisation of the nineteenth and twentieth centuries. Victorian churches litter the urban landscape today because they were needed to cater for rapidly growing urban communities. But in the countryside, the greatest concentration of parish churches by the sixteenth century was in a broad band of the country stretching from the south-west, through the south Midlands across to encompass the south-east and eastern England, and running up to the Lincolnshire Wolds and the Vale of York. Here, in the great areas of medieval prosperity, and especially those of the wool trade, village communities were thick on the ground, and their churches with them. That is why today the Church of England struggles to care for the hundreds of medieval buildings scattered across predominantly rural diocese such as Norwich, Ely, Lincoln and Somerset, when the village communities they serve, never large, have dwindled in size in the modern period.

It is important to remember, too, that in most situations the parish church was the one stone structure enduring through the centuries. Local communities poured their money into the building and adornment of churches. Especially in the wealthier regions, churches were extended, rebuilt, complicated through the addition of chantry chapels, and decorated ever more elaborately with wall paintings and stained glass. Sometimes this was because greater space was needed; but often it must have been because the building itself was a standing testimony to the faith and wealth of its benefactors. The great 'marsh' churches of the East Anglian fenlands, for example, are unlikely ever to have been full. The glorious structure that is Walpole St Peter, west of King's Lynn – 'the finest of all', according to John Betjeman – stood in a prosperous but relatively small community, even by the mid-nineteenth century having a population of just over 1,300, and a Sunday attendance at church probably of around 240, for a building that could hold well over twice that number.[23] Churches were not built simply as vessels to hold specified numbers of people, but as symbols of their place in the hearts and minds of their people.

Here, however, a complication did arise that has remained a feature of the Church of England. Who appointed the parish priest? In some parishes, it was the bishop himself. In others, it was either a monastery or, in a few cases, a wealthy layman who had funded the building of a church. That, at least, was the theory. The parish priest so appointed 'ruled' his parish: he was the 'rector' of it. He was entitled to draw a 'tithe' (ostensibly a tenth in value) from the produce of the land of the parish to support himself; he could also farm his own land, or rather the land that belonged to the parish church, the 'glebe'. He might, particularly in more affluent areas, also levy a small charge for marriages, baptisms and funerals, or perhaps for saying masses for the souls of dead parishioners and their families. In other words, clergy had income, and that opened up the possibility of patrons acquiring for themselves the 'rectorial' benefits of a parish, and appointing someone vicariously (a 'vicar') to do the duty of the parish – say the services, carry out pastoral functions – for a fraction of the income, the balance of course going to the patron. Later in the Middle Ages, when the power to appoint – the patronage – could be bought and sold as a piece of property, called an 'advowson', it became possible for one man to hold several parishes at once, whether as rector or vicar, and to appoint a 'perpetual curate' to do the duty, again usually for a fraction of the income. At the Reformation, this system was to become massively imbalanced in favour of wealthy laity, with the dissolution of the monasteries and the transfer of their property, including their patronage, to the Crown, nobles and gentry.

However the parish priest was appointed and funded, by the late Middle Ages the parish system was well established across England and Wales, and pretty much all the evidence suggests it functioned well. Like all human organisations, theory could be at odds with practice. If, on the surface, the system seemed to offer the prospect of a rough parity between village communities in the way the Church was constituted and supported, in practice there were rich and poor parishes, large and small churches, pious and devout clergy and lazy, inept or corrupt clergy, energetic and committed laity and indifferent and idle laity. But the ubiquitous presence of medieval churches, their evolution as complex sacred spaces displaying in their art a rich and sophisticated world of belief, and the ardour with which, right up to the Reformation, people were pouring money into their improvement and extension, all suggest a system that had developed successfully to cater for the spiritual needs of the population.

PART I

THE AGE OF THE MONARCH

2

REFORMATION AND TURMOIL

Henry VIII and the Break from Rome

The accession of the young Henry in 1509 brought to the throne someone whom no one can have expected to be a threat to traditional religion. Throughout his life, he was devout, almost superstitious, some might say – he received Mass often, and he interpreted daily events as proof of God's favour. The failure of Catherine of Aragon, his first queen, to bear him a male heir who survived to adulthood gradually became, for him, an adverse judgment of God on his marriage. Henry was a man of contradictions – big, brash, physically and sexually energetic, but at the same time religiously conservative, glorying in a love of learning and the arts. Posterity has never quite been able to decide between the idea of him as the 'merrie monarch', big and bluff, and the ruthless and cruel tyrant who did away with wives and courtiers as it suited him. Charles Dickens, possibly following the lead of the radical agitator William Cobbett, called him 'a disgrace to human nature, and a spot of blood and grease upon the History of England'.[1] Such assessments miss what to me seems the key point, however – Henry's almost pathological obsession with consolidating his royal authority and dynastic security.

Henry comes as close to an absolute monarch as any in English history, determined to destroy rivals and to commend his own person as representative of the realm itself. You could call this a monstrous egotism, and it certainly looks like that. But that is to risk psychological reductionism. And it is also to neglect the obvious fact that England had no good precedents for the consequences of a weak monarch and an uncertain succession: his father, after all, had come to the throne after the bloodletting of the Wars of the Roses, in the wake of the fall and death of Henry VI. The real source of Henry's policy towards the Church – what subsequently came to be called the English Reformation – was his desire to enforce his personal authority. Almost all the changes of his reign followed from an essentially conservative or defensive impulse. Undoubtedly much changed religiously in his reign, but it was 'smuggled in' under the cover of a pretence that the position of the Church, and the unity of Crown and altar, was being strengthened by the king's policy.

This explains another paradox – the seeming absolutist who allowed subordinate ministers freedom to pursue policies largely of their own devising. Henry was not interested in the mundane matters of royal administration. In modern management terms, he depended on good delegation. What he was not, however, was a distant and disinterested manager. He was at times (and increasingly towards the end of his reign) a savage and unpredictable intervener. The effects of his ministers' policies always interested him. He wanted to be, and to be seen to be, a mighty figure, noble, powerful and imposing, merciful but intimidating. Hans Holbein painted a mural for the Palace of Whitehall in the mid-1530s, probably during Jane Seymour's pregnancy, which shows Henry VIII standing in front of his father, beside a monumental block which includes the Latin text *Filius ad maiora quiqem procnatus ab aris submovet indignost substitutique probos* ('The son, born indeed for greater tasks, from the altar removed the unworthy and put worthy men in their place').[2] This is a telling insight into the central position of religious policy in the reign. Alongside that image, we should put the frontispiece of the 'Great Bible', commissioned by Thomas Cromwell and completed under the supervision of Miles Coverdale in 1539: this put Henry VIII at the centre of the picture, handing the word of God to the bishops at the top, who in turn hand it on to the parish clergy in the centre, who then teach it to

1. Genealogies of power: an oil painting based
on Holbein's Whitehall Palace mural

the laity at the bottom (bottom perhaps literally in this scheme,
as well as metaphorically).

Little in English policy in the 1520s can have given an impartial observer the thought that within a decade the king would
have broken a millennium-long loyalty to the Pope and taken
the Church of England out of the Roman communion. Up until
then, for most of his reign the dominant minister was his Lord
Chancellor, Thomas Wolsey, archbishop of York and cardinal.
Wolsey had no truck with the new reforming opinion emerging
on the continent of Europe in the 1520s: he prosecuted heretics,
imprisoning and occasionally executing them, and stamped out
subversive literature wherever he could. Wolsey's authority and
status were built on two pillars, both of which were particularly
useful to the king: his evident success in diplomacy and (initially,

at any rate) military policy, and his influence at the Papal court. In the 1520s Henry was in favour in Rome. He was married to the aunt of the Holy Roman Emperor, Charles V, and he was aligned with the anti-Lutherans, in 1521 penning *The Defence of the Seven Sacraments*, as defined by the Catholic Church against Martin Luther. This was the book, probably written in conjunction with Thomas More, which famously brought him and his successors the title 'Defender of the Faith'.

It is worth pausing to ask whether there were other factors at work. We are touching here on one of the most controverted subjects in English history. To put it in a nutshell, was the Reformation in England an act of state, a top-down, centrally imposed programme, or was it rather the outcome of long-term social and ideological pressures that forced, bottom-up as it were, the interests of the Crown in a radically different direction? If history, in the cliché, is written by the winners, then it is understandable that for a long time Protestant apologists were inclined towards the second view. Medieval Catholicism was corrupt and moribund, they said. Ever since the Church's clumsy and only half-successful attempts to suppress the 'Lollard' movement – the movement of reform sponsored by followers of the radical English theologian John Wycliffe in the late fourteenth and fifteenth centuries – little communities of disaffected believers convinced the Church needed reform had continued to exist across parts of the country. People were disillusioned with the clergy, they said, because they were often poorly educated, greedy, and sometimes sexually promiscuous. There was little to distinguish the great leaders of the Church, the bishops, abbots and cathedral clergy, from secular gentry and nobles. Thus, when the movement of protest Martin Luther led against Papal indulgences rapidly fanned out into a wholesale programme of reform, practical as well as theological, it found a sympathetic ear in England. People were of course reluctant to abandon the traditions of centuries; but the change in policy under Henry VIII combined with a cultural, social and theological sea change to alter permanently the religious identity of England. And that, coincidentally, was a sign of divine providence.

This description of the Protestant apology for the English Reformation is of course somewhat exaggerated, at least in the way I have set it out here. But not that exaggerated. The main outlines of this 'Protestant' interpretation have remained in place until quite recently, and elements of it can be found in the writings of respectable academic theologians whose work is still referenced in universities today.[3]

Yet little of it stands up to scrutiny now. There continue to be divergent views about the extent to which Lollardy survived into the early sixteenth century, though most scholars acknowledge that if it did survive, it was relatively unimportant for the course of the Reformation.[4] There was a growing interest in vernacular religious literature in the late fifteenth century and into the early sixteen century, but this was as much a characteristic of 'traditional' Catholic belief as it was of any current pressing for radical reform of the Church – a demand fuelled by the development of the printing press for English language books of hours (collections of prayers and psalms organised loosely around the monastic daily services or 'hours') and even extracts from Scripture.[5] There is evidence of some popular anti-clericalism, but no more so than in other periods of the Church's history, and the idea that it was a significant contributor to a popular movement in favour of an emergent Protestantism is, as one prominent historian has put it, simply a 'fiction'.[6] There is little evidence of widespread refusal to participate in the rites of the Church. On the contrary, in perhaps one of the most decisive interventions in Reformation historiography, the historian Eamon Duffy has demonstrated that late medieval religion at the local level was flourishing right up to the 1530s, with no evidence of popular disaffection.[7] So complete has Duffy's recasting of the argument been that there has been no serious attempt in the last thirty years or so to revive interpretations of the English Reformation based on a bottom-up, rising tide of popular disaffection with the Church.

The shifting argument over the causes of the English Reformation has thus pushed the onus for explaining exactly why it
happened when it happened back on to considerations of royal
policy above all. It is possible to argue that the legislative changes
of the 1530s – the crucial decade – helped to synchronise reforming opinion in England with the direction of royal policy, at least
until Thomas Cromwell's fall in 1540. Protestants – the term is
strictly anachronistic in England until later in the century – could
welcome these changes, and make of them, subsequently, something of a providential argument for the cleansing of the Church
by royal command. They could also, rightly, point out that there
were connections between what happened in England and the
Lutheran and, later, 'Reformed' movements on the Continent.
Moreover, the evidence of dissatisfaction with the Church actually increases for the 1530s, suggesting that as religious change
got under way, ordinary lay people began to be disaffected: clerical recruitment fell dramatically, having flourished in the 1510s
and early 1520s, and cases brought by clergy accusing lay people
of abusing them increased significantly.[8]

But the initiative was firmly in the hands of the king and his
ministers. Nothing would have happened, ultimately, without his
will. That is why the question of Henry's divorce from Catherine
remains absolutely central to the matter, and why the 'origins' of
the Church of England, if we are to pin them to the 1530s, have an
oddly incidental and arbitrary cause. The break from Rome was
a developing crisis that broke one royal servant, Thomas Wolsey,
and made the fortunes of two others, Thomas Cromwell and, as
archbishop, Thomas Cranmer. Henry's failure to produce a male
heir through Catherine, his infatuation with Anne Boleyn, the
inability of Wolsey to persuade the Pope to annul Henry's marriage and Wolsey's subsequent fall, and the alternative scheme
unveiled by Cromwell, with the aid of Cranmer and others –
these were complicated and protracted matters in themselves,
spread over some five to six years. Wolsey's fall provided the
opportunity for Cromwell to propose the taking back of ecclesiastical jurisdiction to England itself, away from the Papacy.

Criticism came to a peak in the aftermath of his fall, in the Parliament that met from 1529, and eventually produced in the House of Commons a 'Supplication' against the Church courts. This was Cromwell's opportunity to take the initiative against those resisting the proposed royal divorce, but it may also have been a genuine expression of pent-up resentment.[9] As the clergy rallied in their own assembly, Convocation, to oppose the Supplication, Henry and Cromwell seized the moment to push through the first of the series of statutes that radically changed the relationship of the English Church to the Papacy. The criticism of Wolsey widened into an all-out attack on what he represented, the 'subjection' of the English Church – and, by extension, under the Papal theory of sovereignty, the realm itself – to the Pope. The first blow, in 1532, was an act suspending the payment to Rome of 'annates' – that is, a year's income on appointment to a new clerical office – in order to put pressure on Rome to grant the divorce. It was a desperate diplomatic manoeuvre that failed, in the face of obdurate opposition from Charles V.

The following year marked an important legislative move, when a statute was enacted prohibiting appeals from English courts to Rome. Here we see the articulation of a principle that would achieve the following year, in the Act of Supremacy, the decisive break with Rome. The Act in Restraint of Appeals contains one of the most famous statements in all English statutory history: 'this realm of England is an empire ... governed by one Supreme Head and King, having the dignity and royal estate of the imperial Crown of the same'.[10] The point, as the preamble laboriously goes on to claim, was that the monarch's discretion to order the affairs of the Church had been eroded by sundry statutes and ordinances which permitted appeals to Rome; these were now abrogated.

In 1534 the Act of Supremacy clarified this principle: the king himself was the supreme head of the Church of England, the *Ecclesia Anglicana*. Henry had simply substituted himself for the Pope. This was as close as any English monarch has ever come to claiming absolute power. The temporal and spiritual 'swords' were united in their obedience to the king. It was not quite a claim to divine right, though Henry certainly thought he was divinely appointed: theories of divine right – that is, of the intrinsic and overwhelming God-given right of a monarch to rule without opposition to or mitigation of their authority – were not worked out in full for another fifty years or more.

By assuming the headship of the Church of England, Henry assumed the power to declare his own marriage invalid, divorce Catherine and marry Anne Boleyn. Cromwell got him out of the diplomatic impasse that had trapped and destroyed Wolsey. For the Church of England, the change was momentous. From this point on, the interests of the monarchy and the Church were inextricably entwined. This has been of enormous significance for what theologians call the ecclesiology of the Church of England. Ecclesiology is that branch of Christian theology that deals with the doctrine of the Church – what it is, what its authority is, how it is ordered, what relation it bears to civil society, and so on. Not all Anglicans, as we shall see later, have agreed about the Church's relationship to the State, and to the monarch; but the Tudor legislation created a bond in practice that had to be reckoned with by all. In the expansion of the Anglican churches overseas, from the nineteenth century on, different models of relationship had to be developed. But in England, and in Wales, until the early twentieth century by far the most important statutory legislation affecting the Church was that enacted under Henry, and then reaffirmed or modified by his successors.

Henry's assertion of authority rested on political and dynastic interest, but it had to be legitimated, and the emergent theology of the Protestant Reformation was useful here, in its understanding of the role of the 'civil magistrate', that is, the secular ruler who was responsible for ensuring the good order of the Church. Political and dynastic interest was also bound up in what eventually emerged, in his son's reign, as the notion of a single settlement for the Church of England, with a single liturgical order, ensuring that, through legislation, through royal injunctions, through careful management of the Church's hierarchy, the unity and uniformity of the Church of England could be imposed throughout the realm. The Henrician understanding of the relationship of Crown and Church became, in a somewhat overused phrase, 'part of the DNA' of the Church of England.

It was, furthermore, the basis of further radical changes in the 1530s, steered by Cromwell. The devastating campaign Cromwell launched against the religious orders necessarily had the support of the king, and it had both political and financial motives. The monasteries were among the richest corporate landowners in the country, an irony – given their vows of poverty – not lost on their critics. There were useful precedents for the reform or closure of small or failing religious houses. But here, the motive was the acquisition of wealth, on the pretext – it was little more than that – that the monasteries were decaying, corrupt institutions that had long ago wandered away from their founding ideals. Cromwell's own motives may have been more aligned with the religious criticism reformers such as Martin Luther made of monasticism, but Henry's views – at least as they had developed by the mid-1530s – were probably a blend of humanist criticism of monkish greed and superstition, and of pragmatism. Cromwell's more cautious, gradualist approach was overtaken in the rush to enrich Crown and nobility.[11] Later, political considerations became more important.

Following the Act of Supremacy, an oath of obedience which recognised the king's marriage and the supremacy of the king was required of all adult males. Some resisted. This led to the downfalls of Thomas More and Bishop John Fisher, and also to those of some members of the religious orders. Henry could tolerate no such opposition. The dissolution was preceded by a comprehensive survey of Church property and income carried out by royal commissioners, which gave the Crown a good idea of the wealth of the Church, and by a 'visitation' of the religious houses specifically, carried out by commissioners personally appointed by Cromwell. The latter had every interest in painting a bleak picture, and they did so. This was the prelude to the dissolution of the 'lesser' houses, enacted by Parliament in 1536. Dissolution of the greater houses – the friaries, the larger priories and abbeys – followed further legislation two years later. The Church of England ceased to be a church in which religious orders were tolerated, until their return, in a very different form and on a much smaller scale, in the mid-nineteenth century.

But more to the point, the suppression of the religious orders transformed social relationships in English society. At a stroke, a whole class of landowners disappeared. At the outset of the dissolution, there were almost 900 houses, spread across the land, accommodating some 13,000 men and women.[12] Most houses also accommodated many dependent laypeople, including the elderly and infirm, and often also servants, and also gave employment through their farms to many thousands more. The orders were by far the largest contributors to local welfare and the relief of poverty. The transfer of their wealth to the Crown and on to the nobility and gentry boosted the status and power of those social groups, thinned out the ranks of the clergy, and deprived thousands of ordinary people of valuable material support.

The great architectural legacy of monasticism was not altogether lost. Six of the great abbeys were converted to cathedrals to support new dioceses – Peterborough, Oxford (retained from Wolsey's new college), Chester, Bristol, Gloucester and Westminster, though the last was only a cathedral for ten years before reverting to 'abbey'. In addition, those ancient cathedrals – such as Canterbury itself – that, in an arrangement almost unique to England, were supported by a monastic community were effectively refounded with cathedral chapters. A number of other monastic churches were retained as parish churches, including Tewkesbury, Selby, Christchurch, Cartmel, Bath, Dorchester, St Albans (later a cathedral) and Sherborne. In other places – perhaps as many as a hundred – parts of the monastic church, or the monastic buildings, were retained for use, while other parts were demolished. The survival of the cathedrals, with their residential chapters, and the colleges of Oxford and Cambridge, kept something of the ideal of a learned religious community alive.

The other radical innovation of the 1530s was an English Bible. Though Protestants were to claim this as uniquely a product of the Reformation, there had been moves in this direction long before the break with Rome. But the real initiative here came from a strongly reforming direction. From the late 1520s until his betrayal, imprisonment and finally execution in 1536, a young English priest from Gloucestershire, William Tyndale, was in hiding on the Continent, where he pursued his dream of translating the Scriptures into his native tongue. The first complete edition of Tyndale's translation of the New Testament, published in 1526 in Germany, drew on the examples of Erasmus's new Latin and Greek editions, on Luther's German Bible, and perhaps also on more clumsy Lollard precursors. Tyndale's combination of an instinctive feel for language and his careful scholarship ensured that the New Testament was opened up to ordinary people in plain, earthy English.

Especially after a revised edition was produced in 1534, thousands of copies of Tyndale's translation were smuggled into England, despite the best efforts of the bishops to suppress them. As is now widely recognised, it was Tyndale's work that underlay subsequent English translations. The 'Great Bible', finally issued under Henry VIII's authority in 1539, closely followed Tyndale's work. The Authorised Version, or 'King James Bible', issued in 1611, which was by far the dominant English translation until the late twentieth century, essentially took Tyndale's work as its main point of departure. All familiar with the resounding opening sentences of John's Gospel from the Authorised Version, for example, will recognise at once how close it is to Tyndale's 1526 rendering:

In the beginnynge was the worde and the worde was with God: and the worde was God. The same was in the

2. Henry delivers the Word: the frontispiece of the Great Bible, 1539

> beginnynge with God. All thinges were made by it and
> with out it was made nothinge that was made.

The rhythm of the language is entirely familiar; what does jar
is that unexpected 'it' in the third sentence. The 'Great Bible'
closely followed this translation, retaining 'it'. Only in 1611 did
the passage settle down into the recognisably more personal
idiom: 'All things were made by him; and without him was not
any thing made that was made.'

To the dissolution of the monasteries and the introduction of
an English Bible we ought to add a number of doctrinal changes.
But here the story is much less straightforward. Henry permitted and almost certainly personally approved what amounted
to an assault on key elements of late medieval piety. Whatever
his views about pilgrimages, relics and the intercession of the
saints before the 1530s – and here there is some disagreement
as to whether he was always sceptical of them on Erasmian,
humanist grounds, or whether, as seems more likely, he genuinely supported them – by the mid-1530s they were changing.[13]
The Ten Articles issued by Convocation in 1536 included a moderate reforming statement on justification, the doctrine at the
centre of Luther's theology, and insisted on the sacrament of
penance as well as baptism and eucharist, but also included provision for reining in abuses of pilgrimage sites, and worship of
images, in the interest of preventing idolatry. In the course of
the dissolution, many famous pilgrimage sites and relics were
broken up or scattered. The shrine of St Thomas Becket at Canterbury – a particularly irritating cult for Henry because Becket
opposed a king – was destroyed at the dissolution of the abbey
in 1538; that of St Cuthbert at Durham in 1539; the shrine of Our
Lady of Walsingham, where Henry himself had paid homage,
was destroyed in 1538, the image of Mary taken to London and
burnt. The royal injunctions of 1538 required that false images
'abused with pilgrimages or offerings of anything made thereunto' in parish churches should be taken down, and clergy were
to admonish their parishioners to avoid idolatry.[14]

All this appears to fit a reforming programme that was to enter a much more radical phase in the reign of Henry's son, Edward VI. But here the complications come into play. Cromwell's fall in 1540, triggered by his disastrous brokering of Henry's failed marriage to Anne of Cleves, and driven by the enmity of court rivals, brought to a sharp end any thought of further reform. Supporters of traditional religion had already come to the fore again. Having achieved his main object through the royal supremacy and the dissolution of the monasteries, Henry had become more cautious, approving six articles on disputed doctrinal points in 1539, all of which restated traditional Catholic doctrine, including clerical celibacy, observing vows of chastity (in other words, requiring former monks and nuns to continue to observe their vows), auricular confession (i.e. personal, private confession to a priest) and transubstantiation. Legislation in 1543 placed limitations on who could read the Scriptures (no men below the level of yeoman, and no women at all, unless gentry or nobility): it was clear that, in Henry's mind, good though it might be for the Scriptures to be read and expounded in English, it was not good that an uninformed reader might do so and form their own conclusions.

Thus, the religious changes of the 1530s had produced several new features of English religion that were in time to be seen as characteristic of Anglicanism: the retention of 'Catholic order' (as later theologians would see it) in the three-fold ministry of bishops, priests and deacons, and the diocesan organisation of the Church, with cathedrals, combined with a rejection of Papal jurisdiction, a more exalted role for the monarch as the 'civil magistrate' who would protect and oversee the good order of the Church, the use of the Scriptures in English, a 'thinned out' calendar of saints' days, and an almost complete rejection (until the High Church revival of the nineteenth century) of pilgrimages, shrines and relics. But all this none the less was compatible with Henry's essential conservatism on certain selective but significant aspects of traditional Catholic doctrine, and especially the Mass.

If we have to assess the impact of Henry's reign in terms of what the Church of England was eventually to become, it is hard to reach a balanced view. The fact that the break with Rome occurred in a context of wider European Reformation misleads as much as it explains. Henry was advised by people such as Cromwell and Cranmer, who evidently had reforming views of their own and were prepared to push them whenever possible; theologians in England were in touch with their Continental evangelical counterparts; England saw a nascent Protestant movement coming into being in the 1520s and 1530s; some of the Henrician legislation was compatible with similar moves elsewhere in Europe – all that is true. But Henry was essentially unclassifiable himself: a conservative Catholic who broke with Rome and suppressed the religious life; a serial adulterer strongly convinced of the value of clerical celibacy; a man genuinely interested in theological debate who was prepared to prosecute and burn those who defied his will. The strong consistent thread of royal policy in his reign was his dynastic ambition, and his assertion of royal authority. All else was subject to that. By placing himself at the very centre of the religious hierarchy in England, Henry was, in effect, placing all his heirs at the very same point – until, that is, royal authority collapsed a century later in civil war. It is not too much of an exaggeration to say that, as a result of Henry's policy and personality, for the next hundred years or so court politics were of greater importance in settling the affairs of the Church than they had ever been before or were to be afterwards, and so was the royal will. Everything depended on the monarch.

Reformation on the Move: Edward VI

Henry's death in January 1547 brought to the throne his longed-for heir, the young Edward. Only ten at his accession, he had the weight of expectation placed heavily on his shoulders by his father. Henry attempted to head off any potential power bids by courtiers by providing for a council of advisers to govern in

his son's minority, but this arrangement fell apart almost immediately. Instead of the feared coup by a traditionalist such as
Stephen Gardiner, bishop of Winchester, it was Edward's own
uncle (on his mother's side), Edward Seymour, who emerged triumphant from the ensuing power struggle. Taking for himself
the title of 'Lord Protector', Seymour also made himself duke
of Somerset, and with his allies at court profited from a general
handout of lands and goods from the dead king's wealth. Once
again, politics at court were central in determining the fate of
the Church of England. Traditionalists were marginalised. Somerset's influence was to last only three years, collapsing in the
wake of rebellion in the West Country, and his ill-fated attempt
to control the young king by kidnapping him. He was succeeded
by John Dudley, shortly to be made the first duke of Northumberland, who executed Somerset, his former ally. This jockeying
for power at court was naturally exacerbated by the king's youth
and inexperience, but it was played out against a background of
continuing tensions over the settlement of religion.

Neither Somerset nor Northumberland were reformers by
conviction, but they had both tied their colours to the mast
of reform. Their support, sometimes active, sometimes tacit,
provided the great opportunity for the quiet man of English
ecclesiastical politics, Thomas Cranmer. Cranmer had proved
himself, under Henry, a principled, even courageous advocate
of reform whose views were moving, in the 1530s and 1540s, in
an increasingly radical direction, beyond the position of Luther
on a range of theological subjects, including sacramental theology.[15] His reputation subsequently as an Anglican theologian
has suffered in comparison with those of Richard Hooker and
the 'Caroline' divines, a number of theologians who came to
especial prominence in the later years of James I's reign, and
who are usually assumed to have shifted the Church of England
once again in a more 'Catholic' direction (we shall see later how
misleading that view really is). But this is unfair to Cranmer.
He was not a systematic theologian to rival Hooker, but his

theological influence on the Church of England, especially as a drafter of liturgy, was second to none.

It has been said that the Church of England's doctrine is to be found especially in its worship.[16] If this is true, then it is above all tribute to the creative genius of Cranmer. And Cranmer, by the time of Edward's accession, was no middle-of-the-road *via media* man. His position on soteriology – the cluster of Christian doctrines concerned with salvation – on the authority of the Bible, on the sacraments, and crucially on Church order – that is, the structure of the Church – put him on the 'left wing' of the Reformation. Cranmer was intent on overseeing a root-and-branch reform of the Church of England. But he was nothing if not careful. Under Henry, he had to tread warily, especially in the turbulent last years of the reign. Even under Edward, with a regime broadly supportive of his ambitions for the Church, he had to reckon with a complex, divided political and religious atmosphere, in which it was by no means clear that there was a broad basis of support for his views.

This has given Cranmer's liturgical and ecclesiastical reforms the appearance of moderation, but the distance travelled in the short reign of Edward was remarkable. The first fruits of Cranmer's efforts to replace the traditional Latin rites of the medieval English Church was an English language litany, introduced during Henry's reign in 1544, which could be used as a penitential rite, in processions. Cranmer translated, reordered and heavily edited the traditional Latin sources, cutting out many references to the saints. Clearly he had a good ear for language, and he was writing, like Tyndale, at a time when what we recognise as modern literary English was coming into its own; also, he was not afraid to draw on good traditional translations when they were suitable. So phrases in this first foray into liturgical English, continued on into later versions, have remained resonant across the centuries up to the present day: 'In all time of our tribulation, in all time of our wealth, in the hour of death, in the day of judgment: Good Lord deliver us.'[17]

But this was just a beginning. Just over a year after Edward's accession, Cranmer introduced a first English communion order, a series of texts – not a complete rite – which could be inserted into the traditional Latin rite most widely used in England, the 'Sarum' rite. It made a number of important innovations, including for the first time providing for all those receiving communion to have both the bread and wine, thus obliterating at one stroke the eucharistic division the medieval Church had made between the priest, who received both bread and wine, and the laity, who received only bread.[18] This was only a prelude to the first complete English prayer book, *The Book of the Common Prayer and Administration of the Sacraments and other Rites and Ceremonies of the Church after the Use of the Church of England*, issued in 1549.[19] Common does not here mean down-to-earth or unadorned, but rather universal, that is, common to all. It was the *only* set of services used in the Church of England. This was Anglican uniformity in action, to be imposed on a still largely unwilling population.

This first Church of England prayer book was evidently intended as a definitely reformed liturgical order, but it satisfied no one. Cranmer had perhaps hoped to disarm traditionalists by retaining some of the traditional calendar of saints' days, as well as a eucharistic order that could be interpreted as allowing belief in the real, bodily presence of Christ, but in this he failed. Stoked up by other issues, including poor harvests, rising inflation and resentment at the seizure and enclosure of common land by private landowners, rebellion broke out in parts of the country, including in the west, where the new service was resisted. It was this unrest that led to Somerset's fall.

But even Cranmer's evangelical supporters thought the book a compromise. The Strasbourg reformer Martin Bucer, newly installed as Regius Professor in Cambridge, wrote a devastating critique of its inadequacies.[20] Cranmer felt his way further forward, to a second *Book of Common Prayer*, in 1552. This looks and feels much like the *Book of Common Prayer* still in use in the Church of England today. Gone was any reference to the

Mass. The order 'for the administration of the Lord's Supper' presented a eucharistic doctrine going arguably even beyond Calvin: Cranmer's theology of 'worthy reception' assumed a real presence of Christ only in the heart of the faithful believer; the whole rite was in effect a series of penitential prayers or acts of contrition by which believers were urged to confess their own innate unworthiness without the supervening grace of God. Nothing illustrates Cranmer's understanding of eucharistic presence better than the words with which the priest gives the consecrated bread into the proffered hands of the believer: 'Take and eat this, in remembrance that Christ died for thee, and feed on him in thy heart by faith, with understanding.'[21]

Cranmer's new English language services thus struck at the root of traditional popular practice, the Mass. It was in Edward's reign that ordinary people first began to see major changes in their local churches. Royal injunctions and specific parliamentary acts carried through other reforms. Chantries – religious foundations established to hold masses for the souls of the dead – were finally abolished at the beginning of the reign, along with collegiate church foundations. This removed at a stroke another widely accepted feature of late medieval religion. Over 2,000 chantry chapels and guild chapels disappeared, though in a few cases – mostly when retained as additional 'side' chapels – the structures survive today, bereft of their original purpose. The assault on the doctrine of purgatory begun in Henry's reign was thus carried further in Edward's. It also meant effectively the end of prayers for the dead, something intrinsically objectionable to reformers as it naturally implied purgatory as an intermediate state. To reformers, the dead were dead, and past change: they were in God's hands already, awaiting judgment. It was a corollary of the reformers' emphasis on justification and the supervening grace of God that nothing human beings could do could alter the judgment of God. But this was connected, too, to the changing understanding of the role of the saints, and thus of intercessory prayer. Since the destiny of the dead could not be affected by human actions, it was an illusion to think that

praying to one or other saint to intercede on behalf of the dead
could be of any value; and likewise, by extension, space for the
intercession of saints even for the living was effectively oblit-
erated. Underlining this, the injunctions also attacked images,
requiring them to be taken down from churches.

It was under Edward that the first concerted campaign of
iconoclasm took place, with windows sometimes smashed or,
more likely, their glass allowed to fade without being replaced,
wall paintings whitewashed, and statues defaced. These changes
were cumulatively a revolution in the Church of England's local
culture and identity. It is tempting to see Edward's reign as some
sort of temporary interlude, an extreme lurch in one direction
that was contradicted by another extreme jolt in the opposite
direction under Mary, only to be modified in turn by a more
moderate correction under Elizabeth. But that is to misread the
Edwardian revolution in worship. Though it did not yet 'take'
at local level, so far as we can tell, none the less it marked the
arrival of a definite, reformed English Church, a truly 'Protestant' church. Elizabeth's settlement of religion was to be much
closer to the situation at her brother's death than the Anglican
'middle way' apologists have conventionally allowed. Things
changed later in the course of Anglican history, but Edward's
reign was no aberration.

Cranmer and his reform-minded colleagues were not content
to alter practice in parish churches. They also wanted to reform
the doctrine and organisation of the Church. Late in the reign
Cranmer drafted a set of forty-two articles on specific or contentious points of Christian doctrine. These have come down to us
as the Thirty-nine Articles of Religion, since they were revised
at the beginning of Elizabeth's reign. But even in draft form
they provided a clear statement of Cranmer's understanding of
a reformed, or fully 'Protestant' doctrine. They amount to a
systematic statement of Christian faith, beginning with belief in
God and the Holy Trinity, proceeding through the authority of
Scripture and the ancient creeds of the Church, to the doctrine
of salvation, and on to the nature and authority of the Church

and the sacraments, then to the civil governance and good order of the Church, and finally to eschatology, that is, the doctrine of the last things. They drew on various Continental Protestant statements of faith, and on some of the earlier articles issued in Henry's reign, and, like the 'confessions' of the Lutheran and Reformed Protestant traditions, they could be regarded as an outline statement of the belief of the Church of England. But they were only ever produced in draft form; Edward's death ensured they went no further.

An equally still-born exercise, this time not resurrected by Elizabeth, was a planned reform of canon law, that is, the law of the Church. It seems extraordinary that the far-reaching nature of the Henrician statutes was never complemented by reform of canon law, though several attempts to establish committees to do so were made, and an outline of a proposed reform projected in 1535. Again, the turn to the left under Edward finally gave Cranmer the opportunity. But it was too late. His proposed reform – the *Reformatio legum ecclesiasticorum* – though drafted, never came into force, and though Matthew Parker as archbishop of Canterbury sought to revive it after Queen Mary's death, opposition from parliamentarians who disputed the monarch's power to reform ecclesiastical legislation ensured it was never adopted.[22]

With all this change being pursued or forced through in a matter of years, it is worth reflecting on what none the less remained untouched by Cranmer's reforms. There is no sign that Cranmer considered abolishing the parish system; indeed, by strengthening requirements to keep parish registers, arguably he underlined its importance to the Church of England. More questionable is the matter of the ecclesiastical hierarchy and the diocesan organisation of the Church, including the cathedrals. There are signs that, had the boy king lived much longer, further reforms would have followed. Much of the traditional structure and organisation of the Church of England remained untouched at Edward's death in 1553. This was to be a Trojan horse for rival theories of the Church in the reign of

Elizabeth and later, with some pressing for more reform to rid the Church of these 'Papist' encumbrances, and others interpreting them as signs of the Church of England's catholicity (its full membership of the universal Church of Christ) and its apostolicity (its fidelity to the form of the Church grounded in the earliest centuries of Christian experience). This survival – which almost certainly boiled down to little more than good or bad luck, depending on your point of view – was to be the source of future conflict. You could say this was the drawback of Cranmer's realism: his refusal to try to change everything at once, and his readiness therefore to try to synchronise the process of reform to accommodate the thin basis of wider political and social support on which it rested, meant that his full vision of a reformed Church of England was only partly achieved. To the organisational and structural shortcomings of his policy, one also has to add various doctrinal and liturgical loose ends, which a longer reign might have ironed out in time – the continued use of liturgical vestments (the white surplice, the coloured cope), parts of the *Book of Common Prayer* itself, and so on. These survivals were not really planned, and were not an intrinsic part of Cranmer's policy; as I have emphasised already, we cannot look to Cranmer for a notion of Anglicanism as a middle way. That would come later.

So Edward's reign was a Reformation only half completed. Even those Anglicans, much later in the Church of England's history, who entirely repudiated the achievements of the Reformation and wanted to see the Church return to a doctrine and practice much more in line with traditional Catholicism, perhaps without Papal communion, could see that the process of Reformation in England was untidy and incomplete. Richard Hurrell Froude, who scandalised his fellow clergy in the nineteenth century by his aspersions on the Reformers, called the Reformation 'a limb badly set'.[23] How an Anglican could apparently think such a view consistent with remaining in the Church of England is a matter to which I will return later, but the point is that even those who largely opposed what the reformers stood for could recognise that contingent circumstances had a significant effect on the outcome of Edward's reign. Since Elizabeth, as we shall see, would not go beyond the limits of what had been achieved in her brother's reign, this half-completed Reformation became the permanent position of the Church of England.

3

REACTION AND SETTLEMENT

Mary: Restoration and Reaction

Edward's half-sister Mary acceded to the throne in July 1553 in circumstances that simply confirmed how precarious England's Reformation was. The rapid failure of Northumberland's attempt to forestall Mary by putting on the throne Lady Jane Grey, a 16-year-old descendant of Henry VII but not in the direct line of succession, showed how little force reformers could muster against a far stronger claimant. Mary entered London as queen to cheering crowds. And yet her posthumous reputation in English history has been appalling. 'Bloody Mary' became the stuff of Protestant propaganda, an incompetent ruler who attempted to turn the clock back and return England to the Papal yoke, alienated her people with an ill-advised marriage to Philip II of Spain, made things worse by her savage persecution and burning of Protestants, lost the last English possession in France, Calais, and failed to produce the heir who would have secured the succession. Mary, it is commonly assumed, turned a people who were half-hearted at best about reform firmly towards Protestantism. If elements of this narrative do hold water, none the less the broader assumption commonly made about the regime as a 'failure' has to be called into question.

There is quite a lot of evidence to suggest that the Marian 'reaction' actually took effect surprisingly quickly and thoroughly at a local level, as well as at the court and in the capital. After all, in large areas of England, religious reform was still only skin deep. Not everything could be switched back promptly, however. Realistically, there could be no wholesale return of monastic property and restoration of monasticism: too many gentry and nobility had benefitted from the expropriation of monastic property, and the regime could not risk alienating them. Pope Paul IV underlined this in 1555 by formalising the dissolution of all those houses closed under Henry VIII.[1] There were a handful of new foundations, including Westminster Abbey, re-established in 1556 as a Benedictine community after having been a cathedral for ten years; but this community lasted just three years, closing down months after Elizabeth's accession, along with other new foundations. The abbey, a royal mausoleum, was preserved by Elizabeth as a royal collegiate church. No immediate move was made against the royal supremacy: Mary needed it in the early months of her regime to force through the repeal of the Edwardian measures. Royal injunctions were used in 1554 to reassert traditional practice and doctrine, including clerical celibacy, heresy, the calendar of saints' days, and the Roman Ordinal as the only acceptable basis for the ordination of priests.

Mary and her advisers recognised the political realities: they had to work through constitutional means. That meant Parliament. Like Edward and her father, Mary used Parliament to ensure that religious reform – now for a return to Catholicism – was enacted by legally recognised means. Reform-inclined bishops, many of them appointed under Edward, were forced out of their sees and replaced by traditionalists. Cranmer himself was deprived of his office, and imprisoned. The Henrician legislation was not repealed until early 1555, some eighteen months after Mary's accession, and *after* England had finally been returned, in November 1554, to the Papal communion.

Careful, but none the less energetic and organised, the Marian restoration was widely welcomed by local parishioners. With the dismantling of the Edwardian legislation went the *Book of Common Prayer*. Much of the paraphernalia of traditional parish worship returned under the royal injunctions of 1554, including Mass books, Mass vestments and vessels, incense, oil of chrism, and the rood and rood loft. It took time for parishes to acquire these things. The revived prohibition on married clergy probably led to the deprivation of a quarter or even more of the parish clergy, leaving many parishes without pastoral provision for a while. New seminaries were founded, but much more time was needed than was in the end available to increase clerical recruitment. Testimony to the speed and effectiveness of change, however, comes from the visitation of Kent carried out in 1556 and 1557. This was a county under the patronage and influence of Cranmer himself for twenty years; but the evidence for the rapid restoration of traditional worship and doctrine is overwhelming.[2] Nicholas Harpsfield, the archdeacon in charge, required information about anyone declining to receive communion under the restored traditional form, or indeed to participate in other traditional ceremonies and rites, and when malefactors were discovered, they were brought before him, interrogated and obliged to conform. Systematic and effective, Harpsfield's work provides a picture of a region returned to traditional worship with relative ease.

Given the brevity of Mary's reign (just over five years), and her failure to produce an heir, the change of policy was short-lived, and perhaps of passing practical significance in a history of the Church of England. Most of the Henrician and Edwardian measures were restored under Elizabeth. But in one important respect Mary had a long-lasting legacy – the effect of persecution and martyrdom. Tudor executions were a public spectacle: people were encouraged to go to them. The theatre of execution was part of the very point of it, to give dire warning to others tempted to follow. Heretics and traitors were executed throughout the sixteenth century, under all regimes. All the same, the Marian burnings stand out for their severity and intensity.

Almost 300 people were burnt at the stake in just four years, under the heresy laws revived against Protestants in late 1554. There were high-profile executions, such as those of Cranmer himself, Hugh Latimer and Nicholas Ridley. But most of those executed were of more humble background, though a significant number were lesser-known clergy, such as John Philpot, former archdeacon of Winchester, who went to the stake kissing it and saying, 'Shall I disdain to suffer at this stake seeing my redeemer did not refuse to suffer most vile death upon the cross for me?'[3] This was not simply a vindictive campaign of terror, relying on arbitrary, jumped-up charges, but a systematic strategy of eliminating the leadership of the Protestant movement, by forcing people to recant, and then executing those that did not. Cranmer was the exception here: he signed no less than five recantations, but was still executed as it was too much of a risk to allow him to live; only when it was clear he would not be spared did he withdraw his recantations and consequently face a brave but perhaps somewhat ambiguous martyr's death. Around a thousand prominent Protestants fled to the Continent to escape arrest and trial. The justification for the campaign of burning – recently restated by the historian Eamon Duffy – was that it applied a limited, last-resort measure of coercion to reinforce the other measures by which traditional religion was being restored.[4]

Without doubt, the burnings were effective. But the collapse of the regime with Mary's death put them into a wholly different context. There is some evidence to suggest that the unprecedented nature of the campaign repelled some people, but too much should not be made of this.[5] Later, Protestant historians claimed the burnings horrified people so much that they finally turned against Mary. Marian restoration became the Marian 'reaction', a top-down, oppressive campaign that failed to take root locally. But, as we have seen, this was largely not so, or at least not exclusively so. The restoration of Catholicism was happening rapidly and successfully at local level, and with considerable – if no longer universal – popular support.

What then of the burnings? Although they didn't tip popular feeling towards Protestantism, they were an own goal, providing Protestant propagandists with a martyrology and myth of Catholic oppression. John Foxe was the most significant of these writers. He first published a collection of stories of martyrdom in 1563, thereafter expanded it considerably and reprinted it. His

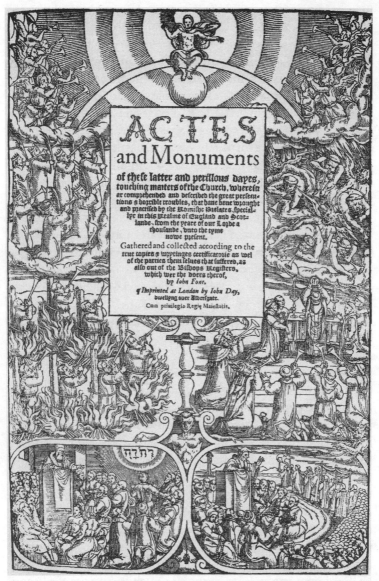

3. Martyrdom and myth-making: the frontispiece
to Foxe's *Book of Martyrs*, 1563

Acts and monuments of matters most speciall and memorable, happenyng in the Church ... as nowe lately practised by Romish prelates ... – invariably known as Foxe's *Book of Martyrs* – became one of the most popular works of religious writing in English history, influencing how generations of ordinary people came to see the Roman Catholic Church as oppressive, and the Church of England as rooted in a heroic history of resistance to Catholicism.[6] It was one of the rare instances in literary history, perhaps, where the sheer size of the book – over 2,000 pages in the last edition published in Foxe's lifetime – actually helped build the book's reputation. It contained more than enough ammunition for those who wanted to use it as a weapon against Rome. But it was in abridged form, in multiple cheap editions, that the text became a familiar one. Foxe combined detailed accounts of trials and deaths with a very evident bias against the inquisitors and judges, putting this all in the context of the long history of Christian martyrdom. It is principally to Foxe that we owe words such as those he attributed to Latimer, burnt alongside Ridley: 'Be of good comfort Master Ridley, and play the man. We shall this day light such a candle, by God's grace in England, as (I trust) shall never be put out.'[7] Nothing serves a cause better than a myth of perseverance through suffering, and that is what Foxe and others gave the Church of England.

But there is an irony in this. Mary's reign marked the point at which the idea that the Church of England could encompass all but a tiny fraction of the English people began to fall apart. The assumption that it was but the continuation of the ancient *Ecclesia Anglicana*, the Church of the English people, continued to shape Anglican thinking for generations to come. It was axiomatic right up until the beginning of the nineteenth century that conformity in religion promoted good order and social peace: along with the pursuit of conformity to the authorised rites of the Church of England, enforced wherever necessary by secular power, ran the ambition of churchmen to seek uniformity in belief and practice. But after Mary's reign, this was beyond the bounds of the possible. The hard core of Protestant activists – clergy, theologians, some gentry – who had fled to the centres of Protestant strength on the Continent mostly settled in towns and cities in or near the Rhineland and what is now Switzerland. These included Strasbourg, Frankfurt, Basle and, of course, Geneva, where from the 1540s the forceful personality of John Calvin was shifting Protestantism in a new, predestinarian direction, one that was later to attract the label 'Reformed', as opposed to the Lutheranism of northern Germany and Scandinavia. Henceforth, Calvin, and not Luther, was to be the dominant theological influence on the development of Anglican theology.

Had Mary lived, who knows what would have become of these expatriate communities? They may have been the militant edge of Protestantism, but it is hard to imagine that even under a long reign Protestant opinion in England would simply have disappeared altogether. Other Continental examples – France, Italy – suggest that more likely would have been the survival of some groups of Protestant worshippers, leading to long-run religious division. That, after all, is what happened the other way round, with Mary's death, when Catholicism became a minority, underground religion, reinforced by missionaries from overseas. But in the end, the counterfactual point is neither here nor there. Mary died in November 1558, and her project of restoration came to an abrupt close. Yet its near success demonstrated how difficult it would be to secure uniformity in religious practice. In her father's reign, dissent was minimal, despite wide disagreements over religion. The switchback of Edward's and Mary's reigns had opened up permanent religious divisions in England.

Elizabeth and Her 'Settlement' of Religion

We can only imagine the desperation Mary and her followers must have felt as she lay dying, knowing that the only credible heir she could nominate was her Protestant half-sister Elizabeth. Their hope was that the new queen would be hobbled by Catholic advisers and bishops, and that, with the success of the restoration project in the parishes, England's newly restored Catholic affiliation would last. It was a forlorn hope, but only just. The inner court was rapidly established, with Elizabeth's friend William Cecil installed as her principal secretary, and the Privy Council purged of its Marian appointees. But fairly brutal arm-wrenching of wavering lords and Members of Parliament, and the emasculation by imprisonment of much of the epis-copate, was required to bed the new regime down in the early months of 1559. There was a lot of resistance, and at first Eliza-beth and her advisers had to tread very carefully. There was, however, no question for them but that the Church would once again come out of the Papal fold. Elizabeth's religious convic-tions were shaped by Protestant, or at least anti-Papal, tutors and advisers as a child, and her circle of favourites, including Robert Dudley and Cecil himself, were firmly Protestant in their beliefs. There was a quite understandable expectation on the part of persecuted evangelicals, both at home and abroad, that her accession would mean the resumption of the Edwardian project of ongoing reform. But Elizabeth was not in that mould. She was, as one of the finest historians of the period has noted, 'an odd sort of Protestant'.[8]

Definitely anti-Papal, while formally she accepted the doc-trine of justification by faith, elements of her personal piety leaned towards a moderate Catholic, perhaps almost Lutheran belief in the real presence in the eucharist. She also willingly received Mass during her sister's reign (though there were obvious political motives for that, too), venerating the symbol of the cross and keeping a crucifix in the Chapel Royal, and favoured the first (1549) English Prayer Book, not the more reformed version of 1552. She patronised Catholic composers, and adored the complex harmonies of Latin motets and set-tings, which she permitted in her own chapels.[9] All of this was anathema to the more consistent or radical evangelicals around her. Here was Elizabeth's predicament, then. English religious life was rapidly polarising, under the pressure of the Edward-ian and Marian switchback. She could perhaps tolerate but not realistically support Catholics, for obvious reasons, and anyway she was in good conscience a Protestant. But she could not go where many of her supporters wanted her to go, further into reforming the Church. It is to Elizabeth herself, and not to any intrinsic quality or theological identity of the Church of England at this time, that we have to attribute what was later often promoted as the virtue of Anglicanism, its 'golden mean' between the extremes of Rome and Geneva.

Her predicament was encapsulated in the settlement of religion in the early months of her reign. It was a matter of practical politics, as much as anything. How could the conflicting expectations of loyal Catholics, cautious and conservative Protestants, as well as firm Protestants be contained peaceably within the one Church? Essentially, the clock that stopped at the death of Edward was dusted down and wound up, only to be stopped again at almost the same point. Royal injunctions repeated most of the prohibitions of the Edwardian injunctions. The royal supremacy was reinstated, but with the concession that the monarch was described as 'Supreme Governor' and not 'Supreme Head' – a concession welcomed by both Catholics (wasn't the Pope the head of the Church on earth?) and Protestants (wasn't Christ the only head of the Church?). Elizabeth lost her battle to have the 1549 Prayer Book reinstated, and the 1552 one was reimposed by an Act of Uniformity, although with some minor but significant changes. The most telling of these was in the order for the Lord's Supper, where the words of administration – the words the priest says when handing the consecrated bread and wine to the communicant – were a simple fusion of 1549 and 1552; 'The Body of our Lord Jesus Christ which was given for thee, preserve thy body and soul unto everlasting life' (1549), returned, but was followed immediately by 'Take and eat this in remembrance that Christ died for thee, and feed on him in thy heart by faith with thanksgiving' (1552). This was a fudge of sorts, but definitely a Protestant one. It was probably as close as the rite could go in seeming to allow a theology of objective real presence (seeming to treat the bread itself as body), but framed within Cranmer's understanding of the eucharist in the second sentence as a 'memorial' by which in faith Christ became really present in the heart of the believer. It might just permit some Catholic-inclined believers to receive communion, and all the evidence suggests that that is what happened.

Even after relations with the Catholic community deteriorated in the early 1570s, it is clear many Catholic families kept their heads down and conformed, at least on the surface; they have been called 'church Papists' by historians.[10] The Forty-Two Articles were amended, and their eschatological clauses removed, to make the Thirty-Nine Articles, which became in effect the Church of England's standard of belief for over three hundred years. A second *Book of Homilies* was eventually produced, to supplement the first. This was all very promising for ardent Protestants, especially the returning exiles, who appreciated the need for some initial caution. But it was as far as Elizabeth would ever go. Once again commissioners were sent out to enforce the changes, in association with the purged and reconstructed hierarchy.

But this was all potentially very unstable, for the obvious reason that it risked pleasing almost no one. The settlement came under pressure from both sides of the religious divide almost immediately, and probably the only reason it held for the duration of Elizabeth's reign was the queen's own obstinacy in defending it, combined with the obvious fact that hers was the longest reign of all the Tudor monarchs, enduring despite constant pressure on the question of dynastic succession, given her refusal to marry. She was, without question, an astute and forceful monarch, though her force was often shown as much in her determination to resist making decisions and the pressure of her advisers, as it was in the taking of initiative. Her dogged refusal to alter the terms of settlement meant, paradoxically, that it practically outlasted the storms and stresses it faced in her reign.

The precariousness of the religious settlement was exemplified in two directions. On the Catholic side, the policy of 'going soft' on Catholic consciences while at the same time firmly putting back a Protestant theology and practice in the Church eventually wore thin. The failure of a plot to marry Elizabeth to the duke of Norfolk, and the ensuing rebellion of Catholic nobles in the north in 1569, set the scene for Pope Pius V's bull *Regnans in excelsis* (1570), which declared Elizabeth a heretic, excommunicated her, and commanded (that is the exact word used) her subjects to disobey her and deprive her of the Crown.[11] Catholics had to choose, then, between remaining loyal to the Crown and treason. This, and Elizabeth's failure to marry, was why the presence in England of the Catholic Mary, Queen of Scots, who had a strong title to the throne, after she had fled Scotland in 1568, became an ever greater threat, and the discovery of her involvement in conspiracy against Elizabeth led inexorably, if slowly and (on Elizabeth's part) reluctantly, to her execution in 1587. By then, an active if covert English Catholic mission to bolster the Catholic community, led above all by the Jesuits, was well under way, producing its equally inevitable executions for treason. Catholics who were not prepared to compromise as church Papists were being driven into the recusant enclave in British society in which they remained for generations, disprivileged and regarded with suspicion.

But by far the greater force destabilising the settlement came from within English Protestantism itself. And here a bugbear word comes into play – 'puritan'. This had relatively little to do with its modern sense of one who dislikes pleasure. It was in Elizabeth's reign that a fissure seemed to open up between those who wanted to 'purify' the English Church and those who were content, perhaps increasingly from conviction, with the 1559 settlement. The word 'puritan', originally a term of abuse, was applied to the former, and it has been tainted retrospectively by its history in the seventeenth century.[12] Anglican apologists, after the Civil Wars, looked back on the Puritan movement as a sort of alien, hostile fifth column in the Church of England, working to undermine its structures and worship in the interests of a radical reformation along the lines of Calvin's Geneva.

The implication was that the Anglican 'mainstream' in Elizabeth's reign stood roughly where it was commonly held to be in the late seventeenth and eighteenth centuries – a *via media*, valuing Catholic order and a sacramental life independent of Rome, with a moderate Protestant theology at its heart.

We shall see in chapter 5 how such a position came to be formulated theologically – and for many, persuasively. But it is not an accurate description of the pre-Civil War Church of England. What some historians have called a 'new paradigm' of Elizabethan religion has upended the conventional relationship of Puritanism and the Elizabethan Church.[13] Puritanism was not a single, compact body of opinion, but a wide range of views which encompassed senior hierarchs who were content with the broad terms of the settlement but wanted to adjust it a little, those who also broadly accepted the settlement but were enthusiastic evangelists and preachers, those who wanted to see definite change but largely in ritual and devotional terms, and those who wanted further root-and-branch reform. What they held in common was religious earnestness – but that is, after all, a very vague term – and some level of dissatisfaction with the prevailing state of English religion. Most Puritans were Calvinist in the sense that they shared a reformed (strictly, we now ought to begin to capitalise 'Reformed' as a distinct position in Protestantism) theology of salvation, stressing not only justification through faith alone, but also predestination. But then the vast majority of ministers in the Elizabethan Church could, by the 1580s and 1590s, in this very loose way be called 'Calvinist'. The Anglican *via media* between Protestantism and Catholicism did not as yet exist. Most Anglican clergy – we cannot realistically make this assertion for many ordinary worshippers, for lack of evidence – were convinced Protestants of a broadly Reformed character. Puritanism was above all a restless, dynamic movement of reform which operated on many fronts and engaged the energies and enthusiasm of many different groups of clergy and people.

Pressure for further reform of the Church came in several

waves, each of which Elizabeth saw off, mostly through inaction. Almost from the off, the newly restored Protestant hierarchy included many clergy uncomfortable with the retention of various 'Popish' practices from the reign of Edward VI, including the use of the sign of the cross at baptism, kneeling (rather than sitting) to receive communion, and the wearing of vestments by clergy, namely the surplice and tippet. The issue of vestments broke surface in the mid-1560s. Open preaching against them by London clergy such as Robert Crowley, with tacit support from Edmund Grindal, bishop of London, provoked a counter-move by Archbishop Matthew Parker, a moderate who was former chaplain to Anne Boleyn. Parker's articles (later called 'Advertisements') enforcing conformity on dress and other matters were, however, not officially sanctioned by Elizabeth, and the crackdown he instigated eventually succeeded only with the forced expulsion of the Puritan leadership from their pulpits.[14]

Further trouble came in the early 1570s with the publication of an 'Admonition' to members of Parliament by Puritan clergy, calling for greater discipline in the Church and for reform to reduce the episcopate to an equality of ministers, with elders in every congregation: 'The model was Geneva, mediated through other reformed churches.'[15] Publications for and against ensued, the argument rumbling on for years. Again matters came to a head in 1575–6, when Elizabeth, facing a new archbishop, the pro-Puritan Edmund Grindal, demanded the suppression of conferences of preachers known as 'prophesyings'; Grindal's refusal to accede, extraordinarily, led to his virtual suspension for the remainder of his archiepiscopate. Perhaps the most significant threat came in the mid- and late 1580s, with a concerted effort by Grindal's successor, the anti-Puritan (but definitely Protestant and theologically Calvinist) John Whitgift, to suppress Puritan preaching, which only served to infuriate his Puritan opponents and to intensify the establishment of unofficial clerical assemblies, or presbyteries, that had begun to form in parts of East Anglia and the Midlands. Again, despite a sympathetic

Parliament actually discussing a bill for further reform of the Church, the moment passed: judicious use of the Court of Star Chamber to prosecute leading ministers, and the dispersal of the conferences, effectively suppressed the dissatisfaction.

But again it is important to emphasise that Puritanism was not a kind of ecclesiastical virus or parasite on the Elizabethan body politic. It is perfectly reasonable to suggest that the outlier, from a broader European Protestant perspective, was not the opinions and causes of Puritanism, but the oddly mismatched religious polity that was the Church of England. Puritans were, in essence, faithful and highly motivated reformed (or rather, in many cases, 'Reformed') Christians who earnestly sought to align the Church with, as they saw it, the true Biblical model of a godly community of faith. Their calling for reform, and for greater Church discipline, was of a piece with what has been emphasised as their preoccupation with edification – their belief that 'all of one's actions must actively work towards salvation or would *actively* lead to damnation'.[16] This is where the later reputation of Puritans for being drab, pleasure-hating fanatics really comes from, but it is a complete distortion of the Puritan spirit. Puritan dissatisfaction with Elizabeth's religious settlement was obviously freighted ominously with dire implications for the future peace of the English Church, should the iron cage that was the royal supremacy weaken or fail. And some Puritans themselves were in any case beginning to question the very foundation of royal authority, arguing – in almost a mirror image of Papal claims – that all temporal authority essentially subserved Scriptural truth, and that monarchs who actively worked against the Gospel could be challenged or even overthrown. This has been called 'monarchical republicanism', but the term misleads if it makes us think of modern republicanism – almost no one at this time seriously thought around the non-existence of monarchy.[17] But Puritans did expect monarchs to be zealous in pursuit of the Gospel and obedient to its commands.

This potential challenge to royal authority was to emerge forcefully in the decades after Elizabeth's death in 1603. The mid-seventeenth-century crisis, which permanently divided and scarred English church life, should not, however, blind us to the momentous implications of the endurance of the Elizabethan religious polity. Anti-Papalism, adhering to the three-fold 'Catholic' order, the *Book of Common Prayer*, the Thirty-nine Articles, the royal supremacy – these features of the Church of England endured even beyond that crisis. This was not, even by 1603, Anglicanism as we have come to know it. But it was the strange hybrid from which such a theological perspective could flower.

4

REVOLUTION IN THE PARISHES

Pre-Reformation Parish Religion

To get some sense of just how much the Reformation changed life for ordinary people, you have to look at the local parish church, and local religious practice. The sixteenth century saw the transition from the layout and decoration of the parish church for traditional Catholic worship to an interior purged and reformed for Protestantism. The extraordinary built heritage in the keeping of the Church of England – over 10,000 medieval churches – is a living museum. But little enough has survived the centuries of change, both from the visual culture of the pre-Reformation Church, and from – more significantly – its rituals and public prayer, to enable us to reinhabit that world fully. It is tempting to lean heavily on the metaphor of a 'lost world' of faith, but it is misleading, because it allows us, if we are not careful, to fall into the lazy way of thinking that traditional Catholic worship was something static and unchanging, rather than a religious culture in constant evolution. None the less, the gap between that world and our own, even for the religious-minded today, is a vast one.

Today, religion is mostly a matter of choice. But for the late medieval mind, one could not really think 'outside' of Christian faith. The Church extended its guidance and its oversight over practically all matters of quotidian life, from the family home, to work, to leisure, as well as to public ceremony and public worship. Christianity was inseparable from the intellectual imagination of western Europe, just as it was inseparable from the way ordinary people thought about times and seasons, life and death, health and illness, success and failure. There was no 'secular' wisdom to rival this, no alternative rational stand-point. If this sounds oppressive – as certainly later generations commonly assumed – actually it may be better perhaps to recog-nise that its ubiquity was its own freedom of expression, its own mental roominess. There were plenty of moral and religious arguments within the late medieval Church, plenty of ways in which ordinary believers could engage more or less intensively with the ritual requirements of the Church. Precisely because pre-Reformation religion was more a question of corporate practice than of the strength of individual confession, personal belief, at least on the part of the laity, was rarely policed, until it transgressed the border between orthodoxy and heresy – but that was rare, though it was at times punished severely.

Traditional parish religion on the eve of the Reformation enabled the ordinary believer to conceive and negotiate a series of boundaries. One was between the sacred and the profane. This was most obvious in terms of spatial location. The church building marked out sacred space, but not uniquely. The land-scape itself was a series of overlapping sacred territories, signalled by sacred wells, by churchyards, by pilgrim routes, and by wayside shrines. Much of this was effectively destroyed at the Reformation, but some sense of it can be gleaned from the experience of travelling in Mediterranean countries even today, when a wayside crucifix or a saint's statue may mark a turning in the road, or the entry to a village, for example. Particular places were singled out as spiritually significant through the presence of shrines and the naming of a saint. The shrine of Our Lady of Walsingham was the most famous, but Willesden, Doncaster, Caversham in Berkshire and Coventry were also marked out in this way.[1] Church dedications might also indicate a special affili-ation to a particular saint, or cultivation of a saint for healing. A rare survival is a shrine to the obscure St Wite, at the church of that dedication at Whitchurch Canonicorum (literally, 'Wite's church belonging to the canons of Salisbury') in Dorset: the saint's bones lie inside a plain casket with holes through which

4. A rare survival: St Wite's shrine, Whitchurch Canonicorum

pilgrims could reach to touch them for healing. There were many such shrines before the 1530s.[2]

But it was inside the parish church that the modern observer would see the most dramatic difference from today. To enter a medieval parish church was to enter a theatre of colour, in which windows and painted statues and walls conveyed the Christian narrative of fall and redemption. So much of this colour has gone that it is very difficult to imagine the spectacle. In some places – Fairford in Gloucestershire is perhaps the most famous example – the survival of significant amounts of medieval glass helps us to imagine it, as it does, too, in some cathedrals, such as York, Canterbury and Gloucester. So ubiquitous was the practice of whitewashing over wall paintings from the 1540s on, that discerning the full glory of painted walls is very difficult. In the nineteenth and twentieth centuries, conservationists began to uncover something of this lost world of religious art. St Cadoc's, Llancarfan in Glamorganshire is a church in which extensive wall paintings, including a spectacular St George and a doom painting have recently been uncovered by careful erasure of the overpainted whitewash.[3]

Saints' statues were the most vulnerable of all these forms of art, susceptible as they were to the accusation of idolatry. Again, to get a sense of just how rich the sculptural interiors (or exteriors) of English churches were, sometimes it is helpful to look at Continental examples, such as the extraordinary façade of Strasbourg cathedral, including a portal with images of the wise and foolish virgins. In England, the west front of Wells cathedral presents a similar richness, though it was heavily reconstructed in the nineteenth century. Parish churches could rarely afford so much carved stone, but wooden carvings abounded, as well as painted images on wooden panels. At Ranworth in Norfolk, the screen that in many churches divides the nave, where parishioners assembled, from the chancel or choir, where the high altar is situated, still has a set of painted images of the saints – a remarkable survival despite the years of iconoclasm in the sixteenth and seventeenth centuries.

These brilliant interiors served a didactic function, in a time when so few people were literate. Biblical stories abounded on the walls and in the windows of parish churches, and were sermons in pictures. But their purpose was more than educative. They were also a setting for the ritual and drama of the liturgical year, and they echoed the sacramental theology central to traditional worship and to its associated notion of contemplation and ascent. The church building was heaven in miniature: to be in church was to enter into a space carrying the believer in spirit upwards to heaven, in contemplation of the saints in heaven, the angels, and Christ ruling on high. The tradition of doom paintings, as at Chaldon in Surrey, was frequently coupled with images of the crucified, risen and ascended Christ. Not only were believers to fear the consequences of sin and lack of repentance, as exemplified in these paintings, but they were also to be uplifted, and inspired, in contemplation of Christ on high. The aesthetics of pre-Reformation churches were saving aesthetics: they aimed to evoke the very experience of the fear and ecstasy of faith.

The buildings and their rich decorations were also of a piece with the rituals of assembly, movement and procession that marked the liturgies of the pre-Reformation Church. In most parish churches, the main part of the nave was not filled with benches, but empty. Congregations might stand, or sit on the floor. Processions might begin in the church, but then move out on to the paths of the parish itself. Some sense of this ritual year, built around the liturgical calendar, can be gleaned from one parish, Long Melford in Suffolk, where, in Elizabeth's reign, the recusant Roger Martin described for posterity both the decorative interior of the church and the main festivals and processions of the ritual year. There were processions for Palm Sunday, Easter and Corpus Christi, for St Mark's Day and for the parish bounds in Rogation Week, bonfires at several points in the year including Midsummer Eve and the eve of St James's Day, and many other festivals and feasts.[4] But even an 'ordinary' or 'low' (in a later terminology) Mass itself was not without its element of drama, when the 'pax board' (usually a mounted wooden disc or board) would be passed round at the peace to be kissed in turn by members of the congregation, usually in descending order of social significance, or when the priest raised the host (the disc of bread) at the consecration, and the sacring bell would be rung.

What anthropologists call the 'rites of passage' enabled people to pass through the stages of life, and thus cross boundaries of growth and personal development. Their associated sacraments – baptism, marriage and extreme unction – bound the Church intimately into this process of growth. But other sacraments also provided means by which the ordinary person could work their way through the perils of life: confirmation, which was really in effect a further initiation rite, marked a stage on from baptism in the growth of the child, coming in effect into a relationship of communion with the Church; absolution cleansed the believer of the effects of sin; eucharist ('Mass') bound the believer into the community of the Church, and into union with Christ.

Another boundary which ritual, art and liturgy helped the believer to negotiate was that between life and death itself. In this life, ordinary worshippers could prepare themselves for death through the ministrations of their parish priest, confessing their sins and seeking absolution before God, putting themselves in a right relation with God. They could prolong life through the intercessory prayers of the saints, or through the miracles that might lift them out of illness at shrines and on pilgrimages. Death was terrifying, because it brought the prospect of judgment and damnation. And yet life itself, in all its complications, could trap human beings in a constant web of self-deceit, lies, jealousy, rage and lust. Meditation on the seven deadly sins, sometimes pictured on the church walls, and on their correlatives, the seven virtues, could help to direct the heart aright. Listening to morally improving sermons, or – for the literate, few as they were – reading improving literature, or praying with a primer could all reinforce the sense that a good life was a preparation for an even better death. The prospect of heaven was a possible compensation for the sufferings of this life. Traditional religion gave ordinary people the opportunity to improve their chances of a good death. But even after death, all was not lost. By prayer, and especially by masses said for the souls of the dead, the duration of purgatory for loved ones could be shortened, the chances of heaven increased. Pre-Reformation belief provided context for contact with the dead, a sense that the dead were in some sense still 'around' or 'here', not altogether unlike the ancestors in many African traditional religions. And even the saints, prayed to, sought out in prayer and pilgrimage for wisdom, captured as personal or household figures, or even, as we have seen, identified with specific locations, were 'wise ancestors' for the living.

At the risk of labouring the point, pre-Reformation religion was a way of life that, for most people, was all-encompassing and yet flexible and adaptable. It had had centuries to develop and change. Despite the growth of the medieval Papacy, with its disputed claims to authority over temporal as well as spiritual affairs, despite the near-ubiquity of Latin as the ecclesiastical and learned language, and despite the accumulated doctrinal deposit of the medieval Church, uniformity was not a notable characteristic of late medieval practice and belief. There was considerable regional variation in liturgy, in custom, in the celebrations of the liturgical year, and in the overlap between 'official' religion – that is, the formal creedal statements and doctrinal positions of the Church – and popular ideas later generations would come to label as 'superstition'. In all these ways, accommodation was made between the spiritual and pastoral needs of people and what they encountered in church and through the clergy. It would be naïve to think that the needs of people and the provision made by the Church for those needs were perfectly matched. But never again, after the Reformation, was it possible to say that one overarching ecclesiastical structure could contain within itself practically the whole range of possible belief and practice in the realm.

The Great Tudor Upending

It is hard to credit how rapidly this world was dismantled. Someone born in the late 1520s would have been baptised and confirmed in the late medieval fashion, an adolescent in the late 1530s and early 1540s as the Henrician changes gathered pace, in their prime in the reign of Edward as radical change swept through the Church, endured or welcomed the *bouleversement* of Mary, only to see things settled again in the manner of Edward with Elizabeth's accession, and still remained a relatively young person. All the really momentous change had occurred in under thirty years.[5]

At what point would ordinary parishioners have become aware of the scale of change? Talk about the royal divorce would have run ahead of any perceptible changes, though perhaps the first real sign would have been the breach with Rome, and the assertion of the royal supremacy. The Henrician injunctions of 1536 required clergy to preach against the 'Bishop of Rome's usurped authority'.[6] Royal coats of arms began to appear in English parish churches in Henry's reign, a trend which over succeeding centuries would see them become entirely normal, just as prayers for the royal family became an integral part of the English language litany. The royal supremacy represented the apotheosis – almost literally – of the new understanding of royal authority over the Church. Nowhere illustrates this better, perhaps, than the chapel of King's College, Cambridge, founded by Henry VI, but completed by the first two Tudor kings, who wanted to associate their new dynasty with the saintly reputation of their murdered forerunner. Visitors today are usually struck first by the sheer scale of the building and by its famous fan vault, but equally noteworthy is the plethora of sculptures outside and in, not of saints, but of royal heraldic symbols – coats of arms, greyhounds, griffins, dragons, lions, portcullises, and the Tudor rose.

Another dramatic change was the disappearance of the monasteries. As they were often patrons and sometimes supplied ministers to parish churches, the monasteries' dissolution probably impoverished some churches, though in other places the community's church building now was handed over to the local congregation. At Wymondham in Norfolk, the local people maintained the nave of the great church for parish worship, as they had used it previously, and allowed the blocked-off eastern half of the church, the choir, to fall into disrepair. In some places, such as Bury St Edmunds, the destruction of the abbey church was complete, but chapels or churches for local laity at the perimeter of the abbey grounds remained in use. At Evesham, not only were two churches within the abbey precinct preserved for use, but so was the great detached bell tower completed just a quarter of a century before the dissolution, as well as the gatehouse. Sometimes parish churches were gifted communion vessels or wooden panels or seats by nobles and gentry enriched by the appropriated lands of the monasteries. Sometimes former monks became parish clergy, simply remaining *in situ*. But in general, the dissolution was a change on a scale transcending that of the local parish church.

If Henry's conservative approach to the Mass meant that its rituals and liturgy were scarcely affected directly, there were other marked changes in the last ten years if his reign. Under the royal injunctions of 1538, each parish church was to provide a Bible in English so that parishioners 'may most commodiously resort to the same, and read it'.[7] Despite later restrictions on who could read it, and with the exception of the reign of Mary, the use of an English Bible was from hereon a routine feature of parish worship. Likewise, the 1538 injunctions also marked the beginning of the campaign against images. It was not an outright ban: clergy were to take down 'feigned' images, that is, those that could be 'abused with pilgrimages or offerings of anything made thereunto'.[8] Candles – 'lights' – were to be retained on the rood loft, on the altar, and at the Easter sepulchre, and clergy were to teach that images only served the purpose of being 'books of unlearned men that cannot know letters'.[9] This was a condition broad enough to allow most saints' images, wall paintings, sculptures and painted windows to survive for the time being. But it did effectively mark the end of the devotional culture of pilgrimages, and it coincided with the destruction of the most famous shrines. Likewise, moves in themselves mild but fraught with peril for the future began to be made against some celebrations on the liturgical calendar, including some processions and saints' days. The Ten Articles of 1536 had banned the doctrine of purgatory, alleging it was something invented by the Pope, but allowed prayers for the dead, and so intercessory prayers to the saints. This was, then, change at the doctrinal level that as yet had only a modest impact on religious practice. Likewise, the move against chantries came only at the very end of Henry's reign and could not be implemented until after Edward's accession.

What remained essentially untouched in Henry's reign was the central, devotional heart of parish worship, the Mass. Along with the retention of the altar and most of the interior decoration, on the surface English parish life appeared relatively unchanged. The suggestion sometimes made that Henry's

Church was the Catholic Church without the Pope is, however, misplaced. The royal supremacy was not a mere organisational device: it carried doctrinal change in its wake, and it facilitated a rolling tide of further liturgical and ritual reform. English parish church life might not have been recognisably 'Protestant' by later standards – but it was not evidently 'Catholic' by those same standards either.

Radical Reversals – Mid-century Crisis

It was the radical changes of religious reform under Edward, Mary and Elizabeth that utterly transformed the ordinary parish church and its life into something recognisably Protestant. This was forced change, conceived centrally and applied with all the rigour available through royal injunction and parliamentary mandate. It is ironic that it was the royal supremacy that was the facilitating mechanism, when Edward himself was in his minority. It was a power exercised on his behalf.

Royal injunctions issued by Somerset in 1547 took the attack on imagery much further, leading to a concerted campaign of iconoclasm. But the main vehicle of change was the English liturgy, and in particular the *Book of Common Prayer*. The deficiencies of the 1549 book, as pointed out to Cranmer by various people, should not blind us to the fact that it was intended to carry a definite 'reformed' or 'Protestant' theology. It was the death knell of the traditional Mass. Cranmer's sacramental and eucharistic theology had changed dramatically in the 1540s, moving him away from a Lutheran position affirming the 'real presence' (a term relatively recent in use) of Christ in the consecrated bread and wine, towards a conviction that the presence of Christ was not objectively there but was rather in the heart of the believer who in faith and genuine penitence received communion. It is not altogether fair to Cranmer's theology to say, as is sometimes claimed, that this meant he had moved from an objective to a *subjective* theory: the presence to the believer was very real indeed. But the effect, in practical terms, was much the same. The communion service was now, in effect, a long, preparatory, penitential rite that aimed, through prayer, reading of the Scriptures, preaching and public confession, to put the worshipper in right relation with God, so that he or she could be deemed 'worthy' to receive the presence of Christ. Out went most of the accoutrements of the traditional Mass – the chanting, the bells, the incense, the special character of the Mass vessels, the hushed, whispered prayers of the priest, the genuflecting at the elevation – along with the fundamental character of the canon of the Mass, including the prayer of consecration as a moment of divine penetration of the material world by the active grace of God. Material things were not, in this new way of seeing things, themselves blessed and raised to divine status. All the special devotion that had once attended the Mass, and which could admittedly morph into the attribution of quasi-magical properties, now began to fall away. The ritual year was severely curtailed, through the deletion of many festivals and saints' days.

Cranmer's liturgy changed more than the devotional or religious life of the community, however. It changed the conception of what the community was in itself, and its relationship to the building in which it worshipped and the area in which it was situated. To a degree unparalleled before, and unmatched since the liturgical reforms of the mid-twentieth century, not just the public worship, but also the personal, private prayer of the community was to be regulated by one book. Once the quality of printing had improved to the point where small, pocket editions became practicable, it was common to publish the Prayer Book along with Coverdale's Psalter. This gave the ordinary literate person not only a book to carry to church for public services, but also to guide them in daily personal prayer. Everything apart from the Scriptures – too big, of course, for binding in with a Prayer Book – was contained in the book, including services for communion, for morning and evening prayer, and for baptism, marriage and burial, collects and other prayers for personal use, a lectionary to guide regular reading of the Scriptures, a monthly

5. Prayer in English: the frontispiece of the 1549 Prayer Book

cycle for reading the Psalms, and a reformed calendar of saints days and festivals. The same book was used by the priest as by the laity, and so by implication the role of the clergy as religious virtuosi was eroded: no longer did they need the elaborate service books, the chants, the breviaries and missals of the late medieval church, and so, as it seemed to some, away then went the arcane incantations of a quasi-magical spiritual elite. One community under God was to worship the same way in public, and to pray the same way in private – or at least, that's what the Prayer Book presupposed. And since the Prayer Book included prayers for the monarch and the royal family, for the governance of the realm, and for the successful resolution of public crises such as drought, war or plague, it made the royal supremacy manifest in the interior spiritual life of ordinary people. The good order of society mapped directly on to the good order and flourishing of souls. With the heavy presence of large tracts of Scripture in the Prayer Book itself, with reading from the English Bible, and with preaching directed or led by the new *Homilies* Cranmer prepared as model sermons on specific doctrinal points, each congregation was to become a 'godly' community. Liturgy here was a means of moral formation and social reform.

To that end, churches' interiors were reorganised and reconceived. With the eradication of painted and carved images, the plain interior of a church concentrated attention on the preached word, and on the drama of the Scriptural text itself. Attention was diverted downwards, and inwards, into what the believer heard and reflected on, just as Cranmer's eucharistic order diverted attention from a presence of Christ 'out there' to a presence 'in here', in the heart. Altars were removed in the reign of Edward, returned briefly under Mary, and disappeared again in Elizabeth's reign, to be replaced by a wooden communion table that to all intents and purposes looked like a domestic dining table. The Prayer Book provided for the minister or priest to stand at the north end of the table, not in the middle facing east, as would once have been usual. In many parish churches, the table was surrounded by seats, and moved away from the

6. The Lord's Supper in Elizabeth's reign: a re-enactment

east wall. Cranmer's liturgy in no way envisaged the demotion of communion in Christian worship: it remained, in theory at least, the centrepiece of worship, or the highpoint of it, with the understanding that the 'godly community' would be most at one, and most closely united to God, in the celebration of communion.[10]

The communion would remain the most important weekly service. But on a long view this proved impossible to sustain. For reasons that are still to some extent obscure, reformed English piety never managed to make the celebration of communion absolutely central to parish worship. Was it that Cranmer's communion rite so emphasised the need for believers to be sufficiently 'worthy' to receive communion that many simply never felt themselves worthy enough? That is certainly arguable. Was it also that, just as many lay people had actually received communion only rarely in the pre-Reformation Church, so in the reformed Church of England the habit of reception simply never took root? That is also arguable. What probably underscored the difficulty was the growing emphasis on the preaching and hearing of the word of God, rather than on the administration of the sacraments.

Over time, churches became more and more like preaching boxes, shorn of their elaborate decoration and side or chantry chapels, with seating facing the pulpit. The installation of fixed seating later in the sixteenth century naturally also changed the interior function of a church. Churches were not needed for processions anyway. Seating – which had earlier been reserved mostly for the gentry – was appropriate for listening to readings and long sermons. But in time it also made possible the allocation of specific seats to families in the parish, and even eventually to the introduction of 'pew rents', charges made for reserving particular seats. Where people sat, and paid for, could become almost a replication of the social order of the parish, with the gentry in the best and most expensive seats at the front and the poor at the back. Richard Gough, living in Myddle in Shropshire in the late seventeenth century, even used the allocation of pews in its church, St Peter's, as a way of describing the history of the families of the village in his *Observations concerning the seats in Myddle* (written between 1700 and 1709, but published in 1834).[11] The interior of the parish church, with rented pews, pulpit, communion table, whitewashed walls, perhaps the royal arms, thus took on a radically different appearance from its pre-Reformation form. What remained of colour were stained glass windows, retained because they were expensive, but replaced usually with clear glass as they faded or broke. Sometimes carvings remained – especially angels supporting the roof beams – with traces of fading colour.

A Reformed Church

Mary's attempt to return England to traditional Catholic worship had, in the long run, little impact on this sea change in religious sensibility, and was little more than a blip. As we saw in chapter 3, that was not because (as was once commonly thought) Mary's policy was strongly resisted across England, though there were pockets of resistance, but because there was too little time to accomplish much before her death. Within two or three years of Elizabeth's accession, the Marian 'reaction' had been largely suppressed, and the reforms of Edward's reign practically reinstated. But this did not mean that England was now firmly and uniformly Protestant. It took two or three generations for the Prayer Book to be widely accepted. Under the royal injunctions of 1559, extensive provision was made not only for the removal of shrines and images ('So that there remain no memory of the same in walls, glass windows, or elsewhere within their churches and houses'), but for enforcing conformity to the royal supremacy and use of the English Bible, for the enforcement of good order in the parish and the distribution of alms to the poor, and for the avoidance of heresy and religious contention.[12] Within the year, the royal supremacy had been fully reinstated, and the Marian legislation (including the heresy laws) repealed. Under a new Act of Uniformity, the second Prayer Book of 1552 was fully reinstated with minor modifications.

But the world of medieval piety did not vanish entirely. Here and there, older traditions about places and saints' dedications survived, alongside the more physical evidence, often damaged or fading, of late medieval art. In places holy wells, perhaps because of their practical use, continued to have people resort to them, and in popular tradition the original dedication and ideas of healing and saints' blessings continued to exercise an influence.[13] Southam in Warwickshire preserves a well to this day originally dedicated to an Anglo-Saxon saint, St Fremund. Folk memory preserved traditions about many of the saints, even as they disappeared from the calendar of feasts and festivals.

Right up into the twentieth century traditions such as that surrounding St Swithun's Day (15 July) – that it would it would be fair for forty days if it was fair on that day, or rain for forty days if raining – continued elements of older patterns of belief. Swithun was a Saxon bishop whose cult as a healer and wonder worker came to an end with the destruction of the monasteries, but his name lived on in church dedications and in the saying itself.[14] Folk songs sometimes testified to older patterns of piety. 'The Joys of Mary', first recorded in 1764, looked back to the medieval tradition of the five joys of Mary, whether from an older or contemporary source:

> *The first good joy that Mary had, it was the joy of one*
> *To see her own son Jesus Christ when he was first her son*
> *When he was first her son, good Lord, and happy may we be*
> *Praise Father, Son and Holy Ghost through all eternity.*[15]

It is doubtful that these survivals were evidence of a deep-seated, tenacious popular Catholicism. They were fragments. A national religious culture that, before the Reformation, encompassed an extraordinary breadth of practice and belief, now gave little weight to notions of sacred space and sacred artefacts. Some popular superstition and magic carried on, seemingly unrelated to the main elements of Protestant belief. It would be quite wrong to think of English Protestantism as, consequently, somehow austere or impoverished: its opening up of the Scriptures in the vernacular to ordinary people, and its habits of prayer and associated disciplines of self-examination in the light of Scripture, in turn led to an effusion of forms of private prayer, meditation, reflection and self-examination.[16] The very richness of this reformed mental universe is a very strong, predisposing reason to think how it could finally gain ground and lodge itself deeply in the consciousness of ordinary people by the early seventeenth century. As one historian has persuasively put it, 'devotional life shows early modern British Protestantism as an *intense*, *dynamic*, and *broad-based* religious culture'.[17] But that it was vastly different from the material, physical, colourful, visual religion of the late medieval church no one could dispute.

A MIDDLE WAY? THE INVENTION
OF ANGLICANISM

The Theology of the Reformed Church of England

The Reformation unleashed over a century of religious conflict in western Europe, and religious positions became ever more polarised. By the end of the sixteenth century, Europe was clearly divided into Catholic and Protestant states, and the terms 'Catholic' and 'Protestant' had come to have seemingly clear, unambiguous application. What gave the Church of England its identity after the break from Rome was above all the royal supremacy, yet royal policy on religion fluctuated wildly in the middle decades of the century. In this context, 'Protestant' was used as an umbrella term at best. It did not really signify a united, coherent body of doctrine. For the mid-century, historians generally prefer to use terms such as 'evangelical' or 'reforming' for views later described as 'Protestant', as they preserve the idea of a plurality of perspectives. There were common convictions, but they were not enough to guarantee unity of belief. They included rejection of the Papal primacy, but also very broadly the three doctrinal points held by most Reformers – as they were put, commonly, in Latin, *sola scriptura*, *sola fide*, *sola gratia*. The first meant the unique appeal to the authority of Scripture: Reformers varied in the degree to which they disregarded the authority of tradition and the Church, but they almost all emphasised the complete dependence of Christian doctrine on the witness of Scripture. The last two were usually two sides of the same coin. Christians were justified – in everyday parlance, 'saved' – by the grace of God alone, through faith. That is, faith alone – not good works – was the means by which salvation came to human beings. But Reformers did not mean that faith itself was a kind of work, a consequence of a human effort of will that in itself would merit grace: rather, the grace of God came before all else, and so the faith that justified was in effect itself an action of God; Reformers would speak of 'justifying faith', conscious and deliberate faith, in an action or grace of God that was 'prevenient'. This was effective faith, a humble acknowledgment of God's saving grace that itself produced good works. As Cranmer put it in the first book of *Homilies*, 'forasmuch as he that believeth in Christ hath everlasting life, it must needs consequently follow, that he that hath this faith must have also good works'.[1]

But these theological tenets did not amount to a systematic theology on their own, and could be worked through in widely varying ways when applied to a whole range of other topics, including the ceremonies, traditions and sacraments of the Church. So we find – as is hardly surprising – English Reformers taking time to develop their convictions, and doing so with much disagreement. Cranmer himself, as we have seen, may have accepted the royal supremacy in the early 1530s, but moved gradually beyond a quasi-Lutheran theology of the real presence of Christ in the eucharist or Mass, not reaching a different conclusion probably until the mid-1540s. Hugh Latimer, probably the most able preacher of the English Reformers, rejected the doctrine of purgatory from the early 1530s, but was still praying for the dead as late as 1550, and did not rethink his view of the eucharist until about the same time as Cranmer.[2] Robert Barnes, burnt by Henry VIII in the wake of Thomas Cromwell's fall, may have preached and written strongly on the doctrine of justification by faith, but he remained – unusually among English Reformers – a convinced Lutheran to the end.[3] The Church of England's theology was in flux for most of the 1530s and 1540s, moving fitfully along a path towards more radical reforming opinion.

Without question, Edward VI's reign saw a decisive move

towards a more thoroughly Reformed position, but Cranmer's work was cut short by Edward's death and Mary's restoration of traditional religion, and what emerged under Elizabeth was a settlement of religion curiously 'frozen' midway through transition. English 'Protestantism' was an almost unique amalgam of Catholic order and a reformed theology. Was it then truly Protestant? Or rather, what kind of Protestantism did it become? The seeds of a distinct position that would later proudly proclaim itself as 'Anglican', and a 'middle way', were there in the amalgam. But they were hardly systematised or even agreed until later in the Church of England's history. The sixteenth century was too contentious for that. Men and women had to take sides, and most English Reformers had no doubt that their sympathies lay with the more sharply defined positions of their Continental supporters. Still, as one eminent historian of the English Reformation has pointed out, the Protestant settlement that emerged in Elizabeth's reign had three main features: a 'distrust' of the doctrine of the real presence in the eucharist; a 'deep animus' against images and shrines; and 'a reassertion of the value of law and moral systems within the Reformation structure of salvation'.[4] All three points were consonant with early Tudor Lollardy, as he notes, and marked a difference from Luther, though whether that is an argument for a powerful undertow of Wycliffite opinion in the mid-sixteenth century is hard to establish. Neither criticism of the doctrine of the real presence nor opposition to images and shrines were unique to England; they were shared with the more radical Reformers of Europe. But the third point was crucial. It derived from the working out of the dynastic and royal preoccupations that had given impetus to reform in England in the first place, and it was present almost from the very beginning of the Henrician reform programme.

Some would even argue that the English Reformation happened the way it did precisely because of England's unique evolution, outside Roman law, of the common law, and of the position of the monarch as upholder and guarantor of the impartial administration of the common law.[5] The common law, it could be claimed, challenged the scope of canon law, and the competition of these rival systems was finally worked out in English history through the royal supremacy itself. If responsibility for the good order of the Church ultimately lay not with the Pope but with the monarch, and yet the monarch's role itself (this, of course, was something that itself became the source of conflict in English political life for the next two hundred years) was also one that could not be above the law, then the role of law as providing a moral framework for the work of the Church was of extreme importance. And since the realm was one, and the Church provided for one uniform mode of worship and ecclesiastical administration, so within the single realm of England and Wales religion and law had to be in harmony. Law was important, too, in containing and, if necessary, eliminating destructive internal divisions in the Church.

Thus, the scaffolding of the Elizabethan settlement, or perhaps we could say of the Protestant Church of England, was a *monarchical* Protestantism, a thoroughly Protestant theology contained within an overarching commitment to the principle of royal authority and good order. This had two implications for the theological history of the Church of England. One was the continuing quasi-spiritual authority accorded to the monarch as supreme governor. Trouble erupted in the seventeenth century when the Stuart kings adopted a 'divine right' theory of monarchy. But the special relationship between the monarchy and the Church of England has never been seriously disrupted up to the present, even though the constitutional position of the monarch has changed substantially over the centuries. The other was the tension that was bound to emerge between the principle of order, with obedience to the law, and the continuing pressure for further reform, mandated by the principle of *sola scriptura*. Here, the theological history of the Church of England was affected by the growing influence of Calvinism, mediated particularly by exiles returning from the Continent at Elizabeth's accession. Application of a more rigorous, more radical reforming agenda via claims that the proper reading of Scripture demanded abandonment of residual 'Popery' produced new models of church order that were in conflict with the requirements of the authorised settlement. A monarchical Protestant church was effectively being weakened from within, by a movement of criticism that yearned to push the Church of England in a more reformed direction.

Foundational Texts

The texts by which the Church of England's doctrine and practice were settled in the late sixteenth century were different from those common in northern Europe, where particular church 'confessions' (condensed formulae summarising essential doctrine) and 'church orders' (legal documents which prescribed doctrine and practice) were the usual means of imposing religious settlement in particular cities and small states.[6] The doctrinal standards of the Church of England were at once more diffuse – scattered over a wider range of texts – and more expansive – applicable as they were uniformly throughout the whole realm. Much more so than in most of the Protestant churches of northern Europe, the reformed Church of England expressed its belief through its liturgy, the Prayer Book.

Public prayer was constituted above all by the orders for morning and evening prayer, or Matins and Evensong. These were constructed by Cranmer from elements of the monastic offices – a sticking point for later critics who resented the retention of such 'Popish' relics. But it is very doubtful that most people would have known this. Rather, these two offices were vehicles for the characteristically English Protestant emphasis on good order and the reading of Scripture. Scripture infused every page of the services, not just in the two readings, but in the psalmody, in the canticles such as the Jubilate (Psalm 100) and the Magnificat (Luke 1.46–55) and the Nunc Dimittis (Luke 2.29–32), and even in the quotations that helped to make up the responses. This combination of Biblical weight and ordered uniformity was carried through into other services, chiefly those of the 'occasional' or pastoral offices of baptism, confirmation, marriage, visitation of the sick, and burial of the dead, as well as Holy Communion. In the catechism, a reformed understanding of the sacraments is presented: there are only two sacraments 'generally necessary to salvation', baptism and the Lord's supper; a sacrament is 'an outward and visible sign of an inward and spiritual grace given unto us, ordained by Christ himself'; bread and wine were the outward part of communion, whereas the inward part, the 'thing signified', was the body and blood of Christ 'taken and received by the faithful'. It is true that the Prayer Book contained much that later generations could interpret or expand in a more traditional or 'Catholic' sense, but this was certainly not intended by Cranmer. The English liturgy was a Protestant liturgy: it gave expression to the key Reformation principles of *sola scriptura*, *sola fide* and *sola gratia*.

So, too, did the Thirty-nine Articles of Religion. At their heart was a series of articles drawing heavily on Continental reformed models, and expounding a doctrine of salvation recognisably reformed.[7] Human beings had no power in themselves to do good works 'without the grace of God by Christ preventing [i.e. going before] us' (article 10, 'Of Free-Will'). It was only through the merit of Jesus Christ that we could be 'accounted righteous before God' (article 11, 'Of the Justification of Man'). Good works could not overcome sin, but were pleasing to God inasmuch as they sprang 'necessarily of a true and lively Faith' (Article 12, 'Of Good Works'). And, most telling of all, in Article 17 the doctrine of predestination was presented in unambiguous form: predestination to life 'is the everlasting purpose of God, whereby ... he hath constantly decreed by his counsel secret to us, to deliver from curse and damnation those whom he hath chosen in Christ out of mankind'. This might sound sectarian, conceiving of the true Church as an elect (and therefore select) body, a church within a church, but other articles made it plain that the Church of England existed to serve all the people of the realm. Article 19, influenced by the Lutheran Augsburg

Confession, described the visible Church of Christ as a 'congregation [i.e. corporate body] of faithful men, in the which the pure Word of God is preached, and the Sacraments be duly ministered' – in other words, the Church was constituted not by particular human rules, but by what the Church did authentically in preaching and ministering the sacraments of baptism and eucharist.

The language was careful: it did not confine such an idea to the Church of England alone – that would indeed have been sectarian. Rather, what was predicated of the Church of England applied to all true Christian churches; the Church of England, by implication, could claim to be just one part of Christ's Church. Elsewhere, and again and again, the Scriptural standard was asserted: purgatory was 'a fond thing vainly invented, and grounded upon no warranty of Scripture' (Article 22); there were only two sacraments 'ordained of Christ our Lord in the Gospel', baptism and eucharist (Article 25); transubstantiation was 'repugnant to the plain words of Scripture' (Article 27). A Protestant soteriology, or doctrine of salvation, and a church order grounded on Scripture were the dominant theological notes of the Articles, supported by a clear distinction between the immutable force of Scriptural injunction and the mutable but none the less legitimate scope of human authority.

These emphases were echoed in the two *Books of Homilies*, the first prepared by Cranmer and published in 1547, the second largely by John Jewel and published in 1562. The *Homilies* have never had a comparable influence to that of the Prayer Book and Articles, though they were for a century or more a ready point of reference for Anglican clergy. None the less, once again their consonance both with the main points of Reformation soteriology and with the more mundane Anglican preoccupation with the practical outliving of Gospel faith (this was particularly the theme of the second book) reinforces the sense that the late sixteenth-century Church of England was in its theology essentially aligned to north European Protestantism.

Theological Apologetics

The formularies of the Church of England, slightly amended in the seventeenth century, remained the main source of official Anglican teaching right up until the twentieth century. They were reinforced by the early seventeenth-century revision of canon law, something often unfairly neglected as an additional source of theology. But the theological sense people made of the formularies shifted considerably throughout this period, and it was somewhere in the middle of that shift that 'Anglicanism' – at least in its modern sense – came into being. Its roots lie in the controversies that beset the Church of England in the long reign of Elizabeth. From the beginning, defenders of the newly re-established reformed Church were obliged to fight on two fronts. The first of these two conflicts – there from the very beginning of the Henrician reforms – was, of course, with the Church of Rome. In trying to make sense, theologically, of the position of their Church, Anglicans were obliged to answer the criticisms of traditionalists and Roman theologians. The other conflict was internal, with those convinced the Church of England was incompletely reformed, tainted by the ceremonies, structures and superstitions it had retained from the 'corrupt' Roman Church. I will take these two conflicts in turn, looking at the work of two individuals who profoundly influenced Anglican theology, John Jewel and Richard Hooker.

It was Jewel more than anyone in the twenty years after Cranmer's death who strove to give the Church of England a coherent doctrinal justification over and against Rome. Exiled to Frankfurt and Strasbourg under Mary, with his close friend the Italian Reformer Peter Martyr Vermigli he defended the use of the Prayer Book in controversy with other British exiles, including the future Scottish Reformer John Knox. It was not only Jewel's Reforming credentials that were useful to the Elizabethan Church, but his depth of learning in the history and theology of the early Church, the age of the 'Church Fathers'. Made bishop of Salisbury in July 1559, for the next twelve years he proved to be an energetic, reforming bishop.

In November 1559, at St Paul's Cross – a large outdoors pulpit by St Paul's cathedral that was probably the most prestigious preaching venue of the age – Jewel preached a sermon that famously threw down a challenge to his Roman opponents. Repeated at court and again at St Paul's Cross four months later, Jewel's 'Challenge Sermon' decisively changed the grounds on which English Protestants and Catholics were arguing. The challenge was this: 'If any learned man of all our adversaries … be able to bring any one sufficient sentence out of any old catholic doctor, or father, or out of any old general council, or out of the holy scripture of God, or any one example of the primitive church, whereby it may be clearly and plainly proved that there was any private mass in the whole world at that time, for the space of six hundred years after Christ', and so on to encompass twenty-seven points of doctrine.[8] Jewel's ground was carefully chosen. He did not claim that *all* Catholic doctrine could not be proven from Scripture or the Fathers, but that certain specific points could not be. It was selective, but very effective. His target was the Roman Church's claim to catholicity and apostolicity. When Catholic apologists argued that their church was the only true Church, tracing back its doctrine and practice to antiquity, Jewel could counter that, on the contrary, significant points of Catholic faith could not be shown to have any ancient pedigree at all. The 'Challenge Sermon' had immediate impact, and drew the Roman controversialists on to a much more challenging ground than they had hitherto experienced.[9]

But Jewel's goal was not merely to discomfit the Roman theologians. He had a much wider and more positive aim in view, brought out more clearly in the short work he wrote in 1561–2 at the instigation of William Cecil, Elizabeth's secretary of state. This was the famous *Apology of the Church of England*. A work of constructive apologetics, the *Apology* rooted the faith of the Church of England in the undivided Church of the early centuries. His aim was to 'show plainly that God's holy gospel, the ancient bishops, and the primitive [i.e. early] Church do make on our side'.[10] Nothing, in other words, was conceded to the *realpolitik* behind the Henrician reforms; the formation of the Church of England was cast in idealised theological terms. Jewel's work was intended to rebut forcefully one of the most powerful criticisms advanced by traditionalists, namely that the Church of England was a new or invented church, with no continuity with the ancient Church of Christ. On the contrary, as Jewel argued, the faith of the Church of England was entirely consonant with the faith of the early Church, clearly grounded in Scripture and in the writings of the Church Fathers: 'we have forsaken the Church as it is now, not as it was in old times past'.[11] Denying the pre-eminence of the Pope, for example, he asserted that 'all the Apostles, *as Cyprian saith*, were of like power among themselves'.[12] He quoted the fifth-century authorities Sozomen and Gregory of Nazianzus in defence of married clergy.[13] He asserted that there were only two sacraments properly so-called, namely baptism and the Lord's supper, as Ambrose and Augustine recognised.[14]

The *Apology* almost immediately attained quasi-official status. Bishop Richard Barnes of Durham provided for a copy to be issued to every parish church in his diocese; others followed suit.[15] Catholic critics – and there were many – were quick to point to the method of convenience that Jewel used, picking his arguments and proof texts with immense care, and he was forced into a prolonged controversy, eventually issuing a massive *Defence* of his own work. Modern scholars likewise have claimed that Jewel was not so much an original theologian as an ecclesiastical pragmatist, defending his position with a scissors-and-paste method that cannibalised texts in the service of a highly selective polemic.[16] But, whatever the accuracy of such a view, it is beside the point. Jewel was not writing as a systematic theologian in the modern sense. Like all the Reformers, he saw himself as standing within the one Church of Christ, justifying the act of reform.

English evangelicals had never repudiated the faith of the early Church: like the great Continental Reformers, they thought that all that they were doing was returning the Church to its origins, *ad fontes*, purifying it of later corruptions, and restoring its apostolic simplicity and purity. But the amplification and defence of this position would be a work of time: it could not be done instantly in the fevered hurly-burly of ecclesiastical politics as it unfolded in the two decades after the break with Rome. In the developing theological conflict with Rome – a conflict that was to last, polemically, at least until the ecumenical movement of the twentieth century – important outposts of the Anglican position had already been laid down. Jewel's work was to provide elements of the infilling, the supply roads and trenches that would support the Church of England in years to come. It was rough and ready work, not elegant, not anything other than a series of elaborate, extended footnotes to the basic claim to apostolicity. But it indicated a strong line of defence that would be deployed and developed again and again by Anglican writers in the following centuries.

Hooker and the Defence of the Elizabethan Settlement

If the main achievement of Jewel was to demonstrate that the Church of England could buttress its claim to continuity with the one Church of Christ by adding the appeal to early tradition to its professed basis in Scripture, for the defence of the Elizabethan settlement against its internal critics we have to turn to a much more capable and original theologian, Richard Hooker. Hooker was the most significant English theologian for the development of the Church of England after the first two generations of Reformers. It is worth looking at his ideas in more detail, because over time they have become so closely bound into the identity of the Church of England, and indeed Anglicanism more broadly, that Hooker has come to be seen as the archetypal Anglican theologian. But he is a complex thinker, and easily and widely misunderstood.

To Hooker is usually attributed the introduction of the appeal to reason in Anglican apologetic, producing the classic Anglican 'triad' of Scripture, reason and tradition. But this risks viewing him in the light of a much later idea that 'reason' could be considered in some sense a rival or parallel source to Scripture itself, qualifying the absolute authority of Scripture. Hooker himself would never have seen things that way. Like Jewel, his purpose was to defend the reasonableness of the existing settlement of Church affairs. Like Jewel, too, he was nothing if not a reformed theologian: his view of Christian faith, and of the doctrine and order of the Church, was grounded first and foremost in Scripture. But Hooker's originality lay in the question he posed to radical critics: how should we *use* Scripture? He was thus attending to a central problem in Protestant theology, namely how the divine commands embodied in Scripture should be applied to contemporary life.

This question had become, by the late 1560s, a burning issue for many members of the Church of England, as we have seen. There were plenty of Anglicans who wanted to see further reform, influenced by the heady currents of theological criticism stemming from Calvin above all. They wanted to get rid of the 'Popish' features of cathedrals, cathedral chapters, bishops and various ceremonies enshrined in the Prayer Book, and in their place erect a form of organisation centred on 'presbyteries', councils of elders or 'presbyters' who would exercise 'godly' discipline in the Church. The mandate for all this was Scripture itself, so these puritans claimed. They could not find the Anglican settlement in Scripture, they said, and so they urged its reform according to a Scriptural model.

But what, in practice, would that mean? That is where Hooker's work proved immensely fruitful. A quiet, unassuming but none the less determined and resourceful man, he was in 1585 made Master of the Temple in London, where he came into conflict with the puritan lecturer, Walter Travers, a kinsman. Clearly by this time Hooker was attracting a reputation as something of a theological maverick. His early sermons often struck an unusual theme, such as that faith might endure even in those uncertain of having it.[17] He had an exceptional capacity for turning a controverted subject on its head, examining it from a more original and more philosophical angle than the polemics that typified the theological exchanges of his age.

This is patently clear from the opening of his great work, *Of the Laws of Ecclesiastical Polity*, eventually published in eight books, only five of which appeared in his lifetime. Hooker begins where almost no other theologian of his stature would begin, namely with the analysis of law. The questions that hang over the first four books, published in 1593, go to the heart of Reformation dispute over the authority of Scripture. What is the nature of divine law, as opposed to human law? Is divine law alone immutable? Is the explicit command of Scripture always applicable in all conceivable circumstances, or is it adaptable and even, in some situations, disposable? Do particular features of church practice that are not referenced in Scripture none the less have sufficient warrant to demand believers' obedience? By beginning his treatise with a typology of law, Hooker was able to argue that divine law was found not only in Scripture itself, as his opponents assumed, but in nature (physical laws) and in moral law; thus, he argued, 'those men which have no written law of God to shew what is good or evil, carry written in their hearts the universal law of mankind, the Law of Reason'.[18] This was not to say that human beings could attain knowledge of divine truth by reason alone: they needed the Gospel, communicated through Scripture. Hooker did not deny that Scripture contained all things necessary to salvation. But applying the law of Scripture did not mean that the practice and order of the Church could only be justified if the exact command for each and every feature of the Church could be found explicitly in Scripture. Such a thing was not even desirable, let alone possible, for, as he said, 'why may we not presume that God doth even call for such change or alteration as the very condition of things themselves doth make necessary'?[19] When circumstances change, the way we apply the commands of God may also change.

But this cuts two ways, and Hooker's later admirers have not always recognised that possibility. If, on the one hand, Hooker plainly was at odds with his puritan critics in arguing that Scripture alone could not provide a blueprint for the Church, but that the application of the divine commands contained in Scripture had to be in harmony with the divine command contained in reason (which Hooker saw essentially as a spiritual principle, an indwelling of the Spirit in human being), at the same time he was not prepared to absolutise features of Church polity and practice that none the less he defended as acceptable for his time and for his people. When he turned to defend the Elizabethan settlement, he did so in terms that were really *sui generis*. Without departing entirely from common Reformation positions and arguments, Hooker essentially justified the position of the Elizabethan Church on ministry, on the sacraments and on the liturgy by drawing attention to the ways in which the law of God in Scripture was adapted, through the historical contingency of the Church of England, to serve the ends for which the Church existed: the Church of England's justification, then, lay in its fusion of custom, tradition, practical adaptation and secular authorisation, with the Gospel and its evangelical purpose.

As one modern Anglican authority has put it, in Hooker there is 'the undoubtedly odd fact that [he] uses what is in some ways a potentially radical apologetic in defence of a conservative and perhaps authoritarian position'.[20] The word 'authoritarian' here strikes a discordant note: Hooker is rarely guilty of that. His arguments unquestionably were deployed in defence of the 'powers that be', but not without caveats and qualifications that would limit the scope of the authority he justified. He defended a moderate sacramentalism. He articulated a theory of the unity of Church and State, but did not defend divine right monarchy. He asserted the divine origin of ministry in the Church, for example, the indelibility (i.e. permanence) of the mark or character of ordination, and even the gifts of the Holy Spirit in ordination ('we have for the least and meanest duties performed by virtue of ministerial power, that to dignify, grace and authorize them, which no other offices on earth can challenge'):

all that makes Hooker's doctrine of ministry sound very 'High Church', as later generations would call it, or 'Catholic'.[21] But he did not assert the absolute necessity of one particular form of ministry, or even of the sign of apostolic succession, the ordination of clergy by bishops themselves ordained by other bishops right back to the origins of the Church. Nor did he insist on the absolute necessity of bishops in the Church, though it has to be said that his view of episcopacy has proved particularly contentious, contained as it is in the posthumously published Book 7 of the *Laws*, which, though almost certainly drafted by Hooker himself, is probably not in the final form he would have wished.

Hooker thus proved to be a somewhat protean authority for later generations of Anglicans, and this has made it difficult at times for historians and theologians to rescue his thought from the 'cocoon of hindsight', as one scholar has brilliantly put it.[22] Both moderate, conforming puritans and anti-Calvinist conformists could quote him as a useful ally, and later generations of Anglicans would find in him support for a bewildering variety of positions. Even today argument about interpreting him continues. Some see him essentially as a Reformed, indeed almost Calvinist theologian, others as a decisive departure from Reformed Christianity.[23] His skill and intellectual resources were marshalled in defence of a settlement of religion that was to be subject to enormous strain and change in the century after his death, and yet the way he mounted his case has proved remarkably effective as an adaptable theological method, combining the appeal to Scripture with a confident use of other ancient authorities and with a readiness to reason carefully about the way in which Scriptural truth should be applied in Church affairs.

Hooker was a theological heavyweight with little popular appeal: his works did not sell in large numbers, and did not reach a wide audience directly. But they were cited again and again as the seventeenth century wore on. Just as Jewel had brought to the fore the appeal to Patristic authority – always in service of the prior authority of Scripture, of course – so Hooker, as much by reputation as by actual argument, brought forward the importance of human reason. An actual, historical church body, such as the Church of England, could never be identified as the 'perfect' church of Scripture, because it was caught up in the processes of history: its polity, its shape, structure and organisation were the products of complex political, social and intellectual arrangements that required analytical justification using the commands and norms embedded in Scripture itself and in Christian history.

Still there was no such thing as Anglicanism, at least not in the sense we would recognise today. Yet *something* had shifted from the middle of the previous century. No longer was it simply the case that the theologians of the Church of England could point to the Reformation of the old Church, assuming that within the exoskeleton of a continuity of structure there was a solid body of Protestant doctrine grounded on *sola scriptura, sola fide, sola gratia*. Anglicans were dividing on different grounds. For many, these 'classic' Protestant maxims had been diluted in practice in the Elizabethan Church: there was not enough *sola scriptura*. The work of Reformation was incomplete. But, for others, a different vision of the Church of England was emerging, one in which the idea of historical continuity, with the early Church at least, but perhaps also with the medieval past, perhaps even (a shocking thought at the time) with elements of the existing Catholic Church, was ever more powerful. Somewhere in this mix, typified by the complexity of Hooker's argumentation, lay principles which could be taken in very different directions in future. Extrapolate and push much further than Hooker would ever have pushed any one of the authorities of Scripture, reason and tradition, and you could envisage the future theological 'parties' of the Church of England.

6

THE ROAD TO CIVIL WAR

James I and the Union Project

At Elizabeth's death in 1603, it was plain for all to see that the Church of England was already a divided Church, and did not command the loyalty of *all* the English and Welsh people. There were 'splinter groups' outside it already who refused to acknowledge that they were part of a national Church. At the extreme edge of Protestant opinion were various groups of separatists, including Anabaptists (this was largely a term of abuse, referring to the suspicion that, because they practised 'believer's baptism' – that is, in adulthood – they actually *re*-baptised those who had already been baptised as children). But they were small in number, and heavily persecuted. At the other end of the spectrum were a much larger number of recusants, Catholics who continued to profess their faith despite considerable pressure to conform to the Church of England. The vast majority of English and Welsh people, however, still attended their local parish church. Yet they were hardly a picture of harmony. The regime's policy of containing or restricting puritan criticism of the religious settlement worked only so far as it could be actively enforced by an energetic administration at local as well as national level. But, given the affinity many English puritans felt with Presbyterianism in Scotland, it is hardly surprising that, with Elizabeth's death, they looked to her successor with anticipation and excitement.

Prima facie, their expectations were perfectly reasonable. There cannot have been a monarch in British history – with the possible exception of Alfred the Great – more learned and competent in theology than James I. Even Henry VIII's vaunted learning pales beside the relish – but also genuine expertise – with which James waded into theological controversy. In a tribute of more than the usual fawning, one of his court preachers, early in his reign, declared the king 'our Solomon or *Pacificus*'.[1] James's religious policy depended on a very high understanding of personal authority and rule, which fitted well with the court politics he had inherited, but went beyond them in his willingness to take an active, even pre-eminent role in hearing and settling disputes. In other words, James was a meddler. In this, he was encouraged by his adoption of divine right theories of monarchy: the king was appointed to exercise his rule by God himself, and therefore was not accountable directly to his people. James was a latter-day Constantine, a monarch who, like a *deus ex machina*, tried to use his royal authority to settle contention in religion. For most of his reign this actually worked rather well: he was adept at steering a course between the more extreme positions on both wings of the Church of England. Only towards the end of his life did the policy begin to fail.

For all his belief in his divine authority, James was nothing if not a wily pragmatist. He was committed to stabilising Church affairs in his joint kingdoms of England and Scotland, but he avoided his son Charles I's mistakes of trying to impose a single model of Church order on both.[2] His 'imperial' project, the idea of a united realm, came to nothing as much as anything because of this pragmatism. He pursued religious unity by persecuting the extreme wing of puritanism and appeasing more moderate opinion by minor concessions. At a conference at Hampton Court in early 1604, called to bring together puritan critics and conforming Anglicans, he resisted radical reform and confirmed the existing settlement of religion in England in all but a few minor points. The *Book of Common Prayer* was affirmed with some very minor amendments. Entirely characteristic of James's approach – and possibly the most shocking moment of the conference to the radical puritans – was his startling intervention in arguments about modifying or abolishing episcopacy, when he blurted out angrily, 'No bishop, no king'![3] James thus hitched the existing polity of the Church of England to his divinely given authority as king. It is to James, then, and to his son Charles that we must look for the highest possible theorisation of the relationship of Church and State in England – something of an irony, when you consider the dire situation in which his son was to find himself by the 1640s, with a religious policy collapsing in on itself on all sides, and contrast that with the brutal assertion of royal power by Henry VIII, who had none the less continued to work in and through Parliament to achieve his ends.

The Hampton Court conference was followed by two further initiatives heavy with long-term significance for the Church. One was reform of the canon law, begun by Richard Bancroft when he was bishop of London, and put into effect when he became archbishop of Canterbury at the death of Whitgift in 1604. This finally achieved for the reformed Church a comprehensive set of canons that had eluded both Edward VI and Elizabeth. The result was an intelligent fusion of ancient precept and modern adaptation, written originally in Latin but translated into English and used thereafter almost invariably in the vernacular. These canons were in force until the revision set in motion by Archbishop Geoffrey Fisher in the 1950s. Their influence in shaping the outlook and development of the Church of England for well over 300 years was therefore incalculable.

The other major initiative was the commissioning of a new translation of the Bible, which eventually appeared in 1611 and quickly established itself as the definitive text in English. The Authorised Version, or King James Bible, was not actually a completely new translation. Much of it was derived from Tyndale, but it drew also on the Bishops' Bible compiled by Mathew Parker in 1568, and also on some earlier Wycliffite texts.[4] However, it was edited and amended by committees of scholars who included many of the ablest men, both puritan, anti-Calvinist and conforming Anglicans. Like the revised canon law, Scripture itself was to be a means of containing division. It is a sign of the success with which the doctrinally mixed committees worked that the Authorised Version came to be widely accepted and used by practically all shades of Protestant opinion in England: the Authorised Version 'silenced arguments about translations and their accuracy or efficacy'.[5]

James's policy of suppressing division by supporting moderate puritan and anti-Calvinist opinion at the same time as upholding vigorously the liturgy and order of the Church entailed some persecution of extremist opinion. This, however, was relatively limited in scope. Some eighty puritan ministers were deprived of their church positions.[6] Despite James's robust anti-puritan rhetoric, in practice he was lenient on conforming puritans. Even deprived clergy might be allowed to take up positions again, if they were willing to muffle their dissent. But, perhaps more surprisingly, given the shock of the Gunpowder Plot, early in his reign in 1605, James also adopted an irenic policy towards those at the other end of the ecclesiastical spectrum, namely Catholics. Here, too, he distinguished between moderates and extremists, making a particular point of associating rhetoric against the Pope as anti-Christ with the Papal claim to authority over secular princes. The imposition of an Oath of Allegiance from 1606 enabled Catholics to enjoy the protection of the law as long as they repudiated Papal claims to the power to overthrow temporal rulers. The effect, however, was limited in practice: both the reluctance of many Catholics to subscribe and the hostility of local Protestant magistrates and notables ensured that the Oath was selectively applied at best.

None of this should give the impression that after an initial flurry of infighting early in James's reign, Church affairs settled down to a steady state. Religious conflict bubbled away throughout his reign. James's 'reconstruction of the Church of England', as it was once described by historians, involved annexing royal power and authority to confirm a religious settlement that a large number of clergy and laity opposed.[7] The institution of episcopacy itself, increasingly defended with an assertion of *jure divino*, or divine right, claims to match those James was making of his own royal authority, the Church courts, the liturgy with its 'Popish' residual signs and texts, the revised canons, were all a far cry from the renewed reformation puritans were seeking. Their criticisms could be muted and contained only because James himself determined it should be so. But even he could not stem the tide for ever.

In the last years of James's reign, the strain of holding together very divergent streams of opinion in the Church began to show. James refused to allow his two kingdoms to be drawn into the Thirty Years' War, which, taking the form of a confessional conflict between Catholics and Protestants but complicated by national and dynastic rivalries, had broken out in Europe in 1618; this was perhaps wise in terms of avoiding unnecessary suffering and expense, but it alienated anti-Catholic feeling in England. Matters were complicated by his archbishop. Richard Bancroft's death in late 1610 had led to the appointment of George Abbot as his successor. Abbot's puritan instincts sometimes led him to decisions or attitudes opposed to the king's will. He was uneasy with the 'Book of Sports', the declaration or list of recreations permitted on Sundays, applied nationally in 1618, which was strongly opposed by puritans offended at its disregard for the Sabbath, and resisted its reading aloud in his diocese. He opposed the ill-fated 'Spanish match' – the proposed marriage of Charles, prince of Wales, to the (Catholic) Spanish Infanta – which naturally scandalised anti-Catholic feeling in Britain. His reputation was damaged by his accidental killing of a gamekeeper while hunting in Hampshire in 1621, and was saved from the ignominy of condemnation by a commission of enquiry only by the casting vote of the king. His strong Calvinism and anti-Catholicism inflamed the hostility of some anti-Calvinists who formed a small but vociferous and ascendant party in the leadership of the Church, and who were indulged by James and enthusiastically supported by his son.

So, even as James struggled to hold his Church together, real divisions were opening up over the nature of religion as a consequence of puritanism. At the risk of over-simplification, it was as if there were two competing models of Christian belonging within the one national Church. One was 'conformity' – to use the word applied by the great puritan minister and writer Richard Baxter – by which I mean an emphasis on observing the Prayer Book services, attending the local parish church and making use of the ministrations of the parish priest. In this version of Christian community, there might be many different levels or intensities of engagement, perhaps many different levels of knowledge of the fundamentals of Christian faith. Those who were not evidently pious might still, rightly, consider themselves included in this idea of the Christian life. The other was the 'godly' vision embraced by puritan ministers, in which popular knowledge of the faith would be improved by preaching and catechising, in which active church membership depended on a conscious, lively faith, in which those born and ostensibly raised in Christian faith might be expected to undergo a real spiritual 'conversion' in adulthood, and in which popular forms of recreation – including drinking, dancing and singing – would be suppressed or purified.

Both of these versions of Christian community were, in principle, inclusive ones: both aimed to draw in as many of the local community as they could. But both had difficulties, too. The 'conformist' view looked lax, undemanding and ineffectual to its critics, and there was much evidence on the ground to justify that view. Born in Shropshire, Baxter later described the region as a spiritual desert: 'We lived in a country that had but little preaching at all ... In the village where my father lived there was a reader of about eighty years of age that never preached'; another who took Orders, having been an attorney's clerk, was, according to Baxter, 'a common drunkard, and tippled himself into so great poverty that he had no other way to live'.[8] The puritan or 'godly' view, however, risked alienating those who were attached to popular customs, or to the Prayer Book itself.[9] Its very rigour was an argument against its likely success as an instrument for holding together the religious impulses of a whole nation.

The Emergence of 'Anglicanism'

So the caricatures that would bedevil later accounts of the dete-
riorating relationship between puritans and anti-puritans in the
English Church were fast becoming set by the end of James's
reign. Puritans were not somehow marginalised in the Church,
but present at every level of it, with supportive bishops: there
was a case for saying that they, as much as their opponents, represented the real 'establishment' of the Church of England.[10]
Anti-puritans were probably a comparative minority. And they
were not simply defending the status quo; their more militant
spirits aimed to push the Church further along the road towards
a rediscovered sacramental and ceremonial tradition, with a
much higher doctrine of the ministry.

It was as much this 'High Church' (the term is really anachronistic) militancy as any pressure from the puritan side that
contributed to the polarisation of English ecclesiastical politics
in the early seventeenth century. One term recently coined for it
is 'avant-garde conformity'.[11] We have already seen how Richard
Hooker could be read this way, though not without distorting
the complexity of his position. The leading spirit of the 'avant-
garde conformists' was Hooker's almost exact contemporary
Lancelot Andrewes. A brilliant linguist immersed in the study of
the early Fathers of the Church, Andrewes was a pivotal figure
at court, while his preaching was almost legendary for its rhe-
torical flourishes, the richness and density of its language and
its wilful subversion of common doctrinal and liturgical positions of his puritan opponents. The chronology of his career, of
course, is crucial: it matches almost exactly that of Shakespeare,
and Andrewes in his own way demonstrated the same ingenuity
and fecundity in language – a reflection, perhaps, of a particular
moment in the history of English when its widespread adoption
as a language of high as well as low culture followed on from
the fading popularity of Latin (though Andrewes was equally
eloquent in Latin anyway).[12]

Andrewes was reluctant to publish his own work, but was
obliged to do so by James I, who adored his preaching and was

even said to have slept with one of Andrewes's sermons under his pillow.[13] James tolerated Andrewes's criticisms of Calvinism, but Andrewes was bold also in his advocacy of a doctrine of real presence. On Christmas Day 1623 he preached before the king:

> There is in Christ the Word eternal, for things in Heaven; there is also flesh, for things on earth. Semblably, the Sacrament consisteth of a Heavenly and a terrene part ... as the two Natures in Christ, so the *signum* and *signatum* in the Sacrament *e converso*.[14]

No wonder Anglo-Catholics in the nineteenth century looked back to him as one of their own.

Andrewes was a conscientious bishop successively of Chichester, Ely and Winchester, but he was kept at court much of the year by James. His influence over the wider Church of England was perhaps more limited. What turned the position with which he is now identified into a controversial political moment was James's death in March 1625, closely followed by his own – for the baton now passed to a much more effective and wily organiser of opinion, William Laud, and to a man seemingly incapable of compromise, Charles I. I will consider Laud's religious policy shortly, but it is worth noting here that it was not force of numbers that eventually resulted in the long-term success of the avant-garde conformists but their closeness to the ruling elite, especially the royal family. They were just one wing of the pre-Civil War Church. They had the advantage of combining conservatism, with all that that signified for stability and continuity, with a radical spirit; the irony was that, in the short term, stability is just what their position failed to guarantee.

So what we often miss, retrospectively, when we look back to Andrewes and Laud, and even to Hooker, is the tenuousness of their position. Andrewes and Hooker, particularly, were seen as typifying Anglican moderation, poised between the extremes of Calvinism and Roman Catholicism. But they did not represent the centre of gravity of the Jacobean Church. A telling illustration is one more figure often associated with the avant-garde conformists, the poet and priest George Herbert. In his poem 'The British Church', Herbert lauded its moderation: 'A fine aspect in fit array, Neither too mean nor yet too gay.'[15] Later generations of Anglicans were to regard Herbert as typical of the mainstream of the Church of England on the eve of the Civil War, a moderate High Churchman who avoided the extremes of Popery and puritanism, and who helped to fashion the moderate, reasonable Anglican 'middle way'. But Herbert was not in the centre of the Church of England of his day. He wanted to see a gulf between Canterbury and Geneva, though he was 'neither Puritan nor Arminian', as one critic has observed.[16] But a significant number of his contemporaries did not see things this way. If we must take poets as typical, the religious sensibilities of the mid-seventeenth century were represented as much by the radical Puritan John Milton as they were by Herbert.

The lens through which we look at Herbert, Laud, Andrewes and even beyond at Hooker today, as well as other significant names such as John Donne and Jeremy Taylor, is one refined in the aftermath of the collapse of the Commonwealth and the restoration of the monarchy, when, as we shall see, a substantial part of the more radical Puritan voices were finally cut out of the Church of England. At that point, the centre of gravity of the Church shifted, and 'classic Anglicanism', as some were to call it, became possible. The view of Anglicanism as a 'mean betwixt extremes' – the phrase is borrowed from Cranmer's preface to the 1549 Prayer Book – depended on the political and legal exclusion of dissenting voices, and not on any intrinsic moderation and reasonableness. Anglicanism has always been a political construct, as well as a religious system. But the fact that the very term 'Anglicanism' was rarely used in the seventeenth century, and really only came into widespread use in the nineteenth, has not stopped many scholars looking back and proposing that the religious views of men such as Herbert, Laud and Andrewes could appropriately be described with that anachronism.[17]

Charles I, Religious Politics and Political Religion

If, by the end of James's reign, the always fragile balance between Puritans and anti-Calvinists was beginning to fail, his son's succession tipped things decisively in one direction. This was catastrophic for religious peace. Charles hooked his conception of the absolute authority of the monarch to the avant-garde conformist position. But all appeared moderation and compromise in the first four years of his reign, when he was attempting to persuade Parliament, with a Commons increasingly dominated by Puritans, to support his foreign policy of war against Spain. There were even those who thought Charles might be sympathetic to Puritanism. But this was a front. His real views were quite different, and were to involve him in the rapidly developing religious conflict between Puritans and Laudians, especially after 1629, when Parliament was dissolved and there was no longer any need to conciliate Puritan MPs.

Like his father, Charles had strong views on religion, but little of his political acumen. He not only favoured episcopacy and 'divine right' monarchy, but swung over wholeheartedly to William Laud's side. He encouraged the Laudian emphasis on sacraments, and especially communion. He supported its reintroduction of ritual and ceremonial that Puritans decried as 'Popish'. And he backed up these changes with the force of royal authority, provoking growing suspicion and ultimately open defiance. Britain's descent into civil war in the 1640s had many causes, but religion was one of the most significant. Charles's vision of the Church, like that of Laud himself, was of a decorous, ordered, ceremonial national Church, united in worship through a common liturgy and a common ministry – hence his (as it was to prove) disastrous policy in the 1630s of trying to unite the two kingdoms of England and Scotland through introducing a version of the Prayer Book in Scotland, along with bishops. This put him seriously at odds with much of the clergy and many influential laity.

Civil war in the 1640s was not something actively sought by either Parliament or the king, but by 1629 it had become a

7. A study in contrasts: the Victorian idea of Puritans

possible outcome of Charles's policy. Parliament's objection to his fiscal and religious policies, in the wake of the assassination of his favourite, the duke of Buckingham, led him to dissolve it, after arresting five members of the House of Commons for 'seditious carriage'. Liberated from the need to work alongside Parliament, for the next eleven years from 1629 (the years of 'personal rule'), both Laud and Charles himself pursued their religious policy with increasing vigour. There is much dispute about who was really the driver: most historians have emphasised the role of Laud, but others have instead stressed the subordination of religious policy to the unfettered exercise of royal authority in these years, with one historian even speaking of the 'Caroline captivity' of the Church of England.[18] This risks becoming a sterile dispute, however, given the close agreement and cooperation between Charles and Laud. At the heart of their policy was the application of legal authority, increasingly exercised through the Court of High Commission, the supreme ecclesiastical court, to prosecute errant or neglectful clergy for failing to observe the provisions of the Prayer Book and canons; in practice, that meant prosecuting Puritans.

Laud was finally raised (as Charles had long promised) to Canterbury in 1633 when the disgraced Abbot died at last. But Laud had been the more powerful figure in the Church long before, along with Richard Neile, bishop of Durham and then Winchester and then, from 1631, archbishop of York. Neile was a thoroughgoing avant-garde conformist, overseeing the transformation of Durham cathedral into a pace-setting exemplar of the 'beauty of holiness' – a phrase taken from Psalm 96 which has been commonly used to describe the Laudian approach to worship, and which included the re-insertion of stained glass windows and colourful fittings into churches.

Beautifying churches was only one aspect of the Laudian policy, however: equally important was the renewed sacramentalism of Laudian worship, reflecting a shift away from the Puritan emphasis on preaching. Most controversial was the 'altars policy'. In essence this meant ceasing to treat the communion table as a domestic table, as it had been following the mid-sixteenth-century reforms, aligned on an east–west axis and placed commonly further down the chancel or choir towards the nave, with benches around it so that the people might even receive communion sitting. Instead, it would be moved up into the east end of the chancel again, as it had been before the Reformation, aligned on a north–south axis and even placed up against the east wall and railed off. Communicants would not cluster around the table, or 'altar', but kneel at the rail to receive the sacrament. This was how the communion table in the Chapel Royal in Whitehall had been arranged since Elizabeth's day.[19] The move to reinstate the table in the 'altar' position, with rails, began in earnest in the late 1620s, at first in select parish churches only, and in various college chapels. St Wulfstan's, Grantham, was a controversial example of the former, the new chapel of Peterhouse, Cambridge, of the latter.[20] In 1633 Neile decreed the enforcing of the railed altar in the York and Chester dioceses, and possibly also in Carlisle.[21] Laud at first was a little more cautious in his own diocese of London, but in 1633 both his own elevation to Canterbury and the settling of a widely publicised controversy over the 'altar-wise' position of the communion table at St Gregory's church, near St Paul's in London, gave him scope at once to widen the campaign and to enforce it thoroughly in the province of Canterbury. Few bishops were prepared to resist; most by then were pro-Laudian anyway.

The Laudian policy went well beyond the interior liturgical arrangement of churches, however, and beyond even the restoration of an ordered ceremonialism reflective of a renewed emphasis on the sacraments. It also encompassed the very principle of authority and order in the Church, and even the scope of ecclesiastical authority. The canons drawn up in 1640 by the Convocations of York and Canterbury exactly reflected this concern. Issued without parliamentary authority – which is why parliament was quick to suppress them – one of their aims was to seize back jurisdiction for Church courts from the common law lawyers whose business had blossomed with the restrictions placed on Church courts from the middle of the previous century. But the bishops were, by then, swimming against the tide. There was growing opposition to the altars policy, especially in parts of the country such as the Midlands and East Anglia where Puritanism was particularly strong. At St Peter's, Nottingham, for example, in 1638 forty-two parishioners, led by the local mayor, refused to receive their Easter communion at the newly installed altar rail; they were prosecuted and forced to back down.[22] Prosecution is hardly a constructive way of persuading anyone of anything, however.

There is an irony in all of this. Despite everything they said against each other, both Puritans and avant-garde conformists prized ecclesiastical discipline and order. Puritans considered anti-Calvinists lax on such matters as observing the Sabbath and preaching; they sought a godly community, a disciplined, faithful community of believers who would truly live out the moral life to which the Scriptures called them. But the Laudians also wanted order and discipline; indeed, they were central to their policy. At root, these were very different visions of a national Church, then – the Puritans (still mostly monarchists) wanted one in which local churches had much more scope to order their own worship and community life, in which leading local laity could act as elders, and in which local presbyters (they avoided the word 'priest') would meet regularly for mutual support and discipline, while the Laudians or 'Anglicans' wanted one in which religious authority was hierarchically and centrally organised.

But behind this lay an even more fundamental division – completely contrasting views of the Christian past. Going back to at least the Elizabethan theologian Thomas Cartwright, Puritans considered much of Christian history a deviation from the original model of Church order and discipleship laid down in the New Testament. As Hooker had pointed out, they attempted to map Scripture directly on to the present. The Laudians, by contrast, saw a strong line of continuity going back through the medieval period to the early centuries of the Church. There had been deviations and corruptions, certainly, but in its essentials the Church of England was entirely consistent with the faith of the early Church, and with the ancient Church of the British Isles, the Church of Augustine of Canterbury, Bede and St Anselm. Where all this was focused most sharply was in differing attitudes to Roman Catholicism: Laudians might be very critical of the Papal claims, and of doctrines such as transubstantiation, but to them Catholics were unquestionably Christians; Puritans tended to see Rome as anti-Christ, Catholics as dangerous fanatics and idolaters, and anything that savoured of Rome in the Prayer Book and ceremonies of the English Church as abhorrent.

With such a gulf between them, it is no wonder that in the years of Charles' personal rule the very aggressiveness of the Laudian policy destabilised English and Welsh society. Later, after the Restoration, many Anglicans counted the 1630s as a time of peace and prosperity for the Church. Looking back, many years later, the diarist John Evelyn recalled 'at this time was the Church of England in her greatest splendour, all things decent, and becoming the Peace, and the persons that governed'.[23] But this was not the view of those many thousands of Puritans who, in the same decade, began their migration to New England, in search of a chance to found a godly commonwealth of their own in America. They felt the religious atmosphere of England was turning against them; later this became a founding myth of flight from persecution, a pardonable exaggeration.

The crisis, when it erupted, was triggered by the king's desire to pull his two kingdoms together in faith and church polity. James had reintroduced episcopacy into Scotland in the 1580s, but had been wise enough not to attempt to replicate the power and authority of the English bishops in Scotland. For the next half century bishops co-existed with a church polity that was essentially Presbyterian. Brought up in England, Charles had little direct knowledge of Scottish society. Using Laud as his chief advisor even in Scotland by the mid-1630s – itself a needlessly provocative move – he devised a common establishment model for the Church across both kingdoms. In 1636 new canons for Scotland replaced Knox's system of discipline, strengthened the power of the bishops, enhanced the power of church courts, reintroduced tithes, and made provision for censorship of publication.[24] The following year a Laudian-inspired Prayer Book was introduced into Scotland. But both the canons and the Prayer Book were widely rejected, and almost all of Scotland was united behind defence of the Reformed system of church government by the 'national covenant' in early 1638; Charles's attempt to impose his reforms by force the following year failed dismally.

By 1639 Scotland had abolished episcopacy and rejected Charles's authority. A second attempt by the king to force the issue in 1640 was disastrous, leading to a Scottish invasion of the north of England, and Charles's reluctant recall of Parliament, without which he could not finance the forces and supplies he needed. Like a house of cards, the Stuart regime was collapsing.

8. Treason as tradition: portrait of William Laud

Once reconvened, Parliament immediately moved to impeach – and eventually execute – the king's chief advisors, including Laud. The Laudian ascendancy was over. Charles's belated concessions to Scottish demands came too late to prevent parallel demands emerging in the English Parliament; his resistance to those ultimately tipped the kingdom into civil war.

The Church of England in Abeyance

Historians have argued endlessly over whether or not the crisis of the 1640s was a 'war of religion'.[25] There were other important presenting causes, including Charles's attempt to rule without Parliament, and his exploitation of fiscal devices which could circumvent Parliamentary approval. But religion was central to the tensions and conflicts bubbling up in the 1630s. The rigorous policy pursued by Laud, backed up by revival of the power of the Church courts, inevitably placed the Church of England at the very heart of the constitutional crisis that ensued.

Evidence for that comes not only from the words and actions of Charles's opponents, but from the petitions submitted to parliament in 1641–2 by almost every English county and the two universities in *support* of episcopacy and the Prayer Book. That from Herefordshire, for example, was signed by 68 'Gentlemen of Quality', 150 clergy and 3,600 freeholders and inhabitants of the county.[26] But in the next five years much of the familiar organisation, liturgy and practice of the Elizabethan and Stuart Church was ripped up. Parliament's 'Committee for Plundered Ministers' ejected somewhere between two and three thousand clergy from their livings in the early 1640s.[27] Episcopacy was abolished in Scotland in 1641, and in England in 1646 at the end of the first Civil War. Laud himself was executed for treason in 1645, some fourteen bishops sequestered (that is, deprived of their offices and associated income and property), while one, Matthew Wren of Ely, was thrown into the Tower of London. The Church courts collapsed in 1641–2, and the Court of High Commission was abolished. Parliament's 'Grand Remonstrance' of December 1641 – before actual hostilities broke out – called for a General Synod of pious and learned clergy to address religious reforms. This was fulfilled in the summoning of the Westminster Assembly in mid-1643, which produced the 'Westminster Confession' of faith and authorised a replacement for the Prayer Book, the *Directory of Public Worship*, in 1645. This was little more than a set of directions for clergy, not texts, giving a great deal of licence to the local minister to frame public prayer as he wished, and revoking virtually all surviving festivals and saints' days. The abolition of Christmas, and the suppression of the holiday and celebrations traditionally associated with it, proved particularly unpopular. The *Directory* was used fitfully, however. That reflected the chaos into which England was falling by the mid-1640s. The hopes of those Puritans who inclined to Presbyterianism that, in place of episcopal governance, a Presbyterian polity would be adopted uniformly for the Church of England were dashed by the growing strength of independency, the belief that each local congregation should be entitled, within the law, to determine its own organisation and worship. With the ascendancy of the independent-inclined Oliver Cromwell later in the 1640s, and the growing influence of radical religious opinion within the Parliamentary forces, the Presbyterian moment passed.

By the time Charles himself was executed in 1649, *his* Church of England had been all but destroyed. In place of a national, episcopal Church polity and liturgy enforced by law and upheld by the monarchy was a regional patchwork of different models of Church authority and organisation. In some places, formerly 'conforming' clergy, whether Puritan or not, remained in post, even sometimes continuing to use the Prayer Book whenever they could. Episcopal jurisdiction had mostly disappeared. The cathedrals were stripped of their clergy and staffed by preachers appointed by Parliament, while debate raged about what to do with them. In some places, a rudimentary Presbyterian system did come into being, with courts of presbyters and elders, but little power of discipline above the local level. Elsewhere, independent-minded ministers gathered together congregations as best they could. A fresh wave of iconoclasm swept parts of the country. The most notorious instance was in East Anglia, where the zealous farmer William Dowsing, in a fifteen-month orgy of destruction as a Parliamentary commissioner, purged the parish churches of Cambridgeshire, Suffolk and parts of Essex and Norfolk of idolatrous images and statues.[28]

Once again, it is necessary to emphasise the implications of all this for the identity of what later came to be called 'Anglicanism'. Those who were Presbyterians and independents, it has to be stressed, were as much, before the 1640s, members of the Church of England as were the now persecuted 'Prayer Book Protestants' and the Laudians. Now, however, the pretence that they were all really part of one national Church had gone. With the collapse of ordered Church government, it seemed that the English reformers' goal of a national Protestant or reformed Catholic Church had failed. The Civil War and the ensuing Commonwealth permanently sealed religious division in England. The idea that the Church of England, after the mid-seventeenth-century crisis, could be the Church for all the English people was an aspiration that could only have value if some way could be found of pulling all these diverse and dissenting strands of Christianity back together again.

The task would prove even harder because the collapse of order and Church discipline allowed a bewildering variety of local sects and radical congregations to thrive. The best-known of these are probably the Baptists and the Quakers. The Baptists could trace their origins back to radical Protestants in the late sixteenth century who insisted on adult or believer's baptism, and largely rejected the Prayer Book and episcopacy. The Quakers were followers of the mystic George Fox, who adopted an itinerant life in the first Civil War, searching for truth and spiritual comfort, and finding none in the clergy. In 1647 he experienced spiritual illumination which liberated him into a life of preaching, with a seemingly heterodox, non-Trinitarian theology.[29] This completely free and unconstrained preaching was exactly what the clergy (including conforming Puritans) had dreaded, before the Civil War. But there was worse, from that point of view. Other groups, more radical still in politics and religion than George Fox, sprang up in parts of the country. Groups called 'Ranters' – a term of abuse, largely, coined by those who objected to their leaders' declaiming divisive and extreme opinions – called for the complete overthrow of the ecclesiastical order, and even in some cases for freedom from moral restraint.[30] All of this confirmed the impression of contemporaries that the world was indeed 'turned upside down'.[31]

Given all the confusion this collapse of order and central direction implied, it is hardly surprising that, as one historian has argued, the attack on the Church of England was 'both haphazard and thorough'.[32] And yet, through all the chaos, a strong residual loyalty to the Prayer Book and to the ceremonies and festivals of the Church persisted in many places. A rebel, episcopal Anglican tradition survived as a parallel religious culture alongside the piecemeal Puritan or independent establishment. But, despite a surprisingly buoyant pattern of diaconal and priestly ordinations carried out surreptitiously by bishops, there were no new consecrations of bishops after 1644. As bishops in office died, their sees became vacant. Just eight were still occupied by the beginning of 1660.[33] Few people at that point would have been confident of the restoration of the pre-Civil War Church.

7

RESTORATION AND REBELLION

Restoration and Its Discontents

Britain's short and turbulent experiment with a republic came to an end on 29 May 1660, when Charles II, on his thirtieth birthday, entered London to cheering crowds. John Evelyn was there, a witness to the

> triumph of above 20,000 horse and foot, brandishing their swords, and shouting with inexpressible joy ... I stood in the Strand and beheld it, and blessed God. And all this was done without one drop of blood shed, and by that very army which rebelled against him.[1]

The panoply of monarchy came with him. Within three months Charles had resumed the ancient custom of touching for the king's evil, having the sick presented to him by one of his chaplains, touching their faces and giving them a gift of gold, as the chaplain said, '[t]hat is the true light who came into the world', with an epistle and prayers to follow.[2] Eight months later Evelyn was again at Westminster Abbey for the coronation. Nothing was spared of ancient ceremony. The dean and prebendaries brought all the regalia. The bishop of London, the newly appointed Gilbert Sheldon, presented the king to the people on every side with quadruple acclamations: 'God save King Charles the Second!' The king was anointed by the archbishop of Canterbury on his hands, his breast and the crown of his head. He was clothed in quasi-liturgical or ceremonial robes.[3] Another diarist, Samuel Pepys, was also there, noting, after the service, the ceremony at Westminster Hall when the King's Champion three times flung down his gauntlet and challenged anyone who would deny Charles to be lawful king.[4] The restored monarchy simply reinhabited the old ceremonies and their associated religious claims and rites. It was as if the civil wars and Commonwealth had never happened.

But this was far from the expected outcome of the death of Oliver Cromwell in 1658, nor even of the eighteen months of confusion and political wrangling that had followed, until near the very end. There was evidently much dissatisfaction with the Protectorate late in the 1650s, and a significant and growing undercurrent of royalist sympathy, but it would be something of an exaggeration to assume – as has been commonly the case in post-Restoration histories – that a great current of popular royalism simply swept Charles back into power as soon as Cromwell and his family were out of the way. The horse-trading that went on between politicians and the leaders of the army, including George Monck, later to be made duke of Albemarle, gradually homed in on restoration of the monarchy when it became clear that no other solution was feasible, and that that was in harmony with the growing tide of public opinion.

The declaration for restoration was not made by Parliament – and a strictly non-constitutional, 'Convention' Parliament at that – until 1 May 1660. Restoration was a process, not a single event. Although republicanism, as the historian Tim Harris has averred, had 'shallow roots' in England, none of the political and religious tensions which had caused the civil wars in the first place had really been resolved.[5] Domestic strife did not cease in 1660. There were abortive rebellions by various disaffected groups in the next few years, none serious enough to threaten the new regime. Popular disillusionment took root quickly, fuelled by rumours of the excess and sexual licence of the court, by plague in 1665, by the fire of London in 1666, by humiliation in the Dutch wars, and above all by continuing instability and uncertainty around religious policy.

Charles's reputation as the 'merry monarch' is, then,

somewhat misplaced. His was a troubled and insecure reign. He was certainly an astute politician, reinhabiting a role that had not been seriously trimmed by the experience of the Commonwealth. His powers as king were little different from those of his father, with perhaps the obvious rider that never again could a British monarch risk all-out conflict with Parliament. He fathered at least eight sons, none of them legitimate. His marriage produced no living heirs. His brother, the duke of York, was first in line to succeed him, but converted to Roman Catholicism in the late 1660s, thereby thrusting anxiety about the succession and the Catholic Church right into the heart of the regime. Charles's rule was an unsteady balancing act, caught between mutually contradictory approaches to the question of religious settlement.

With the goal of a broad and comprehensive settlement before him, in order to give his policy as wide a basis of support as possible, Charles had issued a declaration from Breda in the Netherlands before he set sail for England, in which he promised a general amnesty and religious toleration. He repeated his promise in October 1660, in the Worcester House Declaration, in which he coupled tolerance with the promise of appointment of a commission to review the Prayer Book, and outlined a form of 'reduced episcopacy', with bishops exercising authority with a body of 'grave and learned clergy' in each diocese.[6] This was music to the ears of moderate Puritans and Presbyterians, but not to some Anglicans, including the remaining members of the hierarchy who had endured years of persecution. They wanted a complete restoration of the Prayer Book, the episcopate and the operation of the Church at local level as it had been before the civil wars. That is eventually what they got, though it took some years. But if Charles could not have his comprehensive settlement – and he tried again to promote measures of toleration several times – he was thrown back on the very people who most strongly supported his own very high understanding of royal authority, namely the gentry and former 'Cavaliers' who were suspicious of the republican leanings of some dissenters and wanted nothing if not a return to the status quo before 1642. Charles oscillated, essentially between two different models of settlement, eventually leaning on the narrower version which fully reinstated the position of the Church of England, but left significant numbers of a 'Puritan rump' outside that settlement. The Restoration emphatically confirmed the divisions which had opened wide in English and Welsh Protestantism during the years of the Commonwealth.

The Re-establishment of the Church of England

Whatever Charles's intentions towards Puritans and dissenters, there was a strong undertow towards the more traditional Anglican position. Even one of the earliest measures of the Convention Parliament, the 1660 Act for the Confirming and Restoring of Ministers, which was intended to foreclose radical change in personnel in parishes, had the opposite effect in many places, since its provision for confirming present incumbents in their posts made various exceptions, including of those who denied infant baptism and of those who occupied sequestered livings under the Commonwealth but with their ejected predecessors still alive. Some 700 ministers were forced out by this measure.[7] Although the Worcester House Declaration had been designed to conciliate Presbyterians in particular, the process of appointing bishops to vacant sees, which was pursued vigorously in the early months of the new regime, inevitably had the effect of strengthening the hand of those who wanted a full restoration of a pre-Civil War-style episcopacy, even though many appointees were moderates.

Constitutionally, what emerged from the summoning of the first properly constituted Parliament after elections in 1661 was the repeal of all legislation passed since 1641: bishops were back in the House of Lords, and the Church courts were re-established. This was all in advance of the most important measure, the reimposition of a national liturgy. In April 1661 a conference of representatives of episcopal and Presbyterian clergy met at the Savoy Hospital in London to consider possible alterations to the *Book of Common Prayer*, in order to accommodate Presbyterians and moderate Puritans. But the discussions came to nothing, hindered by obduracy on both sides. Richard Baxter, one of the participants, later accused the bishops of having 'that eminency of power and interest that the greatest lords were glad of their favour, [and] did expect that the presence of so many of them should have awed us into … silence, or cowardliness'.[8] Once again, the undertow prevailed: the 1559 Prayer Book was adopted by the new 'Cavalier' Parliament, with minor revisions (a nod in the Presbyterian direction) and imposed by a new Act of Uniformity in 1662.

The bishops have had a bad press from historians over the years. It is very common to find them and the settlement they promoted described as narrow and intolerant, even as 'uncharitable and schismatic'.[9] But it is possible the shadow of later ideas of tolerance and progress continues to hang over such judgments. It is equally plausible that what the bishops represented was a stronger, more determined form of confessional Anglicanism, refined in the fire of war and persecution, which no longer depended entirely on monarchical fiat for its form and existence – ironically, given Charles I's commitment to the Church, echoed faintly by his son – but was fast becoming, at least in some quarters, a conviction that the order of the Church of England stood on its own, ancient, Catholic authority, independent of the civil power.

The eminent theologian Herbert Thorndike, for example, had developed a theory of the Church's polity which insisted on the prior and distinct authority of bishops apart from the civil magistrate; in the Restoration period, he argued that the Church of England's traditional order, modelled as it was (he assumed) on the early Church, was the true route to comprehension.[10] This was a harbinger of an increasingly confident and assertive High Churchmanship. Provided we do not assume that it was *the* Anglican position, but recognise it as increasingly influential none the less, it does help to clarify just why the bishops and

other clergy were so reluctant to alter the terms of the settlement to encompass significantly different theories of Church
polity and episcopacy.

But the effect, at least as far as many Presbyterian Anglicans
and many moderate Puritans were concerned, was disastrous.
Reimposition of episcopacy and the Prayer Book led to the ejec-
tion of nearly 1,000 parish clergy, bringing the total forced out
since 1660 to about 1,760.[11] They went into permanent separation from the Church. This was the foundation effectively of the
traditions of Congregationalism, or Independency, and Presbyterianism, which evolved into distinct denominations in time
and, with the Baptists and the Quakers, were later called 'Old
Dissent'. For them, 1662 became a defining moment, setting
their identity squarely in a mythology of forced exclusion and
persecution. From this point on, the history of the Church of
England does not as such include them. But their loss to the
Church was – looking at the situation from an ecumenical perspective – a tragedy. There is one more refinement we must
make to this account, however. The Act did not, as is commonly
assumed, exclude *all* Puritan opinion and render the Church
theologically monochrome. A significant number of Puritan
or strongly Calvinist clergy remained inside the Church, ready
to accept with more or less reluctance the terms of Uniformity, perhaps a somewhat troubled minority, committed to the
notion of a national Church, but by no means ready to subscribe
to the views of those such as Thorndike.[12] In some dioceses
these people, at least in the early years of the reign, may even
have been in a majority.[13]

Even with the Act of Uniformity, however, the question of
the limits of the settlement was not completely resolved. The
Restoration Church had to ride a complex and shifting political
and religious landscape, with royal policy changing according to Charles's whims and the alliances and compromises he
was forced to make. The king tried twice again to promote a
broader-based, comprehensive settlement, by issuing a Declaration of Indulgence, suspending penal laws against dissenters and

Catholics, in December 1662, and again nearly ten years later, in March 1672, but on both occasions Parliamentary resistance forced him to back down, claiming the king had no authority to suspend legislation without an act of Parliament.[14]

But if comprehension could not be achieved, the alternative was the far harsher policy of active exclusion of dissenters and Catholics from public office and from freedom to worship. Here, the so-called 'Cavalier' Parliament, which met at intervals from 1661 to 1679, with its determination to erase as much as possible of the Commonwealth and Protectorate legislation, harmonised with High Church opinion, and produced a series of measures which gained notoriety as the 'Clarendon Code', after Charles II's chief minister, Edward Hyde, earl of Clarendon. The Corporation Act of 1661 prevented anyone from taking up local public office unless they received communion in the Church of England, subscribed an oath of allegiance to the Crown and foreswore the Solemn League and Covenant, the 1643 agreement between the Scots and the English to support the Parliamentary cause. Test Acts passed in 1673 and 1678, aimed particularly at Catholics, extended this to a denial of transubstantiation, and confirmed that these provisions applied to Members of Parliament. Conventicle Acts of 1670 (the second of which was called by the Puritan poet Andrew Marvell 'the quintessence of arbitrary malice') penalised 'conventiclers', i.e. dissenters meeting in houses or other places unlicensed for worship.[15] The 'Five Mile Act' of 1665 prevented clergy who had been deprived of their livings under the Restoration legislation from living within five miles of their former parishes, unless they swore a declaration of loyalty to the king and to the settlement of religion.

The details of these measures, and the various devices by which, over the years, their provisions were gradually relaxed, at least for Protestant dissenters, need not concern us here. What is evident is that this flurry of legislation aimed to protect the Church of England's privileged constitutional position. It reflected an abiding conviction not only that such a legislative and constitutional link between Church and State was justified

in the interests of the Church, but that the State had a continuing responsibility to promote religious truth. The State could
not be pluralist. Domestic peace and harmony, once again,
depended on religious unity and uniformity. We are back with
the dilemma of the Restoration regime – comprehend as many
as possible within a broad national Church, or continue to affirm
a more specific perception of ecclesial truth. Even Presbyterians
– or at least most of them – shared the same basic conviction
about the relationship of Church and State.

   But the breaking of this model came initially not from the
side of Protestant dissent, but from Roman Catholicism. Here,
again, dynastic factors came into play. Quite apart from the
suspicion that Charles himself had hankerings after conversion
– and there was to be, apparently, a deathbed conversion – his
failure to produce a legitimate heir meant that the succession
would default to his brother, James, duke of York, who himself
made public his conversion in 1672. James shared his brother's
and father's exalted view of royal authority, and had appeared
a strong defender of the Church of England. But in the years
after his conversion, and especially with Charles's attempted
lifting of penal legislation, anxiety about his real intentions
towards the Church of England began to grow. In the late 1670s
and 1680s, anti-Popery became perhaps the strongest popular
impulse shaping politics. In 1678 this bubbled up in the form of
the absurdly overheated fear of a 'Popish plot', fuelled by the
entirely unreliable ex-convert Titus Oates. Whatever the truth
of Oates's claims of conspiracies to murder King Charles, put
James on the throne and restore Papal jurisdiction – and there
was probably little truth in them – the effect on politics was
electric. James was, temporarily, forced into exile. Parliament
– reconstituted three times in elections from 1679 to 1681 – was
packed with members desperate to exclude James from the
succession.

   The 'Exclusion Crisis', as it is called, polarised political
opinion, not into anti-Catholic and pro-Catholic factions (for
practically everyone was anti-Catholic), but into pro-court and

anti-court. The anti-court group formed the nucleus of those who were fast becoming known as the 'Whigs', loyal in principle to Charles but unhappy with his willingness to accept James as his heir and asserting Parliament's power to effect an alteration in the succession. The pro-court group included many gentry and aristocracy who shared High Anglican commitments to a divine right monarchy, and trusted that James would as king fulfil, as he indicated, his obligations towards the Church. Exclusion failed when Charles prorogued Parliament. But this solidified the hold of the High Anglican / Tory group, who were strengthened by the changing composition of the Restoration Parliament, as a new generation began to succeed the 'reluctant conformists' of the 1660s.[16] The bishops strengthened the hand of this group by the novel use of excommunication as a political tool, since anyone denied the sacrament would fall under the provisions of the Test and Corporation Acts.[17] This was the tense, unresolved state of affairs, with no evident long-term security for the Church against a Catholic monarch, when Charles died suddenly in early 1685.

There is a broader picture for the Church, though, than the political and religious uncertainties that consumed the Restoration regime. Parish Anglicanism had been severely attenuated in the Commonwealth. It was not going to be restored in a matter of months, or even a few years. What was needed was a thoroughgoing process of catechetical, pastoral and disciplinary endeavour, over a generation or two. Charles's reign did at least give sufficient respite at local level to enable that process to begin. Along with reconstitution of the Church hierarchy, clerical recruitment and education had to be enhanced significantly. Church interiors in many places needed to be restored. Infant baptism had fallen away in many places; a new service of baptism 'for those of Riper Years' had to be drafted for the Prayer Book. New 'State' services marking the dates of the death of Charles I, the re-entry of Charles II into London and the Gunpowder Plot were also approved by Convocation and added to the book.[18] The re-establishment of the Church courts,

which lost their power to impose fines, was only partially successful: evidence from the diocese of Winchester and elsewhere
suggests the post-Restoration courts never attained the level of
activity of the early decades of the century.[19] This meant that
the old mechanisms for enforcing church attendance and conformity were increasingly ineffective. So were central attempts
to address some longstanding problems. Measures to reduce
clerical pluralism, to prevent clandestine marriages, to recover
tithe payments, to augment poor livings, to enforce observance
of the Sabbath, and to suppress blasphemy and atheism were
considered by the Cavalier Parliament in the late 1670s, but
were either abandoned completely or passed in neutered or
anodyne form.[20] This was all tribute to a renewed pastoral zeal
and energy on behalf of the established Church, but it faced
formidable obstacles, including sometimes sullen or determined
opposition. Strong or even just residual support for dissent
could co-exist and overlap with popular anti-clericalism, highlighting elements of inflexibility or obtuseness on the part of
some of the clergy.[21] The Restoration Anglican 'project' did not
fail, but nor did it succeed entirely in recovering the ground lost
at mid-century.

      And, briefly, we need to look wider still. This is a history of
the Church of the England as it is now, rather than a history of
global Anglicanism, and therefore the Church's overseas activity
over the centuries does not really feature in this account. None
the less it has to be acknowledged that, as an established Church,
it had an exceptionally close relationship to the people, institutions and processes through which British trade expanded from
the seventeenth to the twentieth centuries, and with it coloni-
sation and imperial rule. The majority of Anglican clergy and
most of the laity probably knew little of this, certainly at first
hand. But overseas commitments without question influenced
and shaped the experience of the Church at home.

      This entanglement with imperial history – for that is what it
was – began in earnest in the Restoration period. American colonies were founded earlier, but expanded through the century.

The reorganisation of the navy facilitated and protected growing trade, assisted by the Navigation Act of 1660. The foundation of the Royal African Company in 1672, following an earlier venture in 1660, was a straight bid to seize the Atlantic trade from the Dutch.[22] And that meant slaves. Over the next century and a half Britain's expanding Atlantic economy depended on the gross inhumanity of the slave trade. The Church of England provided chaplains to the navy, clergy for growing colonies in America, the Caribbean, and eventually Africa and Asia. Families who owned plantations, and therefore benefitted from the human traffic, supported their local parish churches in England and Wales, gave sons to the ministry, and were memorialised in churches at their deaths. Britain's growing influence on the continent of Europe also facilitated greater international contact, especially with leaders of north European Protestant churches. Later still, Anglicans often gave voice to a sense of imperial mission which, with its cultural and racial assumptions, seeped into the attitudes and motives of overseas evangelism. Religion in its practical manifestations can never be disentangled from political ideology, and so it proved for the Church of England.

Glorious Revolution?

The short and disastrous reign of James II, clouded as it has become by the subsequent mythology of the Glorious Revolution of 1688, has often been cast simply as one long downward spiral, driven by growing hostility to James's intention to return his kingdoms to the Roman fold. But it is not at all obvious that that was the direct object of James's policy – at least, not in the first instance. Rather, his popularity and support foundered on the two points of religious toleration, on the one hand, and royal absolutism, on the other. James pursued apparently tolerant policies with the zeal and force of an absolute monarch; conversely, one could say that his absolutist inclinations could countenance toleration of any religious opinion which did not directly challenge his royal authority. This would have been a very difficult balancing act at the best of times, but it proved impossible in the fevered, tense atmosphere of the 1680s. His brother had wisely drawn back from alienating the elite groups most loyal to the monarchy, recognising the limits of his power. James knew no such caution.[23]

His reign began apparently well enough, with a commitment to defend the Church of England, and with the easy suppression of rebellion in Scotland and the West Country. But soon James began to turn his brother's injunctions against seditious preaching against Anglicans publicly condemning Popery, and in July 1686 he established a new Ecclesiastical Commission, packed with his close supporters, to contain the bishops, and to suspend the bishop of London in particular for refusing to discipline an anti-Catholic preacher.[24] Using his dispensing power, controversially, James circumvented the Test Act to insert Catholic officers into the army – this proved particularly unpopular with many existing officers – and Catholics into other public offices including the Treasury and the Privy Council.[25] When he could not corral the House of Commons to support his policies, he prorogued it, and then pursued a campaign of intimidation (called 'regulation') to weed out opponents in the municipal corporations. All these actions confirmed his subjects' worst fears that their king was rapidly moving not only to allow freedom of worship to Catholics, but to subvert the Protestant constitution and the Church of England.

The underlying current of anxiety surrounding James's policy was indeed anti-Catholicism, then, which ultimately proved to be a greater principle of agreement between Anglicans and dissenters than loyalty to the Crown. But this became apparent only with the complete failure of James's attempt to play Anglicans and dissenters off against each other. He could try to court dissenting favour by overturning the legal monopoly of the Church of England, but the very fact that it was quite evident that his real motive for doing so was to enable Catholicism to flourish doomed the project. In February 1687 in Scotland, and then in April in England and Wales,

9. Reverend rebels: the seven bishops

James issued a Declaration of Indulgence suspending all penal laws against nonconformists, including Catholics. As if this was not bad enough in itself for Anglicans, in May 1688 he issued an order in council requiring the declaration to be read aloud in all churches and distributed by bishops to their dioceses. For ardent Anglicans this was tantamount to requiring them to declare the overthrow of their own Church's constitutional position. There was widespread resistance. James's attempt to intimidate seven bishops, including the archbishop of Canterbury, William Sancroft, by prosecuting them for seditious libel and locking them in the Tower, backfired when they were acquitted in court, 'to the inexpressible joy of the City, the army, and the whole nation', as it was somewhat exaggeratedly put by Gilbert Burnet, bishop, historian and supporter of James's usurper, William III.[26] The king's move had decisively settled the Church against him, uniting leading London clergy and formerly loyal figures such as the archbishop himself and leading aristocracy.[27]

By this time, James's daughter Mary and her husband, the Protestant William, Prince of Orange, were already receiving overtures from British opponents, including Whig politicians who had looked to William as a likely heir even before James's accession. Matters were brought to a head by the announcement of the birth of a male heir to James in June 1688.

The mythology of the Glorious Revolution has tended to emphasise the idea of William being invited to take up the Crown after James was deemed to have abandoned his coronation oath. But in fact William's move was much more like a full-scale, external military invasion – the last such on British soil. He landed at Torbay on 5 November – an auspicious date for Protestants – with a fleet of nearly 600 ships and an army of around 15,000 men, most of them Dutch regular soldiers.[28] In theory, James had numerically far superior forces at his disposal, but his support was wavering, and increasing numbers went over to the enemy. Frantic last-minute attempts by James to backtrack on his policies were to no avail, and he fled to the Continent, finally, on 23 December, leaving the kingdom in William's hands.

If the unwillingness of James's erstwhile Tory supporters to stand by him sealed his fate, the outcome of William's accession to the Crown was by no means a new golden age of domestic harmony and peace. The temporary alliance of Whig and Tory

Anglicans and dissenters did not – could not – last. Beyond an aversion to Roman Catholicism and opposition to James's policy, they had little to unite them. One of William's key motives for his actions also had little to do with English religion: he sought to combine British and Dutch interests as part of a great coalition against France – and in this he was largely successful. William himself favoured toleration of dissenters, and was no particular supporter of the established Church, especially its representative institution, Convocation. With the new monarch surrounding himself with Whig advisers, it was always likely that the lower clergy in particular would quickly becoming disgruntled. But some things had shifted decisively. The overthrow of James confirmed Parliamentary authority: the Bill of Rights of 1689 enshrined in law limitations on the powers of the monarch, and also excluded Roman Catholics from the succession.

This had implications for the Church. Though the royal supremacy remained unchallenged, it is arguable that from this point on the Church of England ceased to be a monarchical church, and became instead the privileged and established Church of a constitutional monarchy – although in practice the royal supremacy was exercised through an oligarchy who controlled Parliament. The religious opinions of the monarch lost significance. William was a Reformed Dutchman; later, in the early eighteenth century, the Hanoverians, at least at first, were Lutheran. But provided they upheld the Church of England, and provided they were not Catholic, their own views mattered little. This has remained true up to the present – even monarchs with strong views of their own on Church matters, such as George III and Queen Victoria, and religiously serious monarchs such as Elizabeth II, have had relatively little influence on Church affairs, at least in comparison with their Tudor and Stuart forebears.

A final attempt to achieve a comprehensive religious settlement was made in the wake of William's accession, but failed. Twin measures of comprehension and toleration were put to Parliament. Toleration passed, as the Act of Toleration of 1689.

But comprehension, for various reason, did not. This was not an outcome favoured by Anglicans or dissenters, but it was what it was. Anglicans found themselves confronting not a small dissident rump after the re-absorption of the majority of moderate dissent, as originally envisaged, but a large number of dissenters now fast becoming distinct religious traditions, or 'denominations' – Independents, Presbyterians, Baptists, Quakers. But toleration was grudging, because none of the penal legislation that James had tried to overthrow was withdrawn. Therefore the Church of England remained constitutionally privileged and protected, with many of its clergy committed to the ambition of eliminating dissent by education and catechesis and, if possible, by law. Furthermore, a small number of Anglicans – numerous bishops, including Sancroft himself, and some 400 clergy – were caught by their conscientious defence of the principle of divine right and by their oaths of obedience to James II. Even though most of them had supported James's departure, they could not subscribe to the new king, and were deprived of their livings. These 'non-Jurors' mostly remained attending members of the Church of England, though some founded new, independent Anglican chapels. They also became a conduit for an advanced High Churchmanship which bore fruit much later, in the nineteenth century, though the non-Juring schism itself withered away in the eighteenth century. Finally, 1688–9 marked the decisive abandonment of the constitutional assumption of an all-inclusive national religious Church. It was a momentous step in the long history of Britain's Christian pluralism.

8

THE GREAT CHURCHES

So far I have traced the history of the Church of England through the most turbulent century and a half of its existence. Ordinary churchgoers had seen, in that time, a massive change in religious practice and belief. Yet through it all, the backbone of the Church of England had remained the parish system. Over 9,000 churches had been built before the sixteenth century; that number was almost to double in the great era of population growth during and after the industrial revolution. Yet alongside the parish churches were a small but religiously and culturally significant group of great churches whose history and function set them apart. They were sometimes refuges from wider trends in iconoclasm and reform, preserving practices and treasures which elsewhere succumbed to the destruction of religious radicalism, sometimes experimental sites in which new forms of worship and music could be tested, sometimes moribund, and sometimes lively and engaging intellectual and theological communities. They included the great medieval cathedrals that survived the Reformation, either as 'old' foundations or as old monastic churches refounded as cathedrals of the 'new' foundation. They also included some of the suppressed monastic patrimony – churches such as Wymondham Abbey, Selby Abbey, Christchurch Priory and Tewkesbury Abbey – and a number of large, collegiate churches, some of which (Manchester is the prime example) were later elevated to the status of cathedral. But they also included the college chapels of Oxford and Cambridge Universities, some of them small, admittedly, but others (pre-eminently King's College, Cambridge) of a scale to match the cathedrals and abbey churches themselves, and with choral foundations.

This is an appropriate point to consider these great churches in their own terms, for their history is often sufficiently distinct to warrant that. As we saw in chapter 1, the cathedrals in particular sat at the very top of the territorial organisation by which the Church of England was governed. If the parish church was a genuinely *local* church, a church which people living in particular places could recognise as their church, in another sense the cathedral was *the* local church, because the diocese served a particular region, uniting many parishes, and each diocese was headed by a bishop who had charge of all the parishes and parish clergy in his diocese.

The Reformation and After

All of the Henrician legislation, followed in turn by the successive changes of his children's reigns, impacted directly on the cathedrals and the collegiate institutions of Oxford and Cambridge. Their wealth was a draw for the commissioners sent out by Thomas Cromwell, especially so in the case of the monastic cathedrals (the majority), such as Durham, Canterbury, Ely, Norwich and Winchester; they all lost land and revenue through the changes. They saw their saints' shrines – a valuable source of revenue – broken up and their wealth carried off by the Crown in the general devastation of shrines. The most preposterous violence occurred at Canterbury, where Becket's body was treated as if it were a live person and was accused of treason, his martyrdom denied, and his bones dug up, burned and scattered.[1] The campaign against images that began in the late 1530s at Cromwell's behest, and was carried much further under Edward, affected the cathedrals and other great churches as much as it did ordinary parish churches. At Ely the glorious Lady Chapel suffered appalling destruction under its zealous bishop Thomas Goodrich, its statues pulled down or their faces hacked off, with the building turned into a parish church for the town.

10. Iconoclasm: broken statues in the Lady Chapel, Ely cathedral

A further wave of damage and suppression followed the Chantries Acts of 1545 and 1547, when chantry chapels within the cathedrals were, like chantries everywhere in England and Wales, declared Crown property. At Worcester, even the chantry where Prince Arthur, Henry VIII's older brother, had been buried, was suppressed, and many of its saints' statues defaced. Collegiate churches, including some future cathedrals such as Manchester, Ripon and Derby, had their collegiate foundations suppressed. Only the chapels of Oxford and Cambridge remained largely unchanged.

In terms of permanent change, the creation of the six new dioceses stands out. In each case, an abbey was suppressed, only to be turned into a cathedral and chapter, and some of the monastic buildings adapted to new purposes. Five of these – Gloucester, Peterborough, Oxford, Bristol and Chester – have endured up to the present as cathedrals. Ironically, it was probably its very closeness to the centre of power, and the corresponding usefulness of its buildings, along with its royal associations, that saved a sixth – Westminster. The newly created cathedral had a short life of ten years as centre of a new diocese, and a further six years as a second cathedral for the diocese of London, before reverting to an abbey under Mary, and then under Elizabeth becoming a 'peculiar', a great church under the direct authority of the Crown, not a bishop. Here both the great and the lesser cloisters, the chapter house, much of the abbot's lodging and some other buildings were retained for permanent use.

Elsewhere, extensive demolition of monastic buildings occurred at some cathedrals after they were 'secularised' and their attached Benedictine communities turned into chapters of regular clergy; at both Bath and Coventry the suppression of the priories led to the suppression, too, of the role of the cathedral and priory church, which in both cases had been coupled with another cathedral, Bath with Wells, and Coventry with Lichfield. At Coventry the great priory church of St Mary's – one of the largest in the country – was completely demolished; its successor cathedral, destroyed by bombing in 1940, was a much smaller parish church raised to cathedral status in the nineteenth century. The work of demolition carried on at Winchester into Elizabeth's reign, with the destruction of many of the remaining monastic buildings during the episcopate of Robert Horne. But essentially by then the fabric and appearance of the cathedrals and many of the great churches was much as it would remain for hundreds of years.

The survival of these great buildings was all the more remarkable, given the radical direction of Edward VI's religious policy. Once again it is tempting to indulge in a little counterfactual history. If Edward had lived another twenty years, and Cranmer's programme of reform had gone much further than it did, would the cathedrals have survived at all? It seems doubtful. There was, at the time, little sentimentality about their architectural or cultural importance – quite the reverse. For most English Protestants they were functional spaces. The loss of so many monastic buildings which, had they survived intact, would today be regarded as outstanding monuments – Coventry, Pershore, Chertsey, Bury St Edmunds, Hailes, to name but a few – is a sign of how little regard there was at the time for historic fabric. When not useful for some specific purpose, they were a source of ready-cut stone. Here and there, there were counter-indications of a continuing sense that cathedrals were an ornament to a city – that was certainly the view Elizabeth took of St Paul's, for example.[2] Much of the destruction of monastic property at the cathedrals of the 'new' foundation was not so much an act of religious vandalism as a pragmatic adaptation of spaces that no longer served their original purposes. Probably the cathedral churches themselves were at least partly saved by the fact that most had some sort of worshipping lay congregation.

Although what cathedrals were really for – in contrast to ordinary parish churches, that is – remained a little unclear, there were at least some efforts to turn them to good use. The Lady Chapel of the abbey church of St Albans was made into a school, for example, when the church was turned over to parochial use. At Worcester the monks' refectory was retained and also made into a school. Every cathedral was instructed in Edward's reign to fit up a library with the works of the early Church fathers as well as modern writers such as Erasmus.[3] There was also some attempt to make the cathedrals into centres of reformed preaching; at Canterbury, Cranmer founded a College of Six Preachers in 1541 to supplement the ministry of the Chapter. Under Elizabeth, weekly sermons were required at most cathedrals. Archbishop Grindal required all the minster clergy at York to attend these sermons, taking it in turns to preach themselves.[4] Again, provision was often made for regular lectures in theology. At Durham a prebendary was appointed and paid to lecture two or three times a week in the chapter house. Similar arrangements were made under Elizabeth in many other cathedrals, but also at some parish churches.[5]

The cathedrals and some of the great churches were also

vital in preserving the English tradition of church music. Choral foundations were retained, with vicars choral – the men who were paid to sing for services – usually allowed to retain residences in or near the cathedral grounds. The Elizabethan injunctions included one insisting on the proper maintenance of choral foundations, and on the singing of services in 'as modest and distinct song so used in all parts of the common prayers in the church, that the same may be plainly understanded'.[6] It also permitted additional hymns or 'suchlike song to the praise of Almighty God, in the best sort of melody' – a provision that evidently provided cover for the continuation of the polyphony that in the hands of composers such as Christopher Tye and Thomas Tallis had become a particular glory of the English Church. But in general there was no consistent attempt to reconceive the role of the cathedrals; as one historian has asserted, 'no one took the occasion ... to ask what the cathedrals were actually for'.[7]

Crisis and Recovery

Uncertainty over their role and status marked the next hundred years for the cathedrals and greater churches. Puritan criticism of the remnants of 'Popery' in the Church of England certainly extended to the cathedrals, both for what they represented as relics of a Catholic past and for what still went on in them, including singing, the use of vestments, the use of the *Book of Common Prayer* and the celebration of various saints' days.

The weight of criticism may have been one factor in the apparent neglect of cathedral fabric – certainly there were plenty of instances of that in the early seventeenth century. St Paul's was probably the most notorious example. A disastrous fire in 1561, started by lightning, had destroyed the great steeple and burnt the roofs; though the roofs were repaired, damage done to the vaults almost certainly contributed to the collapse of parts of the walls after the great fire of 1666. The steeple was never rebuilt. There were some efforts made to address the poor condition of cathedrals and churches. Some ruined

11. Even the ruins are destroyed: St Paul's on fire

monastery churches were repaired for parochial worship, including Cartmel in Cumbria and Abbey Dore in Gloucestershire. Several attempts were made to tackle the problems at St Paul's, but the sheer expense as well as the contentious nature of the project stalled matters until, under William Laud as bishop of London and then as archbishop of Canterbury, a concerted plan was put into action with the distinguished architect Inigo Jones as surveyor.[8]

For the avant-garde conformists and Laudians of the reigns of James I and Charles I the cathedrals were particularly important. Efforts to restore something of their liturgical and sacramental life began well before Laud's achievement of high office. At Exeter cathedral, for example, a proper communion table was provided in 1615, and then rails, cushions and hangings, and also new chalices in place of the old communion plate.[9] Laud himself, when dean of Gloucester, moved the communion table to the east end of the cathedral and turned it 'altarwise'.[10] But it was only with his appointments to London and then Canterbury in 1633 that Laud's full programme of reform could finally get under way. With Neile of York, he obtained the appointment of commissioners by Charles I to carry out cathedral visitations in both provinces. These led to specific orders to make good dilapidations and provide 'suitable ornaments' and vestments, including copes.[11] But, as we have seen already, Laud's programme of reform ran out of steam in the late 1630s as the political crisis of Charles's reign deepened.

Once civil war broke out in 1642, the cathedrals were an immediate target for the Parliamentary armies. Almost everywhere, more destruction of stained glass images and statuary took place, sometimes on a catastrophic scale. Organs were a particular target. At Winchester in December 1642, as a Royalist clergyman recorded, Sir William Waller's cavalry 'rode up through the body of the Church … until they came to the Altar; there they began their work, they rudely pluck down the Table and break the Rail … they throw down the Organ, and break the Stories of the Old and New Testament, curiously cut out in carved work'.[12] Destruction invariably followed directly from siege and occupation, partly justified by a Parliamentary ordinance of 1643 mandating the taking down of superstitious monuments. Wells·cathedral suffered twice in 1643, with many images and crucifixes destroyed.[13] Canterbury was damaged early in the war: John Evelyn had visited the cathedral in 1641 and saw it 'then in great splendour; those famous windows being entire, since demolished by the fanatics'.[14]

Nowhere escaped altogether, though a few cities suffered lightly. York was among these, although even here the organ was removed. The windows were saved, however, by the intervention of the Parliamentary general, Sir Thomas Fairfax. At the other end of the scale was the treatment of Carlisle cathedral. Under siege in 1644 and 1645, the city finally capitulated after news of the king's defeat at Naseby in June 1645, and was occupied by Scottish troops. The following year they pulled down the west front of the cathedral and most of the nave to repair the castle; it was never rebuilt, and Carlisle remains an oddly truncated building to this day. Durham and Lichfield also suffered badly, Lichfield in part because the cathedral close itself was fortified; when it fell to Parliament in early 1643 soldiers destroyed the choir stalls, much of the stained glass, images, statues and tombs, and burned most of the library's books.[15]

The destruction marked just the beginning of a decisive move against the cathedral foundations. In April 1649 Parliament passed an act abolishing the foundations altogether, in effect turning out the cathedral clergy from their posts and their accommodation, dissolving the chapters and appropriating the chapter property and revenues. At each cathedral surveys of property documented what was turned over for Parliament's use. These surveys incidentally commented sometimes on the state of the fabric. At Lichfield, for example, 'the whole ffabrick of it is exceedingly ruinated; much Lead and iron was taken away whilst it was a Garrison ... A great part of the roofe uncovered'.[16]

There was no consistent plan for the use of these great buildings. Musical and liturgical life following the Prayer Book ceased altogether. Some of them were used for worship, mostly preaching. Ely was locked for many years on the order of Cromwell. Some were used for stabling horses and for marshalling and exercising soldiers, as was the case with King's College Chapel in Cambridge. A radical proposal before Parliament in 1651 to demolish the cathedrals completely was not passed, but that it could be proposed and seriously debated is a sign of the hostility of the period.

The restoration of the monarchy in 1660 was the saving of the cathedrals and great churches. Making good the depredations of the Commonwealth period took years. Not only did fabric need to be repaired, the buildings themselves refurbished and new sets of liturgical books, vestments and hangings provided, but cathedral chapters had to be re-established, and their property and revenues restored. Much of this work of restoration was still going on in the 1670s and beyond – that at Lichfield took many decades, for example. Even then, it was sometimes merely patching up the effects of previous damage and neglect,

12. Rebuilding the London skyline: the new St
Paul's looms over Wren's parish churches

and did not halt further loss altogether. Part of the north tran-
sept at Ely fell down in 1699, for example, and was eventually
made good under the direction of Sir Christopher Wren.[17] Wren
was involved in restoration and rebuilding at several places.
At Lincoln, for example, he designed a new cathedral library,
partly following his earlier template at Trinity College, Cambridge.[18] And it was Wren, of course, whose (second) design was
accepted for the new building in London to replace the Old St
Paul's which, badly burnt in the fire of 1666, finally collapsed in
1668. The new building, one of the largest Protestant Baroque
churches in the world, took over thirty years to build, and was
not completed until 1710. Along with the physical restoration
went the resuscitation of religious and devotional work. Organs
and choirs were re-established and, with the Church of England
now purged of its radical Puritan wing, cathedral worship

was no longer the subject of such opprobrium from inside the Church itself.

Into the eighteenth century, cathedral life followed the restored pattern and there was little dramatic change. Like much of the rest of the Church of England, these churches acquired a reputation for torpor which is without much justification. There was some turbulence – chiefly the removal of some non-Juring clergy – after the Glorious Revolution of 1688, but thereafter political crises were rare and affected cathedrals little. Music – or rather the maintenance of choirs – continued to be a drain on cathedral finances, and also on some of the greater churches; in general, this is still thought to have been a time of relative stasis for cathedral choirs. All the same, this was the century in which the Three Choirs Festival was founded (1723), involving Worcester, Gloucester, and Hereford.

The main reason for the abiding image of cathedrals as moribund is the nineteenth century's adverse judgment on the preceding century's complicated and compromised financial arrangements. By the late seventeenth century the cathedrals had mostly recovered their pre-Civil War property. But this merely served to ingrain the financial inequalities of a much older system. Cathedrals of the 'old' foundation continued, as they had before, to have separate property portfolios and revenues for each of the prebends attached to a deanery or canonry; this meant the perpetuation of inequality, as well as complicated and cumbersome administration. Cathedrals of the 'new' foundation – in fact the majority – instead held property proceeds in united funds, simplifying administration and giving closer control of stipends. But the wealth of individual cathedrals, and of their clergy, varied enormously. Canterbury was one of the wealthier, but even there the stipend of a canon was around £40 – nowhere near enough to support a married clergyman and his family in comfort.[19] As a consequence, the vast majority of cathedral clergy were pluralists, holding other offices such as parish livings in conjunction with their canonries and prebends. Clergy might be absent for months, paying someone else to

perform their duties; the attraction of holding a cathedral position was obvious for those of independent means, or for those
who were lucky enough to gain a wealthy living elsewhere. It
was not a good system, dispersing pastoral ministry and giving
little stimulus for the development of cathedral worship, but
that does not necessarily mean that the cathedral clergy were
corrupt and lazy. As the Church of England benefitted generally
from rising agricultural rents in the eighteenth century, so, too,
did the cathedrals, and likewise rose the ambitions and the social
pretensions of the clergy.

Reform and Renewal

In the early nineteenth century the cathedrals were in an
uncertain, precarious state. They were among the wealthiest
corporate institutions of the country. Like the colleges of Oxford
and Cambridge, they had escaped despoliation at the Reformation. They possessed extensive landed estates. They gave their
clergy – deans, canons and prebendaries – dignity and status in
county society, in return for duties which often seemed minimal.
Their buildings were poorly lit, cold and closed often during
the day except for services; they in some cases had domestic
buildings – houses and even shops – built up against their walls.
Few people doubted that they were important historic buildings
which ought to be preserved. But they were hardly valued and
accessible in the way we have come to experience them today.
Well into the nineteenth century, cathedrals could be forbidding
places, where even the local clergy felt unwelcome. The clergyman and diarist Francis Witts, for example, attempting to attend
a magistrates' service in Gloucester cathedral in 1827, found the
vergers locking stalls and galleries against him and his group, so
that in the end they had to force entry into a gallery by clamber-
ing over a door; even so, 'the chanter and reader underneath
us were so muttering and monotonous, the altar and pulpit so
distant, and so much of solid masonry interposed that I, at least,
heard next to nothing of the service'.[20]

There was little agreement on what should be done with them. To many people they seemed privileged, remote and of little relevance to the Church at large. On specific ceremonial occasions they sprang to life. But the bishops had little actual power in their own cathedrals, apart from on the formal occasion held every few years when they could carry out a visitation and make criticisms of cathedral management, and recommendations. But it was difficult to enforce these without recourse to lengthy and expensive processes in court. To those critical of the Church of England as a whole – Protestant Nonconformists, radical politicians, a small but noisy band of upper-class religious sceptics – the cathedrals looked especially vulnerable, as the wealthiest and most privileged but most useless part of the Church establishment. The same could be said about the great churches, such as Westminster Abbey and St George's Chapel, Windsor, but also the chapels of Oxford and Cambridge, which were after all outside diocesan control.

It would be easy to exaggerate the poor state of cathedral foundations at this time. The buildings were maintained, if inconsistently; services were performed in them; and the clergy who served them did so often with energy and devotion. But their wealth and lack of evident connection with the work of the Church more widely made them a particular target for those concerned about the Church's inefficiency. The Ecclesiastical Commission, first established temporarily by Sir Robert Peel in 1834, and made into a permanent body in 1836, saw reform of the cathedrals as a key part of its plan to improve the administration and ministry of the national Church.[21] The Ecclesiastical Duties and Revenues Act (sometimes called the Deans and Chapters Act) of 1840 carried out a far-reaching overhaul of cathedral organisation and finances. In essence, it drastically reduced the size of clerical establishments, cutting them down to the basic modern pattern of one dean with four residential canons, who together composed the 'chapter' overseeing the running of a cathedral. It also took away much of the property of the cathedrals, vesting it in funds

administered by the Commission itself, in order to supplement
the stipends of poor parish clergy. The ancient boundaries of
the dioceses had already been revised some years before, and
an act passed enabling the creation of new dioceses to serve the
rapidly increasing urban areas of industrial England. In this way
Ripon and Leeds had been created in 1836, with Ripon minster
becoming the cathedral. The new diocese of Manchester followed suit in 1842, with the collegiate church there made into
the cathedral.

Reform on these lines was only the beginning of a long
process by which the cathedral establishments we know today
came into being. But it was a decisive and momentous beginning, with far-reaching and often unforeseen results. The main
preoccupation of the early Victorian reforms was not with the
functions of cathedrals, so much as with the extent and management of their property, and with their efficiency in performing
the duties they already claimed to fulfil. Although removal of
much of their wealth was done slowly (vested interests were
observed in the lifetime of officeholders), and always with the
intention of leaving sufficient income for the reduced chapter
to perform its duties properly, still the effect was to sharpen
up interest in what cathedrals did, and in the way they were
seen not only by the wider Church, but by society as a whole.
Anthony Trollope's fictional Barchester popularised the image
of the unreformed cathedral establishments, but the point is
that his novels were written against a background of extensive
cathedral reform. Even so, change came slowly at first. Into the
second half of the nineteenth century, cathedrals could be forbidding, underused places. The Norfolk clergyman Benjamin
Armstrong, visiting St Paul's for the evening service in January
1859, found that the people 'seemed to take no interest whatever
in the service ... it is gratifying to find the vast, cold, useless
areas of our cathedrals being turned to some account, but no
serious and devotionally minded person would prefer them to
the regular ministrations of his parish church'.[22]

Reform of governance and financial management

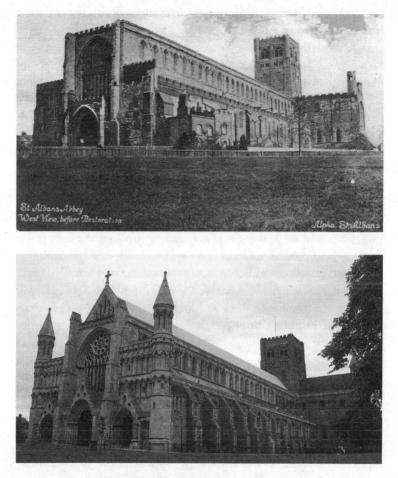

13. Restoration ruined: St Albans before and after

underpinned wider changes. Better, more professional management of a cathedral's reduced resources in turn focused attention on the condition of the buildings themselves. In tune with the revival of interest in Gothic architecture, and with Romantic sensibilities which drove a renewed interest in medieval history, art and architecture, extensive programmes of restoration were undertaken.[23] These required massive financing, and in turn immense effort from cathedral clergy, with the support of influential, wealthy local laity. In some cases, restoration involved rather more new building than, strictly, repair of existing fabric. The most notorious example was the west front of St Albans abbey. Made into the cathedral of the new diocese of St Albans in 1877, what was meant to be the culmination of some forty years' careful restoration of parts of the fabric was ruined by an overzealous, drastic scheme which led to the removal of almost all of the original medieval stonework on the west front of the building, and its replacement by a stylised scheme of the builders' own imagining.[24] Sometimes restoration was forced by circumstances. The spire of Chichester cathedral collapsed in February 1861, leaving a great, gaping hole in the centre of the building. But here restoration was careful, and triumphant: every stone which could be saved was carefully labelled, and reused in a recreation of what had been there before.[25] In general, growing awareness of the need for sensitive repair rather than rebuilding, in harmony as much as possible with existing structures, led to the more conservative but comprehensive approach which came to dominate in the twentieth century, and which was promoted by organisations such as the Society for the Protection of Ancient Buildings, founded by William Morris and others in 1877 partly as a reaction to the ham-fisted restoration at Tewkesbury.

Improvements in the protection and conservation of their fabric were assisted by a growing appreciation of the architectural splendour of these great buildings. This was not just because of a sentimental or nostalgic view of the Middle Ages, though many Victorians had that. Cathedrals recovered a sense of being sacred places, where believers could experience the beauty and transcendence of God in ways that were perhaps impossible elsewhere. This was assisted by the reinvigoration of cathedral music under the influence of the Anglican choral revival in the nineteenth and early twentieth centuries. Overhaul of cathedral worship, opening up the buildings as a resource for the whole diocese, was fuelled by the renewed seriousness of purpose of many Victorian and Edwardian cathedral chapters, under the influence of reforming deans and clergy, such as Richard Church, dean of St Paul's from 1871, who oversaw the reorganisation of the cathedral's finances, restoration of its fabric, and its emergence as a building characterised by great preaching and serious attention to worship.[26] Armitage Robinson, dean of Wells from 1911, had a similar effect there; a still later example might be A. S. Duncan-Jones, dean of Chichester from 1929. The fusion of religious awe, great scale and soaring architecture which a visitor might experience in a cathedral is perhaps nowhere better illustrated than in D. H. Lawrence's 1915 novel *The Rainbow*, in which Will Brangwen and his new wife, Anna, visit Lincoln cathedral:

> Here, the twilight was the very essence of life, the coloured darkness was the embryo of all light, and the day. Here, the very first dawn was breaking, the very last sunset sinking, and the immemorial darkness, whereof life's day would blossom and fall away again, re–echoed peace and profound immemorial silence.[27]

Improvements in building and conservation technology, and the development of a proper regulatory framework in the course of the twentieth century consolidated nineteenth-century advances in building restoration.[28] Even new buildings, such as the great Anglican cathedral in Liverpool, finally completed in 1978 after seventy years of construction, or the cathedrals at Guildford and Coventry, require careful management. State oversight of historic buildings, dating back to the Ancient Monuments Protection Act of 1882, but consolidated in the formation of English Heritage in 1983, means that the fabric of the cathedrals and greater churches is probably better maintained and protected now than at any time in their history.

If, by the beginning of the twenty-first century, the cathedrals and greater churches were better maintained than ever before,

14. Diocesan development: Guildford cathedral under construction

and at the same time more prominent as places of worship as
well as more popular as places to visit than ever before, they were
also better organised as businesses than ever before. The nineteenth-century reforms, in removing much of their inherited
income, had also removed their financial cushion. Throughout
the twentieth century cathedral finances proved to be insecure,
and although the seriousness of this varied from place to place,
even the introduction of charging for tourist admissions late in
the century did not prove enough to stabilise the costs of running
these great buildings. In addition to the stipends of clergy and
other employees, the costs of maintaining the fabric under
the more intense and demanding state regulatory framework
posed severe challenges. Some cathedrals sought to respond by
attempting to exploit or dispose of historic assets, such as hiring
out precious documents or selling off libraries, while others

faced sharp internal conflict over what to do. By the 1990s, the controversies sparked had brought cathedral organisation once more into the spotlight. A Cathedrals Commission, reporting in 1994, recommended new changes to cathedral governance, expanding the governing chapters to include lay representatives who could bring specialist legal, financial or other expertise to bear, and creating governing councils drawing on lay and clerical representation from across the diocese though this last provision was to endure only twenty years before further reform.[29] This was a significant change in the ethos and organisation of cathedrals, reflecting a renewal of the sense that the cathedral was there not just to serve its own congregation, and also the floods of tourists and pilgrims who visited it, but also as 'mother church' of the wider diocese.

PART 2

THE AGE OF THE OLIGARCHY

9

CONSOLIDATION AND CONFORMITY:
THE LONG EIGHTEENTH CENTURY

The so-called 'Glorious Revolution', the last political upheaval in British history to dethrone a monarch, marked the end of a tumultuous era of civil war and instability. But tension and conflict endured beneath the surface throughout the 'long' eighteenth century, the period from 1688 to 1832: dynastic anxieties did not disappear; fault lines opened up in the governing elites (including those of the Church of England) over political and religious reform; and demographic, industrial and urban change eventually resulted in a challenge to the hegemony of the landed aristocracy.

For the Church of England, this was an era of consolidation *and* turbulence. The impression of a time of ease and prosperity gifted later generations with the image of a Church too enmeshed in the lives of the landed elite. But immense effort had to be put in to re-establish a routine liturgical life where it had been severely disrupted in the early and mid-seventeenth century. Even the reconstruction of a local, religious idea of time immemorial – epitomised in Thomas Gray's 'Elegy Written in a Country Churchyard' of 1751, with its appeal to the 'narrow cell' where 'The rude forefathers of the hamlet sleep' – was actually a *recent* work, and never really carried through to completion. If the Restoration Church of England was developed, as one historian has put it, 'within a Petri dish of festering political affairs', this was hardly much different after 1688.[1] Well into the eighteenth century the memory of civil strife troubled the Church's leaders. The impression of order and stability was something of an illusion, then. Protestant dissenting communities clung on in places, as did the English Catholic community; the Church of England was simply unable to bring them all back into its fold. Even in the seemingly more placid years of the eighteenth century, the aspiration of a comprehensive national Church for *all* the kingdom's people was irrecoverable.

Strife and Stability

The foundation of the eighteenth-century Church of England was therefore ambiguous. The presumption that, legally and constitutionally privileged as it was, all the people of the realm were its pastoral responsibility, was challenged by groups of separatist or dissenting believers who could not in good conscience accept the Anglican settlement. But 1688 had changed the Dissenters' constitutional position – from now on, the capital 'D' is appropriate for a permanent body of opponents to the religious settlement. When the French philosopher Voltaire wrote of England nearly half a century later, 'This is the land of sects. An Englishman, as a free man, goes to Heaven by whatever route he likes', it was the presumed effect of the Toleration Act he had in mind.[2] But though the Act conceded the existence of Dissenting communities, it in effect contained and regulated them. It was a grudging, second-class form of toleration, by modern standards. Yet although its goal remained defence of the Anglican settlement, in the long run it created 'a religious market place in eighteenth-century England'.[3] Moreover, by removing the obligation to attend the local parish church, the Act eviscerated the Church courts, making the enforcement of conformity impossible. In that sense it was a crucial step in the long-drawn-out process by which England and Wales became the paradox of a religiously pluralist state incorporating an established or 'State' Church.

At the very head of the constitution rested the monarch. The Church of England looked first and foremost to its supreme governor to defend its rights and privileges. But the succession itself was uncertain, with no living heirs for William and Mary, nor for Anne, who succeeded her sister Mary on William's death in 1702. The Stuarts in exile remained a threat, if an attenuated one. 'Jacobite' rebellions in 1715, 1719 and 1745, limited in scale and, except perhaps briefly in 1745, almost completely ineffectual, were a reminder of dynastic insecurity. But this now mattered less, perhaps, than before. The cumulative effect of the overthrow of James II and of the formal union of the two kingdoms of England (with Wales) and Scotland in the two Acts of Union passed in both countries in 1706 and 1707 was to seal the religious identity of the constitution and the idea of national destiny and national identity as inescapably Protestant.[4] The Act of Settlement passed in 1701, with an eye on the continuing Stuart threat, excluded Roman Catholics from the line of succession: religion trumped primogeniture. Henceforth, the monarch *must* be Protestant – or, in the explicit provision of the Act, in communion with the Church of England.

Not that everyone was in agreement about this, even within the Church. The crucial point at issue was not Church doctrine and order, but the relationship between the Church and the State, and by extension the role of the monarch and the proper attitude towards Dissent. True to the origins of the term in the support given by many nobles and gentry to the succession of James II, Tories were sympathetic to legitimacy and the Stuart claim, even after some had allied with the Whigs in 1688 to defend the Protestant constitution and the Church of England. High Church Toryism defended divine right, and the principle of passive obedience; at the same time it sought to uphold the rights and privileges of the Church of England, and to limit or even reverse concessions to Dissent. Tories received covert support from Queen Anne, but were checked by the Whig ascendancy under the Hanoverians.

But the establishment of the Church of England depended in turn on the pervasive connections between the Church hierarchy and the governing elite. Protected by the overarching umbrella of the Restoration legislation, when it came to legislative action, to civil governance at local level, and to the 'soft power' of informal networks of social influence, Anglicans held most of the cards. Increasingly the episcopate was drawn from the same background as the gentry and aristocracy. This had not always been so. Some eighteen out of seventy-three bishops who served in the Church of England at some point under Charles II, for example, had had 'plebeian' origins, compared with only five from the nobility.[5] By the late eighteenth century the proportion was reversed. Of course, it was consistently true that the majority of bishops were from gentry or, broadly, 'genteel' backgrounds; nevertheless the virtual disappearance of men of humble origins, and the growing prominence of those of aristocratic origins, is striking.

The bishops and clergy even had their own representative assemblies, at first – the ancient Convocations of Canterbury and York, which had fallen into abeyance, but were revived after the Glorious Revolution, only to be prorogued in 1717 in order to prevent differences between a 'Tory' lower house of clergy and a 'Whig' (effectively pro-Hanoverian) upper house of bishops from breaking into open conflict. After that, the bishops were increasingly at the mercy of Parliamentary timetables and machinations. They had to tread a fine line between asserting the authority of their office in defence of the Church when necessary, and staying close to the dominant group in Parliament, the Whigs. Orthodox in belief, most bishops seized whatever opportunities they could to defend Church interests: they exemplified, in the words of one modern historian, 'High Church Whiggery'.[6] The most astute leaders of the Church in this period – men such as Edmund Gibson (bishop of London from 1723 to 1748) and Thomas Secker (archbishop of Canterbury from 1758 to 1768) – were determined to work with, not against, the prevailing tide of political opinion, recognising their dependence on it. [7] As Gibson put it, 'my political reasonings proceed upon these two positions ... that there is no way to preserve the Church but by preserving the present establishment in the state'.[8]

If the close interdependence of the Church and landed society suggests a harmony of interests, it would be wrong to give the impression that by the turn of the nineteenth century English religious affairs were settling into a placid pattern. After all, the existence of Dissenting communities in England and Wales, and of an English Catholic or 'recusant' community, consistently challenged Anglican hegemony. Elimination of Dissent was virtually a missionary mandate for Anglicans. Questions about its extent were part of the routine process of visitation by which bishops and archdeacons examined and tried to control what was happening at a local level. Different strategies for accommodating or resisting it partly dictated different political outlooks. The Tories had at best reluctantly accepted the post-1688 settlement: they were wary of Dissent, and were in this supported by many parish clergy. The Whigs, by contrast, had broken decisively with divine right, and favoured contractual theories emphasising a communion of interests between ruler and ruled. In political theory, John Locke was to become their favoured theorist. In political theology, the names of the century on the Whig side included: Benjamin Hoadly and William Walburton. Hoadly, bishop of Bangor, who provoked a storm of controversy with his 1717 sermon, 'The Nature of the Kingdom, or Church, of Christ', in which he denied that any particular model of Church government was sanctioned by the Bible, so that the polity of the Church could vary according to circumstance and the will of civil government. William Warburton, in *The Alliance between Church and State* (1736), defended an establishment based on the principle of mutual interest. The conflict between these two different understandings of establishment – Tory and Whig – was at its greatest at the turn of the century.

In essence, it was a stand-off between those who accepted – even if reluctantly – formal tolerance for the majority of Dissenters, and recognised the Church of England's monopoly had gone, and those High Church clergy who continued to assert the exclusive privileges and constitutional necessity of the Church of England. But the High Church–Tory 'agenda' remained effectively elimination of Dissent. Champion of that position at the turn of the century was Francis Atterbury, later bishop of Rochester. His *Letter to a Convocation Man* (1696/7) was, as one historian has put it, 'sensational' in its effect, stirring up High Church antipathy to the Williamite policy.[9] An even more incendiary clergyman was Henry Sacheverell. A drinker and intemperate preacher, Sacheverell went too far in a sermon at St Paul's in 1709 in which he launched a blistering attack on Dissenters, who had made, he said, the Lord's house not only a 'den of thieves', but also 'a Receptacle of Legions of Devils'.[10] Sacheverell was impeached before the House of Lords, and punished with a three-year ban on preaching. By now, the strength of support among gentry and the parish clergy for the Tory position was a positive brake on the ambitions of the Whigs.

In the last years of Queen Anne's reign, a Tory administration formed in the wake of the reaction against the Sacheverell impeachment attempted, with the tacit support of the queen, to impose further restrictions on Dissent. But the measures were abandoned when Anne died. Anne had also overseen the establishment of Queen Anne's Bounty, a fund to augment poorer livings, which over the next century gradually made a significant difference to clerical poverty. With the accession of George I, and the decisive victory of the Whigs in the Parliamentary elections of 1715, the brief Tory ascendancy was at an end. For the next sixty years, the Whig vision of the Church's establishment prevailed. It forced the clergy to defend Church positions strenuously – hence the residual conflict between a 'Tory High Churchmanship' at local level and an episcopate obliged to make peace with monarchs and ministers, though this conflict faded as the Hanoverian succession bedded down and as Whig and episcopal patronage gradually exerted its subtle pressure.[11]

Augustan Assurance?

The Victorians came to believe the eighteenth century was a time of foxhunting and port-swilling gentrified clergy, neglectful of their duties. Looking back, in a historical survey of the era, the writer and divine Richard Church claimed that the blot of the Church of England was its 'quiet worldliness'.[12] There was some justification for this view, in light of the persistent problems of clerical poverty, pluralism and non-residence. And yet so varied were these conditions from place to place that an overall picture is hard to describe. Some modern historians have defended the Church's reputation forcefully, arguing that non-performance of duty was rare, Anglican pastoral practice was largely effective, and that parish churches were not generally neglected by their parishioners.[13] Against that, some continue to insist on organisational obstacles and pastoral inefficiency.[14] Still others stress that the diligence of many clergy should not blind us to the divisive effects of the strategies of coercion and conformity which the Church adopted to try to minimise Dissent.[15]

How successful was the Church at implementing and enforcing its national, parochial provision? Several attempts were made to measure the real strength of the Church on the ground, but none were comprehensive enough to settle the matter. The Compton Census of 1676 attempted to assess how much of the kingdom formally conformed to the Church of England. Data were compiled for each diocese, counting Conformists, Nonconformists and Papists in each parish. The findings suggested that, overall, less than 5 per cent of the population in most dioceses were Nonconformists, and less than 1 per cent Catholics.[16] But although the best available recent work on Church affiliations tends to confirm this broad picture, most scholars agree these figures are an underestimate, and anyway there are many gaps and omissions in the surviving data.[17] There was to be nothing like it again until the mid-nineteenth century.[18]

If we take the findings at face value, however, they indicate significant regional variations, and that is confirmed by patchy later evidence. In the diocese of Chichester, for example, statistics collected by the bishop in the 1720s suggested that Dissent was in decline even from the probably low estimate of the Compton Census.[19] Canterbury, on the other hand, was historically 'in the vanguard of radical Protestantism', and recorded much higher numbers of Dissenters.[20] Even here, though, there was a clear decline underway early in the century. For a variety of reasons, as time passed members of established Dissenting families began to conform to the Church of England. John Potter, bishop of Oxford from 1715 to 1737, then archbishop of Canterbury to 1746, was the son of Thomas Potter, a Dissenter in Wakefield; his father accused him of having 'too great a love of the World' – probably a common charge from those Dissenting communities left behind by conformity.[21]

If Dissent was on the wane, was the Church clawing its way back into unchallenged dominance? Yes and no. For the vast majority of parishes before the industrial revolution, the location of the church building in a particular settlement, and the boundaries of the parish it served, had been laid down centuries before. The size and distribution of parishes therefore continued to reflect an early medieval pattern, despite the intervening centuries of economic, social and demographic change. In upland parishes, spreading across the north of England, much of Wales and the west Midlands of England and down into parts of the West Country, parishes were large, their settlements scattered and thinly spread. Distances to walk to church might be long, and maintaining religious discipline proportionately more difficult for distant settlements. Perhaps an extreme example is that of Stanhope in County Durham, on the northern Pennines, which, with over 55,000 acres, was one of the largest parishes in England (though most of its neighbours were also large).[22] Elsewhere, dioceses frequently faced a high concentration of settlements and associated parish churches inherited from the Middle Ages. In the growing towns and cities churches were even closer together. These differences were reflected in patterns of worship. In the north of England, for example, it was more common for parish churches to have two services on a Sunday – in scattered upland settlements, double provision would increase the likelihood of attendance – whereas in the south (and especially in rural areas) the tendency was for just one.[23]

Moreover, the Church faced significant internal and organisational challenges. One was the extent of clerical poverty. This existed in all dioceses, but it was especially prevalent in the upland parishes of Wales and northern England. Despite the work of Queen Anne's Bounty, by the mid-1730s over 5,500 livings still received an income of less than £50 *per annum*, the absolute minimum requirement for a clergyman.[24] On its own, clerical poverty was sapping enough. But its chief disadvantage, from the point of view of an effective pastoral ministry, was that it was almost certainly the most pressing reason behind the twin evils of pluralism and non-residence. As ever, generalisation is difficult. The 'starveling hill clergy' of the Lake District were not generally pluralists.[25] But pluralism was a natural and commonly accepted way for clergy to ensure they could attain an income suitable for their social expectations, as a way of supplementing the income of office if it was inadequate, and of ensuring sufficient support for their families. Pluralism existed at all levels of the hierarchy, but most pluralists were not senior clergy, and the livings they held jointly were adjacent, or at least relatively close to each other. Very few parishes were not served by a resident clergyman, however, since a pluralist incumbent had to employ a curate to perform duty if he could not do it himself, and in many cases clergy holding adjacent cures would travel between parishes on a Sunday to take services, much as their thinly stretched modern counterparts in the countryside do today. None the less, the system did not serve the Church well, and impeded the exercise of an efficient local ministry.

Condemnation of these features of the eighteenth-century Church is easy. Understanding just how difficult it was to reform the system is not. There was little recognition that the problems of the Church required concerted, centralised national effort, since that would have entailed a completely different understanding of the Church's polity. At almost every point, the scope of what would today be called the 'senior leadership' of the Church was severely curtailed by the fusion of ideas about property rights and the derivation of income from fees, tithe and the produce of Church land (the glebe) with the ancient titles and theories of office-holding in the Church. It would be a simplification – but not an implausible one – to say that, on a long perspective, the ancient idea of a celibate, largely poor hierarchy had, over centuries, become wholly enmeshed with a quite different set of values that effectively treated Church office like secular office, with the income derived not from national provision (a sort of 'national health service' idea of organisation) but from holding the office itself. More prosaically, as one historian has put it, 'the medieval system of funding for celibate clergy remained in place to fund a largely married clergy'.[26]

Protection for the holders of ecclesiastical office came from the treatment of their positions much like private property. All of this helps to explain just why in the eighteenth century, even when the deficiencies of the system were evident, and when bishops made strenuous effort to rein in those deficiencies, the actual incidence of pluralism and non-residence increased. For all its defects, bishops had to make the system work. They were like master puppeteers who had only a limited set of strings to pull to keep everything going. When the pressures on the system were growing, with increased population and social and economic change placing ever greater demands on parochial provision as the century advanced, all they could do, realistically, was to use the means available to them, through patronage, through their informal influence, through exploitation of ties of kinship, rewarding loyalty and diligence here and there whenever they could.

Nineteenth-century critics easily confused the weaknesses of the system with the idea of its absolute failure. But the evidence is not compelling, at least for the early part of the eighteenth century. To the contrary, all the signs are that the Church of England was consolidating its position in the towns as well as in the countryside. Episcopal visitations suggest parishioners were generally assiduous in attending services, and there was even demand for an increase in the number of Sunday services to accommodate the routines of agricultural work.[27] Furthermore, although it was not generally a great period of church building, there were significant efforts to extend pastoral provision where it was needed. This could be by building chapels of ease – supplementary church buildings in a parish to 'ease' the pressure on the parish church – especially in increasingly populous areas. Sometimes dilapidated churches might be demolished and replaced. This happened, for example, in Battersea in the mid-1770s, when the growing, fashionable population of the district petitioned Parliament to allow them to demolish the 'very ruinous' medieval church and replace it with a more capacious building.[28] More commonly, existing parish churches where the strain of numbers was felt would be 'improved' by the addition of nave galleries for additional seating, a supplement to the process of installing boxed pews which could be rented out to regular attenders. Victorian reformers would regard these galleries as ugly and restrictive intrusions into the soaring aesthetic of the medieval idea of sacred space, but they were practical answers to a practical problem.

You can get a strong impression of how much these interior alterations affected the aesthetic of medieval churches by looking at the few remaining examples of eighteenth-century interiors which survived purging by Victorian church restorers. St Mary's, Whitby, is by far the best known, a large medieval church standing high above the town, cluttered up by galleries and pews. St Peter's in Petersham, Surrey, is another. Typical of the eighteenth-century interior is the prominence given to the pulpit – and the similarity these interiors had to the layout of a theatre is not accidental. Even when the theology of the incumbent was High Church, and sacramental, the greater part of worship was not eucharistic. A renewed emphasis on preaching was a feature of post-Restoration worship, and it led to a situation – confirmed in many lay diaries and letters of the late seventeenth and eighteenth centuries – in which the laity had such high expectations of preaching that they found services devoid of a sermon boring: 'The spatial heart of Restoration

and Hanoverian church building,' argues the historian Mark
Goldie, 'was the pulpit, not the altar.'[29]

The Prayer Book and sound preaching were at the very
heart of regular Anglican worship in the eighteenth century,
and to that extent it was a static, formal and conventional tradition of worship, at least by contrast with the more emotional
style associated with Methodism and with the more elaborate
ceremonial and sacramentalism of the High Church revival of
the nineteenth century. All the same, even where communion might only be celebrated four times a year – at Christmas,
Easter, Whitsun and on Trinity Sunday – there is much evidence
that lay people regarded it highly, prepared themselves carefully
for it, and saw it as an essential part of religious devotion.

The relative success of the Church's pastoral mission was
also reflected in the strength of lay religion. Ordinary people,
if literate, displayed a hunger for devotional reading which
involved published sermons and improving literature as well as
the Bible itself. Lay religious associations and clubs, especially
common at the turn of the eighteenth century, were a sign of
this. Perhaps the best-known examples were the Societies for
the Reformation of Manners, formed after 1688, which were
mainly led by lay people, mostly Anglican, to promote popular
piety but also to correct impropriety. In fact, such was the apparent success of these societies at first that they even began to
alarm magistrates, who feared civil disruption as a result of the
practice of employing paid informers to produce prosecutions.[30]
But they were relatively short-lived; perhaps of more long-term
significance was the charity school movement, again led particularly by Anglican laity. But there is a deeper and more pervasive
point behind this evidence. For all its institutional challenges,
its internal arguments and its political tensions, the eighteenth-
century Church was strong and relatively stable simply because
religion remained absolutely central to the experience of the
English and Welsh people. Churchgoing, commentary on
church attendance and church affairs, and attention to preaching were a natural part of life for most people.

An Age of Enlightenment?

Victorian criticism of the eighteenth-century Church was aimed not just at its organisation, but also at its theology. The Victorians accused the Georgian Church of elevating reason above faith, natural religion above revelation, and the critical spirit of the human sciences above the authority of Scripture. But Anglican 'orthodoxy' was not monochrome; it contained a wide range of opinion, from the High or 'hyper' Calvinism of those who were inheritors of the Puritan tradition, through 'Latitudinarians' who were prepared to tolerate theological disagreement and were relatively indifferent to the finer points of ecclesiology, to High Church and often Tory churchmen loyal to the sacramental tradition of the Caroline divines of the early seventeenth century.

The intellectual history of the eighteenth-century Church has been dominated by the assumption that in Britain, as on the Continent, it was an age of 'Enlightenment', exemplified by the emergence of a new spirit of free enquiry, and a confidence in human reason over traditional religion. There is some truth in this. For example, in *A Treatise of Human Nature* (1739) the philosopher David Hume – a Scot, and a name of international renown – asserted that all human knowledge essentially had its basis, not in revelation, but in a 'science of man' based on 'experience and observation'.[31] But much more typical of eighteenth-century thought was a moderate rationalism which, far from rejecting religious belief, affirmed it while expressing faith in language and concepts emphasising the harmony of Christian doctrine and human reason. Locke's *The Reasonableness of Christianity* (1695) set the tone for a whole genre of Christian apologetic, even as it provoked many readers by its apparent sympathies with Socinianism, the denial of the divinity of Christ. Even the great Joseph Butler, perhaps the most influential Anglican philosopher and theologian of his generation, while in *The Analogy of Religion* (1736) arguing that nature was no more secure a foundation for faith than Scripture, none the less held that revelation and human reason were entirely

consonant.[32] Towards the end of the period, William Paley, in
A View of the Evidences of Christianity (1794), argued that natural
religion and human reason provided compelling support for
Christian doctrine. The emergent emphasis on reasonableness,
moderation and the influence of human reason probably owed
much to Newtonian cosmology, but also to the determination
of many churchmen to avoid the vicious divisions of the seventeenth century.

Miracles were certainly a prominent point of controversy,
with a tendency at the more 'Latitudinarian' or 'liberal' (another
anachronistic word) end of Anglican theology, either to dispute
the possibility of supernatural intervention in human affairs
altogether – admittedly a rare position – or to assume that miracles were strictly rationed by God to Jesus's own life and work
and also to the early apostolic age, when the Church was establishing itself in the world. The anti-miracle advocates included
the historian Edward Gibbon, the first volume of whose *The
History of the Decline and Fall of the Roman Empire* (1776–88)
attempted to describe the rise of Christianity in non-miracu-
lous terms, emphasising 'the human *causes* of the progress and
establishment of Christianity'.[33] An Anglican clergyman who,
in his time, caused greater controversy was Conyers Middleton,
Fellow of Trinity College, Cambridge, and an extreme Latitudinarian whose views verged on Deism. Towards the end of his
life Middleton published *A Free Inquiry into the Miraculous Powers*
(1749), which passed over the miracles of Jesus but launched a
vicious attack on the 'quackery and imposture' of those of the
early Church.[34]

The extreme anti-miraculous position assumed that specific
divine intervention in the world was neither necessary nor
plausible, and this extended to revelation itself. Religion was
grounded in natural reason, and was essentially an ethical
system. The freethinker John Toland had summed up this position in *Christianity Not Mysterious* (1695/6): God was a remote
first cause uninvolved in the world. But it was a small minority

of thinkers who thought like this. On the contrary, the Deist controversy was widely perceived to have been won by the arguments of theologians such as Edward Stillingfleet, whose *A Discourse in Vindication of the Doctrine of the Trinity* (1697) was praised as a decisive attack on Toland, Locke and others. None the less, radical questioning of aspects of the Biblical basis of Christian doctrine by English writers influenced new currents in Biblical criticism, especially in the German universities.[35]

The religion of reason was certainly a distinct, even new dimension of Christian religious thought. But it was not simply a stage on the way to an emptying out of faith, as if the real motor of intellectual change was outside Christianity altogether and the Enlightenment was a movement antithetical to religion. In fact, almost the opposite was true of most of those who wrote on theological and philosophical matters. Their aim was *not* to dilute or undermine Christianity, but to strengthen it, if need be by reforming the institution of the Church and by moderating and improving the bad behaviour of Christians themselves. The hostility of the 'enlightened' to arbitrary imprisonment, to torture, and to unnecessary suffering exemplified a Christian humanism liberated – as they saw it – from the antagonistic certainties of the previous century. This widened in time into an understanding of human dignity and human rights that would drive the opposition to the slave trade, pressure for penal reform, hostility to the exploitation of the labour of children, and even to inherited privilege and extremes of wealth and poverty. In that sense, the Enlightenment in Britain was the parent of movements of humanitarian reform active outside as well as inside the institutional boundaries of the Church. But it was as much a religious movement as anything else. Not for nothing has it even been described as a *clerical* Enlightenment, for so many of the writers and thinkers of the age were clergymen, whether Anglican, Dissenting or Catholic.[36] The language of reason served an apologetic purpose. But faith lay at the heart of eighteenth-century thought in England.

The Church of England mostly managed to contain a wide

range of disagreement on important doctrinal and ecclesiological issues, without much fundamental division over the limits
of true Christian identity. The Deist controversy had raised
arguments about the nature of God himself, and especially
the doctrine of the Trinity. Orthodox Anglican controversialists, such as Stillingfleet and Daniel Waterland, seemed to have
settled the matter by the mid-century, but it flared up again
towards the end of the century in the hands of Dissenters
such as Joseph Priestley, who argued that the doctrine was a
corruption of the original belief of Christians. Another area
of controversy concerned Church order. Although, after 1662,
there was little internal disagreement over the need for episcopacy, there were continuing divisions over the nature of the
Church's authority, and especially between 'High' and 'Low'
views. In the nineteenth century, the term 'Low' came to mean,
essentially, Evangelical, but in the eighteenth century it referred
to a plain, practical view that denied to the ministry and structure of the Church any intrinsic spiritual authority. This was a
position associated particularly with the more extreme end of
Latitudinarianism. Its most controversial representative, probably, was Benjamin Hoadly, whose 1717 sermon on *The Nature of
the Kingdom, or Church, of Christ* sharply separated religious and
temporal authority: Christ had left behind him no visible sign of
his authority; the civil power could not, and should not, support
one particular interpretation of Christian truth. As many of his
opponents pointed out, this seemed to undermine completely
the Church of England's claims.[37] The 'Bangorian controversy'
drew down upon Hoadly's head the opprobrium not only of
High Church Tories, but also of Whig churchmen and moderate Latitudinarians, ending for a couple of generations any
serious possibility of amendment of the Act of Uniformity and
of the Test Acts.

None the less, the settlement of Church and State could
not remain out of discussion for ever. Modification of the
terms of settlement was a permanent goal of Dissenters and of
more radical Latitudinarians. In 1772, the 'Feathers Petition' (so

named after the tavern in which it was conceived), advocating relaxation of clerical subscription to the Thirty-nine Articles, was drawn up by the Latitudinarian Francis Blackburne and his followers. Their petition having been decisively rejected by Parliament, some of Blackburne's supporters, including his son-in-law Theophilus Lindsey, seceded from the Church. Lindsey himself noted with exasperation that one of the Parliamentary opponents of the petition, Edmund Burke, the Irish Whig politician and man of letters, had 'declaimed most violently against us in a long speech, but entirely like a Jesuit, and full of Popish ideas'.[38] Lindsey scarcely did justice to Burke's defence of the Hookerian ideal of the essential unity and harmony of Church and State. The real issue, Burke observed, was not the question of *toleration* of diversity of opinion, which Dissenters already possessed, but the terms on which diversity of opinion ought to be rewarded with preferment: 'If you will have religion publicly practised and publicly taught, you must have a power to say what that religion will be which you will protect and encourage.'[39] But Burke's re-presentation of Hooker was only one version of the argument for establishment. Others were possible. William Warburton's *Alliance between Church and State* (1736) had supplied an essentially Utilitarian argument: since the partnership between Church and State rested not on religious truth as such, but on mutual benefit, the State ought therefore to support that religion which was numerically the greatest. The argument upheld the position of the Church of England, and justified continued discrimination against Dissenters, but High Churchmen saw little comfort in it. The difference between Burke's position, Warburton's and Lindsey's – I am taking these three authors as symbolic of the divisions amongst Anglicans – indicated a practical uncertainty about the basis of establishment that would evolve in the nineteenth century into a prolonged conflict over Church–State relations.

So Anglican orthodoxy in the 'age of Enlightenment' was far from being an intellectually moribund tradition rapidly giving way to a discourse of human reason and natural religion that contained the seeds of Christianity's future downfall. On the contrary, it bore up well, encompassing much of the literature of critical interrogation of tradition that conventionally has been folded into a narrative of imminent secularisation. True, Anglican use of the language of reason served an apologetic purpose, and new critical insights were often brought to bear precisely in order to defend traditional Christian doctrine. But there was no widespread flight from Christian orthodoxy on the part of writers, philosophers and intellectuals.

Admittedly, what I have been describing was the religion of the clergy, which we can establish with relative ease from the many published sermons, pamphlets, books and other works they produced. What theological themes and convictions drew the attention of ordinary churchgoers, many illiterate, and many at best ill-informed about the formal content of the formularies of the established Church? We can be sure that the language of the Prayer Book and of the King James Bible was the staple in which the religious experience of most ordinary people was captured, supported perhaps by John Bunyan's *The Pilgrim's Progress* (1678) and by Foxe's *Book of Martyrs*. It seems probable that the Christian conscience of many people did not consistently reflect traditional Anglican belief, nor was it likely to be a self-consistent system. Popular piety was probably a collage of fragments of folk belief and 'superstition', including a significant residue of magic, and elements of official doctrine that touched particularly closely on the key moments of life, drawing again on the pastoral offices of the Prayer Book. It did not exclude the possibility of moments of excitement, of belief in the miraculous, and of an obsession with prognostication.

Here and there, apparently against the grain of rational religion, figures appeared like the extraordinary Mary Evans from Anglesey, who around 1780 declared herself to be the bride of Christ and gathered a following who called her a prophetess, dressed in white mantles on Sundays, and tried to delay her burial when she died in 1789 in the hope she would be quickly resurrected.[40] Even more extraordinary was Joanna Southcott, a Devonian farmer's daughter born in 1750 who, in her forties, received a divine command to write down prophecies and became convinced that she was going to give birth to Shiloh, the child mentioned in Jacob's deathbed prophecy in Genesis 49:10. Joanna's following reached many thousands, but the movement collapsed with her death in 1814.[41] Religion in the age of Enlightenment was a complex and many-sided thing, and Anglican clergy, despite their best efforts, could not hope to make all their parishioners the informed, penitent, faithful and devout believers postulated in Cranmer's liturgy.

Clouds on the Horizon

If the Church in England and Wales was in as robust a condition as I have described, why did such a seemingly successful institution face growing criticism by the turn of the nineteenth century? What had changed in the previous fifty years or so? The Church had, by the 1740s, made up much of the ground lost in the conflicts of the seventeenth century, although it had had to accept the permanent existence of Dissent. Thereafter, however, it began to cede ground again. Numbers of Dissenters began to increase from around the middle of the century and, as they did so, the privileged position of the established Church looked less secure. Its institutional weaknesses were exposed by the gathering pace of social, political and economic change, and in turn by critical philosophies and radical political positions attracting new support for the overthrow of the establishment altogether.

As we have seen, the Church was beset with structural weaknesses and limitations. Mitigation of these was possible only if the demands placed upon it did not intensify faster than its ability to adapt. But it was not well placed to implement organisational change rapidly. It lacked the means to formulate and propose its own legislation. Without enabling legislation, the creation of new parishes and changes in existing parish boundaries virtually required a separate parliamentary bill for each new context.

If a bill could be formulated, vested interests might come into play: patrons who did not wish to see their power of patronage eroded; incumbents unwilling to jeopardise sources of income; parishioners resistant to the erection of new buildings or the subdivision of the parish. There was a leadership question, too. Though the Church of England was hardly a centralised system, and bishops' power to effect decisive change was limited, at the same time little could be effected without constant episcopal goading and oversight. Yet the political and constitutional demands placed on bishops kept them in or near London for long stretches of time, and in an age of poor transport it was time-consuming and difficult to move backwards and forwards between their dioceses and the capital. None of these were absolutely crippling limitations, but they certainly impeded the Church's ability to meet the challenge of rapid change.

And dramatic economic and social change was coming upon Britain in the mid- and late eighteenth century. Chapter 16 will look more closely at the impact of industrial and social change on the Church. Here it is enough to emphasise that it was this that finally overwhelmed the apparent stability and success of Georgian Anglicanism. The intimate connection between the Church and local society, including the ease with which clergy and gentry shared values, outlook and social life, simply could not be replicated in the new industrial conurbations. The geographical and social differentiation of these areas placed special burdens on a Church which essentially conceived of itself in terms of settled parish life. As recruitment to the clergy, and especially senior clergy, had become increasingly dominated by the affluent classes in the eighteenth century, the gulf that opened up between working-class communities and the lives and expectations of the clergy became acute. In these rapidly changing, sometimes turbulent contexts, it was much easier for Dissent to thrive. It was not bound by the legislative and ecclesiological paraphernalia of the established Church. Congregations might meet in cottages, or in small hired rooms. Ministers would be supported by their congregations, and anyway rarely had the social aspirations of the Anglican clergy. Dissent was very varied by the early nineteenth century in any case. While some denominations, such as the Independents, or Congregationalists as they were increasingly called, Unitarians and Presbyterians might have an especial appeal to more affluent social groups, others such as the Primitive Methodists and Baptists were often much closer to plebeian culture. But this very differentiation helped Dissent to spread rapidly in situations in which Anglicans struggled to make much headway.

Worse still for the Church of England, social and economic change accompanied the re-emergence of radical political and social philosophies hostile to its privileged position. The American Revolution from 1776 to 1783 was an early indication of how sharply circumstances could change for the Church. Although it had proved impossible, for political reasons, to establish new Anglican dioceses in the colonies, in some of them Anglicanism was none the less virtually an established or official denomination. However, Anglicans in America were placed in an ambiguous position by the war, caught between loyalty to the Crown and the evident need to protect their church communities in a newly independent state. What emerged eventually was a new model of Anglican identity, an episcopally ordered Church completely separate from the State, and – significantly – gifted the succession of bishops not from its parent Church of England, but from the equally 'unofficial' or dissenting episcopal church in Scotland. In America, the anti-clerical, sceptical philosophy of some Enlightenment thinkers did gain a foothold, and Americans welcomed the revolution that broke out in France in 1789, though in the end the United States demonstrated a new way of combining high religiosity with a formal separation of religion from civic order.

At the time, that seemed threatening enough to many Anglicans. It was as nothing, however, compared to the radical dismembering and then persecution of the French Church that occurred from the summer of 1790 onwards. In Britain, political radicals, fired up by events in France, saw a pattern of political reform that could be imitated in their own country; many of them combined quite naturally their conviction that the British constitution needed to be thoroughly overhauled with an equally passionate belief either that the established Church ought to be forced to widen its scope to include Dissenters or be overthrown altogether. Even so, few of the political radicals were out-and-out atheists. Even Thomas Paine, whose *The Age of Reason* (1793/4) was treated throughout the nineteenth century as a vicious and emblematic assault on Christianity, was in fact a Deist whose aim had been to uphold belief in God against the (as he saw them) absurd claims of traditional religion.[42] Much more threatening to the position of the Church of England, however, was not the hard-edged religious radicalism of Paine, but the growing strength of an evangelical Dissent (which nowadays we would consider doctrinally and morally conservative) which found common cause with radical Whigs and democrats against the constitutional privileges enjoyed by Anglicans.

The eighteenth-century Church of England was not the supine, ineffective institution its critics assumed it to be, and certainly did not justify the largely negative judgments of posterity. But it was facing wholly new and unprecedented challenges by the turn of the nineteenth century, and the practices and organisational devices that had operated more or less effectively for so long were being rapidly undermined. However much Church leaders and their supporters in Parliament strived to find ways of addressing the structural deficiencies of the Church, they could not move far enough and fast enough to cope with the gathering momentum of social change. They were not alone. Growing calls for political reform, including the widening of the franchise, were voiced by those social groups, including factory workers, skilled labourers, manufacturers, merchants and shopkeepers whose expansion was driving industrial and urban change. Not just the Church of England itself, but the entire political and constitutional settlement was under threat. Evangelicalism complicated this growing constitutional crisis, inspiring and energising those very Dissenting communities the Church of England had once hoped to suppress or to win back. It was not, in the end, the seventeenth-century crisis that finally put paid to the Tudor ideal of a unitary confessional state, but Britain's economic and social transformation over a century and a half later.

10

THE EVANGELICAL REVIVAL

Why Evangelicalism?

A new, vigorous movement of renewal began to sweep through European and American Protestantism in the early eighteenth century. Americans have given this movement the name 'The Great Awakening'; in Germany and Scandinavia, where it remained mostly within state churches, it has been called 'Pietism'; and in Britain it has been called the 'Evangelical revival'. It had small beginnings, in scattered local contexts, sometimes attracting large crowds to open air preaching, but more often cultivating small, even intimate study groups and prayer groups which operated alongside formal parochial provision. It spread not only within the Church, but into Dissent. Its main expression in the mid and late eighteenth century, Methodism, eventually passed outside the Church of England and became a distinct denomination, later itself fragmenting. But Anglican Evangelicalism did not collapse with the Methodist schism. By the nineteenth century it had become firmly embedded as a distinct wing of the Church, just as Evangelicalism was the dominant form of piety in Dissent.

Evangelicalism's ability to cross denominational boundaries is a sign that, ultimately, it was not only a resuscitation of forgotten elements of Church doctrine and practice but something much more adaptable – a style and mood of piety, a fresh set of emphases, an appeal to common experience, an attempt to propagate a simple or basic Christianity that transcended specific traditions. Contemporary critics used the word 'enthusiasm' dismissively of it, seeing it as the effusion of a primitive, subterranean passion which eroded 'rational' religion.[1] Yet there was little truly irrational or anti-rational about Evangelicalism. It was actually a rational, systematic approach to the interpretation of the Bible, and to the pedagogical work of the Church.

More to the point, the psychological pathology of Evangelicalism offered believers a new way of interpreting and internalising their understanding of faith. Rather like contemporary identity politics, Evangelicalism gave believers a key for transforming their sense of self in the light of the imperatives of their faith. That is why the language of new birth, or rebirth, was so powerful. It had Biblical roots, especially in the third chapter of John's Gospel, where Jesus describes a new birth of water and spirit as the entry to the kingdom of God (John 3.3–7). Evangelical pathology presumed a life of sin, and perhaps also a lax or formalistic faith, giving way through the troubling of conscience and then the active intervention of God to a 'new birth' in conversion in which the individual would be transformed into a new person. The powerful emotional and psychic forces unleashed in this passage from one form of life to another were perhaps comparable in intensity to other forms of radical transition in life, such as 'coming out'.[2]

Over thirty years ago the historian David Bebbington produced a definition of Evangelicalism which has become widely accepted as classic.[3] It had, he said, four features: conversionism; activism; Biblicism; and crucicentrism. A formal, received faith involving regular worship and prayer was insufficient without a personal experience of the transforming effect of God's grace. Activism involved an intense, outward-looking evangelism and pastoral engagement. Motivated by their conversion experience, Evangelicals poured immense energy into saving souls and promoting works of philanthropy, bypassing more conventional approaches to pastoral care. Third, Evangelicalism was Biblicist: it put the Bible at the very centre of faith. Evangelicals were not necessarily literalists in the modern sense. They held a variety of theories about inspiration, though all saw the Bible as the inspired word of God. But Evangelical piety was a Biblical piety.

The Bible was studied and quoted extensively for daily inspiration, copied and printed in cheap editions, translated into newly discovered languages as Britain's overseas empire expanded, fought over and argued over as never before. Fourth, Evangelicalism was crucicentrist, that is, it reasserted the doctrine of the atoning sacrifice of Jesus Christ on the cross. This was the heart of the Christian understanding of salvation, Evangelicals claimed. Christ had released human beings from the burden of their sins by taking all their sin upon him and, in his willing death, deflecting the righteous anger of God from humanity: by his sacrifice, human beings were freed from the terrible doubt and anxiety that otherwise a life of good deeds and earnest endeavour could entail. So the cross was the doctrinal correlative of conversion: the despair believers felt on realising how inescapable their sins were, how every human effort to follow the moral life risked repeated failure, was negated by the conviction that the burden of sin was lifted by Christ's death on the cross.

This four-fold description, though widely accepted, is not exhaustive.[4] All four features were in themselves not new. Many Christian movements have been activist.[5] Famous conversions in Christian history long predating Evangelicalism include those of St Paul, St Augustine and Martin Luther, the last two significantly leaning heavily on Paul's theology. Biblicism had roots in the Reformation doctrine of *sola scriptura*. And the theology of the atonement that Evangelicals emphasised was certainly not new: it was derived largely from medieval ideas of atonement, especially St Anselm's articulation of the 'substitutionary theory' – the idea that Christ took upon himself on the cross God's punishment for humanity's sin – in his great treatise *Cur Deus Homo* (c.1098).

If these individual elements of Evangelical theology and practice were not necessarily original, why did Evangelicalism seem so new and why did it provoke the strong reactions it did? Two further, perhaps less ubiquitous aspects of Evangelicalism help us to see why it felt so different from contemporary

Anglican worship: emotionalism and personalism.[6] The emotional expression of Evangelicalism included greater freedom in using language of the heart and the feelings in hymnody, prayer and preaching. Sometimes it extended to more extreme, unbridled displays of excitement and even ecstasy. Evangelicalism was 'heart religion'.[7] Again, this kind of language was not completely new. Anglicans and Nonconformists alike often emphasised the heart-rending nature of particular passages of the Bible. Matthew Henry's life of Richard Illidge, a conforming Anglican well before the revival, testified that he prayed, drawing on James 5.16, 'that every Prayer may come warm from the Heart, may be an *effectual fervent Prayer*'.[8] But Evangelicals intensified this emotionalism, alarming those of a more sober faith. To this was often added a conception of Jesus Christ as a personal friend and saviour, addressed in language again of warmth, welcome, love and friendship. The most familiar and homely expressions of this sense were a later development in Evangelicalism – one thinks, for example, of Joseph Scriven's mid-nineteenth-century hymn 'What a Friend We Have in Jesus' – but the attractiveness and intimacy of the Evangelical sense of God's presence and love was there right from the beginning.

Why did this potent cocktail of Reformation theology, organised piety, emotional resonance and psychological reassurance emerge at this particular juncture? Evangelicals themselves often ascribed their movement to a reaction against the dry formalism, as they saw it, of contemporary Anglican worship. Some argue that the apparently cavalier way in which the Whig administrations of the 1730s and 1740s treated the Church was a vital context for the reactive force of Evangelicalism, and others that the Deist controversy, which came to a head in the 1720s and 1730s, likewise provoked a devout reaction.[9] Both of these explanations are plausible, but insufficient. It is also relevant that these years were a time of heightened confessional tension in Europe, with the Habsburgs and other Catholic princes making inroads into Protestant communities in central Europe.[10] The Moravians, religious exiles from central Europe, were particularly important for early English Evangelicalism, establishing themselves in London in the early 1740s, where their combination of evangelism, intense personal prayer and mutual confession and regular organisation was profoundly influential on the Wesleys.[11]

In the end, the question of timing and origins is elusive. More certain is the fact that Evangelicalism marked a departure from established Anglican pastoral practice. The parish system presumed long-term settlement and pastoral care from cradle to grave. But it rarely attended to the intensity and authenticity of individual, interior religious experience, and it appeared to make no distinction between the merely conforming and the seriously devout. Baptism was the point of entry into the Christian community. Children were baptised within a few days of their birth, in case of premature death. The Prayer Book doctrine of baptismal regeneration assumed that, as the parents and godparents made religious commitments on behalf of the baptised, in baptism children were assured of their salvation: baptism, then, wiped away the taint of original sin. It was a saving ordinance. Without altogether denying this doctrine, for Evangelicals baptism itself could *not* be the 'new birth' by water and the spirit mentioned in John 3, and its connection to salvation was much more uncertain. As Wesley himself argued, 'To say ... that there is no new birth but in baptism, is to seal all under damnation', because everyone was likely to sin after infant baptism.[12]

Without rejecting the rites and ordinances of the Church, Evangelicals privileged the intense, interior process of confession of sins and acceptance of a living faith in Christ: *that* was what truly made a Christian. The very term 'evangelical' came into common use as a way of characterising an approach to faith that went beyond the formal and external; this was how, for example, the great John Newton was using the term as early as the 1760s, though its widespread use to describe a party or group – the 'Evangelicals' – mostly dates from half a century later.[13] Conversion was a third birth, after natural birth and the new birth of baptism. For Evangelicals, the converted were the true Church existing within the visible boundaries of the institutional and legal framework of the Church. Evangelicals thus opened up a serious internal challenge to the way Anglicans conventionally thought of the Church. All the external requirements of formal religious observance were ultimately beside the point. You could attend church regularly, do your best to follow Christian moral precepts, call yourself a Christian, even read devotional literature avidly, without having experienced the direct infusion of God's liberating grace that Evangelicals believed occurred in conversion. Pushed to its extreme, this effectively marginalised the whole edifice of Anglican pastoral and liturgical practice.

But this was not how the Evangelical leaders initially saw their task. They began mostly inside the established Church, seeking to renew or revive its teaching and ministry, and to renew the faith of ordinary people. Their goal was intensity. They wanted to make concrete and real not just the experience of justification, through the new birth of conviction of sin and conversion, but the fruits that would flow from an intense living faith, including acts of love and the purification of local life. Drawing on a variety of sources, including High Church devotion, the Puritan tradition of the seventeenth century, the influence and example of the Moravians, and contacts with fellow Christians in America, they promoted a way of being Christian that was to change the Church of England profoundly.

Methodism

Methodism was by far the most innovative product of Evangelicalism in Britain. Provoking sharp reactions from many contemporary Anglicans, it became a permanent, new religious tradition in Protestantism, with over 39 million members today.[14] Why devote much space to it in a history of the Church of England? For most of the eighteenth century, Methodism was a renewal movement *within* the Church of England, however deep the tensions which were eventually to lead it to separate. Methodism permanently influenced the culture of the Church, not just through the manner of its going, which sharpened awareness of the Church's organisational deficiencies, but in its hymns, its missionary zeal and evangelistic methods, and its close attention to lay piety and religious education. Within sixty years of Methodism's separation, the Church of England had changed so much that many of the matters that led to the division had ceased to pose a challenge for those Evangelicals who had remained. By then, however, Methodism itself had split several times, and developed in a direction the Wesley brothers might not have welcomed. Anglican intransigence, incomprehension and lack of imagination contributed to a second wave of Dissent, a 'new' Dissent to stand alongside the 'old' Dissent of the mid-seventeenth-century crisis. The loss of Methodism was a further setback for the idea that the Church of England was the Church for all the people of England and Wales.

The history of Methodism conventionally begins with John and Charles Wesley and George Whitefield in the 1730s, but they were not the first Evangelicals in Britain. That honour goes to some remarkable preachers a few years earlier in Wales, including Griffith Jones, rector of Llanddowror in Carmarthenshire, and his pupil Howel Harris.[15] Among various factors which may have influenced religious revival in Wales were the survival of a strong Puritan influence in some areas, the relative poverty of Church of England livings, the difficulties of ministry in two languages, and the work of charity schools.[16] By the late 1730s Harris was travelling far afield within Wales, building contacts with others inclined to his views, preaching widely, and gathering the rudiments of an organised movement, a sort of 'para-church' made up of local societies organised into a formal association, alongside the official Church.[17]

But it is with the Wesleys that any account of the foundation of Methodism must really begin. John and Charles were the sons of a clergyman who had abandoned Dissent for Anglicanism, as had his wife, Susannah. Both were educated at Oxford, where John began to organise the 'Holy Club', a group of students who met to pray and study the Bible; the name 'Methodism' came from their methodical approach. Despite some tensions, they worked closely together in ministry for the rest of their lives. In 1735 they went to Georgia in America, John acting as a missionary for the Society for the Propagation of the Gospel in Foreign Parts (SPG) in a new colony, where they encountered Moravian refugees. Returning to London in 1738, they founded a new society in Fetter Lane, where both of them had spiritual crises resulting in conversion, Charles first on 21 May, and John on 24 May, when, reading the preface to Luther's *Commentary on the Epistle to the Romans*, he felt his heart 'strangely warmed': 'I felt I did trust in Christ, Christ alone for salvation, and an assurance was given me that he had taken away *my* sins.'[18] What was integral to this experience for John was not just the sense of sins forgiven, but the conviction of Christian perfection as a humanly attainable goal. Over the next year he began his extraordinary career of itinerant, open air preaching. Charles soon abandoned itinerancy for marriage, family and a more settled ministry in London.

George Whitefield must share equal credit with the Wesleys for giving the initial impetus to the Methodist movement. He joined the 'Holy Club' at Oxford, and underwent conversion in 1735, three years before them.[19] He went out to Georgia just as the Wesleys were returning, beginning a lifelong association with the colonies that took him frequently to America. But it was his open air preaching in and around Bristol that began the movement in England. Whitefield had, by reputation, probably the most compelling 'pulpit' presence in British religious history. His fine voice, his use of gesture and changes of pitch, his repeated honing of his sermons – he is said to have preached over 18,000 times – so that he could recite them without hesitation like the great actor he is supposed to have once aspired to be, and his emotional charge, all produced an extraordinary effect on his listeners.

Unfortunately Whitefield lacked tact, and offended as easily as he inspired. He spent much of his later life trying to undo the damage his vehement criticism of Church leaders early in his ministry had caused. His deference to his lay patroness, Selina Hastings, countess of Huntingdon, was so cringing it is reminiscent of Mr Collins and Lady Catherine de Bourgh in *Pride and Prejudice*: 'Tears trickle from my eyes, whilst I am thinking of your Ladyship's condescending to patronize such a dead dog as I am.'[20] Idolised by Howel Harris, Whitefield forced Harris's own fiancée Elizabeth James, against her own inclinations, to marry him, breaking Harris's heart, who none the less was persuaded to give her away at the wedding; unsurprisingly it was an unhappy marriage.

Celebrated as a great defender of the American colonists in their struggles with the British government, Whitefield was the proud owner of a slave plantation in South Carolina, wrote in defence of slavery, and raised money to buy more slaves in order to boost the income of the estate in support of his philanthropic plans.[21] Unlike the Wesleys, Whitefield was a convinced Calvinist: he did not believe in Christ's offer of salvation for all, but for the elect predestined to salvation, and he was highly critical of the Wesleys' doctrine of Christian perfection.[22]

This was more than a trivial disagreement over a minor point of Christian doctrine: it became a permanent rift, marking profoundly different views of the Christian life and affecting Methodist organisation accordingly. For Whitefield, preaching to persuade his listeners of the need for conversion was the entire point of human effort in evangelism, for once the sinner is convinced of his or her own sinfulness, and acknowledges Christ, then whether they are elect or not is not something within their own grasp; it is a gift of God, and since God has predestined some to salvation and others to damnation, Whitefield himself could do no more for them. For the Wesleys, since Christ's salvation is open to all, and the eternal destiny of individuals is still to be determined by their own Christian life, what happens subsequent to conversion remains an open question, something that has to be pursued through a disciplined life of faith, through study of the Bible, through attentiveness to prayer and worship and to the needs of others.

This Arminian theology, as it is called, mandated much more attention to the careful cultivation of the life of the Christian community. Even as they created new societies of Methodists inside the structures of the established Church, the Wesleys continued to emphasise the pastoral ministry of the parish priest. Methodism was to be complementary to the Church of England, renewing it from within. Whitefield, for all his famously conflictual comments about the leadership of the Church's leadership, did not necessarily seek separation either. But he was seemingly uninterested in devoting any time or energy to planning the community life of the people persuaded by his preaching, and at the same time he was more open to those who – like the Calvinistic Methodists increasingly sponsored and supported by the countess of Huntingdon – were content relatively early in the movement to seek a permanent status apart from the established Church.

The congregations Whitefield founded faded away quickly, or were absorbed into the small group of Evangelical churches known as the Countess of Huntingdon's Connexion.[23] The Wesleys, by contrast, quickly established a para-church structure within the established Church, using what one historian has called a 'ragbag of pragmatic innovations borrowed from Moravians, Quakers and others', with local societies organised around small groups constituting 'class meetings' (which were often ticketed affairs) of about a dozen people, or even smaller meetings called 'bands', used for the sharing of intimate stories of conversion, and prayer meetings, with hymn-singing and preaching led by local lay preachers, all eventually organised into regional clusters called 'circuits' served by itinerant ministers, and finally, at a national level, from 1744 on an annual conference serving the whole 'connexion', as it was called.[24] The Methodist formula was an astute combination of inspiration and organisation, a 'disciplined commitment to self-improvement combined

with a fervent belief in divine intervention in daily life'.[25] Those
hearers of the Wesleys' and others' preaching, moved often to
tears or even to wild, ecstatic utterance by the realisation of
their sins and their need of redemption, having made a public
confession and received God's grace, were instantly drawn into
a mutually supportive association, itself serviced and sustained
by a rapidly evolving national organisation.

Perhaps the greatest cultural legacy of Methodism, however,
was its hymns, and here the real genius of the movement was
Charles Wesley. It would be more accurate to call him a religious poet, because much of his output was in the form of
religious lyrics which subsequently found appropriate settings
in music. But he did write explicitly for singing, too, and hymns
were an essential part of all Methodist meetings, especially open
air gatherings. The Wesleys published thirty books of hymns,
and appropriated, amended or recycled already popular hymns
for their own purposes.[26] But Charles wrote some 9,000 religious poems himself, of which possibly up to two-thirds were
set to music. Among his output were abiding favourites right up
to today, including, for example, 'Lo! He Comes with Clouds
Descending', 'Hark! The Herald Angels Sing', 'Soldiers of
Christ, Arise', 'Love's Redeeming Work is Done', 'Love Divine,
All Loves Excelling', and 'O Thou who Camest from Above'.

Methodism was not, however, particularly large, at least for
much of the eighteenth century, and it is easy to exaggerate its
impact. We don't have reliable statistics for the first two decades
of the movement, but we do know – because the connexion
started to record formal membership – that in 1767 there were
some 22,410 adult members in England, and a few hundred in
Wales.[27] By the time of Wesley's death in 1791, those figures had
more than doubled to 56,605 and 534. Membership probably has
to be multiplied by a factor of three to reflect the actual number
of people attending Methodist meetings, including children. But
the population of England and Wales in the early 1790s was over
8 million, so that, even assuming a total Methodist affiliation of
around 200,000, they made up no more than about 2.5 per cent

of the total population. These figures cannot of course take into account the large numbers of people who, particularly in the early years of Methodism, went to hear the Wesleys, Whitefield and others preach, but did not become members. Also, many Methodists continued to attend their local parish churches as well. These relatively small numbers were not spread evenly around the country. There were clear areas of strength, including the West Country (especially Cornwall), north Wales, Yorkshire and the north east.[28] Methodism particularly thrived in parts of the country where the ecclesiastical establishment was thinly stretched. By the end of the century, Methodism was on its way to becoming the largest single denomination in Cornwall, having a particular appeal to miners and fishermen; by 1851 over 40 per cent of the adult population of Cornwall was Methodist.[29] Cornwall was a stand-out case, however. The most dramatic period of growth occurred after Methodism's separation from Anglicanism in the 1790s, when it benefitted from the great upsurge in population and urbanisation of the early nineteenth century.

There were tensions in the movement from the beginning between the ordered, often conservative approach of the Methodist leadership and a plebeian, frequently unrestrained and exuberant element. Methodist meetings were often accompanied by waves of excitement that seized members of the congregation and threw them into ecstatic fits or wailing. Yet Methodism stirred up as much passionate hostility as it did enthusiastic support, and that hostility was spread across all social groups, from gentry and clergy down to labourers. Reasons for this were many: Methodists were often seen as outsiders, 'Popish' in their methods (meeting secretly in cottages and at night), and intent on ruining popular leisure. Rioting against Methodist meetings and open air preaching alarmed magistrates. It was the dual perception that this was a form of religion that undermined the social order while at the same time sidelining the official ministry of the established Church that raised so much suspicion. Without any doubt, most Church leaders failed to recognise why Methodism was taking root in the first place. It was a cultural movement from below, despite its educated leadership: it empowered the labouring poor, artisans, craftsmen and shopkeepers to talk about their religious experiences. To have retained it within the Church of England would have required a degree of imagination and an organisational flexibility beyond it.

By the 1780s the Methodist experiment was increasingly at odds with official Anglicanism. Whitefield was dead, and the Wesley brothers were ageing, but their success in creating a permanent organisation was challenging Anglican pastoral ministry. The new Methodist communities, increasingly building their own chapels, required some form of ministry to sustain them into the future. It was, famously, John Wesley's reluctant ordination of ministers first for America, then Scotland, and finally, in 1788, for England that appeared to mark the ultimate break from the Church of England, for under the Anglican understanding only bishops could ordain, and Wesley was not a bishop. But in reality the separation was a much longer process and, even at the end of his life, Wesley, like his brother, refused to abjure the Church of England. None the less, the damage was done. The Methodist connexion was mutating into an altogether separate denomination, with its own structure, rules, ministry and forms of worship. That development continued on into the nineteenth century, taking the movement further and further away from its Anglican roots.

Evangelical Anglicanism

Though the Methodist secession was another blow to the idea of a comprehensive national Church, it did not take Evangelicalism out of the Church altogether. Its departure allowed a different form of Evangelicalism to flourish, one more accepting of the historic structures of the Church, more rooted in the educated elite, and more prepared to exploit its social influence to transform the ethos of the Church. Today Evangelicalism constitutes one of the strongest subcultures within the Church of England, and also within the worldwide Anglican Communion. Its roots may be entangled with those of Methodism, but it evolved differently.

Mainstream Anglican Evangelicalism may have differed significantly from Methodism in its approach to Church order, but there was no sharp difference in core theology. As we have seen, the division between 'Calvinists', who believed in the predestination of the elect to eternal salvation, and 'Arminians', who opposed strict predestination and supported the possibility of salvation for all, already existed within Methodism, between Whitefield and the Wesleys; but it is also existed in the Evangelicalism that survived in the Anglican Church after the Methodist secession. As we saw earlier, a Reformed, predestinarian theology remained a powerful element of the late seventeenth-century and early eighteenth-century Church.[30] Theologians like the redoubtable John Edwards, who spent the last thirty years of his life writing an immense number of tracts attacking Latitudinarian opinion, defended the whole range of doctrine classically associated with the magisterial Reformation, including a strongly predestinarian theology.[31] Edwards firmly supported the order of the Church of England; there were plenty of other Anglican clergy of 'Reformed' views on soteriology who none the less on issues of Church order (especially episcopacy) could even be described as 'High Church'. Some of the early Evangelicals not drawn into Methodism probably came from this surviving Reformed tradition.

Whatever the threads of continuity, by the 1730s and 1740s there were identifiable clergy, loyal to the Church, who expressed sentiments similar to those of the Wesleys, and yet were aloof from their movement. William Romaine is one of the best known of these transitional Evangelical figures, becoming pivotal for the movement in the capital.[32] But he is not as famous as John Newton, author of 'Amazing Grace' and a one-time slave trader. His conversion, in 1748, actually predated his last slaving voyages in the 1750s, and there is little explicitly articulating regret about his slaving past in his autobiography, *An Authentic Narrative of Some Remarkable and Interesting Particulars in the Life of John Newton* (1764). This was before he was drawn into Evangelical circles, however. The conscience-stricken supporter of abolition was a later development, when he was a Church of England clergyman, and perpetual curate of Olney in Buckinghamshire, later moving to London.[33] At Olney, Newton pursued what was in many ways to be a typical Evangelical parish ministry, visiting and supporting the poor, keeping friendly relations with local Dissenting ministers, welcoming other Evangelical clergy to his pulpit, speaking outside his parish at cottage prayer meetings, and encouraging lay religiosity. We can find many more clergy like Newton and Romaine, alongside lay supporters and sympathisers, in the mid-eighteenth century, though until the 1760s and 1770s there was little sense of a group identity.

That began to change as Methodism grew further apart from the Church of England. Newton's move from Olney to London can stand as a symbol of what was happening to Anglican Evangelicalism in the late eighteenth century. A once scattered movement, spread widely across the country but in relatively isolated or unconnected situations, was becoming organised, and even fashionable, not only in the capital itself but increasingly in the major towns and cities, and in the professions. In the capital, but also in country houses, and in the town houses of the burgeoning mercantile classes, Evangelical clergy and laity were in communication with each other, supporting each other, building up the networks that would enhance and project their influence into the next century.[34]

Newton was consulted in 1785 by perhaps the most famous Evangelical layman of all, William Wilberforce, in the process of his own conversion. The son of a Hull merchant, Wilberforce was elected as an MP for Yorkshire at the remarkably young age of twenty-one. His later conversion brought him decisively into the orbit of London Evangelicals, especially the circle around the banker John Thornton, who lived in Clapham, and whose son Henry was the centre of the group later called the 'Clapham Sect'. Wilberforce was lively, fun-loving (he was an indulgent father), but also intensely serious. His political ambition, wedded to earnest religiosity, gave him remarkable single-mindedness in pursuit of particular religious and moral purposes. But, in this, he was only one among many. Others of his connexion included: Thomas Clarkson, indefatigable campaigner against slavery; Thomas Babington, politician; Zachary Macaulay, merchant; Henry Venn, clergyman; his son, John Venn, also a clergyman; and James Stephen, lawyer – all of them ardent Evangelicals. They came from the rising professional and middle classes, were comfortable in each other's company, and co-operated on a wide range of Evangelical causes. They formed such an influential and cohesive group that they have been called, variously, the progenitors of the Victorian 'intellectual aristocracy' and the 'Fathers of the Victorians'.[35]

For most of this group – and they were joined by other, humbler figures equally influential in their localities – the finer points of Calvinist doctrine were of secondary interest. They were symptomatic of the evolution of Anglican Evangelicalism away from preoccupation with arguments over predestination towards a more practical interest in transforming the world for the better. Another symptomatic figure was Hannah More, who in the course of her long life journeyed from aspirant writer and dramatist in the circle of Johnson and Burke to energetic philanthropist and propagandist for Evangelicalism.[36] Her tracts sold by the hundreds of thousands, and her books such as *Practical Piety* (1811) brought a popular, eclectic Evangelicalism to an enormous readership. In More, as well as the other leaders of the Clapham group, one can see just why these privileged Anglican Evangelicals attracted as much criticism as praise, and an ironic sobriquet, the 'Saints', for their alleged sanctimony.

An equally influential figure was Charles Simeon, for fifty-four years vicar of Holy Trinity, Cambridge. Through mentoring hundreds of students at Cambridge who were subsequently ordained, Simeon brought Evangelical principles and preaching to parishes up and down the country. With the aid of money bequeathed by John Thornton he established a trust to buy up

15. Converting culture: the writer Hannah More

parish advowsons (the right to make a presentation to a living)
'on a grand scale' so that the service of clergymen of sound
Evangelical principles could be secured in perpetuity in particular parishes.[37]

This exploitation of a mechanism for propagating Evangelical opinion was typical of elite Evangelicals' organisational
ingenuity. They were born managers and organisers. Their

A View from S.t MARY's Church. CAMBRIDGE.

16. Charles Simeon preaching

characteristic instrument was the voluntary society, gathering influential figures into an organising committee, preferably under royal or aristocratic patronage, raising funds through their social networks, and forming local branches wherever necessary to mobilise and organise local support. Frequently the societies were interdenominational. The Church Missionary Society was founded in 1799 to promote missionary endeavour in Africa and Asia, becoming by far and away the most successful Evangelical Anglican mission agency. The Religious Tract Society was founded in the same year for the publication and distribution of religious propaganda (Hannah More was a favoured author). The British and Foreign Bible Society, more commonly known as the Bible Society, was founded in 1804 to promote translation of the Bible into foreign languages, and the distribution of Bibles in cheap, accessible editions across the globe. Eventually there was a voluntary society for almost every worthy cause one could think of, including debt relief, the relief of poverty, prevention of cruelty to animals, opposition to gambling, temperance, and even the suppression of vice (which was interpreted very liberally to include prostitution, Sabbath-breaking, pornography and fraud, but which attracted the unintentionally suggestive name of the 'Vice Society').[38]

Not all of these causes were exclusively Evangelical, but Evangelicals were actively involved in all of them, and prominent in most. The greatest cause of all was abolitionism. Here again Evangelicals were not exclusively at the forefront of the campaign, but many of the leading abolitionists were Evangelical in religion, though some ardent defenders of slavery, such as the plantation owner George Hibbert, were also Evangelicals. Hibbert actually worshipped at the same church as Wilberforce.[39] Wilberforce's Parliamentary activity was dominated by the cause of abolitionism. Some historians have minimised the impact of abolitionism, attributing the ending of the British slave trade in 1807, and of slavery itself throughout the empire in 1833, to changing economic opportunities.[40] They have pointed to the many elite families who owned slave plantations and justified the trade, including of course members of the Church of England. But it does not seem necessary to see things as so polarised. The ending of the slave trade was surely a multi-layered and multi-level phenomenon, engaging a wide range of

17. Abolitionism: Am I not a woman?

views, enjoying growing support in the country as well as (eventually) in Parliament, accelerated by the witness of freed slaves such as Olaudah Equiano and changing economic and social circumstances.[41] In this very complex mix – and no one has yet been able to settle the debate decisively – the mobilisation of Evangelical opinion was a vital element.

But the debate is symptomatic of the difficulties of holding together, in one interpretative move, both the 'central' perspective of the metropolitan elite and the changing currents of opinion in the country at large, or rather in specific local contexts. These things went together in the case of Evangelicalism. Evangelicals got their hands dirty. The very conversionist, activist imperative Bebbington described propelled them into local endeavour on a panoramic scale. They set out to reform not just the worship and prayer life of ordinary congregations, but local social life and morality. Their earnestness and dedication went hand in hand with a canny awareness of the importance of public profile and image, and of what we would now call 'communication skills'. The combination of theological seriousness, social prominence, organisational ability and sheer drive was a winning one.

By the 1820s Evangelicalism had ceased to be marginal. Over the next thirty or forty years Evangelicals moved into the very centre of the ecclesiastical hierarchy, appointed to bishoprics by politicians nervous about the 'Romanising' reputation of the new breed of High Churchman. The appointment of the prominent Evangelical John Bird Sumner to Canterbury in 1848 sealed the movement's influence in the Church.[42]

In the early nineteenth century its reforming zeal, however, was reserved essentially for the pastoral spirit and missionary endeavour of Anglicanism, and not its liturgy and order. It remained tenaciously loyal to the Prayer Book and other formularies of the Church of England, and determined to work constructively within its existing structures. Only later did tensions begin to emerge over the adequacy of the Prayer Book as a vehicle for popular worship, over the significance and interpretation of the Thirty-nine Articles, and over the authority of Scripture. Evangelicals were to be at the heart of Anglican opposition to Anglo-Catholicism, fearing it would undermine the Protestant character of the Church. They were prominent in attacks on 'Liberal' or 'Broad' Church leaders and theologians who questioned and reinterpreted traditional doctrines and the literal truth of the Bible. Increasingly they found the Anglican formularies an inadequate defence.

In the Gorham Case of 1850 an Evangelical clergyman in the diocese of Exeter called George Cornelius Gorham resisted his bishop's insistence that the Prayer Book baptismal rite required acceptance of the doctrine of baptismal regeneration, which, as we have seen, was anathema to some Evangelicals because it implied an objective character to the salvific nature of infant baptism and thereby seemed to sideline justification through a mature faith and conversion.[43] The courts eventually found in favour of Gorham, but this Evangelical victory merely demonstrated the fragility of the Prayer Book as a satisfactory embodiment of authentic Reformation principles, at least for the nineteenth century. As both of the other emergent wings of Anglicanism were also finding, widening internal theological disagreement was rendering the traditional formularies incapable of expressing harmoniously the teaching of the Church.

The 'trade' Evangelical newspaper, the *Record*, founded in the 1820s and merged in 1949 into the *Church of England Newspaper*, through its 'vitriolic partisanship' in the nineteenth century stirred up hostility against other Anglicans and aggressively defended Evangelical principles.[44] The use of Church patronage, the development of distinct Evangelical theological colleges such as the London College of Divinity, St John's Hall (founded 1863), Wycliffe Hall (1877) and Ridley Hall (1881), and the work of all the many voluntary societies together helped to cohere and shape a distinct Evangelical Anglican identity that was eventually – though far into the twentieth century – to issue demands for new forms of worship, new approaches to mission and to Church management, and new relationships with other Protestant traditions.

11

THE FORTUNES OF CLERGY:
FROM PATRONAGE TO PIETY

Numbers and Status

The Church was arguably the one organised, national, professional service in early modern England. Looking at the life experience of the clergy themselves takes us closer to the heart of what the Church *aspired* to be and to do than could studying any other section of the community. Accordingly, at this point we break again from the broadly narrative approach to look at that experience over roughly two hundred years, from the Restoration to the mid-nineteenth century. In each settlement, the clergyman was the visible incarnation of the Christian Church, because he was the one person uniquely charged with the pastoral and spiritual responsibility of its people.

As an occupational group, the clergy were a pyramid with a very wide base and narrow apex. At the bottom were the parish clergy, composing some 94 per cent of the total figure of around 13,000.[1] At the very top were the diocesan bishops, some twenty-seven in all (including the bishop of Sodor and Man, who did not sit in the House of Lords). In between, composing a layer of 'middle managers', were archdeacons, cathedral deans and other cathedral clergy and the two chapters of the royal peculiars of Westminster Abbey and St George's, Windsor – nearly 800 persons in all.[2] The natural inference from this bottom-heavy structure – that senior clergy were too few to exercise really close management – is underscored not only by the sheer physical constraints of poor transport and communication, but by the historic, legal realities of parish organisation. Once appointed to a parish, vicars or rectors – 'incumbents' – held their positions effectively as property, and could be disciplined or dismissed only with the greatest difficulty and at great cost. (This remained the case right up to the late twentieth century.) A subclass of vulnerable clergy existed, in the form of assistant curates, whether temporary (serving a title before going on to secure an incumbency for themselves) or permanent, dependent on the bishop's licence and the incumbent's willingness to appoint and to pay over a portion of his income as stipend, and with little or no job security. Somewhere between incumbents and assistant curates were 'perpetual curates', clergy with defined duties but no right to tithe and glebe; perpetual curates were usually appointed where additional churches had been built within an existing parish. But the apparent neatness of all of this was compromised by considerable inequalities in income. For some parish clergy, fortunate enough both to secure a comfortable living and to have come (as was often the case) from a moneyed background, the style of life to which they could accustom their families was a world away from that of impoverished post-holders without private means. For much of the eighteenth century, and well into the nineteenth, there was a class of poor clergy who struggled to make a living and to care for their families. They were far from illiterate, and often devout and diligent, but their educational opportunities were limited, and without the support of a wealthy lay patron or senior clergyman, they were condemned to a succession of short-term curacies, or poorer livings. They could be found in most dioceses, but notoriously many of the extended parishes of the highlands of northern England, and Wales, were in their hands.

The social status and identity of the clergy were, accordingly, very broad, even if – until late in the twentieth century – their gender was not, for of course they were all male. The growing tendency for an increasing number of sons of aristocracy and landed gentry to seek ordination certainly cemented the Church of England's influence at the very highest levels of society, but it accentuated the social difference between the upper levels of the hierarchy and the poorest clergy. Standards of education varied, too, though the Reformation and post-Reformation pursuit of an educated clergy, literate and fit to be authoritative readers and preachers of the Word of God, had left its mark. By no means were all clergy able to avail themselves of an education at Oxford or Cambridge, but a majority were, and the proportion increased in the early nineteenth century, from almost 60 per cent of new deacons to just over 80 per cent by the 1820s, while all clergy were supposed to submit to examination by an ordaining bishop.[3]

At a time when religion remained central to popular culture and social life, the local clergyman was an axial figure in the local community. Until reform of the Poor Law in the 1830s, clergy were closely involved in the administration of poor relief, as well as dispensing informal relief themselves. In the absence of a police force, it was often the clergy who monitored local behaviour and initiated action against malefactors, working closely with the local magistracy; increasingly, from the mid-eighteenth century they were often themselves magistrates. These were overlapping, intricate networks of responsibility and relationship.

Local prominence did not compensate poorer clergy for their lack of material means. The abandonment of clerical celibacy at the Reformation really did change the relationship clergy had to their surrounding culture, because wives and families had to be fed and provided for, and the 'middle-class' enculturation of the clergy over time was probably an inevitable consequence, fuelled in the eighteenth century by agricultural prosperity, as so much of a clergyman's income derived ultimately from land and the use of land. Although there were wide variations in income and background, the proportion of 'plebeian' or lower-class background clergy declined considerably in the period. In Canterbury diocese, for example, around half could be described that way in the late seventeenth century; by the early nineteenth century, the figure had fallen to around 10 per cent.[4] But even

18. Rising affluence: a late Georgian rectory in Berkshire

those, increasingly from upper-class backgrounds, who reached the very summit of the hierarchy had usually had to perform parish duty at some point. On the whole, despite the absence of a formal, national professional structure for recruitment and training, the clergy demonstrated a strong sense of professional and vocational identity.

The high and secure social standing of the clergy did not mean that they were above criticism. Generally they were held in high estimation, though, and the greatest criticism was reserved usually for those who fell short. Lay people were particularly quick to criticise the clergy they knew for hypocrisy, especially in their preaching. 'Larry' Banville, a Norfolk gamekeeper who was Irish Catholic by upbringing but a regular attender at Anglican services, noted in September 1827:

Went to church, heard a good sermon preached by Mr

Glover all about charity, but he would have none of it. I
suppose he would not give a penny to a poor man if it
would save his life.[5]

Banville was a good example of the apparent contradictions of
those who were drawn to anti-clericalism, personally attentive
in his churchgoing but sometimes dismissive of the parsons,
socially resentful yet loyal to his master. And clergy were always
susceptible to abuse from the drunk and discontented. The
diarist Francis Kilvert, curate of Clyro in Wales, tried to admonish a drunk parishioner, Ben Lloyd, only to find himself pursued:
'he began to roar after me, but he could only stagger very slowly
so I left him behind reeling and roaring, cursing parsons'.[6] There
was always criticism, to which bishops were not immune either.
Bishop Edward Stanley, a reforming Whig bishop of Norwich,
appalled the Evangelical William Andrew, vicar of Kettering-
ham in Norfolk; of a confirmation that the bishop conducted at
nearby Wymondham, he wrote: 'O how much did the Bishop
say in his address to wound everyone acquainted with the Gospel
of Christ.'[7]

For much of this period, however, as a class or vocational
group clergy were not particularly prone to 'status anxiety'.
Their place in society was assured. The one obvious challenge
to their role was the existence of Dissenting communities. Even
though the number of Dissenters remained small for much of
the period, the clergy of the established Church were understandably anxious about their existence, given that it called into
question the very *raison d'être* of a national Church. But even
then, especially in Evangelical circles, Anglicans often made
common cause with Dissenting ministers in pursuit of particular
moral and social goals. By the mid-nineteenth century, however,
intense rivalry between Church and chapel had become part
of the religious landscape for most parish clergy, even in the
countryside.

The Search for Place and Income

But how did someone get a position in the Church? In a few dioceses, especially parts of Wales, a significant number of men seeking ordination had not gone to one of the ancient universities. In St David's, for example, only just over a tenth of those ordained between 1760 and 1824 were graduates.[8] This was an extreme. The major problem in Wales, apart from poverty, was the need for clergy who could speak Welsh fluently, and this limited recruitment from outside. But for the majority of clergy, if not education in a special clerical school, Oxford or Cambridge was a necessary first step, followed by willingness on the part of a bishop to examine them and then ordain them, usually to a 'title' – a first appointment as curate of a parish.

Getting an incumbent willing to take you on as curate could itself be quite a task, though. There was no centralised appointments system, no clear national standard, no mechanism by which candidates could be matched efficiently to vacancies. Everything depended on personal contacts. The key was to get recognised by a bishop, preferably with the aid of someone who acted as a patron, who could recommend you to an incumbent. Ties of kinship mattered enormously. So did social standing. All this made things peculiarly difficult for those from humble backgrounds. And this was just the beginning. Ordained as 'deacon' for a title position, and then usually within a matter of months as 'priest', a clergyman would naturally want a permanent position in charge of a parish as incumbent, that is, as rector or vicar. Here, though, the formal position of the 'patron' was pertinent, for appointment was mostly in the hands not of bishops but of corporations, cathedrals, some clergy for familial reasons, and laity from the gentry or aristocracy. Acquaintance, family ties, mutual obligations, personal wealth, the readiness to offer a *quid pro quo* – all came into play for clergy seeking a living, and had to be exploited to the full. In return, to try to retain some degree of active management of their dioceses, bishops had to duck and weave through the complexities of the social hierarchy, rewarding loyal friends, appeasing enemies, exerting informal

19. Parson Woodforde: the only known portrait

pressure. Much of this could seem mystifying to parishioners. 'The Bishop do barter and bargain away things strangely,' one clerical daughter remarked in the mid-eighteenth century.[9]

The procedural tergiversations this jostling for place could involve were to shock later generations, and certainly on any view they were hard to reconcile with the idea of a stable, responsible pastoral ministry. The diarist James Woodforde's life was full of these aspirations and manoeuvres. Shortly after his ordination in 1763 he went to assist his father as curate at Castle Cary in Somerset, following a man who was presented to the living of nearby Evercreech which he was to hold 'for a minor (Justice Rodbard's Son of 12 Years old)' – Woodforde passes no comment on that – as well as taking on another parish, Babcary.[10] Woodforde had to fill this post, which he held from a Mr Wickham for £30 per annum plus surplice fees, along with a perpetual curacy at his birthplace at Ansford. But he was always fearful of losing one or other of these three positions, as in 1772, when he recorded a conversation with the bishop about 'the usage my Uncle has treated me with, & that I was to be turned out of my Curacy at Ansford'.[11] He had to resist at the same time pressure from parishioners at Castle Cary to increase the services there from one to two on a Sunday, but noted – it seems with approval – that the bishop would not suffer this 'as it has not been usual'.[12]

Woodforde was eventually forced to leave Ansford when his cousin Frank was inducted there in July 1773, giving James notice which he thought 'not only unkind but very ungentlemanlike'.[13] Not much of this had anything to do with a sense of vocation as a later generation would see it. Eventually, in December 1774, Woodforde obtained the valuable (£400 *per annum*) incumbency he wanted. But this was not without a struggle. By then living at New College, Oxford, as Sub-Warden, he entered into a competitive election with another Fellow for the college living of Weston Longville in Norfolk; this required a meeting of the whole of the Fellowship, with discussion ('Many learned & warm Arguments stated & disputed') going on for two hours, and a vote, with twenty-one votes for Woodforde, and only fifteen for his opponent.[14] At last Woodforde was now permanently settled, remaining at Weston Longville until his death in 1803. For many clergy, ministry was a lifelong battle against economic insecurity and successive disappointment.

It is worth pausing to note just why clerical income was so problematic. There was almost no professional Church bureaucracy. Everything depended effectively on local resources, and variedly wildly from place to place. The most important source of income locally was theoretically the tithe, the legally required tenth contribution from the produce of the land. This could be collected in kind, posing a practical challenge for parson and farmer alike, though it was often commuted to a cash payment. In 1783, for example, Woodforde noted with approval (and perhaps surprise) receipt of £286 and 15 shillings, with 'a very agreeable meeting ... no grumbling whatever'.[15] But collecting it all was difficult, and a priest was in a vulnerable position trying to enforce the demand, especially in years of poor harvests or returns.

Fees could be charged for the pastoral offices – baptism, marriage, burial – and a contribution required for some other services, such as the 'churching' of women, that is, the giving of thanksgiving in church after childbirth. But in small country parishes this would never yield much. In some towns, there was a local rate, substituting generally for the tithe, but this was often resented by Dissenters and increasingly resisted in the nineteenth century. In many places in practical terms the most important element in the clerical economy was income from the glebe, the land in effect attached to the living. Some clergy farmed this themselves, with pigs, chickens, even sheep and cows, as well as growing crops. Elsewhere, the glebe was let out to tenant farmers, though it was rarely substantial enough to provide more than a meagre rental income. Even for those from a professional background, questions of income and expenditure remained crucial. With little or no pension provision until the twentieth century, clergy of limited means simply clung on until illness and death in post.

All these features of the clerical economy – multiple sources of income, wide variations in income, patronage, the advantage of private means – were interdependent. Long before the reforms of the nineteenth century, critics had noted that pluralism was a common concomitant of the poverty of many livings. And a further implication was non-residence, with clergy performing Sunday duty and the pastoral offices in parishes where they did not actually live or engaging a low-paid curate to do their duty for them. But despite acknowledged weaknesses of the system, few could afford the luxury of a principled refusal to engage with it, and so the vast majority simply tried to find whatever opportunities they could within it.

Nor did parishioners necessarily get short shrift from their clergy. On the whole, the system functioned effectively enough, at least in areas of modest, gradual population growth. Francis

Witts was a typical pluralist, being rector of Upper Slaughter in the Cotswolds from 1808 to 1854, which he combined with the living of Stanway – some twelve miles away – from 1814 to 1854. But he was conscientious enough. He performed his parish duties at Upper Slaughter and relied on a curate at Stanway, but made the journey over there regularly to carry out various duties and keep an eye on things. He swapped duties with his curate when he felt that some special event at Stanway required his personal presence, attending, for example, to preach after 'recent irregularities' there which led to the birth of three illegitimate children 'seemed to require animadversion from the pulpit, which they accordingly received from the Vicar'.[16] Like many of his contemporaries, Witts was also a magistrate. Today most clergy would probably find the combination of pastoral and judicial responsibilities a downright conflict of interest, but Witts had no such compunction.

Did pluralism, clerical poverty and the constant jostling for wealthy livings signify a deep corruption in the established Church, a culture of subservience and venality? Later generations thought so, but again the evidence is mixed. Certainly, patrons often appointed men likely to support their own point of view, especially in politics. One study of clerical appointments in Norfolk, for example, noted a very close correlation between patrons' views and those of the clergy they had appointed.[17] And this is surely what we would expect. But it is not the whole story. There is equally compelling evidence to suggest that many patrons did not merely seek the advancement of likeminded mediocrities, but rather to make the best appointments they could. The system could not function without personal acquaintance and ties of loyalty and dependence, in the absence of any systematic way of assessing competence such as competitive examination or recognised professional standards: 'Nepotism may not have been disadvantageous for diocesan administration.'[18]

Proof that patronage did not simply replicate the political opinions of patrons is the otherwise inexplicable paradox of a

strong vein of clerical Toryism thriving throughout the eighteenth century, despite the general dominance of the Whigs
in Parliament. There were many motives for the exercise of
patronage, in any case: Oxford and Cambridge colleges used it
to favour Fellows who wanted to marry (they could not hold a
Fellowship and reside unless single) or to support and enhance
the careers of Fellows, municipal corporations (which lost the
ability to hold patronage in 1835) to favour those with local ties
of kinship or interest, and gentry to look after younger sons. All
these motives were perfectly compatible with the appointment
of able candidates. Bishops in particular might use the power to
appoint to a living, or a canonry or a prebend, to reward able
candidates or shore up the careers of otherwise struggling but
diligent clergy.

Culture and the Life of the Mind

Underpinning the social and civic significance of the clergy was
their educational status. In rural parishes, the clergyman might
be the only university-educated person, or equivalent, in the
community. He was likely to have much wider reading habits
than anyone else, a collection of books, a study, and a practice
of reading and writing that formed the very basis of his profession. But many clergy saw their intellectual role in even broader
terms. Frequently they participated in local learned and literary
societies, met sometimes in study and prayer groups, promoted
literacy through founding schools, and contributed actively
to debate on controverted issues. From the late seventeenth
century on, encouraged by the Society for Promoting Christian
Knowledge (SPCK), they often founded parish libraries, making
a limited but none the less much-used range of books available
to their local communities. These were particularly common in
towns, where naturally there was greater demand.

In almost every branch of science and literature in early
modern Britain clerical scholars made an important contribution. Two of the most important eighteenth-century

philosophers, Joseph Butler and George Berkeley, were clergy, though Berkeley served mostly in the Church of Ireland. Clerical writers and poets included Jonathan Swift, Lawrence Sterne and George Crabbe. Thomas Malthus, the political economist, was rector of Walesby in Lincolnshire. Gilbert White, the naturalist, was curate-in-charge of his home parish of Selborne, in Hampshire, for forty years. These are all household names, but there are many other lesser-known clergy who made forays into scholarship and literature. The antiquarian William Stukeley, rector of All Saints', Stamford, from 1730, wrote two of the earliest thoroughgoing studies of the prehistoric monuments at Stonehenge and Avebury, though his association of these sites with the Druids mentioned in Caesar's *Gallic Wars* has not stood up to critical scrutiny.[19] One estimate is that a third of county histories written in the eighteenth century were by clergy.[20]

But the literary productivity of the clergy was even more substantial, if one takes into account the huge variety of controversial pamphlet literature and tracts published in this period. Practically every doctrinal dispute and political crisis involving the Church between the late seventeenth and mid-nineteenth centuries generated thousands of pages of disputatious writing. Many pamphlets would have had small print runs and limited circulation, and no longer survive. But sufficient exist in university, college and cathedral libraries to give an indication of the vitality of this world of religious argument. Cambridge University Library alone lists over 400 individual items relating to Benjamin Hoadly, bishop of Bangor, most of them provoked by his *Original and Institution of Civil Government* (1709) and his 1717 sermon on the variability of Church order. Another genre of literature was the hortatory, evangelistic or devotional tract. Again, vast numbers of these were published and the SPCK was instrumental in promoting them. The Religious Tract Society, founded in 1799 by an interdenominational group including Anglicans, supplied vast numbers to clergy and missionaries throughout the succeeding century.

But the most important intellectual activity of the clergy

was preaching and catechising. Congregations were hungry for good sermons, and clergy sometimes reported numbers attending church declined when there was to be no sermon. Published sermons were avidly consumed by literate laity as reading material. Given the importance of preaching, some clergy could be remarkably reticent in composition, relying on sermon outlines or on pre-prepared sermons – even if their own – rather than those composed on each and every occasion as required. It must be remembered that sermons were not the short 'thought for the day' discourses of today, but commonly a good three-quarters of an hour or more – more like lecture-length. In an age of scratchy quill pens, sermon writing was laborious work. Woodforde declined to preach in Somerset while staying there 'as I brought no Sermon with me – The last Time I was in the Country I had some Sermons with me and was never asked to preach therefore I thought it of no Use to bring any now'.[21] Even so, Woodforde was generally diligent in sermon preparation. A little later, but still before the High Church revival, Francis Witts thought country clergy neglected the composition of original sermons: 'disuse begets distrust of one's own powers, and a disinclination to the labour'.[22] A common practice was the preparation of a full text, which might be repeated on several occasions, sometimes with variations to suit different circumstances. Catechising was also an intrinsic part of the responsibilities of parish clergy. This was commonly connected with preparation for confirmation, and performance of the duty varied enormously from place to place and time to time, partly given the equally haphazard (though common) prevailing practice of public confirmation, with hundreds of candidates presented at once from many parishes for a rite that only the bishop could perform.[23]

The duty of catechising leads on to education of the young in basic literacy and numeracy. Here, there were again wide variations in practice. Many market towns and some larger settlements already had grammar schools, often founded as acts of charity by gentry in the sixteenth and seventeenth centuries, and usually connected with the parish church. But it was the prospect of permanent Dissenting communities after 1689 that led to the widespread creation of charity schools, in which the clergyman often had a central role. These were small, usually aimed at the poor, frequently meeting in a parish room or the room over a church porch, and included catechising and other religious instruction among their tasks. Clergy were usually trustees and could even be teachers themselves, or employers of teachers, as well as giving a hand in classes from time to time.

The SPCK actively encouraged the formation of these schools, often underwriting their costs. Charity schools usually met during the week, but, by the late eighteenth century, the Sunday School movement was gathering momentum. These probably grew out of the charity schools, either as a cheaper alternative or as a supplement. Impetus was given to the movement by the support of the Gloucester printer Robert Raikes, who encouraged the creation of Sunday Schools by Anglican clergy at first in the Gloucester region, and then further afield. Exact numbers are hard to come by, but it is reckoned that by 1833 over 1.5 million children may have been attending Sunday Schools, with perhaps over 40 per cent of these in schools attached to Anglican parish churches.[24] Again, some clergy taught in Sunday Schools themselves, but more often than not they oversaw volunteer female teachers. Until their sharp contraction and then near-collapse in the mid-twentieth century, Sunday Schools were a major means for inculcating religious belief and values in the young, used to the full even by families who rarely attended church itself.

A further contribution to education by clergy was the establishment of parish elementary schools in the nineteenth century, the forerunners of the still existing network of Church of England primary schools. Again, the parish clergyman was usually the key local instigator, drawing on the support and sponsorship of the National Society for the Education of the Poor in the Principles of the Established Church (the 'National

Society', as it is usually known), founded in 1811. By 1824, over 3,000 National Society parish schools were educating some 400,000 children; the figure continued to rise throughout the nineteenth century.[25]

Moral Guardians

Clergy in early modern England and Wales were not only expected to preach and teach Christianity – at least, in its established, Church of England form – to all their parishioners, but to act as moral and spiritual leaders of their communities, inculcating the precepts of their faith by example as well as teaching. The growing wealth and social expectations of clergy throughout the eighteenth century, however, made this a more difficult task perhaps than it had been when the social division between clergy and parishioners had not been so great. The assimilation of the clergy to the gentry and professional middle class may have helped standards of education to rise, but it came at a cost. There were always exceptions, especially in the poorer livings of upland northern England and Wales, but the social status of the clergy echoed the fine gradations of hierarchy and deference that structured rural society and filtered into social relationships even in the towns.

Even in church, with a gospel of liberation from sin and equality before God, you could not escape social hierarchy. Joseph Arch, for example, the leader of agricultural trade unionism, 'the revolt of the field', in the late nineteenth century, recalled how, in the Warwickshire village of his youth in the 1830s, his 'proud little spirit smarted and burned' when he saw his father, a labourer, waiting to receive communion:

> First, up walked the squire to the communion rails; the farmers went up next; then up went the tradesmen, the shopkeepers, the wheelwright, and the blacksmith; and then, the very last of all, went the poor agricultural labourers in their smock frocks. They walked up as if they were

unclean – and at that sight the iron entered straight into my poor little heart and remained fast embedded there.[26]

Clergy who aspired to a gentry lifestyle inevitably stretched and broke the links that had once – long before – bound those such as Chaucer's 'poor parson' to the soil. That did not mean they ceased to care for the poor, or do their best to oversee their welfare. Regular visiting of the poor was a model enjoined by George Herbert in his *Priest to the Temple* (1652). It gave clergy an opportunity to chide and correct as well as to encourage their flocks and attempt to deter them from attending Dissenting chapels, and to dispense practical relief. William Holland, a splenetic Somerset parson active at the turn of the nineteenth century, typified the combination of pluralism, conservative politics, prejudice about Dissenters and Papists and delight in the produce of his glebe that, in the eyes of a later generation of reformers, gave the eighteenth-century Church of England a bad name. But Holland was determinedly dutiful, and in his own way diligent and compassionate. Late in his life, and suffering frequently from painful facial tremors, he none the less set out to look after his scattered rural people. In April 1816, for example, he wrote that

> I rode out and called on many of my Old and Poor Parishioners and I found out at last Old George Adams at the end of a long lane in Cockercombe. He is 86 and came out at last, weak and with a long beard. I gave him some of the Sacrament Money. God Bless you said he I have no one but you and Madam to look after me.[27]

These acts of charity were doubtless of help to those who lived in conditions of precarity, but they would have been intermittent and fitful. Clergy, one way or another, were also often involved in the more formal and systematic provision of parish relief established under Elizabethan legislation. Overseers of the poor were elected in each parish to administer the distribution of money raised from the neighbourhood to those fallen on hard times and those unable to work, and the management of alms houses for the elderly and infirm. The parish priest could act as a conduit for information, making recommendations about who should receive relief, chairing the vestry meetings at which overseers were elected, and acting as chaplain to alms houses. The oversight of the system exercised by Justices of the Peace brought clergy into a more formal role, as they took up magistrates' responsibilities increasingly in the eighteenth century. By the 1830s around one in six clergy was a magistrate, with the overall proportion of clerical magistrates rising to above 40 per cent in some dioceses.[28]

Yet the traditional responsibility of the parish priest for the moral well-being of his community was fast in decline during this period. It had not altogether disappeared. Clergy frequently corrected abusive and drunken behaviour, and clearly could exercise some influence on local morals through their pastoral visiting and their preaching, and through administration of the rites of passage. But their power to enforce was weak. With the Church courts in decline after the Restoration, the only public means of correcting immoral but none the less legal behaviour had largely gone. With the failure of the short-lived Society for the Reformation of Manners in the early eighteenth century, any concerted effort to re-impose ecclesiastical discipline on worship and public morality had come to an end.[29] A fresh attempt was made by the Evangelical Society for the Suppression of Vice at the beginning of the nineteenth century. But by then the legal enforcement of morality had become virtually impossible, and the only available means was moral suasion.

Clergy sometimes attempted to use the ancient penalty of excommunication – refusing to give communion – as a means of putting pressure on the recalcitrant, but this was rarely an effective remedy, and in practice had little legal force.[30] To make matters worse, the survival and then, in the late eighteenth century, growth of Dissent seemed to pose a direct challenge to Anglican notions of good order and public morality. This was hardly fair to Dissenters, but it was a strongly felt opinion. William Holland, for example, was utterly convinced that Methodism led to flagrant immorality:

> another Methodistical man is come into the Rectorial House ... He has got a woman with him by whom he has had a child and is parted from his wife. This is Faith assuredly without Good Works with a Vengeance. Their Doctrines lead to these enormities.[31]

Holland was solidly a 'Church and King' man.

A figure like Holland might seem to us a caricature or throwback. How typical his views were is hard to say, though they were not uncommon. More to the point, the social world he represented was very different from what we would recognise as the context of the clerical life today. Holland exemplified a world passing away, a world so vividly and eloquently described in Anthony Trollope's Barchester novels.

By the early nineteenth century, the criticisms of the Church's ramshackle structures were mounting, as rapid social and industrial change increasingly exposed its struggles to adapt to new situations as quickly and efficiently as its supporters wanted. Reform of those structures was long overdue, and it was to impact vitally on the clerical life. But the change, which some have labelled 'professionalisation', was one driven by the newfound energy and commitment of clergy themselves. By the mid-nineteenth century, the combined effects of the Evangelical and High Church revivals were manifesting themselves in a much more energetic and rigorous conception of the clerical task.

To get a sense, briefly, of the change, we need to leap forward a little while. A good example is Benjamin Armstrong, the High Church vicar of Dereham in Norfolk, who took up his charge in late 1850 and remained there until 1888. In autumn 1852 he undertook a complete visitation of his extensive parish, including outlying settlements such as Northall and Etling Green. He carefully recorded the statistics, noting the numbers of poor households visited, how many Dissenters there were, how many houses had Bibles, how many parishioners were unbaptised, and how many were communicants.[32] He improved and built local schools. He organised bread and soup distribution for poor families.[33] He was even looked to for mediation in a dispute over street lighting with the local gas company.[34] Armstrong was not unusual in all of this. He was symptomatic of the effects at local level of what was by any standard one of the most far-reaching periods of national reform in the Church of England's history, a period almost as significant as the Reformation itself, and it is to that 'crisis' of reform that we must now turn.

12

THE CRISIS AND REFORM OF
THE CONFESSIONAL STATE

Popular images of the Georgian Church of England thrive on the impression of rural stability, privilege, polite conversation and the social whirl of dinners, balls and whist drives. If you think that the egregious Mr Collins in *Pride and Prejudice*, pre-occupied alternately with pleasing his patroness and getting married, his mind about as far from concern about the spiritual welfare of his parishioners as it is possible to get, can really stand as a symbol of the detachment and calm in which the Church found itself at the beginning of the nineteenth century, you would be wrong.

Europe was in turmoil from the 1790s to the 1810s. The sense of growing crisis was everywhere, triggered by events in France. The largest power in Europe, with a population three times the size of Britain and Ireland combined, France's descent into internal chaos when a moderate constitutional revolution in 1789 turned violent, had echoes of the mid-seventeenth-century civil wars in Britain. But in France a new political ideology of equality and liberty, informed by an authoritarianism influenced by Rousseau's idea of the 'General Will', posited not only a new political and constitutional order but a violent social revolution, too. Systematic persecution of the French Church followed the Papacy's rejection of a revolutionary programme of ecclesiastical reform. Order was restored under the dictator Napoleon, who concluded a concordat with the Papacy, but imposed stringent conditions on the Catholic Church in France. Only with Napoleon's final collapse at Waterloo in 1815, after over twenty years of almost continuous war, did a full restoration of the Catholic Church in France take place. In these years, the 'Enlightened' values of the French Revolution were exported across Europe by the French armies. The Revolution acquired with Protestants and Catholics alike a reputation as a godless, destructive threat, ever to be invoked as a warning to complacent established regimes.

In Britain the example of the Revolution was profoundly divisive. It coincided with the rapid growth of Dissent, both 'old' (Baptists, Quakers, Independents, Presbyterians, Unitarians) and 'new' (Methodists). The total number of Methodist members – that is, signed-up, full members; attenders would always have been a larger number – in England and Wales more than tripled from 57,000 in 1790 to over 186,000 twenty-five years later.[1] Dramatic growth rates were also experienced by the older forms of Dissent, revitalised by Evangelicalism. One estimate is that in 1790 some 90 per cent of the population of England and Wales were adherents of the Church of England, but that by 1815 that proportion may have fallen to 66 per cent.[2] Wesleyan Methodists were mostly conservative in politics, but that was not the case with old Dissent, after decades of hostility and marginalisation. Dissenters' grievances about establishment made common cause with a political radicalism inspired by events in France. In cities like Derby, strongly Nonconformist and politically Liberal, clergy could be very unpopular, being associated with a political and religious privilege which supporters of reform hoped 'would be swept away'.[3] Ever more relentlessly, the weaknesses of the Church of England were being exposed.

Establishment and Its Defence

The Church was not supine, however. The assumed blindness and complacency of the Anglican hierarchy is a common way of explaining the ensuing political crisis of the early 1830s and government-imposed Church reform. But this does not hold water because there were concerted efforts to reform the Church from well before the end of the eighteenth century. In fact, so significant were the changes put in place during the Napoleonic Wars, and shortly afterwards, that arguably they demonstrate the very reverse – the resilience and energy of the established Church. More drastic reform was forced on the Church, but it did not come for lack of serious effort by churchmen themselves.

In the 1800s a series of government measures aimed to increase the Church's effectiveness. An 1803 'Residence' Act gave enhanced powers to bishops to regularise and curb non-residence. Under Spencer Perceval, who has the distinction of being the only British prime minister to be assassinated, grants were made to increase the value of poor livings. Further measures came in peacetime. In 1818 and in 1824 Lord Liverpool's government made grants totalling £1.5 million to support the building of new churches, through the establishment of the Church Building Commission. This was matched by voluntary Church effort, with the creation in 1817 of the Incorporated Church Building Society to raise funds for new churches. All this was surely a sign of the Church–State link working well.

These measures reflected contemporary views on the necessary connection between Christian belief and public morality: a devout people would be an ordered, respectful people. Preachers declaimed the importance of obeying established authority. But if clergy and laity alike widely assumed the social utility of the Church, they were no less in earnest about the transforming power of the Gospel they preached. Across Europe, this was a common reaction to the social upheaval triggered by the French Revolution. In 1802 in France, the monarchist writer François-René de Chateaubriand published his *Génie du christianisme*, a defence of the Catholic faith which helped stimulate religious revival there. In Prussia Friedrich Schleiermacher's *Reden über die Religion*, published in 1799 and best known in English by its title *On Religion: Speeches to Its Cultured Despisers*, was an irenic defence of Christianity which again came to stand as a symbol of a reviving religious confidence. In Britain, there were parallels

in the turning of the great Romantic poets William Wordsworth
and Samuel Taylor Coleridge, and their friend and collabora-
tor Robert Southey, away from the political radicalism of their
youth towards Anglican orthodoxy. The lax, superficial, nominal
Christianity Wilberforce had criticised in his *Practical View* was
fast giving way by the 1810s to a renewed zeal among the governing classes. Evangelicalism had something to do with this.
So did the belief that the 'Enlightened' values of the previous
century had led to the chaos and disorder of France. Renewed
commitment to the established Church was evident in a dramatic increase in the number of men entering the ministry,
from an annual average of 277 in the 1800s to almost double
that number in the 1820s.[4] Training establishments for clergy
were created at St Bees in Cumberland in 1816, Lampeter in 1822,
King's College, London, in 1828, and Durham in 1831. At local
level, in the dioceses, bishops began to revive the office of rural
dean, and to institute more frequent visitations ('inspections')
of parishes.

These initiatives were effective, up to a point. But they were
at best modest amelioration, not fundamental reform. Rates
of clerical residence improved in many dioceses in the early
nineteenth century, but non-residence was still a weakness, not
helped by enduring income inequalities. The likely consequence
of the general uplift in agricultural prices from the late eighteenth century was to widen the gap between the poorest and
richest benefices. The work of Queen Anne's Bounty, along
with agricultural prosperity, certainly helped to improve the
situations of the poorest clergy. Whereas in the mid-eighteenth
century over 5,000 livings were worth less than £50 *per annum*,
by 1809 the number was under a thousand.[5] Further improvement came with Parliamentary grants from that year on, but by
then the social and material expectations of the clergy had risen,
and £150 *per annum* was widely recognised as the minimum
necessary to support a clergyman and his family. Recruitment
was improving, but problems of job insecurity, unpredictable
income and ineffective disciplinary mechanisms continued to

impair the work of the clergy. New churches were being built, but not on a scale and at a speed commensurate with the soaring rates of growth of the new urban and industrial centres, and the Church lacked adept and efficient machinery to subdivide parishes and create new ones. For all that the establishment of the Church was not moribund, it was hampered by its historic structures and faults.

The Crisis of the Confessional State

To make matters worse, the combined efforts of Church and State to strengthen the Church's ministry only exacerbated the criticism of establishment put forward by political radicals and politically minded Dissenters. The post-1815 years were a time of extraordinary political ferment in the new manufacturing areas of the north and Wales, the time of the Peterloo Massacre in 1819, of the beginning of the campaign for factory reform, of early trade unionism, and of experiments in social organisation such as Robert Owen's socialist industrial community at New Lanark. For the Church's critics, opposition to establishment was often a principled objection to a State-supported Church enjoying the resources of the nation to further its particular view of religious truth. The fact that the established Church was seemingly riddled with corruption and inefficiency simply underlined this.

The attack on the Church actually combined different groups, including outright atheists such as the followers of the Utilitarian philosopher Jeremy Bentham, whose *Church-of-Englandism and Its Catechism Examined* (1818) assumed the irrationality of Christianity, and also theologically orthodox Protestant Dissenters. But this was a vital reason eventually for the survival of the establishment – effective Church reform would drive a wedge between moderate and radical critics. The radical template was exemplified in the journeyman woolstapler John Wade's *The Black Book, or Corruption Unmask'd* (first published in 1820, but revised and reprinted several times), which enumerated the

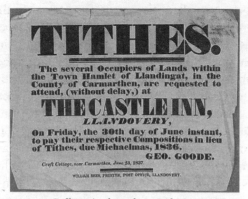

20. Collecting the tithe: a tithe notice

faults of both Church and State. Wildly inaccurate though the book was, most of its many readers had no opportunity to cross-check its 'facts', and the general impression it gave was enough – the mud stuck. Another widely read publication was William Cobbett's newspaper *Political Register*. This carried his 'Rural Rides', in which he commented not only on the living conditions of the labouring poor but on the oppressiveness of the tithes, on the self-serving arguments used by the richer clergy of the established Church, and on the common cause the clergy had made with oppressive landowners.

Renewed pressure on the Church came above all, however, from Ireland. The constitutional crisis of 1828–32 was not so much the product of long-term grievances in England and Wales as of desperate measures to resolve a political impasse on their periphery. Since 1801, the established Church of Ireland had been combined with the Church of England to form a single establishment. But the two churches had very different contexts. In Ireland Anglicans were a minority, easily outnumbered by Roman Catholics. Encouraged by the willingness of Lord Liverpool's government to support the established Church, the Church of Ireland in the 1820s embarked on an aggressive campaign of evangelisation and education. But despite early successes, this so-called 'Second Reformation' in the end was counter-productive, provoking the Catholic Association, led by Daniel O'Connell, to launch a mass movement in favour of Catholic Emancipation, which would entail lifting the penal legislation which prevented Catholics from participating fully in public life. O'Connell's success left government ministers such as the Home Secretary, Sir Robert Peel, little room for manoeuvre.

But Catholic Emancipation would imply, as a precondition, abolition of restrictive legislation on Protestant Dissent. Though many Dissenters had qualified for public office by occasional acts of conformity, the restrictive legislation was still a standing offence to them. So it was that, in 1828, the Test and Corporation Acts were at last repealed, as a prelude to the more controversial measure. From now on, Dissenters could qualify directly for public office, as magistrates, municipal officers, elected officials and Members of Parliament. The following year the administration of the duke of Wellington passed the Roman Catholic Relief Act, repealing the penal laws against Catholics.

It is worth pausing a moment to consider the implications of all this. They may be hard to grasp for a modern audience likely to think of these controversies as remote and abstruse. But this was a turning point in the position of the Church of England. The Church has faced three times in its history when its relationship to the State, and through that to the wider society, has changed fundamentally. The first was of course the Reformation itself, when the Papal supremacy was abolished in England and replaced by the royal supremacy. For over a hundred years the medieval assumption of the intrinsic unity of Church and State held formally, despite the evidence of dissent from recusants (traditionalists who remained loyal to Rome) and separatists (Protestants who broke away from the Church of England). The position of the Church was supported by active persecution of those who dissented.

The second period was the prolonged crisis of the seventeenth century, when the Anglican hegemony was challenged and broken during the Commonwealth, re-established at the

Restoration, and then amended in 1688–9. From then, until 1828–9, the Church of England remained in a privileged and protected position, with the formal unity of Church and State still in place, and with restrictive legislation limiting the constitutional participation and status of Catholics and Dissenting Protestants, though active persecution was at an end. In turn, that position began to unravel in 1828–9.

The removal of the civil disabilities applied to Dissenters and Catholics spelt an end to the idea – stated most eloquently for Anglicans by Richard Hooker – that there was a harmony of interest between the Church and the State, such that the State would accept a direct responsibility for the promotion of Christian truth as expressed in the formularies of the Church of England. This was not perhaps a revolution, though some historians have claimed it was.[6] It was on the surface a modest adjustment, largely concealed by the continuing prestige and constitutional prominence of the Church. But its implications were momentous. The Church moved into a position of being, *de facto*, partially disestablished. And there it remains today. The monarch is supreme governor of the Church of England. Bishops sits in the House of Lords. Major moments in national history – royal weddings, coronations, state funerals, acts of commemoration – are officially celebrated at Anglican churches such as Westminster Abbey and St Paul's. Parish clergy still have some distinct powers and responsibilities, such as the ability to act as civil registrar for church weddings. But little else remains of the Church's former constitutional position. The last direct grant of money from the State to the Church was in 1824. The operation of most parts of government was based increasingly on the presumption of religious neutrality. In its essential workings, the State increasingly became a secular organ (the standout exception here was education). This left the established Church, largely shorn of its legislative defences, in an ambiguous position. Even within Anglicanism, argument has raged since the mid-nineteenth century over whether establishment as it is now is a hindrance or a help for the Church.

Parliamentary Reform of the Church

Even after these changes, it was still possible to maintain that Parliament had a particular responsibility to uphold the interests of the established Church. As if anyone could doubt the seriousness of the change, however, the measures of 1828–9 were swiftly overtaken by a groundswell of opinion, from a temporary alliance of working-class and middle-class pressure groups, in favour of a reform of Parliament itself, ultimately achieved in the 'Great Reform Act' of 1832. Parliament was, if anything, even more vulnerable to allegations of corruption than was the Church. Representation in the Commons was tied to constituencies which reflected the premodern economy and society, with little weight given to the new industrial and urban centres, no secret ballots, huge variations in the franchise from one place to another, and elections wide open to the bribing of electors by candidates. The problem for the Church of England was that the bishops sat in the House of Lords and so would be called upon to take a stance on reform one way or another. In fact, most sided with the Tory opposition to measures introduced by Earl Grey's Whig/Liberal administration, and provoked popular outrage as a result, leading to rioting, the burning of bishops in effigy and even the destruction of the episcopal palace in Bristol in 1831. The public reputation of the episcopate was at an all time low. It was this crisis, coming hard on the heels of Catholic Emancipation, which convinced many churchmen that the very existence of the Church of England was under threat.

The spotlight now moved on to reform of the Church itself. A concerted Dissenting campaign in favour of disestablishment got under way in the early 1830s, emboldened by the prospect of increased representation of Dissent in Parliament after the removal of civil disabilities in 1828 and Parliamentary reform. If the establishment of the Church of England was to survive, the Church needed urgently to address its structural weaknesses, and find the energy and resources to rise to the challenge of rapid social and demographic change. Yet churchmen found themselves in a bind. Distrust of the Whig government elected after the 1832 Reform Act meant that few expected strong support from that direction. Yet the Church had no means to put its own house in order. It did not have a central assembly, nor legislative powers, nor any corporate means of expressing its mind clearly on anything. Church reform could only be achieved through State action. There were plenty of ideas circulating about how it should be done – a veritable storm of pamphlets, speeches, published letters and tracts.

From all this noise of ecclesiastical controversy, two contributions stood out, for radically different reasons. In 1832 Robert Henley Eden, an Evangelical lawyer, published his *A Plan of Church Reform*.[7] Lord Henley, as he was known, proposed a far-reaching yet rational, constructive programme of reform, including the creation of new dioceses, the equalisation of bishops' stipends and the size of dioceses, the creation of a representative body for the Church, the reduction of cathedral chapters and the appropriation of some of their revenue to create a fund to increase poor livings, and the vesting of the management of Church property and funds in a new, independent body of Ecclesiastical Commissioners. Henley's proposals were made without significant implications for the worship and doctrine of the Church.

That was not true of the notorious *Principles of Church Reform* (1833), published by the great headmaster of Rugby, Thomas Arnold. Arnold shared some of the same practical goals as Henley, but proposed to reassert the national character of the Church by adjusting its liturgy and formularies to include all Trinitarian churches apart from the Roman Catholic Church. This was the old Latitudinarian idea of comprehension in a different key. Baptists, Methodists, Congregationalists and Presbyterians would be brought in under the umbrella of the established Church again. Neither most churchmen nor most Dissenters liked the idea. But it did concentrate attention on the shrinking hold the Church had on the active loyalties of the English and Welsh people. Arnold was a strong defender

1. Chaldon 'doom' painting

1554   1600

RICHARD HOOKER.

2. Richard Hooker: a Victorian window in Chester cathedral

3. Charles King and Martyr, a modern icon

4. Painting of Elizabeth kneeling at prayer

5. Georgian Anglicanism: interior of St Mary's, Whitby

6. John Wesley preaching from his father's tomb at
Epworth: a painting by George Brownlow

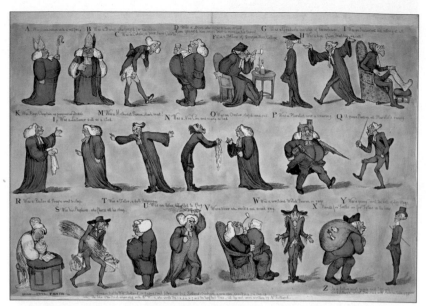

7. Pre-reform clergy: *The Clerical Alphabet* by Richard Newton, 1795

8. Opposition to reform: the burning of the Bishop's Palace, Bristol, 1831

9. Medievalism recovered: the interior of All Saints, Margaret Street

10. Hardly the preferential option for the poor: *The Free Seat*, by James Lobley

11. Momentous change: women celebrating the Eucharist

21. Building the city: a Commissioners' church at St Luke's, West Norwood

of establishment, but he did not underestimate the difficulties it now faced: '[If] we do not root out Dissent, and so keep the Establishment co-extensive with the nation, we must extend the Establishment or else in the end there will and ought to be no Establishment at all, which I consider as one of the greatest evils.'[8]

The Whig government fell in the summer of 1834 and gave way to a brief, minority Tory government led by Peel. Still labouring under the reputation of being the Tory turn-coat who had brought in Catholic Emancipation, Peel was a firm supporter of established churches, however. Henley's proposals were taken off the shelf and dusted down. With

the connivance of the vigorous, reforming but much-loathed
bishop of London, Charles James Blomfield – one of his
modern biographers notes his 'impetuosity, relentless administrative energy, self-confidence, and pomposity', a combination
unlikely to have endeared him to many – Peel created an
Ecclesiastical Commission to examine the condition of the
Church of England and make recommendations for its material improvement.[9] It comprised five bishops (the archbishops
of Canterbury and York and the bishops of London, Lincoln
and Gloucester) and five lay members, including Peel himself.
At first temporary, it was made into a permanent body by the
Whig government of Lord Melbourne and its membership
expanded in 1840 to include all the bishops, some cathedral
deans, further laity and three Church Estates Commissioners,
two of whom were appointed by Parliament and one by the
archbishop of Canterbury, and who acted effectively as the
treasurers.[10] The new Commission worked quickly to produce
a series of comprehensive reports surveying the administration
of the dioceses, clerical incomes, pluralism and non-residence,
and the cathedral chapters.

Three pieces of legislation followed, which provided the
backbone of the administrative regulation that has steered the
Church of England ever since. The Established Church Act of
1836 equalised the stipends of bishops, apart from a number
of senior bishops whose prestige and enhanced responsibilities were considered to set them apart, rationalised diocesan
boundaries to make dioceses a little more equal in size, and
authorised the creation of new dioceses for Ripon and Manchester, thus making provision for populous, industrial areas.
Since no one wanted to increase the number of bishops in Parliament, and yet churchmen did not want to see bishops ending
up permanently outside the Lords, the Act also suppressed two
sees by attempting to fuse St Asaph with Bangor and Bristol
with Gloucester. The former proposal was never actually put
into effect, and the latter lasted no more than sixty years, when
continued population growth required the separation of the

sees again. Continued political in-fighting, internal controversy and defence by entrenched interests slowed down the other two measures.

In 1838 the Pluralities Act severely restricted the holding of livings in plural and non-residence. Clergy could not hold more than two livings each, and those two could not be more than ten miles apart, amount to more than £1,000 in income a year, and have a population of more than 3,000 in each of the parishes. However, the measure did not apply to existing appointees, and so pluralism and non-residence were slow to disappear altogether, although the Act's provisions began to shape the profile of diocesan clergy quickly. In Lincolnshire, for example, within fifteen years of the passing of the Act, the proportion of incumbents appointed after 1838 who were non-resident had fallen to 3 per cent, compared with 25 per cent of those appointed before 1838.[11] Finally, the Ecclesiastical Duties and Revenues Act of 1840 abolished a wide range of sinecures and non-resident prebends, and imposed a maximum number of resident canonries at four for most cathedrals, though with a slight increase to five or six at the larger and busier establishments. The estates of the deans and canons – though not the corporate estates of the chapters as such – were vested in the Commissioners when the current holders died or resigned, yielding a surplus of some hundreds of thousands of pounds to increase the stipends of poor livings. The personal patronage of the deans and chapters was also removed, and transferred to the diocesan bishop, though again the corporate patronage was left untouched. It was this measure that also turned the Ecclesiastical Commission into a permanent body and enlarged its membership.

These measures were not the only significant acts of reform carried out in the mid-nineteenth century, but they marked a turning point in the fortunes of the Church, wresting it away from the odour of 'old corruption' that had hung about it in the pre-reform days. With the constitution of the Ecclesiastical Commission itself – in the twentieth century to become the Church Commissioners – they created the pattern according to which the Church has continued to evolve ever since. Within a generation the Commissioners and the reforms they had sponsored had come to be accepted as a permanent and necessary part of the ecclesiastical landscape. If we play the superficial and suspect game of trying to pinpoint the moment when the 'modern' Church of England came into being, this is surely it. Yet the measures were unpopular at first. Many Evangelicals and moderate High Churchmen welcomed the reforms, recognising the dire situation in which the Church had found itself in the reform crisis.[12] But reform offended vested interests – families depending on patronage and place to provide for sons, cathedral clergy convinced of their utility, ambitious clergy eager to supplement their income, among others. A flurry of pamphlets opposed one or other aspect of the schemes proposed.

There were the predictable criticisms from radicals and pro-disestablishment Dissenters that the reforms did not go nearly far enough, since they left the basic fact of establishment in place, and merely tidied up the more obvious weaknesses of the current system. The Utilitarian philosopher James Mill propounded an alternative scheme in the *London Review* for a national Church that would be rather like a civil service for non-dogmatic moral teaching, overseen by 'inspectors' rather than bishops. But Mill no longer believed in anything closely resembling the historic Christian faith. He scorned prayer, the sacraments and any form of religious doctrine, for such a State religion 'ought to be stripped of all which is separating'.[13] More common was the stance adopted by one of the leaders of militant Dissent, Edward Miall, founder of the journal *The Nonconformist*, which campaigned for the separation of Church and State. To Miall, the idea that Dissenters could be assuaged by addressing specific grievances had been a fatal mistake: '[Dissenters'] aim must … involve a noble principle. It must be honest, direct, and final. THE ENTIRE SEPARATION OF CHURCH AND STATE is really their object.'[14]

But there were voices inside the Church itself resistant to reform anyway. The most strident and, ultimately, influential were those more radical High Churchmen who broke with the moderate High Church consensus represented by Bishop Blomfield and his ilk. To the leaders of the Oxford Movement and their sympathisers, the Ecclesiastical Commission was the autocratic device of a State intent on subjugating the Church and curtailing its intrinsic spiritual authority. One of the Oxford Movement's leading figures, Edward Pusey, wrote a long article (his articles were never short) attacking the proposals of the Commission in the *British Critic* in April 1838: this seems, he said, 'more like one of those rapid transformations, which in boyish days one saw on the stage effected by the wand of a magician, than a real act, intended by real bishops to consolidate and strengthen the government of a portion of the Church of Christ'.[15] But there were also criticisms from a more pragmatic position, evocative of once widely accepted assumptions about property and religion. Sydney Smith, the celebrated Regency wit, was a pluralist clergyman, combining a rectory in Somerset with a canonry at St Paul's. Smith lamented the Ecclesiastical Commission's haste to tear up a system which, he believed, attracted men of talent and energy into the Church.[16] They had gone too far and too fast: instead of a 'quiet and cautious mode of proceeding', he said, 'all is change, fusion, and confusion': '[The] fact is, that the respectability of the Church, as well as of the Bar, is almost entirely preserved by the unequal division of their revenues.'[17]

It is a measure of how much things have changed since the early nineteenth century that the kinds of arguments Sydney Smith made would cut little ice today. What looked like an attack on the rights of property and on the deferential and hierarchical relationships by which the Church, like other professions, was sustained, was in retrospect a vital moment in the Church of England's modern survival. It was a forced transformation from being a relic of the old regime to the beginning – for it was no more than a beginning, and yet the most important part of that beginning – of a long period in which the Church's structure, culture, expectations and professional *modus operandi* were completely overhauled.

The Local Establishment

These constitutional reforms were not only a change at the very centre of government, but affected every community. The association of Crown and Church was celebrated and prayed for in the liturgy, marked by the royal coat of arms displayed in churches, affirmed in the loyal oath sworn by clergy at ordination, and reinforced through the performance of public prayers in times of war and national emergency. The parish priest in early modern England and Wales did not minister to a specialised, distinct group of Christians self-defining as 'Anglican', nor did he conceive of his task as exclusively concerned with religious needs; he served and led a whole community, assuming that all members of that community were his pastoral and moral responsibility by virtue of living within his parish. Only by degrees, hard-won at that, were Dissenters able to achieve concessions that eventually gave them some scope to exist as distinct communities themselves within the larger community of the parish. So the constitutional changes of the late 1820s and early 1830s were bound to change local perceptions of the parish clergy. Moreover, further reforms with a direct impact on local communities followed in the wake of parliamentary reform. Municipal corporations were reformed in 1835, opening up the government of some 178 towns to Dissenters and Roman Catholics, and creating a uniform system of rolling, annual council elections. From now on, Dissenters had a much stronger voice in local politics. Reform of the Poor Law in 1834 created the hated 'Union' workhouses, diminishing the influence of the local clergy. Legislation in 1836 for the first time created a national, secular or civic system for registering births, deaths and marriages, with a General Register Office in London. While parish clergy remained civil registrars for weddings conducted in the parish church, weddings could take place in Dissenting and Catholic chapels, and be registered quite separately from the Anglican arrangements, as were now all births and deaths.

The cumulative effect of these changes became evident only in time. Particularly in towns where Dissenting communities were prosperous and expanding, the mid-Victorian years were a time of intense, local sectarian rivalry. Commonly, an older, predominantly Anglican landowning and mercantile elite found itself challenged on a range of local issues by Nonconformist clergy, businessmen and traders making common cause with political Liberalism. The most intense battles often took place over the issue of church rate, a local tax on the propertied which could be applied by a vote of householders in an open vestry meeting, chaired by the parish priest, to support the upkeep of the parish church. A notorious example was at Braintree in Essex, where in 1837 the churchwardens, despite failing to gain a majority in favour of a rate in the vestry meeting, nevertheless imposed it on the parish on their own authority; only in 1852, after a protracted legal battle, was the decision overturned.[18] But such conflicts were common. Even in a town such as Croydon, long before it was absorbed into greater London, and where Dissenters could never muster sufficient numbers of ratepayers in a vestry meeting to overthrow the parish proposal, the issue was sufficiently toxic to ensure protracted local wrangling, led by Edward Miall's son-in-law.[19]

In rural parishes, the conflict between Anglicanism and Dissent was often much less open, and the historic pre-eminence of the local clergyman faded more slowly. But just as constitutional and administrative reform were everywhere transforming the position of the established Church, the ongoing process of diocesan reform underlined a shift in the public understanding of the clergyman. The process by which the Church of England overhauled its own machinery, and at the same time came to terms with a more constrained constitutional position, effectively illustrated the process sociologists

of religion have called 'denominationalisation'. The argument
runs like this. Churches like the Church of England – national,
historic churches, that is – could lay claim to the title 'Church'
precisely because originally their ambitions and reach were universal, aiming to encompass a whole society. Religious groups
that broke away from them would be called, in the terminology,
'sects', because they cultivated a small group of like-minded
followers. But in the modern era both 'churches' and 'sects',
under the impact of social, demographic and political change,
had to rationalise and streamline their structures and practice
in order to survive, and in the process developed an accommodation with other religious groups: so both converged on
a new category of religious organisation, the 'denomination',
which maintained a professional ministry and bureaucracy,
and a national organisation, and reconciled universal religious
claims with a *de facto* acknowledgement of religious pluralism.

Like all sociological theory, the idea is both illuminating and historically elusive. But it does point to a shift in the
Church's self-understanding forced on it by the changes of the
early nineteenth century. The work of reforming bishops like
Thomas Burgess, bishop of St David's from 1803 to 1825, and
his successor, Connop Thirlwall, who between them established schools, voluntary associations to encourage religious
education and theological study, a new college – St David's at
Lampeter, encouraged the learning of Welsh, revived the office
of rural dean, and built new churches, both steadied the work
of the Church at local level, and at the same time effected a
definite shift away from the cluster of social assumptions that
had shaped the outlook of the parish clergy in pre-reform days.[20]
This took time. The gradualist nature of reform meant that,
even in the late Victorian period, features of the older establishment sometimes persisted. Pluralism did not disappear
overnight, for example. Into the 1850s and 1860s there were
egregious examples of it. William Jackson, for example, who
was chancellor of the diocese of Carlisle from 1846 to 1855, also
drew stipends as rector of Lowther and rector of Cliburn, which

together brought him an additional £450 p.a., as well as holding a Fellowship at Queen's College, Oxford; when he gave up the chancellorship to become Provost of Queen's, he retained his northern preferments.[21] But Jackson was a figure of the past. The age of oligarchy was at an end. The onward march of reform could not be resisted for long.

PART 3

THE AGE OF THE PEOPLE

13

THE HIGH CHURCH REVIVAL

Before the constitutional reforms of the 1820s and 1830s, most Anglicans agreed on the authority and utility of the established Church. The effects of the Evangelical revival were being felt in a reinvigorated parish ministry in many places, in a new idealism and zeal for overseas as well as domestic mission, in education and in moral and social causes such as abolitionism. But Evangelicals rarely positioned themselves polemically over and against High Churchmen, even if some High Churchmen were wary of the 'saints'. All that was to change. The political changes of these years triggered internal disagreement between Anglicans over Church authority that widened into internal conflict, leading to the emergence of distinct church 'parties' in the middle of the nineteenth century. It is from this time that we can date the modern typology of Anglicanism, its strange accommodation of three quite distinct, even sharply different, approaches to Christian belief – the Evangelical, the Anglo-Catholic, and the Liberal.

High Churchmen took an active part in efforts to revive the national Church before 1828.[1] The 'Hackney Phalanx', for example, a circle of High Church clergy and laity centred around the wine merchant Joshua Watson, included a bishop of Durham, a Master of Trinity College, Cambridge, and a number of prominent High Church theologians.[2] They strongly supported the National Society, published journals, encouraged church building, and were instrumental in the creation of King's College, London. Many of the bishops stood in this tradition, too. William Howley (pronounced 'Hooley'), for example, bishop of London from 1813 and then archbishop of Canterbury from 1828, was satirised by Jeremy Bentham as the 'Prostrator-general of wills' because he had argued that the true Christian shows 'a prostration of the understanding and will' to the authority of the Church, a classic High Church emphasis.[3] But Howley, as his modern biographer argues, was in fact an active, reforming bishop, who, in concert with Charles Blomfield, oversaw the work of the new Ecclesiastical Commission. Before the 1830s Church 'party' lines were fluid, however. There were no substantial differences between them in forms of worship and liturgy, nor in clerical dress. There were not even sharply divergent practical approaches to the sacraments. There were some theological differences over the doctrine of salvation, including predestination, and the relative authority of Scripture. There were also cultural and devotional differences of language and tone, and distinct social networks. But as yet these had not hardened into defining battle lines.

Evangelicals and High Churchmen alike supported the close partnership of Church and State, but on different grounds. Evangelicals mainly viewed establishment instrumentally, as a providential means by which the work of the Church, and so the proclamation of the Gospel, could be promoted. Church order could change; any specific form of it was not absolutely validated in Scripture, though Christians were obliged to respect the authorised form embodied in the Church of England. This position is sometimes labelled 'Erastian', that is, assuming the subordination of the Church to the State, though that is not strictly fair to the Evangelical view of the supremacy of Scripture.[4] For High Churchmen, Scripture and Church tradition were in harmony, reflecting a corporate, historic idea of the Church independent of the State. But State and Church were organically connected, pursuing correspondent aims. In this view, the historic order of the ministry and the sacraments not only had an 'objective' character, acting as conduits of divine grace in and of themselves, but, in theological language, they participated in the reality they represented – they were not merely instrumental, they were, in some sense, 'divine', as the presence in history of the body of Christ. High Churchmen at this time were loyal to the Prayer Book, but they saw it not so much as a Reformation departure from the liturgy and traditions of the pre-Reformation Church as a purified continuation of them.[5] For High Churchmen, the weakening of the main legislative props of the confessional State was a catastrophe. But they reacted to it in strategically different ways. Some, like Howley himself, while regretting the Church's loss of its preferred constitutional position, believed it was all the more urgent to protect the Church against further depredation by moderate, efficient reform, freeing it to pursue a much more vigorous policy of evangelism and expansion. But others took a very different line.

The Oxford Movement: Rather More than Twelve Years ...

No aspect of the history of the modern Church of England has been more celebrated and deplored, mythologised and anatomised, than the Oxford Movement. The name is usually applied to a small group of idealistic High Church clergy based in Oxford who, for twelve years, from 1833 to 1845, led a campaign to restore to the Church the theology and practice it had lost since the Restoration. John Henry Newman, John Keble, Edward Pusey, Richard Hurrell Froude and their disciples are commonly held to have restored neo-Gothic aesthetics, a revived colourful ceremonial ('the beauty of holiness') comparable to that of the Catholic Church, and a more intense sacramentalism. The idea of the twelve years has been fixed firmly in the consciousness of the modern Church by two texts from long afterwards, Newman's spiritual autobiography, *Apologia Pro Vita Sua* (1864), a classic of Christian writing, and a history of the movement written by Richard Church, *The Oxford Movement: Twelve Years, 1833–1845* (1891). Following Newman, Church accepted Keble's 'Assize Sermon' of 1833, which protested against the Whig government's plan to reform the Irish Church, as the beginning

22. An extreme between two means: Pusey, Newman and Keble, flanked by rival archbishops Manning (Catholic, left) and Wilberforce (Anglican, right)

of the movement, and Newman's own conversion, which he labelled 'the catastrophe', as its effective end.[6]

But although Oxford was the epicentre of the movement, it was always a broader phenomenon that stretched over a much longer period of time. Its real origins lie in the coalescence of friendships and intellectual interests around Keble, Froude and Newman at Oriel College in the late 1820s. It was the political conflict over Catholic Emancipation in 1829, stirred up in Oxford by having Sir Robert Peel as its MP, which marked the real start of the movement.[7] Ever more convinced of what they took to be the Patristic model of the Church as standing on no other basis than its own authority as a divine society, the 'extension of the incarnation in time', the Oxford leaders deplored Liberal or rational attempts to downgrade traditional doctrine, and the idea that the State had a responsibility to order the affairs of the Church.

As a campaign in defence of the traditional position of the

Church of England, at first the movement attracted support across the Church. The series of tracts, collectively called the *Tracts for the Times*, which Newman and others began publishing from Oxford in the same year, 1833, gave the movement another name, 'Tractarianism'. But there were other initiatives, too, including a loyal address to Archbishop Howley signed by some 6,500 clergy, and another one signed by some 230,000 lay heads of household.[8] The charismatic, quietly forceful Newman – probably the most brilliant English theologian of his age, and perhaps of any age – was the most creative and dominant personality of the group. But his central role should not obscure the extraordinarily fertile nature of the Tractarians as a whole, nor the impact of other powerful personalities within the group, such as Pusey and Keble. The year 1845 may have marked a caesura in the movement's Oxford progress, but it did not at all end its influence.

By the early 1840s Newman's position anyway had become so controversial that even sympathisers were wondering how compatible it was with historic Anglicanism. John Burgon, for example, later dean of Chichester, and a 'high-churchman of the old school', was appalled by the 'mischievous effect which Newman's lapse to Romanism' had had; it was a 'master-stroke of Satan's policy', effectively paralysing the Church's newly-recovered life.[9] Far from fading from view as it was replaced by the brighter, sharper lustre of Tractarianism, the movement of Catholic renewal in Anglicanism always had a much broader base than Oxford, and exerted a profound influence throughout the century, fusing, blending and sometimes distinguishing again in unexpected ways various different hues of High Churchmanship.

Yet, conceding that much, the central role of the Oxford leaders cannot be denied. Just how and why, then, did the Oxford Movement go from widespread support in 1833 to hostility and division by 1845? In a nutshell – though this is cutting a lot of corners – it began by reasserting supposedly neglected elements of the High Church tradition in defence of the Church's spiritual independence, developed these in ways that brought it into conflict with the bishops, and finally fragmented into radical and more moderate segments, at odds with each other over the view they should take of Rome. In this trajectory, Newman's role was critical. As an Anglican, he was a fissile combination of breadth of imagination, logical deduction and intellectual risk-taking. For him, the movement was above all about recovering a coherent, systematic understanding of Anglicanism as a *via media* between Protestantism and Roman Catholicism. In his *Lectures on the Prophetical Office of the Church* (1837), he argued that the Anglican *via media* was the closest approximation to the Church of the Fathers. Both Protestantism ('Popular Protestant-ism', by which he meant principally Evangelicalism) and Roman Catholicism had substituted something else for the testimony of 'primitive' (i.e. ancient) tradition – in the former case, a plain assertion of Scripture which, without any notion of mediation by the Church, resulted in an undue emphasis on subjective, private judgment and, in the latter, an opposite assertion of the authority of the Roman hierarchy, or the Church as presently constituted. But Newman was realistic enough to realise that what he was sketching was not actually what most Anglicans believed: it was a 'paper theory', needing to be embodied in practice, and recognised as the true spirit of Anglicanism.[10]

But that did not happen. Instead, the movement was drawn into a series of controversies which cast it, not as the true inheritor of the authentic Anglicanism, but as a divisive splinter group, intent on subverting the Church's Protestant character and easing the path to Rome. Anti-Catholicism was still deeply embedded in British society, and reinforced by Prot-estant nationalism. From a strategic perspective, the actions of the Oxford leaders were disastrous, alienating significant sections of support in the Church and giving their opponents enough ammunition to discredit them as 'Papist' fifth-column-ists. Opposition to the appointment of a Liberal theologian in Oxford offended 'Broad' or Liberal churchmen as well as some traditional High Churchmen. Publication of Froude's literary

Remains (1838) after his premature death, with their disparaging comments about the Reformation, appalled a wide range of opinion.[11] The Tractarians' queasiness about the construction of a memorial to the Protestant Reformation martyrs in Oxford – a proposal that was in itself deliberately provocative – underlined Evangelicals' growing suspicion of the movement.[12]

The heaviest blow was Newman's Tract 90, *Remarks on Certain Passages in the Thirty-nine Articles* (1841). His aim was to show that you could subscribe to the Articles conscientiously while holding to Catholic doctrine. When Article Twenty-two condemned, for example, the 'Romish doctrine concerning purgatory', Newman claimed this could not possibly include *both* the early Church's understanding of the doctrine and the position agreed by the Catholic Church at the Council of Trent. Accordingly, this article could be affirmed 'by the Anglo-Catholic as a matter of private belief', i.e. without repudiating purgatory.[13] The argument persuaded few. It merely convinced many, including most of the bishops, that Newman and his followers were already practically Roman Catholic.

The reaction of the bishops unsettled Newman so much that he began a protracted withdrawal from his ministerial and university responsibilities. Through the *Apologia*, we can discern his intellectual journey, from the realisation that the 'paper theory' of the *via media* was just that, unrealisable in practice, to a growing conviction that it was the Church of England that had departed from the spirit of early Christianity, not Rome: 'The proof of the Roman (modern) doctrine is as strong (or stronger) in Antiquity, as that of certain doctrines which both we and Romans hold.'[14] Newman's conviction of the historical and theological correctness of the Tractarian position evaporated. A few hundred clergy and laity seceded to the Roman Church, as did Newman himself in 1845. But Pusey and Keble did not, and nor did many others.

Although Newman's loss was a heavy blow, in retrospect it did not fundamentally change the direction of the Anglo-Catholic or High Church revival. By the mid-1840s, even the more distinctive theological emphases represented by the Tractarians were already becoming embedded in parishes outside Oxford. Pusey was now clearly identified as the leader of what remained of the movement. In 1843 he had preached a sermon, *The Holy Eucharist a Comfort to the Penitent* – 'perhaps the most important sermon of his life' – in which he asserted a strong doctrine of the real presence and of eucharistic sacrifice: as the eucharist repeated the sacrifice of Christ on the cross, it became a 'comfort' to the penitent.[15] Like Newman had, Pusey faced rebuke in Oxford and was inhibited from preaching for two years. But the sermon marked out what was to be an ever more significant double emphasis in the liturgical and devotional practices of the Tractarians, namely a rediscovery of the 'Catholic' doctrine of the eucharist in Anglicanism, and a recovery of the theology and practice of sacramental confession. In both respects, Keble, Pusey and others continued well into the second half of the nineteenth century to take Anglo-Catholicism in a direction barely laid down in outline before Newman's conversion.

What made Tractarianism distinct in Anglicanism was that, at first at least, everything flowed from its understanding of Church order. In the first of the Tracts, Newman had asserted boldly that the authority of the ministry stood above all on its historic connection back through the centuries to the Apostles themselves, a connection mediated in time through the laying on of hands in ordination by bishops, the 'apostolic succession'. When Newman said that this 'sacred gift' was 'the real ground on which our authority is built', he meant that the ordained ministry could not ultimately be beholden to civil or State authority; the Church was in principle and in origin independent of the State, and was not even an equal partner but of higher or superior standing to secular authority.[16] This went beyond traditional High Churchmanship, and could even be described as 'theocratic'.[17] That is why the Tractarians so resented government-led reform of the Church, though they were mollified when the Ecclesiastical Commission was expanded to include all the bishops.

But this political theology was only a starting point. Its salient feature was an intensified emphasis on apostolic succession.[18] The Tractarians insisted, not just on the authority and providential character of the succession – the traditional High Church view – but its *necessity* for the Church: they 'supercharged' the doctrine, making it a guarantee of the Catholicity of the Church. The eucharist was only valid when celebrated by a priest or bishop ordained in the line of apostolic descent: they maintained the '*exclusive* validity of the orders and sacraments of episcopal ministries'.[19] This had two important consequences. First, in Tractarian eyes, it cut the Church of England off from other Protestant churches, and denied that they were truly part of the Christian Church. This was startling, since most Anglicans saw their Church as part of the family of Reformation churches, closer to them than to the Roman Church. Second, it raised the spiritual significance of the ordained ministry higher than it had ever been. It smacked to contemporaries of 'priestcraft', the word of abuse levelled at the Catholic clergy. With this raised status went new forms of clerical dress (the white collar, the black cassock rather than academic gown, the vestments worn by priests celebrating the eucharist), a renewed interest in clerical celibacy and devotional discipline, a revived practice of personal confession and sacramental absolution, and the rearrangement of liturgy and the internal ordering of churches to give expression to the growing emphasis on the eucharist.

Critics were quick to see in these developments an effeminate, un-English interest in the aesthetic and flamboyant, but this was to underestimate the theological seriousness and ascetic spiritual drive of the Oxford Movement. A reading of Keble's or Newman's parish sermons is a sober corrective to any suggestion that theirs was a superficial religion. They shared an earnest commitment to saving souls with the most ardent Evangelicals. But for the Tractarians conversion was a lifelong process, a living into the pursuit of holiness that depended first and foremost on observing the disciplines of the Church, beginning with baptism and proceeding through catechism and confirmation to communion, with regular confession and penance. For Keble the whole of life was to be lived in anticipation of death and judgment. Christians needed to avail themselves of all the supports the Church could provide through the ordained ministry, especially confession and absolution, for 'all have need of penitence', even – astonishingly, to modern eyes – Keble says, the youngest children, for even a child but a day old 'has need of penance, i.e. of God's corrective discipline. For it is a sinner in the sight of God, and subject to His wrath, having in it, that seed and spark of original sin.'.[20] This was a demanding, severe religion. The Tractarian spirit was not first concerned with the external aspects of religion – the dress, the ceremony and ritual, the music and architecture – but with the inculcation of a high, demanding view of the Christian life, no less demanding than that of Evangelicals.

Yet the spirit of Tractarianism was not puritanical. For all that it elevated the doctrine of the Church and ministry, it did not make a sharp division between the Church and the world. Its equal attention to the doctrine of the incarnation – Christ's coming in human flesh – as to atonement meant that it was open to the aesthetic, and to the idea that the material world was a type or pattern of the divine (an idea that has obvious consonance with sacramentality). And that was also typical of its roots in Romanticism, the movement of thought and feeling that rose in reaction to the perceived rationalism of the Enlightenment. Keble's popular book of poetry, *The Christian Year* (1827) – a genuine bestseller, published many times in the nineteenth century in hundreds of thousands of copies – combined High Church theology with a Wordsworth-like appreciation of the natural world. Although a renewed interest in medievalism, and especially in Gothic architecture, predated the movement, its religious sensibility worked in harmony with Gothic revivalism.[21] In all this, the Oxford Movement, like the High Church revival in general, was of a piece with the Continent-wide movement of Catholic renewal that began in the early nineteenth century, as a reaction to revolutionary radicalism and as a determination to renew the faith and community of the Christian past in Europe.

Ritualism – A Second Wave?

The aesthetic appeal of Tractarianism led to one of the most controversial developments of the High Church revival, 'Ritualism'. Attracting accusations of flamboyance and a preoccupation with mere externals, Ritualism has had a lasting effect on Anglicanism. It aimed to give much greater ritual and ceremonial expression to the liturgical theology of High Church Anglicanism, and especially its sacramentalism, including processions, colourful liturgical dress and the use of incense. Scholars have disagreed profoundly about the relationship of Ritualism to the Oxford Movement. Some have seen it as a natural development of Tractarianism, others as a significant departure from Tractarianism's pastoral and devotional spirit.[22] In favour of the former view is the fact that Ritualism was not doctrinally creative, but took its theology almost entirely from Tractarianism. On the other hand, the Tractarians themselves were mostly unconcerned about ritual development, and anxious about its provocative effects, which jeopardised the dogmatic gains of the movement. Ritualism, which really began to manifest itself in the Church of England in the late 1850s and 1860s, was certainly at the very least a step on from the movement's Oxford origins, and you can find examples of clergy in the 1860s and 1870s embodying the more cautious Tractarian spirit without Ritual experiment, and Ritualist clergy with (as far as we can tell) very little interest in or understanding of the austere piety of the Oxford Movement.

So the High Church revival was a broader movement than Tractarianism, encompassing not only Ritualism, but also the 'older' High Churchmanship: the fusion of critical scholarship and High Churchmanship that came to be called 'Liberal Catholicism', and the sacramental edge of the Christian Socialist movement associated with figures like Stewart Headlam, ardent defender of theatres and bail for Oscar Wilde, and Conrad Noel, turbulent vicar of Thaxted.[23] Ritualism was based above all on the centrality of the eucharist in worship. The greater frequency with which High Churchmen urged that communion should be celebrated, the link between communion and the pursuit of holiness, and the creation of parish organisations which aimed to bring communicants together for social and devotional occasions outside the communion service itself – all encouraged a reshaping of the practice of liturgy and its ceremonial expression in a more extravagant direction.[24] They had an evangelistic purpose: rather like the marching bands of the Salvation Army, so it was claimed, the colour and movement of Ritualism were more likely to appeal to the labouring poor than the dry formalism of traditional High Church worship.

Ritualism's significance must also be seen in the context of early nineteenth-century liturgical design and practice. In many churches, the interior was organised around the preaching of the word. While high-backed or boxed pews and galleries for further seating cluttered up the nave and transepts, the choir or chancel was often used merely as a place of storage, and a high 'three-decker' pulpit, with the pulpit itself above and clerk's and officiants desks below, dominated the interior. Music was provided by a church band in one of the galleries, usually at the west end of the church. This is a generalised description. Almost universally, by the standards of High Church worship today, ritual and ceremonial were minimal. Very few churches had choirs. It does not require much imagination to see how it was likely – highly likely – that sacramental renewal would promote the reorganisation of liturgy and church interiors. An early example was the proprietary chapel in Margaret Street, west London (later to become All Saints), where the incumbent, Fredrick Oakeley, cleared out the three-decker pulpit, galleries and box pews in the early 1840s, installed an altar instead of the communion table, instituted a surpliced choir, began using coloured altar frontals and candles on the altar during service, and added musical embellishments to the liturgy of the

23. Rescinding the Reformation: Ritualism

Prayer Book.[25] These were modest changes in comparison with the development of full-blown Ritualism at mid-century. They were controversial enough, however, as were ritual innovations at the new church of St Paul's, Knightsbridge, in 1847–50, and then most notoriously at St George's-in-the-East, Whitechapel, ten years later, when the incumbent's use of coloured eucharistic vestments, candles on the altar and other changes provoked months of turbulence and disruption by crowds objecting to his 'Popery'.[26]

The Ritualist movement was particularly stirred up by publication of the *Directorium Anglicanum* (1858), edited by John Purchas and subtitled 'Being a Manual of Directions for the Right Celebration of the Holy Communion ... According to the Ancient Uses of the Church of England'. The Ritualists claimed to be rediscovering and restoring ancient usage, but the *Directorium* was actually a blend of ancient sources, guesswork and influences from contemporary Catholic practice. It provided a model for innovation, however. For more than two decades, the Church was riven by a series of legal disputes in which ritual and liturgical innovations were challenged by disgruntled 'Low Church' or strongly Protestant laity and clergy. An early case, Westerton versus Liddell, in 1855 established the legality of modest practices such as having a cross behind the altar, the use of candles as lights on the altar and a credence table (a small table on which the bread and wine, the chalice and other receptacles could be kept) in the sanctuary. In the Mackonochie Case of 1868, the popular, dedicated 'slum' priest Alexander Mackonochie was prevented from using incense in worship, from elevating the paten containing the 'host' (the communion bread at consecration) above his head in the prayer of consecration and from mixing water with wine in the communion service. By then, the battle lines were very clearly drawn, with the broadly Evangelical 'Church Association' promoting and supporting legislative action to put down Ritualism and the English Church Union, an Anglo-Catholic defence body formed in 1860, in turn supporting Ritualist clergy against complaints and prosecution. Ritualist supporters increasingly emphasised what came to be called the 'six points': the use of incense; lighted candles on the altar; eucharistic vestments; the mixed chalice; wafer bread (rather than ordinary bread); and the eastward position (when the priest faced east to celebrate, rather than standing at the north side of the table or altar as the Prayer Book directed). Five of these six points – incense being to some extent the exception – related directly to the celebration of the eucharist.

Most modern churchgoers would probably react to these controversies with amazement that such seemingly harmless matters could prove so divisive. Why not live and let live? But there were deep matters of principle involved. For opponents of ritual, the very character of the established Church, and its Protestant identity, were threatened: there was something dishonest

HEIGHT OF FASHION.

24. *Punch* on the foppery of Ritualism

and idolatrous about Anglo-Catholics adopting alien practices and beliefs which had been firmly rejected at the Reformation.[27] For Ritualists, what they were demanding was, on the contrary, not at all antipathetic to the traditions of the Church of England, but recovering and manifesting its truly Catholic character. Without their innovations, the English Church remained hampered by its inability to embody in its worship and practice its true inner, spiritual life; in other words, *not* to put these changes into practice was to continue to live a lie.

And the bishops? They were divided, both about the desirability of the changes and about how to deal with the stubborn and mostly intractable Ritualists. Successive bishops of London had enormous difficulty in trying to contain ritual innovation – London was a particular 'hotspot' for Ritualism. A commission established to examine the issue in 1867 eventually issued in the one concerted attempt to legislate on the matter, the Public Worship Regulation Act of 1874, which established a

new civil court to deal with ritual matters, though it retained
an episcopal veto over proceedings. But this was to prove a
dead end. A spate of ritual prosecutions followed. But where
the bishop's veto was not used, in several cases the offending
clergyman simply refused to submit to the court's ruling, and
as a result was sent to prison. This happened five times. The
evident sincerity and determination of Anglo-Catholic clergy
began to turn public opinion in their favour, and discouraged
bishops from allowing prosecutions to go forward. Further tensions at the end of the century, and a Royal Commission on
Ritual in 1903–6, ruled out any more legislative attempts to
ban or contain ritual.[28] Once again, the permissible latitude of
belief and practice in the Church of England had been pushed
outwards. The liturgical style and practice of modern Anglo-
Catholicism had found a permanent, if sometimes reluctant,
home in the Church.

The Culture and Diffusion of Anglo-Catholicism

The continuing controversy over ritual and liturgical innovation
pointed to an obvious truth – Anglo-Catholicism, far from being
suppressed or in some way marginalised as eccentric or even 'un-
English', was in fact thriving in parishes up and down England
and Wales. It came in many varieties, including an extreme
'Roman' version which looked explicitly to the Catholic Church
for guidance on what should be said, worn or done in church
(and even included a few – admittedly very few – parishes that
experimented with using the Latin rite), and a more common
'English' or 'Prayer Book' style which ostensibly remained faithful to the Prayer Book, but added to it gestures, prayers, actions,
processions and such like that enabled Anglo-Catholics to reconcile, as they thought, the Anglican tradition with the common
Catholic culture of western Europe.

Prayer Book Catholicism was projected through manuals
and directions such as *Ritual Notes* (first published in 1894, but
frequently republished) and then the popular *Parson's Handbook*

(published in 1899, and also frequently republished) by Percy Dearmer. Certain of its practices, such as the use of incense in worship and the reservation of the sacrament (that is, the placing of consecrated bread to one side after the eucharist in an 'aumbry' or 'tabernacle', for communion of the sick and also for prayer and adoration) were never adopted by more than a small minority of Anglican churches. But others – surpliced choirs, candles on the altar, a cross or crucifix on the altar, eucharistic vestments and the changing colours of the liturgical year – came to be, by the middle of the twentieth century, so widely accepted that they ceased to carry any 'party' significance.

Various national organisations, such as the Confraternity of the Blessed Sacrament and the English Church Union, had local branches in some churches. Despite its elevation of priestly status, Anglo-Catholicism gave lay people many opportunities for participating in the life and work of the church. Servers, including crucifers and candle bearers, were needed for the complex liturgies. Generally these were male, until the second half of the twentieth century, but from the late nineteenth century women often took part in parish choirs, and men and women could work as volunteers in the plethora of parish organisations supported just as much by late nineteenth-century Anglo-Catholic churches as by other brands of Anglicanism, including district visitors, Sunday Schools, the Mothers' Union, the Church of England Men's Society, the Church Lads' and Girls' Brigades, the Church of England Temperance Society and charities such as coal and clothing clubs.

Women were prominent in another major development within Anglo-Catholicism, which really merits much more attention than I can give it here – the revival of the religious life. Apart from a few brief, ill-fated experiments such as the Little Gidding community, created by Nicholas Ferrar in 1626, which was really an extended household marked by a practice of daily prayer and Bible reading, the religious life had completely disappeared from Anglicanism with the dissolution of the monasteries. Partly stimulated by the renewed conception of a disciplined spiritual and devotional life, which for some High Churchmen included clerical celibacy, and partly influenced by the extraordinary revival of religious orders in mainland Catholic Europe, monasticism was a natural development of the High Church revival.[29] Newman briefly established a small monastic community at Littlemore, just outside Oxford, in the early 1840s, before his conversion. Other small, usually short-lived experiments were tried. But by the 1850s, small communities were being established in various places, often at first as adjuncts to the local parish, or for specific pastoral duties. What came to be called the Community of St Mary the Virgin, at Wantage, for example, was founded in 1848 by the vicar of Wantage, William Butler, a disciple of the Tractarians, as a parochial sisterhood, using two cottages in the town. The sisters helped with parish work, particularly teaching, followed a rule of life including their own corporate worship, and joined regularly in the worship of the parish.[30] In time conventual buildings were erected, and the dress more commonly associated with nuns adopted, though these things were done slowly, given the abiding strength of popular anti-Catholicism. Another example was at East Grinstead, where in 1855 John Mason Neale, one of the founders of the Cambridge Camden Society and an ardent scholar of liturgy, began a community of sisters who would be, first and foremost, nurses to the poor of the area around Sackville College, the alms houses where he was warden; this became the Community of St Margaret.[31]

Male communities included Benedictines and Franciscans, but also new orders that did not follow existing Catholic models, such as the Society of the Sacred Mission, founded in 1894 by Herbert Kelly, which eventually settled at Kelham, in Nottinghamshire, and the Community of the Resurrection, founded by Charles Gore and Walter Frere, among others, which eventually settled at Mirfield in Yorkshire. Both of those communities are very good examples of the later development of Anglo-Catholicism, because their founders, while influenced in part by the ideals of the Oxford Movement, were also shaped by the social and theological ideals of the moderate High Churchman or 'Liberal' (a term he disavowed), F. D. Maurice. By the early twentieth century, then, the somewhat shaky attempts to recreate the religious life in Anglicanism had definitely taken root. These communities were never very large, nor very numerous, and they have suffered decline in the late twentieth and twenty-first centuries.

If the general effect of the High Church revival can, predictably, be seen in a greater interest in liturgical reform and sacramental theology, in a new interest in ecumenical relations with the Roman Catholic and Eastern Orthodox churches, as well as other episcopal churches such as the Old Catholics and the Church of Sweden, nevertheless the movement exercised a wider influence still. It inspired artists, poets, writers, musicians and architects. In the nineteenth century the novelist Charlotte M. Yonge and the poet Christina Rossetti stand out as noteworthy, as well as John Keble himself and the Welsh Tractarian poet Isaac Williams. But in the twentieth century the movement continued to exert a literary attraction, counting among those writers influenced by it T. S. Eliot, Dorothy L. Sayers, Rose Macaulay, Barbara Pym and even W. H. Auden.[32] Artists influenced by its affinities with medievalism included members of the Pre-Raphaelite Brotherhood, particularly William Holman Hunt.

There were, again, obvious interconnections between the Oxford Movement and Ritualism and the neo-Gothic revival.[33] Many of the best-known British religious architects of the nineteenth and early twentieth centuries found in the movement a stimulus for the freer exercise of their imagination, including George Gilbert Scott, along with his sons George and John and his grandson Giles, George Frederick Bodley, John Loughborough Pearson and Ninian Comper. Pearson's St Augustine's, Kilburn, for example, consecrated in 1880, could stand as a late-nineteenth century model of an Anglo-Catholic church interior, incorporating colourful wall murals and stained glass, a stone rood screen and a high stone altar in the sanctuary. The Gothic style was infinitely adaptable, lending itself to railways stations

(St Pancras), museums (the Natural History Museum), town
halls (Manchester) and country houses (Tyntesfield), as much
as to churches. Yet in the fusion of building design and liturgical
arrangement of the church interior, arguably Gothic revivalism
found a perfect fit of form and function.[34]

The achievement of these architects in the second half of
the nineteenth century was immensely facilitated by the work
done by the Cambridge Camden Society, with its journal *The
Ecclesiologist*. Founded in 1839 by a group of Cambridge under-
graduates inspired by the Oxford Movement, foremost among
whom was J. M. Neale, the society (which sometimes attracted
the name 'The Cambridge Movement') promoted the medieval
church as an aesthetic and religious ideal.[35] The High Church
revival also profoundly affected the development of church
music, it almost goes without saying. This will be covered in
more detail in chapter 14, but again it is not difficult to see how
the creation of surpliced choirs worked in harmony with both
the Gothic space and liturgical and ritual innovation, and helped
produce a second golden age of English church music.

It is very difficult to assess the numerical strength of High
Churchmanship by the end of the nineteenth century. It certainly had pockets of strength – including London, Brighton,
the West Country and parts of Yorkshire – and areas of relative
weakness. Like Evangelicals, High Churchmen organised themselves, founding theological colleges to promote their distinctive
theology, working through various national societies such as
the English Church Union and the Society of the Holy Cross,
and exploited patronage to protect the Anglo-Catholic character of particular churches. Without doubt, just as certain ritual
and devotional practices remained controversial, others were
widely adopted and became part of mainstream Anglican life.
By the mid-twentieth century it was even claimed that Anglo-
Catholicism had become the dominant strand of Anglicanism,
capturing a greater proportion of the episcopate than other
church parties, and mobilising large numbers for the various

Anglo-Catholic Congresses that were a feature of the 1920s and 1930s.

Its relative success in taking root in parishes was aided by, or perhaps it helped to cause – it is very difficult to assess which came first – the decline of popular anti-Catholicism. The last great anti-Catholic upsurge of opinion in England and Wales occurred in 1850–51, when the Roman Catholic episcopal hierarchy was fully re-established here, and such was the hostility aroused that there was even a Parliamentary act, the Ecclesiastical Titles Act of 1851, passed to prevent Catholics using the titles of existing Anglican dioceses. But this was another instance of prematurely obsolete ecclesiastical legislation. Once passed, the Act was never formally applied, and Roman Catholics continued the gradual process of assimilation into English society that had begun even before Emancipation in 1829.

By the end of the century, although there remained various centres of sectarian conflict, not just in Ireland but on the mainland, including in Glasgow and Liverpool, where the Irish Catholic communities were particularly strong, 'No Popery' protests were fast becoming a thing of the past. Catholicism within Anglicanism benefitted from that. The hard work done by many Anglo-Catholic clergy in poor urban areas – the 'slum priests' of Anglo-Catholic mythology – assisted this process of growing acceptance, even though again it is easy to exaggerate this and to downplay the immense contribution of Evangelicals and Broad or Liberal churchmen to church life in the more deprived areas of the great cities. No matter – the point here is the journey of Anglo-Catholicism from the provocative, controversial history of the Oxford Movement to broad acceptance as an intrinsic aspect of modern Anglicanism.

14

WHERE CHOIRS SING: ANGLICANISM'S CULTURAL EXPERIMENT

The Medieval Legacy

If there is one feature of the contemporary Church of England that has an international appeal, it is the great tradition of choral music that people the world over associate with Anglican worship. Many people would say that one of the Church's great achievements has been to preserve this timeless cultural heritage. But what we recognise today as the 'choral tradition' has changed considerably over time, and it is as much a product of modern innovation and interpretation as it is of the preservation of ancient musical form. Once again, what looks like historic continuity masks a much more complex history.

England already had a reputation for excellent music before the Reformation. Though only a fraction of their music has survived, composers such as John Dunstaple (also spelt 'Dunstable') were known throughout Europe. Dunstaple's music mostly used three, four or five parts, all of which would have been sung by men and boys or just men. It was in the religious houses, cathedrals, greater collegiate churches and some colleges that choral foundations existed capable of singing the work of composers such as Dunstaple. A few great collections of the music of these communities survive, such as the 'Old Hall' manuscript, now in the British Library, and the *Eton Choirbook*, an assembly of sixty-four pieces which once formed part of a larger volume.[1] But most of the religious music of the Middle Ages was lost in the dissolution of the monasteries. Sometimes musical books were simply burned, sometimes they were broken up to bind other works or used for other purposes, and anyway the religious purposes for which they were produced rapidly changed in the course of the sixteenth century.

Most ordinary parish churches would have had nothing like the complexity and sophistication of this music. Although the only church music worshippers would have encountered would have been the chanting of the priest, in Latin, there was probably a lively 'folk' tradition of popular religious songs. We have some surviving vernacular religious poetry from the Middle Ages, and the few surviving cycles of 'mystery' plays, which were common across parts of Europe as well as Britain, featured retellings of Biblical stories, mixed up with more mythological or comic elements, and would have been accompanied by instruments and song. But these, though Christian in the broadest sense, were performed largely outside churches and had little direct impact on the development of English church music. In such a situation, and given the expense involved in supporting choirs to sing the more complex church music, it was hardly surprising that the church music we think of today as late medieval or early modern was mainly an elite phenomenon.

The Reformation in Music

Here, as in so much else, the Reformation marked a decisive shift in devotional culture, though perhaps not as consistently as many leading Reformers would have wished. The ascription of a distinct Anglican approach to church music is a hazardous exercise. Clear principles of liturgical reform – doctrinal purity, accessibility and simplicity – enunciated by English as well as Continental Evangelicals had implications for music. Doctrinal purity entailed the purging of 'superstitious' or idolatrous elements from the liturgy and so, accordingly, also from the music sung in church. This could be done negatively, through the excision of doctrines such as purgatory, the invocation of saints, ideas of eucharistic sacrifice and transubstantiation, prayers for the Pope, and so on, and through the termination of various services and processions. Settings of Marian texts, for example, fell out of favour, as did many other late medieval settings accompanying worship. The more positive or constructive approach to doctrinal purity implied the writing of texts specifically to illustrate reformed doctrine, and this was perhaps not so evident in new music in England, though indirectly it occurred through the eventual setting of parts of the *Book of Common Prayer* itself to music.

A second principle was accessibility. This meant abandoning Latin in favour of English. Cranmer's justification for use of the vernacular – 'the service in this Church of England these many years hath been read in Latin to the people, which they understand not; so that they have heard with their ears only, and their heart, spirit, and mind, have not been edified thereby' – applied just as much to singing as it did to speaking.[2] Particularly important here was the work of John Marbeck, a Reforming sympathiser who produced *The Booke of Common Praier Noted* in 1550, providing musical chants to express parts of the liturgy. Marbeck's work was not widely adopted in the sixteenth century, however; its influence on Anglican church music really belongs to the choral revival of the nineteenth century. The 1552 Prayer Book removed most references to the singing of the service, and so Marbeck's work, which perhaps reflected a Lutheran outlook that was already out of favour in England by then, was quickly set to one side.[3]

The third principle, simplicity, was also evident in Marbeck's work, and that of many others. Reformers – Cranmer notable among them – disparaged the complex harmonies and elongated, melismatic phrases of late medieval and Renaissance polyphony, and encouraged the close matching of notation to the spoken word, syllable by syllable. At its best, in the work of many late Tudor composers, the consequence was an effective, spare clarity and succinctness of expression.

A fourth principle or feature was implicit in the very idea of Common Prayer – the use of liturgy as a way of directing the public worship and private piety of the kingdom as a whole, ending division, ensuring social peace. The imposition of liturgical and doctrinal uniformity through the Prayer Book ended geographically variable traditions. This included Wales: the Welsh version of the Prayer Book, *Llfyr Gweddi Gyffredin*, contained no significant variations from the English original. There is, however, one important caveat. Although there had been probably close on 200 'professional' church choirs before the Reformation, and the dissolution destroyed a large number of them, nevertheless some forty or so remained, in the choirs of the cathedrals, some Oxbridge colleges and a few large urban churches. Here, a different practice continued from that of the vast majority of parish churches: more complex music could be performed, including some Latin motets and canticle settings. This was true above all of the Chapel Royal, which under Elizabeth became an oasis of musical excellence, and a refuge for composers who continued to write music for choral performance.[4] In musical and liturgical matters, then, pre-eminently the Chapel Royal, but also the cathedrals and other choral foundations were out of step with the general thrust of the Reformation in music.

The Chapel Royal was a magnet for leading composers. The two greatest composers of the Tudor age, Thomas Tallis and William Byrd, both served there. Byrd especially, but perhaps also Tallis, had Catholic sympathies, and wrote a large amount of music for Latin texts. In 1575 they collaborated in producing a published collection of Latin motets, *Cantiones quae ab argumento sacrae vocantur*, but sales were small, and the music would have been well beyond the capabilities of most churches. Some of Tallis's work remained in favour at the very few places where it was sung through the seventeenth and eighteenth centuries. So did Byrd's, though his reputation fell somewhat behind that of Tallis until the late nineteenth century, perhaps affected by the clear turn to more explicit Catholic writing in his later years[5] – the queen was remarkably tolerant of that. Other composers of the late sixteenth and early seventeenth centuries whose music was sung at the Chapel Royal, or who worked there, included Thomas Weelkes, Thomas Tomkins and Orlando Gibbons.

Given that all these composers' works are regularly sung today, it would be easy to assume they were the foundation of English church music, but their music would have been heard by only a fraction of the worshipping population. Theirs was music for the rich and powerful, requiring trained singers and instrumentalists, and dependent on expensive royal, noble and ecclesiastical establishments. There is no sense in which we can say confidently that *this* was the English tradition of church music. We like to think it was, but if we do that, we are rubbing out of the record the music that the vast majority of the English and Welsh people would have encountered in church and sung themselves.

For that, we have to turn to the single most important musical product of the Reformation in England and Wales, the sung vernacular psalm. Since the Prayer Book made little provision for singing, churches which did not have expensive choral foundations – that is, almost all parish churches – could make little or no use of music as part of the service itself. What we now commonly recognise as choral Evensong, with hymns, sung responses and psalms, and choral settings of the canticles and anthems, simply did not exist. Music was not completely absent from church, however. The Prayer Book did make allowance for the psalms to be said *or sung* at morning and evening prayer, and although at first in practice psalms were sung before or after the service, later it became much more common for that to happen during the service, at the appropriate point. But these were not Coverdale's psalms, the translation later published with the Prayer Book. They were versified translations, suitable for singing by people who had little or no formal musical education. They are usually called 'metrical psalms', because they followed a regular metre, verse by verse.

For over a century the most commonly used collection constituted translations by Thomas Sternhold and John Hopkins, and published as *The Whole Booke of Psalmes, Collected into English Meter* (1562), also known either as the 'Anglo-Genevan' psalter, or more simply as 'Sternhold and Hopkins'. It was the mainstay of parish psalmody until superseded by a new metrical psalter by Nicholas Brady and Nahum Tate published in 1696. Welsh versions were also eventually prepared, led by Edward Kyffin's translations, and first published on his death in 1603. The Anglo-Genevan psalms generally used the so-called 'ballad' metre, a metre of 8–6–8–6, i.e. four-line stanzas of alternating eight and six syllables. Most of the melodies were Genevan. The advantage of the uniform metre was that knowledge of only a handful of tunes was necessary to sing the whole book. A few remain in common use today, the best-known perhaps being that now called 'Old Hundredth', usually sung to William Kethe's version of Psalm 100, 'All people that on earth do dwell', though here the metre is 8–8–8–8. There was usually no organ accompaniment (indeed no organ), and no harmony, just the melody. The congregation would sing line by line, following the parish clerk, a practice called 'lining out'. The affinity of these metrical psalms with popular song is evident – the ballad metre, singing in unison but with different registers, familiarity, reliance on oral transmission, and so on. *This* was the music of Anglican worship for over two hundred years.

Plebeian Praise and Polite Music

In music, as in so much else, the Commonwealth was a time of enormous disruption. Essentially, almost everything that I have described as the 'High' tradition of choral music came to an end. The choral foundations were disbanded everywhere, as the tide of the conflict turned in favour of Parliament. In January 1645, the *Book of Common Prayer* was suppressed. The Puritan agenda, stirred up by resentment at the Laudian 'project' of elaborating and decorating worship in church, was to eliminate anything that could serve as an obstacle to the hearing of the word of God. It was summed up in Nathaniel Holmes' criticism of cathedral singing:

Yea nor do they all sing together, but first one sings an

anthem, then half the choir then the other tossing the word of God like a tennis-ball. Then all yelling together with confused noise.[6]

Metrical psalm-singing, however, was another matter. It was the one form of musical expression the *Directory for Public Worship* encouraged. The psalter, the earliest English form of sacred hymnody, thus remained central to popular religious experience even through the turbulence of the 1640s and 1650s.

At the Restoration the choral foundations were quick to begin re-establishing themselves, though recruitment was difficult at first, even for the Chapel Royal. But stylistically things did not simply pick up where they had left off in 1642. New fashions in music were coming in. Partly this was the influence of Continental models, especially French, which the new king had experienced in exile. Partly it was the influence of lay patrons of music, as the Church had now lost its virtual, pre-civil war monopoly on the commissioning of music. Partly it was simply the evolution of musical style. It is associated particularly with Henry Purcell, another product of the Chapel Royal, where he sang as a boy and was taught by John Blow and Christopher Gibbons, son of Orlando, and was himself later organist. Purcell's originality and immense talent was evident almost from the beginning. In his short life, compositions for the Church and for secular audiences poured out of him, but in a style distinctly different from many of his precursors, and drawing on new methods of harmony and instrumentation. Now anthems could expand into dramatic sequences of varying tempo and intensity, with soloists and chorus in dialogue. If he was the standout musician of his age, Purcell was not alone in his commitment to writing music for the Anglican service: his brother or cousin Daniel Purcell, John Blow himself, Pelham Humfrey and others composed music sung in cathedrals into the eighteenth century.

But this was still music of the 'high' or 'art' tradition, requiring highly trained singers and instrumentalists. There were steps in the late eighteenth century to adopt this style of music in some parish churches, and new anthems, canticle settings and responses continued to be produced throughout the period. In order to sing them, choirs were sometimes organised from the scholars of local charity schools, or engaged from local singers. But the achievements of these parish choirs were limited. Theirs was not the music most ordinary congregations heard or sang. The staple remained simply the metrical psalms. In some churches in the late seventeenth and eighteenth centuries, simple settings of the responses were also used, with the parish clerk singing the versicles, the opening sentences to which the responses of the congregation replied. The psalms were accompanied by a number of additional songs, a few of which have survived in common use, including the carol 'While Shepherds Watched Their Flocks by Night', sung to the melody 'Winchester Old', which goes back to the late sixteenth century.

By the nineteenth century, church reformers saw this metrical psalm tradition as dreary and shambolic. Their belief was reinforced by the rise of the choir band, or 'west gallery' music. Rather than relying on the clerk to lead the whole congregation, a small group of singers might be formed as a choir, standing usually in one of the galleries, commonly the west gallery, supported often by a group of instrumentalists playing the fiddle, a couple of wind instruments and some brass, and sometimes by a small organ. The disappearance of this west gallery music as a consequence of nineteenth-century musical reform is still significantly under-researched. But some local studies have suggested that at least half of parishes might have had some variant of it in the late eighteenth and early nineteenth centuries.[7] And there are good grounds for questioning the condescension of a later period. There was little overlap between west gallery music and the cathedral style. In many places, if not most, the choir and band would have played at secular gatherings and celebrations as well as in church, and probably few of the performers could read music; theirs was almost certainly a practice based on oral tradition and on families of amateur music-makers – 'Like country dialects, it was assimilated through upbringing and exposure.'[8]

It is impossible to know how exactly they performed, but recent scholarship has suggested affinities with other 'folk' performance, with loud voices, a high nasal tone and musical interludes between verses which were like (and probably drew on) popular dance tunes. This was music not just for church, but for taking out of the church building at funerals, for example, and for social occasions.[9] It blurred the line between secular use and religious use – indeed, that was one of the objections later raised against it. But it has a good claim to be a genuinely popular form of church music, even a 'plebeian' one counter-posed to the 'high' art tradition of the cathedrals, and it did not depend on the importation of trained experts from outside the community to organise and lead musicians.

Its suppression in the nineteenth century highlighted a growing division between elements of popular culture and the middle-class, professional values of the modern Church. We have seen already how the Reformers aspired to a learned clergy and encouraged education, and how the growing assimilation of the clergy to the culture and living standards of the gentry in the late seventeenth and eighteenth centuries placed them as a profession apart from the social horizons of the labouring poor. The musical revolution about to come upon the Church in the nineteenth century was to emphasise how church music had to be distinct and different from that of the home – even the middle-class home, let alone the cottages and taverns of the labouring poor. But in this, unfortunately, it only served to widen the already existing gap between ecclesiastical culture and popular culture. Not until the late twentieth century, when many Evangelical churches adopted rock, jazz and pop music, was the gap to be narrowed again.

Perhaps the most striking feature of the age was the popu-larity of the religious oratorio, the pattern set by the success of George Frideric Handel. Handel wrote some church music, principally for the Chapel Royal, Westminster Abbey and St

Paul's, but it is probably for *Messiah* (first performed in 1742) that he was best known even in his lifetime. Following his influence, amateur singing in local choral societies provided another opportunity for church musicians. Oratorios became a staple, for example, of the Three Choirs Festival, founded in 1715 for the choirs of Hereford, Worcester and Gloucester cathedrals. The other great stream of innovation in eighteenth-century music was the hymn. The initiative here lay in Dissenting chapels, not Anglican churches. The hymns of the early eighteenth-century Independent minister Isaac Watts stand out particularly. To his work and that of others must be added the extraordinary body of hymnody of Charles Wesley. But many Anglican clergy rather frowned on popular hymn singing, and considered it brought indiscipline and excess into worship.

The Choral Revival of the Nineteenth Century

Yet church music was caught up in religious renewal in the nineteenth century. It is too simplistic to use contrasting labels of 'Evangelical' and 'Tractarian'. We find High Churchmen who were not Tractarians supporting the reform of church music, Evangelicals sharing, if not the enthusiasm for surpliced choirs and Gregorian chant of the Tractarians, none the less a desire to make church music orderly and efficient, and so on. But pressure for reform did intensify in the 1830s and 1840s, and is especially associated with the High Church revival.[10] The 'beauty of holiness', the mark of High Church aesthetics, spread into music.

The aim of these reformers could be summed up in a single word – 'reverence'. The accusation that popular metrical psalmsinging, the west gallery music, and even the charity school choirs were 'irreverent' was a constant refrain in reformers' description of parish music. They wanted orderliness, restraint, attentiveness to the words and mystery of worship, a harmonious and clean sound, and a clear distance from the more raucous style of secular singing. The Tractarian clergyman William Bennett claimed,

> There is hardly a church in our country ... where there
> seems any degree of command or self-restraint ... All seem
> to do just what they please – say what they like, sing what
> they like ... without any rule, and without any principle.[11]

Choral reform was about spiritual renewal, through discipline, obedience and attentiveness in worship. It required not only a raising of general standards (according, that is, to 'high art' ideals), with all the education and training that implied, but a change in the nature of the music itself.

The choral revival was a concerted movement drawing on the energy and vision of a number of talented musicians, the foundation of new institutions for the promotion of music, and a minor industry of scholarship and publication. It was aided by the development of a national system of education, since music became firmly rooted in schools and training establishments as an adjunct to the curriculum. Government funding, for example, was behind the wildly popular massed singing classes organised by John Hullah at Exeter Hall in London from 1841 to 1843. The appointment in 1842 of Thomas Helmore, clergyman and musician, to the new Anglican foundation of St Mark's College, Chelsea, a teacher training institution with its own chapel, was instrumental. Helmore introduced daily choral services, with a choir singing a wide repertoire, including works by Tallis, Byrd and Gibbons, as well by more recent composers. A little later, in 1856, Sir Frederick Ouseley founded St Michael's College, Tenbury, as a school especially aimed at teaching choral and instrumental music, with choral services daily in the chapel, in order to furnish, as its statutes said, 'a model for the choral service of the Church in these realms'.[12] As a boarding school, St Michael's was aimed at the children of the middle classes, striking out in a new direction from the cathedrals which relied on local boys.[13]

The Society for Promoting Church Music, instituted in 1846 by Robert Druitt, High Churchman, doctor and enthusiastic musician, provided a national organisation for choral renewal.

25. A school for music: St Michael's, Tenbury

Its journal, *The Parish Choir*, disseminated news about the changes clergy and musicians were putting into place up and down the country, but also supplied a rolling portfolio of church music: rather like modern magazines that include parts of the very model or artefact that the magazine itself is promoting, so subscription to *The Parish Choir* over five years furnished a complete, basic repertoire for a modest parish church choir.

The momentum generated by the revival is reflected in the roll call of talented musicians it attracted, among others: Thomas Helmore himself; his brother Frederick, who worked as an itinerant choir trainer and was nicknamed the 'musical missionary'; Frederick Ouseley; the organist and composer Samuel Sebastian Wesley, who is particularly remembered as one of the first masters of the introduction of a cathedral-style choir at a parish church in Leeds; another organist and composer, Thomas Attwood Walmisley, who transformed the choirs of Trinity and

St John's Colleges in Cambridge; and John Stainer, composer, student of Ouseley and organist at Magdalen College, Oxford and St Paul's.[14] Later still was Charles Villiers Stanford, composer, and academic, whose settings of the canticles remain among the most popular works in the choral repertoire today.[15]

So what were the innovations of the revival? In summary, reformers aimed to apply the cathedral model in a parish setting. Not *all* of the features of cathedral music could be used indiscriminately. There was a particular division among reformers themselves over the place of plainsong or plainchant. The common standard in cathedrals was what is called Anglican chant, the singing of the psalms (not metrical psalms) to three- or four-part harmonies; this was adopted by many parishes. But congregation members could not realistically join in, just as they could not join in the responses and the canticle settings. So some reformers advocated the use of Gregorian plainchant, adapted to English texts: the simplicity of the single line closely matched to text in theory made this much more suitable for congregational singing. But in practice successful plainchant requires a discipline, restraint and musicality difficult to achieve with an ordinary congregation, and it never really caught on at parish level.

Almost by default, choral reform fell into the 'cathedral' style of the choir singing and the congregation listening. The choir would be surpliced, it would be placed in the chancel or sanctuary, in rows facing each other, usually trebles in the front row, other voices behind them. They might process in, perhaps singing an opening hymn, and out again at the end. The choirs were almost invariably composed of men and boys, not women and girls. The belief that boys' voices were purer than girls – a belief roundly exposed as false by more recent experience – and perhaps a lingering view that the attentive, restrained 'reverence' of male choirs would not suit the temperament of women – another plainly erroneous opinion – kept women and girls out of church choirs until quite late in the nineteenth century.

There were other innovations. Although much of the

repertoire was really for Matins and Evensong, which remained the most popular services in Anglican parish churches until well into the twentieth century, there were determined attempts to produce and adapt music for accompanying the communion service. At last John Marbeck's adapted plainchant for the English service came into common use.

All of these innovations required the suppression of the choir–band tradition of music-making. In most churches the only instrument used to accompany choirs became the organ. The irregular, loud, assertive, high-voiced style of singing went out completely, to be replaced by the formalised, restrained, even-toned voices associated with the singing of church music in four-part harmonies. Congregational participation remained minimal. What we think of as choral Evensong, that much-vaunted glorious tradition of historic Anglicanism, is, at least in parish churches, really a product of nineteenth-century revival.

There was a definite loss in this. Just as the exclusion of the plebeian tradition of church music widened the expressive gulf religiously between middle-class culture and that of the labouring poor, so the highly specialised, trained surpliced choir reflected a definite shift in the liturgical place and role of music in church, from being a collective articulation of the participation and religious aspirations of the people to being part of the paraphernalia of the new, High Church clerical ideal. Placed in the sanctuary or chancel, choirs were physically separated from the congregation and identified more closely with the clergy. They wore a special dress, namely cassocks and white surplices, which were also shared with the clergy. They were conceived as providing music *for* the people, rather than music *of* the people.

There was, however, one very important exception – the absorption of hymn-singing into mainstream Anglican worship. Congregational hymns were, as we have seen, particularly popular in Dissenting chapels. Some Anglican churches followed suit by continuing to use metrical psalms before and after the service, even when also chanting psalms during the service. But under the influence of High Church interest in the early

26. Giant of the choral revival: Thomas Helmore

centuries of the Christian Church, and in the Latin worship of medieval Christendom, some choral reformers wanted to use Latin hymns and songs – even relatively modern ones, from Catholic sources. This touched acutely on sensitivity about 'Popery', however, and it was easier to provide English translations that could match harmonised adaptation of the plainchant melodies. So favourites such as 'O Come, O Come, Emmanuel' – the music adapted by Thomas Helmore – came into use. But settings of modern texts – from Keble's *Christian Year*, for example – were also adopted, and others borrowed from further afield, from the Wesleys, Watts and other Dissenting writers.

Many books were produced in the mid-nineteenth century, but the publication in 1861 of the first edition of *Hymns Ancient and Modern*, edited by the composer and organist William Henry Monk, was a watershed. It was a runaway bestseller, having the tunes and harmonies on the same page as the text, and organised into sections to match the liturgical year. At last parish churches had a single book which combined popular hymns from an eclectic variety of traditions with the best of modern settings and modern texts, alongside the riches of the past. In hymn-singing, choir and people could join in together. With many melodies, and some texts, already popular in the 'plebeian' tradition of religious music (even if performed somewhat differently), the practice of hymn-singing was the one aspect of the choral revival that joined old and new local church traditions. The proof, perhaps, is in the way some hymns have outlasted their church contexts, becoming anthems for football and rugby matches, tunes for military brass bands to play, and carols for street singing and school concerts.

It is hard to credit just how quickly the new model of choir took root. Within two generations controversy about surpliced choirs had died down, and the pattern of choral Matins and Evensong adapted from cathedrals had settled into its groove. The speed of change was aided by the reform of theological education for clergy and the foundation of new theological colleges. It was always difficult to sustain a full choir in a small, far-flung parish church, but most churches had a choir by the beginning of the twentieth century, and, to an extent that would have seemed unimaginable fifty years before, there was a common choral culture – chanted psalms, hymns, sung responses, canticles and anthems, and organ voluntaries before and after the service.

Ironically, change was not so evident in the cathedrals, colleges and greater churches. Partly this was because they already had in place many key elements of this choral culture, but partly it was because the main challenge facing them was not so much innovation as improving standards. Here, the obstacle was usually the paucity of financial resources available, though it was sometimes also the obduracy of the clergy. In many of these choirs the adult parts – alto, tenor, bass – were sung by poorly paid lay clerks, who supplemented their income by other employment, had no pension provision and were often

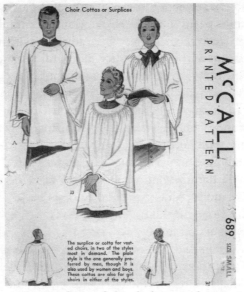

Choir Cottas or Surplices

The surplice or cotta for vested choirs, in two of the styles
most in demand. The plain
style is the one generally preferred by men, though it is
also used by women and boys.
These cottas are also for girl
choirs in either of the styles.

27. The popularity of church choirs: make-your-
own choir surplice patterns, 1930s

poorly trained in the first place. Arrangements for recruiting
and training trebles varied, but commonly again they often had
little musical education or, recruited from a few local families,
were of variable quality. But there were none the less champi-
ons of revival and improvement who managed to achieve great
things in the cathedrals, with the right combination of ability,
resources and clerical support. Stainer, for example, had a vital
impact on the music at St Paul's, aided by a particularly sympathetic dean in the form of the Tractarian Richard Church and by
the cathedral chapter.[16] And he was not alone.

Consolidation, Decline, Experiment

In the early twentieth century choral music experienced probably its greatest period of consolidation and flourishing, before
the winds of change swept over it and changed dramatically its

context and character.[17] A lively culture of amateur musician-
ship sustained parish worship. The Church's near-monopoly
of funerals, weddings and baptisms, as well as its historic and
civic prominence, gave the Anglican choral service a powerful hold on Christian life in Britain, which it retained until long
after the Second World War. Further elements of consolidation
were the publication of the *English Hymnal* in 1906, edited by
Percy Dearmer and Ralph Vaughan Williams, with its move
away from *Hymns Ancient and Modern*'s Victorianising adapta-
tions of pre-nineteenth-century music and its use of many folk
melodies, and the foundation of the School of Church Music
by Sydney Nicholson in 1927 (later renamed the Royal School of
Church Music, or RSCM), as a resource and training institute for
choir directors and organists.

There were also new currents of composition. If this chapter
so far has given the impression that English church music was *sui
generis*, an isolated national tradition, that of course was never
wholly true. It was never completely detached from wider, continental trends. Composers like Vaughan Williams, Gustav Holst
and Edmund Rubbra wrote music for church use, but with their
grounding in the development of a different tonal landscape from
a previous generation, they fused the established choral forms
to new, innovative musical languages. Later composers such as
Benjamin Britten, Kenneth Leighton and William Matthias went
even further. Church music was a small part of their output.
Another was Herbert Howells, whose works for churches form
a major part of his output, but who also wrote ambitious secular
pieces. There were many others who worked as cathedral organists and choir directors but also composed almost exclusively
for performance in church. Something of an outlier was John
Tavener, most of whose music has an overtly religious dimension, even if not always specifically for a church context.

The new technology of broadcasting and recording helped
to sustain the national and international profile of English
church music into the twenty-first century. The BBC first broadcast its weekly 'Choral Evensong' in 1926; it has been almost

continuously in production since then. The runaway broadcasting success was carols from King's College, Cambridge. First
transmitted on Christmas Eve on radio in 1928, the 'Festival of
Nine Lessons and Carols' quickly established itself as almost a
national institution, followed later by the televised programme
'Carols from King's'. The advent of the LP, then CD, then digital
recording brought the highest quality of choral music into the
home.

All this helped to make the reputations of the new kinds
of choral ensemble that were established from the 1960s and
1970s to sing church music in a concert setting – Scola Cantorum
of Oxford (formed 1960), the Tallis Scholars (1973), the Sixteen
(1977), to name but a few. Many of these ensembles recruited
from the chapel choirs of Oxford and Cambridge, as well as
from other university chapels. By the beginning of the twenty-
first century, most Oxbridge colleges had adopted a full, mixed
choir singing choral Evensong and other services, and even
appointed professional musicians as directors of music. The
reasons for this are many, but clearly the opening up of male
colleges to women from the 1970s made the creation of balanced, high-achieving, mixed choirs possible across the ancient
universities to a degree inconceivable years before. Incidentally,
a parallel process was at work in many cathedrals and greater
churches, where girls' choirs were often formed alongside the
traditional boys' choirs – Salisbury was first, in 1991 – to sing the
same pattern of service.

But just as the Anglican choral tradition was, through
broadcasting and recording, reaching a wider audience than
ever, parish church choirs began to struggle. The inescapable
reason is the decline of organised religion in Britain, and especially of attendance in the mainstream denominations. The pool
of youth from whom many parish choirs hoped to recruit was
shrinking rapidly by the 1980s. At the same time, the liturgical heart of the Anglican choral tradition, the *Book of Common
Prayer*, was being displaced. Liturgical revision not only modernised the language of worship but changed or replaced many

of its texts. Traditional settings of the responses became redundant. Psalters had to be revised. But in any case, the influence of the Liturgical Movement in England, as elsewhere, encouraged the marginalisation of morning and evening prayer, and the reinstatement of Holy Communion, or the eucharist, as the main Sunday service.[18] In other words, the very pattern of worship for which the vast majority of Anglican choral music had been written had changed dramatically by the end of the century. It was perfectly possible to produce new music for the new services, but the changing context of worship strained parish musical resources just at the point when many churches were finding it harder and harder to keep choirs going.

This was one – but just one – of the reasons why many churches began to look elsewhere for music from the 1960s. If a choir was unsustainable, and it was proving difficult even to find a competent organist, then some palatable alternative had to be found. Some parishes relied on taped accompaniment to hymns and abandoned other musical input. But under the combined influence of the charismatic movement and the exponential growth of pop culture, many churches instead began to experiment with a completely different approach, adopting electric guitars and synthesisers, even a complete rock band, to sing songs and choruses which were much closer to rock or pop music than to anything else previously sung in churches. Screens on which the lyrics of worship songs could be broadcast even took the physical place of the choir sometimes. The BBC's Sunday television programme, *Songs of Praise*, has charted the history of the change since its first broadcast in 1961.

Other influences that cut right across traditional church music included the contemplative, simple music of the Iona community, and the repetitive, tuneful chanting pioneered at the Taizé community in Burgundy. Through Christian youth and family festivals such as Greenbelt (begun 1974) and Spring Harvest (1979), a vibrant Christian pop and jazz music scene came into being. This was clearly part of a wider cultural change. The fall in churchgoing, the decline in traditional school assemblies, the collapse of Sunday Schools, the loss of basic Christian knowledge even among those born into ostensibly Christian families – all implied a rapidly deepening unfamiliarity and discomfort with much of the music of the Anglican choral tradition. Paradoxically, it is argued that the cathedrals and greater churches may have retained or even grown their congregations precisely because of the collapse of traditional music and liturgy in many parish churches.[19]

Another important development underlining this shift away from a sort of musical monoculture towards the end of the century was the growing impact of Gospel choirs, both within Anglicanism and outside it. Here the vital factor was the growing cultural, ethnic and religious diversity of British society. Nothing signalled this better, perhaps, than the enthronement of Archbishop Justin Welby in Canterbury cathedral in 2013: along with traditional hymns and anthems and Benjamin Britten's *Te Deum* in C were sung a Punjabi hymn and a Ghanaian chant accompanied by African drumming. By the turn of the twenty-first century, it was impossible to know for certain what musical tradition you would find at any one parish church, so great was the musical diversity within the Church of England. In the cathedrals, college chapels, greater churches, and still in a significant number of parish churches, the model of choral music established in the nineteenth century continued to flourish, albeit with greater difficulty in recruitment. But elsewhere, no common pattern could be discerned, except that it could be said that overall the last fifty years had marked a progressive movement away from the assumption that 'reverence' required something different from popular secular music. There were obviously gains and losses in this.

15

LIBERALISM

By the middle of the nineteenth century, the Church of England was not so much one theological tradition, however vehemently various factions in the Church might shout aloud for their own convictions, but a composite body in which a variety of positions competed for the moral high ground. To outsiders it may have looked and felt like a mighty religious engine, confident of its status and authority, deeply embedded in the governing structures and the social elites of England and Wales, and assured of its wealth and political influence. But those outsiders could hardly ever agree on what it actually was, or whereabouts in the spectrum of Christian belonging it sat. To Roman Catholics, it was a Protestant, State church, the progeny of schism and individualism. To Protestant Nonconformists, despite affinities with Anglican Evangelicalism, it was a hair's breadth away from Rome, its liturgy, order of ministry and cathedrals testimony to an incomplete Reformation, and a State church unfairly privileged and set on eliminating other traditions. Both of these perspectives were to some extent correct. But whatever its origins as a unified State church, Anglicanism had become a hybrid tradition. Both Evangelicals and High Churchmen could claim with some justification that the history of the Church of England validated their own position.

Into the seemingly sterile conflict of High and Low, however, a third term began to be introduced by the middle of the century – Liberalism, or the 'Broad Church'. The credit for this term is generally laid at the door of William Conybeare, who wrote an article for the *Edinburgh Review* in 1853 on the subject of 'Church parties'. Conybeare was not of course celebrating Anglican sociability, but analysing the division of the Church of England into distinct groups, each with its own theological position, national figures, publications and even organisations, like political parties. His method was Aristotelian: he identified the essence of a position, drawing on supposed empirical evidence to demonstrate its relative strength, and then described its radical and conservative extremes. No one can have been surprised by his account of the Low and High traditions – by then the conflict of the two, intensified by the Oxford Movement, was notorious. It was his delineation of the 'Broad Church' that gained attention, not least because it was the position he himself celebrated as most distinctly 'Anglican': 'Its distinctive character is the desire of comprehension. Its watchwords are Charity and Toleration.'[1]

But the idea of a nineteenth-century 'myth of origins' for Liberalism is somewhat misleading. The central predicament of Anglican Liberalism was, and has always remained, the paradox that Christianity is a historical religion, rooted in a particular historical revelation in a given time and given place, loaded with all the time-specific assumptions that that particular context has given it (just think about the assumptions historic Christianity made about human sexuality, about disability, about gender roles, about slavery, to name but a few ...), and yet it is professed and articulated in the language and thought forms of a constantly evolving social reality. That is a predicament – or perhaps I should say simply a necessary feature – of all religions that claim to have a particular historical foundation. It may not have been described in the terms we would apply today, but the problem of trying to find new language to explain and adapt older ideas goes right back to the earliest centuries of the Christian Church.

The religious Liberalism of the nineteenth century had antecedents not just in the general awareness of this central predicament, the cultural clothing, of Christianity, but in certain specific attempts to reinterpret the faith in response to contemporary challenges. In particular, Anglicans could look to antecedents in the previous two centuries, to the theologians and church leaders of the English religious Enlightenment who had begun to address critical historical questions about the Bible and about the history of the Church. In the seventeenth century, members of the Great Tew Circle around Lord Falkland before the civil wars, later the circle of the Cambridge Platonists, later still into the eighteenth century those who were called 'Latitu-dinarians', were all claimed as precursors. But the issues they had grappled with were very different in scope and intensity from the challenges of the nineteenth century. The particu-lar focus of much earlier discussion had been on the extent to which particular church doctrines or features of church order were, or were not, essential to Christian faith as it was professed by the Church of England. The label 'Latitudinarian' had come to be applied to those who emphasised the category of 'things indifferent', or, in the commonly used Greek term, *adiaphora*, to draw the limits of the established Church wider than some of their more 'orthodox' or conservative High Church rivals were prepared to do.

But by the nineteenth century, the challenges of new criti-cal approaches to philology, to texts, to the history of religion and culture, and even to science, were becoming much more serious for Christian belief. The most famous of these chal-lenges was that of the new evolutionary biology pioneered by Charles Darwin and Alfred Wallace, and endorsed by the geol-ogist Chares Lyell. But although the resulting conflict between Darwinian theory and conventional Christian accounts of the origin and development of life – especially the various narratives of creation in Genesis – has captured the popular imagination, actually by far the more pressing challenges to conventional belief were those presented by critical study of the historical formation and context of the Biblical texts, or, as it was called at the time, the 'higher' criticism (the 'lower' criticism being the more technical study of the language of the texts).

The 'lower' criticism mostly could sit comfortably with orthodox beliefs about Biblical truth and inspiration: close study of the Biblical texts might elucidate new elements of meaning, or demonstrate seemingly hidden connections and parallels, without fundamentally challenging the conventional understanding of Biblical truth. Erasmus of Rotterdam, in the sixteenth century, could be described in nineteenth-century terms as a 'lower' critic, questioning the received Latin text of the New Testament, the Vulgate. Yet Erasmus died a faithful Catholic. It was much harder to sustain an orthodox faith when the verisimilitude of the Biblical narrative itself was at stake. Although British critics had been ahead of the game in the early eighteenth century, by the nineteenth century it was German Protestant scholarship that was doing the running.

Many of the Germans' arguments would come to seem crude or obvious to later generations of scholars. Had Moses really written all of the first five books of the Old Testament, the Pentateuch? Why then were there no less than three different creation stories in Genesis? Why were different words used for God – Yahweh in some places, Elohim in others – in these texts, if they were all apparently written by the same hand? Why did there seem to be discrepancies between different accounts of the origins of the Jewish law? And turning to the New Testament, isn't it obvious that the thought world of the fourth gospel, John's Gospel, is radically different from that of the other three gospels, and that its narrative is different at key points? Why are there significant differences, none the less, even between the gospels of Mark, Matthew and Luke? Don't they suggest, not the *literal* truth of texts divinely inspired, but rather the perfectly natural and predictable variations in accounts of the same founding events that arise when different authors, from different perspectives, try to account for what they have seen and heard in their own terms?

These and other such questions pose no problems at all for modern Biblical critics, who are perfectly comfortable with the assumption that the Biblical texts were the products of the human imagination, albeit (as they may suppose) written by authors inspired by what they had seen, heard and experienced in, for example, the witness and life of Jesus Christ. To suppose that the Biblical texts were written by human authors, inspired but not infallible, and therefore somewhat at variance, is perfectly compatible with the assumption that none the less they convey vital truths of faith. But Christians can think that today largely because, in the nineteenth century, orthodox believers confronted the radical challenge of higher criticism, and in a sense faced it down, showing they were unafraid of its implications.

As it eventually turned out, then, Christianity did not necessarily have much to fear from close analysis of the historical context and literary construction of the Bible. But at the time, such a conclusion seemed wildly optimistic and dangerously complacent. Near the beginning of the century the poet and thinker Samuel Taylor Coleridge, best known today as author of 'The Rime of the Ancient Mariner', and as an opium addict, but who deserves greater popular recognition as a religious and philosophical thinker of genuine depth and originality, wrote a passionate and lucid defence of the principle of reading the Bible as literature (in other words, just like any other literature) because, as he believed, doing so would reveal the intrinsic merit – the exalted inspiration – of the Biblical text. But Coleridge realised that his *Confessions of an Enquiring Spirit* (1840) could not be published in his lifetime; his thoughts were too heretical. Coleridge's instinct on this matter was astute. Whatever the complexities of English religious and intellectual life – and they were great – the sheer success of the Evangelical and High Church revivals in the first half of the nineteenth century ensured that the Church of England would be, on the whole, barren land for critical, historical analysis of the Bible, at least at first. As a consequence, Liberals and 'Broad' churchmen, were generally regarded by others as dangerously loose rationalists, insecure in their hold on Christian orthodoxy and likely to undermine the faith of ordinary people.

Liberalism and Establishment

All this was ironic, for the truth is that most Anglican Liberals were – and probably still are – quite conservative. On the whole they were not arguing for the dissolution of traditional Christianity. They were certainly not the rationalists their opponents accused them of being. It was possible to claim their intellectual system was essentially parasitic: they assumed the basic truth and continuing relevance of historic Christianity, but then poured all their energy and passion into positions which modified, adjusted, limited or arguably undermined traditional ideas of faith. To their contemporaries, then, it looked as if all their work was set deliberately to undermine the simple faith of ordinary people. The most pointed criticism of them was probably that they, as educated, privileged, middle-class people (as they were in the main) did not care what effects their arguments might have on faithful Christians: they put their intellectual presuppositions ahead of their pastoral and spiritual concerns. So it was alleged, anyway. But this was neither true nor just. Liberal or 'Broad Church' arguments were eminently pastoral in intent. The whole point of trying to reinterpret traditional faith for the contemporary era – as Liberal Anglicans saw it – was precisely to make it relevant, to bring people to see how important it was for their moral and spiritual well-being that they laid hold properly of the truth of faith, and not of some empty, repetitive formula repeated mindlessly from age to age. Liberals did not want to undermine the Church of England but to strengthen it, to expand it, to make it once again a church that could encompass all the people of England.

This was, after all, the goal of Thomas Arnold's *Principles of Church Reform*, which, as we saw earlier, argued for the radical alteration of the Church's formularies so that Trinitarian Dissenters could once again enter the national Church. But Arnold's proposal was so radical it was not followed directly by many Anglicans. Its significance above all lay not so much in its actual, practical content – it was not until late in the twentieth century that Anglicans and Free Churchmen (as Dissenters were increasingly called by the late nineteenth century), partly from necessity, partly from idealism, began to consider how they might share buildings and conceive of a future, reunited church – as in the underlying theological argument. Arnold was not prepared to see as church-dividing many of the doctrinal principles about which his contemporaries argued: they were of relative importance only, for him. The Church of England should state broad principles and preach a simple gospel, so that as many people as possible might follow its teachings and find their spiritual and pastoral home within it.

All of this may sound attractive today, when Christians sometimes have a bad name for dogmatism. But the position Arnold represented was intrinsically conservative. In effect, he prioritised the political status of Anglicanism. He wanted to uphold the Anglican establishment, to continue its close association with political order, and to support and defend its relationship with the ruling elites – and he assumed that Anglicanism simply *was* the religious expression of historic English national identity. Broad Churchmen generally followed suit. In an age of Romantic nationalism, they emphasised the 'Englishness' of the Church of England – a cultural and even racial concept about which they were happy to be somewhat flexible, expanding it to include the Welsh and the Irish as it suited them.

The most creative, but also elusive, expression of this apparent 'fit' between English nationalism and Anglicanism was the theology of F. D. Maurice.[2] Maurice was, after John Henry Newman, arguably the most innovative Anglican theologian of his age. In his most famous and influential work, *The Kingdom of Christ* (1842), he assumed the Church of England, for all its faults, was the essence of the Christian Church as it was to be found in England: all other Christian traditions, by comparison, fell short. But he was not narrow-minded. He did not think Anglicans, and Anglicanism, perfect. Nor did he think other Christian traditions (and indeed other faith traditions) valueless: they contended, he believed, for important positive principles in their different ways, and these positive principles were important for a reunited Christian Church.[3]

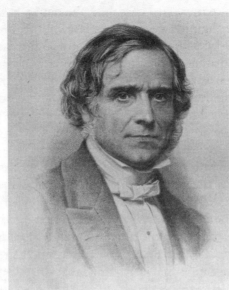

28. The gentleness of moderation: F. D. Maurice

Maurice was the first great theologian of the modern ecumenical movement, the movement for Christian unity. He genuinely believed Christians of different traditions could move closer together if they studied each other's belief and practices sympathetically. But he also believed in a strong association of Church and nation. He practically divinised them, along with the family, as part of a 'divine order' established by God on earth, though expressed in myriad different ways in history.[4] Nations thus had for Maurice a quasi-providential aspect: national identity was an important step in realising on earth the divine ordering of humanity. Maurice's argument, while not presuming some sort of practical reorganisation on Arnoldian lines, did imply that the Church of England was in essence the true Church of Christ (in England and Wales), and that its mission was to draw back together the separated branches of Christianity. Once again, the effect was to reinforce the national Church argument: there must be a church of the nation to provide for, preserve and religiously promote the community of the nation.

Maurice's theological project was remarkably complex and sophisticated, and it is difficult to do justice to it in a few sentences. It was also difficult to appreciate in his own age. He inspired strong opinions, for or against, but there were enough who read him with interest to ensure he was a powerful and influential voice in Victorian debates. We could summarise his contrast with Arnold this way. Arnold thought the national Church could be made truly comprehensive again by a structural rearrangement that would enable different churches to come under its umbrella. Maurice thought that structural arrangements of this kind were utterly useless unless undergirded by a genuine, mutual theological sympathy and convergence. The Church of England needed to realise its national vocation fully, to articulate properly the way in which its worship and practice were themselves already sufficient to draw back the separated or disillusioned, if only Anglicans could become truly or fully themselves. It may sound a wishy-washy or vague aspiration, and so it has seemed to many of his critics, but for some it was an inspiring vision of Anglicanism as an inclusive community of believers.

Except in a few cases, we do not know how much ordinary clergy were inspired by reading Maurice to express similar convictions about the national Church. But we can certainly find practical clergymen who put a vision of the Church of England as the national Church at the centre of their ministry. The Liberal or 'Broad Church' idea of the national Church was unquestionably irritating for the Free Churches, and for Roman Catholics. It seemed to them to align the intellectual, political and social elite with a State church they often experienced as oppressive and dismissive. But it proved enormously influential. It made Liberal Anglicans much more vulnerable to contemporary ideas of nationalism and even, in a few cases, racial distinctiveness than were Evangelicals or High Churchmen. Charles Kingsley, the novelist, clergyman and disciple of Maurice, for example, resorted to racial stereotypes and myths to justify his support for British forces in imperial conflicts such as the Indian Mutiny and the Opium War.[5] Evangelicals put the saving of souls first: they were not immune to the cultural assumptions of their day (who is?), but there was an essential, reductive egalitarianism in their ideas of salvation – all had fallen short, all needed saving. High Churchmen were suspicious of the claims to authority of the State, and often suspicious of ideas of cultural superiority: for them, the Church had an independent, spiritual authority all of its own, and that trumped all ideas of secular political community.

And yet the idea of the national Church proved to be resilient and long-lasting. Its greatest advocate was probably William Temple, the dominant Anglican personality of the mid-twentieth century. The son of an archbishop, Temple was born and raised a Victorian, and nineteenth-century battles over the nature and limits of the national Church were never far from his mind. The idea of the Church of England as a church for *all* the English people found a particularly persuasive voice in him, in the crisis years of the 1930s and the Second World War, not least because he always saw its mission as essentially social as well as religious, expanding the reach of the Church to encompass all those on the margins of society, as well as at its centre. But his debt to the nineteenth-century idea was immense.

Doctrine and Faith

The really controversial dimension of Anglican Liberalism did not concern its political theory, but its religious content. Anglican Liberals found themselves committed to doctrinal revision across a wide spectrum of belief. They were aided, unintentionally, by the very attempts of the episcopal hierarchy, and the courts, to rein in more extreme positions from Evangelical and Anglo-Catholic wings of the Church. So internal Anglican argument only helped to consolidate the position of the controversial Liberals, because it made all attempts to argue that 'such and such' a view was the only authentic Anglican position unsafe.

The most testing challenge to traditional doctrine came from new approaches to the ideas of heaven and hell.[6] Popular preaching – especially, but not exclusively, in the Evangelical tradition – dwelt on the risks of a life lived without conscious attachment to faith. Neglect of the moral law risked the eternal salvation of the person. The alternative to eternal salvation, and eternal bliss, was eternal damnation and everlasting pain. Popular evangelists loved to dwell on the risks of non-believing, whether it was an actual repudiation of belief or a practical indifference or neglect that underpinned wrong actions. As a result, popular preachers were easily cast as cynical manipulators of human emotion, playing on people's vulnerabilities to threaten and cajole people into church. Such a view unfairly distorts their sincerity: they were undoubtedly motivated by a genuine concern for the saving of souls. But the effect of their preaching, as F. D. Maurice and others pointed out, was to turn Christianity into a system of rewards and punishments, enforced alternately by bribes and threats: act well and great would be your reward in heaven; act badly and Satan and all his torments were waiting for you. Faith was not about the here and now so much as the future state, after death. And what did all this say about God? God, it seemed, was not the loving God of the New Testament but a willing inflictor of eternal pain.

To many Anglicans, this was a travesty of the Gospel. It turned the loving Father of Jesus into a sadistic monster. Wasn't the Father the source of all life and love? Maurice, for example, claimed eternal life was not – for Jesus – a future, post-death condition alone but began in the here and now.[7] The kingdom of God was now. Eternal punishment was not inflicted deliberately by God as a penalty, but simply the consequence of a determined, human refusal to seize on faith. Hell, in other words, was the turning away from God; human beings were the agents of their own fall and judgment. This view, which has become commonplace in modern theology, was heterodox enough to cost

29. Benjamin Jowett, editor of *Essays and Reviews*, 1860

Maurice his chair of theology at King's College, London, in 1853.[8] Nearly twenty-five years later Frederic Farrar, a canon of Westminster famous for a somewhat sentimental *Life of Christ* (1874) and an equally sentimental school tale, *Eric, or, Little by Little* (1858), preached a similar doctrine in Westminster Abbey and still provoked criticism and controversy. His *Eternal Hope* (1878) emphasised the moral force of objections to the idea of eternal punishment. Theologians like Maurice and Farrar were responding to the pastoral anxieties of sincere churchgoers offended by the fire-and-brimstone preaching of popular evangelists, and there is evidence that their views helped to reconcile uneasy consciences to the Church. But others were less impressed. The writer Molly Hughes, for example, had an erratic, fault-finding aunt whose religious views fluctuated between Nonconformity and extreme High Church, but never embraced the Broad Church, 'where, Mary dear, they do not believe in Hell'.[9]

By far the greatest controversy over the advance of the 'higher criticism' was triggered by a volume of essays that appeared just a year after Darwin's *On the Origin of Species*. *Essays and Reviews* (1860) was edited by Benjamin Jowett, Fellow of Balliol and classical scholar, who had assembled a group of writers to illustrate 'the advantage derivable to the cause of religious and moral truth, from a free handling, in a becoming spirit, of subjects peculiarly liable to suffer by the repetition of conventional language'.[10] Beneath that leaden Victorian prose was an alarming idea. The term 'free handling' threatened the accepted authority of traditional approaches. It was exactly calculated to infuriate High Churchmen and Evangelicals suspicious that 'private judgment' was being set against the authority of the Church and the Bible. All of the essays in the volume professed to be defending Christianity by adapting its presentation to the needs and challenges of the day. Even just thirty years later, such views would seem uncontroversial. But at the time they were profoundly shocking.

To give just one example, in his essay on 'The National Church', Henry Bristow Wilson freely admitted that there were considerable difficulties in the way of reconciling the picture of Jesus as presented in the gospels of Matthew, Mark and Luke with that presented in the writings of Paul and the gospel of John, or, as he said, 'At any rate, there were current in the primitive Church very distinct Christologies'.[11] The idea that the New Testament contains different perspectives on Jesus Christ is widely accepted across the Christian churches today, but in the mid-nineteenth century it seemed a direct contradiction to the unity and coherence of the Biblical witness. The reaction to the *Essays* was extreme. Up and down the country meetings were organised and petitions gathered against the essayists, bishops condemned them, and a serious attempt to prosecute charges of heresy against two of the writers was mounted, though it was ultimately to fail. It was very easy to attack *Essays and Reviews* by selective quotation. At a meeting of deanery clergy, Benjamin Armstrong, High Church vicar of Dereham, Norfolk, led the charge against the 'infidel and unsettling tendency of the book'; since no one else had read it except him, he produced from his pocket 'a long list of quotations ... which was read to the meeting' and the protest was signed unanimously.[12]

Clergy reacted this way because they were convinced that a small core of rationalist theologians were hell-bent on revising traditional doctrine, and that any attempt to do so would undermine the Church. To many it seemed as if there was a steady flow of heterodox publications picking up insights and arguments from a rag-bag of German theologians, sceptical philosophers and hard-bitten historians calling into question the wisdom of the ages. Just two years after *Essays and Reviews*, another English theologian, John William Colenso, now a missionary bishop in Zululand, produced the first volume of a critical commentary on the Pentateuch and the book of Joshua that cast doubt on the Biblical accounts of the Exodus by demonstrating the physical impossibility of the recorded numbers of people, their travels and their provision. Colenso's metropolitan bishop tried to prosecute him for heresy, tipping the South African church into schism.[13] In 1865, J. R. Seeley, professor of Latin at University College, London, published *Ecce Homo*, an attempt to apply classical methods of literary and historical analysis to the New Testament, producing in the process a picture of Jesus as an ethical prophet largely stripped of its miraculous and metaphysical content. Seeley intended no disrespect to traditional Christianity; none the less the book's controversial reputation reflected the fevered atmosphere in which new critical insights were being received.[14]

The accumulating sequence of controversial books and pamphlets had a numbing effect over time. Many clergy were prone to exaggerate the dire implications. On a long perspective the 'crisis of faith' of Victorian England, as it has sometimes been called, was less a crisis than a shiver of anxiety.[15] Victorian Anglicanism mostly absorbed the new criticism, just as it absorbed new theories and discoveries in science, with relative ease. There was a flurry of controversy in 1889 when a group of young Anglo-Catholic writers, including the Principal of the newly established Pusey House in Oxford, Charles Gore, published *Lux Mundi*, a collection of essays on the doctrine of the incarnation which demonstrated a freedom in handling critical enquiry, including the theory of evolution and idealist philosophy, that would probably have appalled Pusey himself.[16] But the outraged Henry Liddon, Pusey's disciple and biographer, died himself the following year, and with him died, mostly, the notion that High Churchmanship was inimical to critical enquiry. By then, too, a group of mostly Cambridge-based theologians, including two successive bishops of Durham, J. B. Lightfoot and B. F. Westcott, had themselves pioneered a synthesis of conservative Anglicanism and critical methodology, albeit from a position of 'central' churchmanship. By the end of the nineteenth century, if the touchstone of Liberalism had once been a readiness to handle confidently critical and historical methods in defence of Christianity, then Anglican Liberalism had become mainstream.

But the wider diffusion of critical enquiry did not prevent the formation of a distinct position within the spectrum of Anglican opinion which could be described, then and later, as 'Liberal' or 'central' churchmanship. That Liberal or 'Broad' Anglicanism had become established effectively as a third church party in the Church of England can be seen in the life and work of parish clergy such as William Fremantle and Samuel Barnett. Fremantle was a protégé of Benjamin Jowett, and for seventeen years rector of the west London church of St Mary's, Bryanston Square.[17] Notoriously, in his *The World as the Subject of Redemption* (1885), his vision of the Church was inclusive almost to the point of being universalist. Barnett was one of his curates at Bryanston Square, but it was among the poor of Whitechapel that his most famous work was done. Here, with his equally famous wife, Henrietta, Samuel turned the national Church ideal into a practical pastoral vision, establishing clubs and classes for the poor, experimenting with alternative forms of worship and imagery, and above all founding a non-denominational 'settlement',

Toynbee Hall, to bring university students into contact with the poor and to provide social services for the area.[18]

Barnett's social commitment illustrates neatly the double legacy of late Victorian Anglican Liberalism. One aspect – Fremantle himself was a perfect example – was the growing readiness to push the boundaries of Anglican belief outwards, beyond the doctrinal certainties professed with equal vehemence by High Churchmen and Evangelicals. Fremantle was one of the founders of the Churchmen's Union for the Advancement of Liberal Religious Thought, in 1898. The Churchmen's Union, later retitled Modern Churchmen's Union (and today called 'Modern Church'), rapidly became the organisational hub of advanced Liberal Anglicanism. 'Modern' here was deliberately annexed to an idea of intellectual and religious progress implying that more traditional understandings of Christian doctrine were otiose. It gave some encouragement, then, to a more radical phase of Liberalism, an Anglican 'Modernism' that in some respects, and chronologically, paralleled the even more controversial Modernist movement in Roman Catholicism.[19]

Anglican Modernists included Hastings Rashdall, who advanced a radical revision of traditional doctrines of the atonement, James Thompson, whose *Miracles in the New Testament* (1911) was dedicated to proving their impossibility, and Henry Major, whose *English Modernism* (1927) was virtually a programmatic statement. The high water mark of Anglican Modernism was a conference at Girton College, Cambridge in 1921 on Christology, which attracted press notoriety in a slack season, with misleading headlines about heretical deans and dons.[20] It overreached itself in the person of Ernest Barnes, mathematician and bishop, advocate of an ethical Christianity largely shorn of its miraculous elements, vigorous opponent of Anglo-Catholicism, and a feisty controversialist who preached what were nick-named 'gorilla sermons' asserting evolutionary theory.[21] In 1947 he published *The Rise of Christianity*, a late efflorescence of Modernism which drew down on his head public censure from Geoffrey Fisher, archbishop of Canterbury.[22] By then the moment of Anglican Modernism had passed. Although there was no such thing as a theological consensus in the Church of England, more conservative theologians had absorbed and synthesised the critical currents on which Barnes and others had drawn, and theological orthodoxy was flourishing.

The other aspect of the Liberal inheritance was the strengthening of a distinct tradition of Anglican social theology. Admittedly this crossed Church party lines. Many High Churchmen who were theologically orthodox in the late nineteenth century were drawn to the social implications of Christian faith mapped out by F. D. Maurice and others. The history of a distinct Anglo-Catholic 'sacramental' socialism belongs elsewhere, but it had a shared spirit with many 'Broad' or 'central' Anglicans. The Barnetts' *Practicable Socialism* (1888) covered subjects of general social ethics such as poverty, Poor Law reform and unemployment, but also practical matters such as children's holidays.

By far the most famous exemplar was William Temple. Temple's Liberal pedigree was impeccable, his archbishop father, Frederick, a contributor to *Essays and Reviews*. As a young man, his ordination was temporarily obstructed by his doubts about the doctrines of the virgin birth and resurrection. By 1908 his faith had settled into an orthodox mould, though his theology was always a somewhat awkward mix of idealist philosophy and traditional Christian doctrine. Temple's meteoric rise is testimony to his intellectual brilliance, his boundless energy and his personal charisma: headmaster of Repton at thirty-three, rector of St James's, Piccadilly at thirty-five, canon of Westminster at thirty-eight, bishop of Manchester at thirty-nine, archbishop of York at forty-eight, and finally archbishop of Canterbury at sixty-one. His politics were centre left, and his ecclesiology profoundly attached to the national Church ideal.[23] Somehow the unlikely fusion of establishment Anglicanism, philosophical theology and leftish sympathies appeared utterly natural and unforced in him. It was exemplified in his war-time bestseller

Christianity and Social Order (1942), and also in his chairmanship of the Church of England's first Doctrine Commission, which, provoked by Anglican Modernism, sat fitfully from 1922 until it produced its report, *Doctrine in the Church of England*, in 1938. It has been called a 'pondered, dull document', but this is not really fair to the wide-ranging ambition of the report, which tried to capture the breadth and diversity of Anglican convictions, and could be said to mark officially at last a sort of truce between Liberalism and its former High and Low Church opponents.[24]

Despite doctrinal difference, this Anglican Liberalism generally varied little from its Low and High rivals in its ethical assumptions. Liberals were more likely to countenance divorce, and to favour birth control, but that was about as far as their ethical progressivism went, and even then opinion was to shift slowly, and did not, at least on sexuality, move much beyond that point. Not until the second half of the twentieth century did Anglican Liberalism begin to move significantly further on sexuality and marriage, matching broader trends in British society.[25] Nor did it have distinct liturgical practices. Most Liberal clergy shadowed either Low Church simplicity in worship, or a diluted form of High Churchmanship, following the Prayer Book with some ritual and sacramental observances.

16

THE CHURCH IN INDUSTRIAL SOCIETY

Workshop of the World, or Dark Satanic Mills?

At the cusp of modern British history stands that great period of social and economic change called, in the convenient shorthand, the industrial revolution. It had extraordinary implications for all the British churches. An immensely complex subject, it has a vast scholarly literature.[1] Its central features, for our purposes, can be briefly listed, however. Economically, it marked a shift from the dominance of agricultural production to manufacturing, the factory system, financial services and mechanised transport. Socially, it entailed a fundamental move away from a population based mostly in the countryside to one living in concentrated, industrial conurbations. The population of England and Wales increased rapidly, from around 5 million at the beginning of the eighteenth century to over 20 million by 1871, and continued growing thereafter.[2] This increase was probably caused above all by rising fertility, but it was not evenly spread, either between country and city or between different regions. The rising population was sustained by remarkable increases in both agricultural and industrial productivity, as well as by growing trade. This massive economic expansion led to Britain being dubbed the 'workshop of the world' in the nineteenth century. It fuelled ideas of British might and exceptionalism that were to find their most controversial reflection in the fantasy of imperial destiny.

The idea of a sudden, dramatic change in the late eighteenth century has been rejected latterly by most economic historians, who instead posit a process that was long in the making, its origins lying much further back in British history than was once thought. In the eighteenth century, growth and change were continual, but gradual year on year; only in the early nineteenth century, especially from around the 1820s on, did they begin to gather pace so much that we can then genuinely speak of a revolution in economy and society. This is not to deny the social dislocation worked by industrialisation and urbanisation. There is still no consensus on whether living standards rose or fell for most of the poor, but increasingly the evidence suggests that: overall in England and Wales, wages were high (relative to the rest of Europe) in the eighteenth century and prices modest; industrialisation did not lead to a general collapse in living standards in the early to mid-nineteenth century; and a gradual improvement did begin somewhere around the third quarter of the century.[3] However, all generalisations are suspect here: there were serious pockets of deprivation, poor living standards and health in many cities, and cycles of boom and bust that made life very insecure.

Until recently, most historians agreed that industrialisation and urbanisation were disastrous for the churches. Church leaders often thought this themselves. False ideas of a 'golden age' of faith in the past have misled people into assuming that low or declining church attendance showed that secularisation – the falling away of people either from active church participation or even from any form of serious belief – was an intrinsic aspect of the emergence of a modern society in Britain. This led very quickly and easily to the crude assumption that religion was 'outdated', and that a modern society was a secular one. An article in the *Westminster Review* in 1862 on the '[r]eligious heresies of the working classes' claimed, for example, that 'there are large classes not ostensibly connected with any denomination, and to whom religion has long since become an unreality'.[4] Even the more proletarian denominations, such as the Primitive Methodists and the Salvation Army, had little grip on the working classes overall, it was assumed. The Church of England, led by the sons of landed gentry and the learned professions, educated often at the ancient universities and sharing the aspirations of their class, was surely not able to have much traction with factory workers, miners, dockers, or the urban poor generally. Besides, the Church's institutional strength lay in the countryside, where the vast majority of its parish churches were placed; the pace of industrial and urban change would leave it effectively stranded, increasingly marginalised by the onward march of industry and technology.

The Church of England had many institutional failings. Many of its clergy and leading laity definitely did not understand or appreciate the magnitude of the changes British society was undergoing. Their political sympathies were often at odds with those of the emergent working class. Their services frequently offered little attraction to the urban poor, and, as we saw in an earlier chapter, even the very strategies of renewal adopted by many Anglicans in the nineteenth century widened the gap between the Church and popular culture. The 'church condescending' was how many working-class people experienced the Church of England.[5]

But a number of powerful myths do need to be contradicted. The first is that the Church of England simply failed to adjust its organisation and pastoral provision to the new industrial society. On the contrary, though it faced formidable obstacles, the Church did engineer a remarkable institutional revival in manufacturing areas as much as elsewhere in the nineteenth century. The second is that there were no working-class Anglicans. Anglicanism did not at all escape class bias, and had a differential social appeal. But there were many working-class Anglicans. The third, more pervasively, is that the hierarchy were simply complacent about the changes going on around them. In fact, you could characterise the experience of the Victorian Church as one long experiment in mission and evangelism. And finally, perhaps the biggest myth of all, is that the birth of industrial society marked simultaneously and inevitably the death throes of religion in Britain.

Numbers, Regional Strength, Class and Gender

The starting point for any discussion of the Church of England's relative success in the nineteenth and early twentieth centuries has got to be the apparently simple question of numbers. Did it grow or did it shrink? Did it keep pace with, or even overtake, population growth, or did it fall behind? Unfortunately, these are not straightforward questions. The Church of England had no clear-cut definition of membership. Everyone in England and Wales in theory could be deemed members. Even baptism was not a simple marker, because it was possible (though rare) not to be baptised but to attend, and certainly common to be baptised in an Anglican church but belong to another denomination or not attend at all.

Generally historians have tried to measure affiliation in three ways. First, some sort of yearly, identifiable point over a long period. Easter communicants is a good example, and commonly used, but we have no adequate figures nationally before 1885, and even then large numbers of Anglican attenders did not receive communion at Easter, despite it being a canonical requirement.[6] Second, the pastoral offices – baptism, marriage, burials. We have parish registers from the mid-sixteenth century, but they are very patchy (many have been lost or destroyed) and cannot easily be gathered into a national series. We have national baptism numbers only from 1885 again. Third, church attendance. But regular, national censuses of churchgoing exist only from the late twentieth century.[7] We do, however, have the only, official national census of churchgoing in Britain, which was taken in 1851.[8] It was a controversial exercise, never repeated. Interpretation of its statistics is very difficult, particularly because there was no decisive way of excluding double attendances (though the report did try). But it does give a useful snapshot of mid-Victorian religion. Its overall conclusion was that the total of attendances (note, not attenders) at services on the census Sunday represented 60 per cent of the population of England and Wales, though that figure comes down to about 42 per cent for attenders when various stratagems for excluding 'twicers', i.e. double or triple attendances, are used. It was shocking enough that it seemed that less than half of the population attended church. But the proportion of Anglican attendances was only 48 per cent of the total number.[9] The Church did not have the active support, it seems, of a majority even of regular churchgoers in England and Wales. As there was only one national census, it is impossible to use it on its own to determine whether churchgoing was increasing or declining. Various local censuses of churchgoing, especially in the second half of the century, do however enable us to aggregate sources in some areas.

What do all these statistics tell us, overall? The broad conclusions are perhaps surprising. Attendance at Anglican churches in England and Wales almost certainly *increased* during the nineteenth century, certainly in absolute terms – in fact, it probably continued growing absolutely into the 1930s – but also in relative terms (i.e. relative to population growth) perhaps until some point round about the 1850s or 1860s, when it began to plateau and then perhaps to decline gently on into the twentieth century. Once we have ditched the idea of a golden age of churchgoing, and recognised that – as we saw in earlier chapters – the mechanisms for enforcing church attendance had fallen largely into disuse as long ago as the late seventeenth century, and that there has never been a time when all of a community regularly went to church, it is not so surprising that a church steadily overhauling its organisation and pastoral provision should see an impact in numeric terms.

There are two crucial qualifications, apart from the general difficulties of interpreting the statistics. One is that the Victorian period was the first great age of systematic statistics. So church leaders in a sense intensified the problem they encountered: they measured numbers, and found them falling short of their ideal of maximum attendance, and so imagined a terrible falling away where none really existed, at least as a recent phenomenon. But, second, by defining affiliation increasingly in these active terms, they allied concepts of belief to middle-class norms of behaviour, and excluded from consideration, and denigrated, religious opinions and behaviour that did not easily match these norms. The figures point to a sustained Anglican revival through the nineteenth century, and do not support the idea that the industrial revolution was a disaster for the Church. But they do indicate a second broad conclusion that cuts across the first. If we measure the strength of the Church by active participation, such as churchgoing, it is clear that Anglicanism had lost ground to other denominations in the late eighteenth and early nineteenth centuries, and never recovered it. This of course had very troubling long-term implications for those wedded to the concept of a national Church.

There was much regional variation, caused by many different factors – pre-modern patterns of settlement and church distribution, occupational patterns, landownership, the relative strengths and weaknesses of other denominations, migration, even different theologies of mission and pastoral service, to name only a few. In 1851 the contrasts between mainly rural counties and those dominated by industry were already apparent. In Kent and Sussex, for example, over two-thirds of attendances were Anglican, whereas in the West Riding of Yorkshire only a third were.[10] Similar variations existed between towns and cities. In Worcester, 70 per cent of attendances were Anglican, but in Bradford just 22 per cent. Most extreme was Wales. Overall, excluding Monmouthshire, Anglicans made up less than 20 per cent of attendances throughout Wales; in Merthyr Tydfil the figure was as low as 6 per cent.[11] In general terms, Anglicanism was stronger in the countryside than in the towns – no surprise there – and stronger in the south and west of England than in the west Midlands, north-west and north-east, and in Wales.

Undoubtedly there was a falling away of regular attendance between the countryside and the cities, giving rise to clerical perceptions of the 'godlessness' of the cities. But again there were surprising features of this. As you would perhaps expect, Roman Catholics were concentrated mostly in the industrial cities, dependent on Irish immigration. But in Liverpool, for example, where they made up a third of attendances, Anglicans were actually higher, at 40 per cent. In Birmingham Anglicans made up 47 per cent of all attendances, Catholics just 6 per cent. These many local differences are not susceptible to a handful of variables; each locality had its own complex history. But if we take even the most basic conclusion from 1851 – that, despite its growth, the Church of England had lost its majority position – none the less there is a counter-conclusion. That is that Anglicanism retained a pan-national presence, a presence in every community. Moreover, the census only measured actual attendance. Once we factor in the very high numbers of those who continued to seek baptism, marriage or burial according to Anglican rites, attended Anglican schools and Sunday Schools, or in one way or another had some sort of contact with Anglican churches, it is not difficult to see why the loss of a churchgoing majority proved not to be as catastrophic for the Church of England as many feared.

The only exception here is Wales, where the really marked growth of Dissent set the scene for the disestablishment of the Church of England in Wales in the early twentieth century. But even here we should be cautious about assuming the virtual collapse of Anglicanism in south Wales, something that is part of the local mythology of the region. In many parts of south Wales the Church of England remained the largest single denomination right through into the early twentieth century, completely overshadowed as it was by all the combined forces of Dissent.[12] That provided the platform for the perhaps surprising consolidation and recovery of the newly disestablished Church in Wales in the twentieth century. Elsewhere, even in the new industrial heartlands, the Church of England's presence was far from negligible at mid-century. In Oldham and its surrounding townships, for example, just over a third of all attendances in 1851 were Anglican – more than double those of the next largest denomination, the Wesleyan Methodists.[13]

That brings us to a further dimension of complexity – social class. A great deal of nineteenth-century commentary assumed the appeal of the Church of England to the upper and middle classes, and to the rural poor who, it was commonly believed, had little choice but to obey the whims of local landowners and pitch up at the parish church. Much of this description is, regrettably, true. The culture of deference that saturated Victorian society, especially in the countryside, undoubtedly played into the hands of the common alliance of squire and parson. The continuing grip of the established Church on the upper echelons of society meant that there was a strong 'pull' into Anglicanism for those upwardly mobile merchants, traders, craftsmen and others who were building their fortunes in the rapidly expanding Victorian economy. The tendency of sons and daughters of rich Nonconformist tradesmen and entrepreneurs to marry into or convert to the Church of England was an observable phenomenon. The clergy echoed the values of the professional and landed classes. To read their letters and diaries of the period is often to catch this world of deference and – in our terms – snobbery. When Fredrick Helmore, the 'musical missionary', went to East Farleigh in Kent in December 1843 to begin training Henry Wilberforce's choir, he found the new recruits waiting for him in the servants' hall at the vicarage.[14] That captures an inescapable aspect of the Victorian Church.

This class bias was reflected in differential patterns of church affiliation and attendance. Both in the industrial towns and cities, and in the largest and most complex expanding city of them all, London, there was an almost inevitable broad correlation between areas of affluence and Anglican strength. In Shoreditch, Southwark, Finsbury and Stepney in 1902–3 less than 5 per cent of the population attended regular services in Anglican churches; in Ealing over 28 per cent did.[15] In Leeds in 1851, Anglican attendances, at 16 per cent of the population, were outnumbered by the Methodists at 19 per cent.[16] But again there was significant internal variation in the city, from the huge numbers attending the newly rebuilt parish church in the centre of Leeds to the relatively sparse congregations in some of the industrial suburbs such as Holbeck and Hunslet.[17] But the contrast risks obscuring something important. For all its class bias and differential class appeal, there were substantial numbers of working-class attenders at Anglican churches. They may have made up a fraction of the population of a district, but they were not negligible. Three Anglican churches in Holbeck and Hunslet recorded total attendances (including Sunday scholars) of nearly 3,000, which would probably translate into something like 2,250 individual attenders – hardly a trifling figure, even if it was outdone by Nonconformity. In the barracks city of Colchester at the beginning of the twentieth century 'by far the majority of people in the pews were drawn from the working classes'.[18] A Southwark vicar claimed in 1962 that 'what we will not face is that the industrial working-class of England as a class has never been to church'.[19] This is simply not true. In the deprived borough of Southwark itself in 1902–3 some 12,000 attendances were recorded in Anglican churches; again that was a fraction of the total population, but still a considerable working-class constituency.[20]

Gender was also a differentiating factor. The leadership of the Church of England was almost uniformly male. There were a few leadership positions for women, in the new sisterhoods, and in the order of deaconesses created in the 1860s, following the Lutheran model established at Kaiserswerth in Düsseldorf in the 1830s. There were, again, powerful women who made important contributions to church life in the era of industrialisation, such as Florence Nightingale and Mary Sumner, founder of the Mothers' Union. But these significant women were dwarfed in numbers not only by the many thousands of male clergy, but also by the almost complete monopoly men held of political office and business leadership. The laity who led church building committees, chaired or sat on the committees of Anglican voluntary organisations and took a leading role in education and church politics were almost all men. There were, admittedly, some opportunities for women – especially middle- or lower middle-class women – as teachers, visitors and volunteers in parishes. But women were silent in church. And yet by the early nineteenth century – probably beginning long before then – congregations were disproportionately dominated by women. In 1902–3 some 24,000 men attended Anglican churches in Greater London in the morning, but 42,000 women did.[21] This female predominance was not confined to Anglicanism. It was probably greater in working-class communities than in middle-class congregations. In middle-class households in the nineteenth century it was common for the father of the house to take the lead in family prayers, but in working-class households much more common was the assumption that religion, church and Sunday School were the preserve of the mother. This was reinforced by the virtual absence of women from the clubs and pubs that were the staple of male working-class leisure.[22]

Reaching an assessment of the overall performance of the Church of England in the era of industrialisation requires the careful balancing of innumerable variables and the avoidance of melodramatic generalisations. In the heyday of secularisation theory in the 1960s and 1970s it was common to claim that the Church of England had been in decline since the early nineteenth century. This perspective held sway because it appeared to be supported by the first detailed study of religion in an industrial city, Sheffield, which appeared in 1957.[23] But not only was the Sheffield study flawed in its historical methodology, it was also very clearly shaped by a theological conviction that modern society was intrinsically hostile to institutional religion and demanded a radical reconception of Christianity.[24] The conventional view was a gross and misleading oversimplification.

For much of the period of rapid industrial growth in the nineteenth century, Anglicans, in competition with Nonconformists, were engaged in an immense programme of church building and evangelistic effort, and the number of churchgoing Anglicans increased, until it began a gentle decline relative to the expanding population sometime around the third quarter of the century. Industrialisation and urbanisation were not catastrophic for the churches. There were significant numbers of working-class Anglican attenders, though they were probably

well outnumbered by non-attenders, Catholics and Nonconformists in most industrial and urban areas. On the other hand,
Anglicanism was not uniformly popular across all social classes:
if the poor continued to have recourse to the Church of England
for its pastoral offices and also for education and charitable help,
none the less they were well under-represented proportionately in its congregations. The Church also fared better in some
regions than others. Like all denominations it had demonstra-
bly less appeal to men than to women. When it began to lose
ground in the late nineteenth century, its relatively thin support
in some areas was to prove a poor basis from which to launch
the many strategies attempting renewal and growth it was to
adopt in the twentieth century.

Mission and Ministry

What were the institutional mechanisms and strategies that lay
behind the Church's adjustment to industrialisation and urbanisation? Without question, the package of reforms ushered in by
the Ecclesiastical Commissioners did help the Church to adapt
more rapidly and effectively than it had managed at the beginning of the century. The reorganisation of dioceses, reform of
cathedral chapters, new curbs on non-residence and pluralism
and the redistribution of income to augment poorer livings
were all necessary initiatives. They went hand in hand with a
plethora of other changes, many begun at local level, such as
the revival of the office of rural dean, the overhaul of diocesan
administration and the creation of new training institutions.
The Victorian period was a time of prodigious investment of
human and material resources in the Church, and scarcely any
aspect of its life and work was left unchanged by it.

Church building was probably the biggest single area of
investment. A growing population needed new or expanded
churches to accommodate larger numbers of worshippers. In
some places the Church's record of adaptation is impressive.
In Oldham and Saddleworth, for example, the building of new

IRON BUILDINGS & ROOFING
CHEAPEST HOUSE IN LONDON FOR IRON ROOFING.

New and Second-hand Churches, Chapels, Mission and School Rooms, Cottages, Shepherd's and Keeper's Huts. Stables, Coach-houses, Farm Buildings, Sheds for Manufacturing Purposes, &c. Several Buildings always on view, and 100 tons of Iron kept in stock. Plans and Estimates for every description of IRON BUILDING and ROOFING free on application. Buildings shipped and erected (if required) in any part of the World.

W. HARBROW'S Works, Brixton Station, LONDON, S.W.

30. Tin tabernacles from the catalogue

chapels ('chapels-of-ease', as they were usually called) in the eighteenth century apparently outpaced population growth.[25] By contrast, in Whalley, also in Lancashire, churches failed to keep up with the three-fold growth of the population.[26] And this was a common pattern. By the early nineteenth century it was widely acknowledged that there were simply not enough churches in the new urban and industrial areas, and the Church was ceding ground to Dissent.

The creation of the Incorporated Church Building Society in 1817, closely followed by government action with the formation in 1818 of the Church Building Commissioners, created two central agencies, voluntary and governmental in turn, which coordinated building programmes. One hundred and eighty-eight new 'Waterloo' churches, as they were called, were built by 1831.[27] In London, determined action by Bishop Blomfield in the 1830s and 1840s led to the formation of the Metropolitan Churches Fund and a programme for building fifty new churches. By mid-century, over 300 new Anglican churches a year were being built; by 1875 nearly 3,500 had been completed.[28] Legislative action was needed, too, to create new parishes for these churches. In 1843 Peel's government passed legislation for populous areas to this effect, where necessary overriding the rights of existing incumbents. By all these means, extraordinary progress was made in mapping out the urban parish system that still prevails in towns and cities today, though many churches have been bombed, demolished or abandoned from 1939 onwards. A famous example was, once again, Leeds, where Walter Hook subdivided the massive historic parish with its eighteen chapels-of-ease serving a population of 150,000, and built thirty-one new churches.[29]

So extensive and successful was the Victorian (and Edwardian – it carried on into the twentieth century) strategy of church building, that it has led modern-day critics to claim that too *many* churches were built, even at the time, for the number of people who were likely to attend. The problem of oversupply became evident in the following century as congregations declined.[30] Today, as the empty shells of abandoned Victorian churches litter the urban landscape, often boarded up, their sites scheduled for redevelopment, it is very tempting to assume that churches were thrown up too quickly, before any substantial congregations had been gathered. But by the late nineteenth century, church 'extension', as it was called, had become a much more flexible, adaptive process.

Beginnings were almost always very small-scale, with the evangelising of a district, the formation of the nucleus of a new congregation, the purchase of a site and erection of a temporary corrugated iron 'mission hall', often purchased from another local church or from a supplying company via a catalogue of church furniture and furnishings. A building committee would be formed, composed of local worthies willing to contribute financially. If the congregation grew, then thoughts would turn to a more permanent structure, which would be built in stages matching the growth of a congregation. Many of these iron mission stations were indeed not needed in a couple of generations, and never became permanent buildings. When permanent buildings were put up, many of them were never finished. Almost always the last part of a permanent structure to be constructed was the tower or steeple. Incidentally, the adaptive strategy of building was sometimes responsible for the notion that humble temporary or small-scale buildings were deliberately put up for the poor to keep them away from 'respectable' worshippers. This was rarely the case. But by the late nineteenth century church builders had learnt not to commit large resources to permanent buildings without evidence of local commitment, and it was often in working-class areas, where churchgoing was, as we have seen, generally much lower, that new congregations proved particularly difficult to cultivate.

There was also a flood of experiment in organisation, mission and even worship. They included new forms of ministry – the deaconess movement, lay pastoral assistants, male and female religious orders, district visitors. The formation of the Church Army in 1882, at the instigation of Wilson Carlile, created a parallel evangelistic body to the Salvation Army, working from within the parish system. Other new organisations sprang up for a wide range of needs and people: the Church of England Temperance Society to marshal Anglican support for limiting alcohol consumption; the Church Lads' Brigade and Church Girls' Brigade; the Church of England Men's Society; the Church Benefit Society; the Church of England Children's Society (for long known as 'The Waifs and Strays'); lobbying organisations such as the Church Defence League; and organisations supporting specific doctrinal perspectives such as the Church Association (Evangelical) and the English Church Union (Anglo-Catholic), among many others. New techniques of evangelism were tried, including open air preaching in cities, and short, intensive parish 'missions' in which missionaries would visit a parish over a couple of weeks and carry out a packed programme of meetings, lectures, visits and worship. New forms of liturgy were experimented with, including short services of prayer and praise and, after the passage of the 'Short Services Act' of 1872, adapted use of the Prayer Book and Bible with hymns for special occasions. All this is testimony to the creativity of the Victorian Church.

The Church may have been a hierarchical institution, perme- ated by class bias and the culture of deference, but nevertheless in many parishes the clergyman had to work as part of a large team. The late Victorian parish was often a complex organisa- tion, with schools, Sunday Schools, a long list of charities, lay workers and assistant clergy, and a practice of dividing up the parish into districts – usually just a handful of streets – to each of which a 'district visitor' (usually female) was assigned for handing out literature, visiting parishioners, assessing pastoral and material needs, and acting as a channel of communication to the clergy. The work of these visitors was often assisted by nurses, and was one of the streams which fed into the emer- gence of social work in Britain.[31]

All of these organisations required a small army of volun- teers, sometimes with a few lay professionals as well. Towards the end of the century, voluntary church councils began to be formed, particularly in urban parishes, in order to give volunteers and church organisations a way of consulting and coordinating their work. All this effort was underpinned financially by a shift away from pew fees, the use of glebe and local church rates as ways of funding the local church, towards voluntary giving. The taking of collections during services became characteristic in the Victorian period, particularly as a way of offsetting losses from the practice of renting out pews to local families, like num- bered theatre seats, which many considered (perhaps wrongly) a serious hindrance to attracting the poor.[32] The commutation of tithe into a cash charge absorbed into rent, via legislation in 1836, removed a longstanding source of resentment in the countryside. Church rates were finally abolished in 1868. But the creation of a centralised and equalised system of funding professional ministry had to wait until well into the twentieth century.

Finally, new conceptions of the Church's relationship to society and to politics emerged in direct response to the chal- lenges raised by the deprivation and hardship of industrial and urban areas. Systematic attempts at organising the plethora of local charities were made, through, for example, the Charity Organization Society (COS), formed in the late 1860s. The COS generally operated within the moral framework of Victorian philanthropy, highlighting the contrast between the 'deserving' and 'undeserving' poor and, sceptical of aid dispensed by the State or local government, its impact was, accordingly, limited. Some clergy became more sympathetic to a greater role for government in ameliorating poverty and providing social services. The roots of this shift could be found partly in the moral crusades of many Evangelicals such as William Wilberforce and Anthony Ashley Cooper, 7th Earl of Shaftesbury. But they also lay in the experience of ordinary parish clergy, such as the famed (and somewhat mythologised) 'slum priests' of the Anglo-Catholic tradition – men such as Robert Dolling, who is supposed to have said, 'I speak out and fight about the drains because I believe in the Incarnation.'[33] Others began to articulate a conception of the social implications of Christian theology that had clear affinities with socialist ideas, and were eventually to lead, as we saw in the last chapter, to the tradition of Anglican social criticism we associate with, in the twentieth century, William Temple, William Beveridge and the foundation of the Welfare State.[34] There were practical outcomes, such as the Anglican contribution to the 'Settlement' movement, the brief trend at the end of the nineteenth century to found communities in poor parts of the great cities in which clergy would work with local volunteers and with students from universities and the public schools to run clubs, charities and classes.[35]

The Church of England's engagement with the new industrial society was often constructive, creative and immensely varied. As such it cannot be called a failure. Yet neither was it an unmitigated success. It lost ground relentlessly to the Free Churches. Its active support was disproportionately concentrated in the middle and upper middle classes. Not until much later, in the late twentieth century, did it begin to break through the barriers of class, gender, race and educational experience that had confined its professional ministry to a small section of

31. William Temple: Churchill called him 'the only half-crown article in the sixpenny bazaar'

the population, and even then its record remained patchy. By then, anyway, its congregational base was undergoing persistent, dramatic decline and, although the overhaul of its ministry was, as we shall see later, an attempt to respond to that decline, it had a long way to go to match the social diversity of British society.

Anglicanism in the Industrial World

Although Radical politicians saw the emergence of representative democracy in Britain as a struggle for power between the old aristocracy and gentry, and the rising middle and working classes, in fact the grip of 'old money' on politics, the economy and the learned professions was tenacious even in the industrial age and beyond. The last aristocrat who was prime minister was Alec Douglas-Home in 1963–4. In that world, Anglicanism remained supreme. There were some noble and gentry Catholic families, but very few Nonconformists indeed among the nobility and landed gentry. With this social presence, and through its links with the Royal Family, Parliament and the armed forces, the Church of England retained its social and political prominence at the heart of government, even after the diminution of its constitutional privilege in the early nineteenth century. Yet it also helped to determine a specific sense of national identity that attracted some of all classes throughout the period – not just a Protestant identity, but one with conservative, royalist overtones, an appeal to Empire and a sense of distinct national destiny and character.

Instead of solid horizontal religious and political affiliations, however – a Tory and Anglican gentry, a Liberal and mixed Anglican and Nonconformist middle class, and an indifferent, Catholic or passively Anglican working class – as we have seen, differences in religious affiliation and activity were just as complex within the social classes, i.e. 'vertically'. In the middle classes at all levels were found active Anglican congregations. The distinction between the world of work and the domestic sphere was important in middle-class religion, not because the working environment was seen as somehow godless, but because the home and family were quintessentially the arena in which faith was to be nurtured and its moral codes enforced: 'The Linkage of Christianity, godliness and the family was crucial.'[36] Fathers might have been involved in supporting churchgoing, family prayers and Bible reading, but generally these activities were in the hands of mothers. Religion was probably more bound up with the home than it had been at any time since the Middle Ages.

Molly Hughes, author of the *London Girl* autobiographies, was brought up in the affluent area of Canonbury in the late nineteenth century, and was a devout High Anglican churchgoer all her life. Her home was not especially pious, but Christian faith was central to it. Her education until the age of eleven was at home, and centred on the Bible: 'I had to read aloud the strange doings of the Patriarchs ... occasionally mother's pencil ... would travel rapidly over several verses, and I heard a muttered "never mind about that".'[37] Sunday meant church in the morning, and an avoidance of most forms of amusement except reading. The piety of Hughes's home came mostly from her Cornish mother, but although the afternoons 'hung heavy' and it 'seemed always to be 3 o'clock', religious talk was rarely inflicted on her and her brothers, and her father's Sunday efforts 'weakened towards evening', when he would read aloud from Shakespeare or books such as *The Ingoldsby Legends*.[38]

There was one occupational group who straddled the middle and working classes – domestic servants. There were over a million of them in Britain in 1851, around a twentieth of the total workforce, 90 per cent of whom were women.[39] Whatever their religious background, they were also shaped by the religious values of the homes in which they worked. Obligatory family or household prayers and reading of the Bible formed a common bond of experience for servants and their employing families, and a form of catechesis and religious education that might have been lacking for servants otherwise. Since entry into domestic service could be as young as twelve or thirteen, the impact of the Prayer Book and the King James Bible was often lifelong. On the other hand, servants might also be deprived of the opportunity to go to church themselves, if their employers needed them at the house. William Taylor, a footman in London who kept a diary in 1837, noted simply one Sunday: 'This is Sunday and I have *realy* [sic] been to Church' – that is, he could attend the service himself rather than simply take the family there and back.[40] Later in the year he went to church, 'but it was so full that I could not get inside the door, therefore I took a walk and called at a Methodist Chapple [sic]. There I stayed but a very short time.'[41] As Taylor's experience attests, the propagation of religious values and knowledge, even in this society of deference, did not simply flow downwards, but was owned and professed by individuals themselves, as part of their own culture and identity. Anglicanism in these circumstances could cross all classes and form a bond of common commitment.

But the statistics are clear. Anglicanism may have had substantial working-class adherents, but they were a minority everywhere. Was there in any sense a characteristically *Anglican* working-class religious culture? It is difficult to argue that. But just as Disraeli claimed to have released the 'angels in marble' through enfranchising the skilled working class in 1867, so there was always a Conservative-inclined, royalist, Anglican strand in working-class culture that sat entirely at odds with notions of class consciousness.

The extraordinarily complex and proactive organisation of the parish in this era rested not only on the assumption that middle- and lower middle-class volunteers would come forward to staff charities and societies, but that their services would actually be used by the people at whom they were aimed. And there is plenty of evidence of that. An 'Anonymous Navvy', writing in *Macmillan's Magazine* in the early 1860s, testified at several points to the practical help he had received from clergy. Living a tramping existence for some years in search of work, with drink and brawling recurrent difficulties, he broke his ankle, and a local parson 'used to come and sit with me, and I could talk to him and ask him questions. I found out more from him than from any other since I came out of Lewes Gaol.'[42]

Even so, it was just as common for working-class people to turn away from the Church of England and find solace in Dissent. The proportionately greater growth of Dissent in the late eighteenth and early nineteenth centuries must have included, as a cause, a significant trend away from the established Church. After all, the class bias of clergy, with their preaching on social order, would have alienated many workers. Memories of clerical magistrates, the alliance of landowners and clergy, the social stratification of parish church congregations, the social gulf that existed between the clergy and many of their parishioners – all these things made the ministry of the Church increasingly difficult in working-class areas.[43]

Finally, though, there is a wider question of working-class religious culture that we have to take into account. If actual church attendance was a minority habit, there were other ways in which Christianity was widely diffused in industrial society. Hymn-singing, cheap religious tracts, the huge numbers attending Sunday Schools, religious education in elementary schools, popular religious prints and scriptural texts all contributed to shaping a popular culture that remained profoundly Christian throughout this period.[44] Outright atheism was rare, the organised secularist movement always small. Some have used terms like 'diffusive Christianity' to describe the all-pervasive nature of belief outside the official activities and services of the institutional churches.[45] Use of oral evidence, drawn from interviews with people living in the late nineteenth and early twentieth centuries, has yielded a picture of popular belief that takes us beyond the simplicities of earlier historians' assumptions that working people were alienated from Christianity.[46] In many working-class families, contact with a local church might be through just one member of the family, through whose affiliation the whole family would perceive themselves as churchgoers – 'religion by deputy'. The very visibility of churches, and the presence of their clergy, made them prominent locally and likely to be approached for material help, and perhaps pastoral comfort and occasional spiritual guidance. The Church of England may have long lost its hold on even a bare majority of the churchgoing public, but its physical and cultural reach was still impressive.

17

THE RESHAPING OF THE VICTORIAN
AND EDWARDIAN CHURCH:
BUREAUCRACY AND TRADITION

Synods and Suffragans

Reform of the Church of England's organisational structure continued into the early twentieth century. The Ecclesiastical Commission may have constructed much of the main framework of the modern Church in the mid-nineteenth century, but vital elements still remained to be put in place. Organisational reform – particularly, for some reason, church reform – is hardly the stuff of drama and romance, but it is vital to understanding how the Church adjusted to the stresses it faced in the twentieth century.

Bishops and dioceses were a key part of this process. Why create new dioceses, new bishops, new cathedrals? Residual elements of medieval and early modern prelacy – the historic palaces, the presence of the Lords Spiritual in Parliament – masked a fundamental change that was under way in the very idea of what a bishop was for. Their constitutional and courtly role was fast becoming a formality at best by the 1840s; they were becoming, instead, hands-on senior managers or overseers.[1] Diocesan finance and organisation were becoming more complex. Bishops needed to be active on the ground, visiting parishes, fronting up fundraising, addressing societies and stirring up the many mission initiatives of the Victorian and Edwardian Church. Overlarge and unwieldy dioceses were a hindrance to all this; the growing weight of business brought many bishops

32. The beginning of central organisation: Church
House, Westminster, as designed in 1890

close to physical collapse. The role of the bishop as the only minister of confirmation and ordination in Anglicanism, if anything,
underscored the need for more of them. Twelve new dioceses
were created between 1876 and 1914; another seven came into
being between 1918 and 1927. Eleven of these nineteen – Liverpool, Newcastle, Southwell, Wakefield, Birmingham, Sheffield,
Coventry, Bradford, Blackburn, Leicester and Derby – were in
the Midlands and north. Assistant bishops and suffragan bishops
were also appointed in growing numbers from the 1860s, using
an existing but dormant legal provision dating from the Reformation. The overhaul of training and education for the ministry
also continued, including the foundation of many new theological colleges in the second half of the century.[2] Along with this
went the development of theology as an academic discipline, at
first with a more or less explicit purpose for supporting professional ministry; only later did it come to be conceived, at least
in the universities, as a neutral or 'objective' study among the
humanities.[3]

But reformers increasingly encountered a difficulty: as the

established Church, the Church of England required Parliamentary action to put its intentions into effect, but with the greater complexity of the British State in the nineteenth century and its demands on Parliamentary time, that was proving more and more difficult. The problem existed to some extent even in the eighteenth century: out of 14,217 Acts passed between 1660 and 1800, only 373 fell into the category of 'religion', and even then not all of these related to the Church of England.[4] By the late nineteenth century this reliance on Parliamentary consent was becoming a serious impediment to Church business. The admission of Dissenters and Catholics to the reformed Commons after 1832 added principled objection to the practical one: now those who did not worship according to the rites of the Church of England could none the less have a say in its business. This was Keble's 'national apostasy'. So what was the answer? Surely the revival of the Church's own representative assemblies of Canterbury and York, the Convocations, in abeyance effectively since 1717. Without such a mechanism, Anglicans could have no independent means of determining Church policy and proposing legislation.

The revival of the Convocations was controversial. Many bishops feared they would provide a vehicle for troublesome junior clergy, especially of the Tractarian kind. It was only in 1852 that the Convocation of Canterbury met to consider business; the Convocation of York did not meet until 1861. Yet these were only for clergy. The pressure to include an element of lay opinion began to grow. Here, perhaps, two different 'models' were more or less unconsciously at work, one based on the early precedent of the Councils of the Church, mostly involving clergy, but at times summoned by lay rulers (such as the Emperor Constantine at the first Council of Nicaea), and the other centred around the Parliamentary model of representative government.

When the laity were donating money in unprecedented sums for church building and other causes, and volunteering in ever increasing numbers to run parochial and diocesan agencies, it would have been inconceivable not to have developed a mechanism for consulting them. But this could not be, at least at first, formally part of the Convocations. So the pressure for a three-tier system – bishops, clergy and laity – began to build. Quite quickly, a voluntary representative system emerged, with lay representation. Bishop Browne of Ely led the way with the first diocesan 'conference' in 1866. By the 1880s almost all dioceses had them. Four principles came to the fore: separate but parallel representation for clergy and laity; the linking of representation to traditional ecclesiastical units (parish, deanery, diocese and province); a hierarchy of these authorities; and indirect rather than 'direct' or democratic representation at the layers above the parish. Laity were not represented nationally until the 1900s, and were excluded from discussions of doctrine. Voluntary as it was, the system was not uniform; by the 1890s many urban parishes had councils, but they were rare in rural areas. In 1903 the Convocations were brought together with parallel lay assemblies to form the Representative Church Council (RCC), the first truly national assembly of the Church of England in modern times. But it was still a voluntary, patchy system, and the Church was entirely dependent on Parliament for legislative authority.

The franchise in this system was restricted to men, and usually based on confirmation, not baptism. This naturally reflected the influence of High Churchmen, who were particularly prominent in the agitation for self-government. They assumed the power to determine representation should lie with those most committed and engaged in church work. Baptism was too wide and indiscriminate a basis. Confirmation and communion were the real marks of active church membership.

Pressure for legislative autonomy came from three sources. The Liberal landslide victory of 1906 brought into power a government shored up by ardently anti-establishment Dissenting MPs. Welsh disestablishment followed. Fearful of the argument extending to the Church in England, in 1913 the archbishops established a committee to propose a scheme for the full integration of lay opinion. But the case was also theological: High

PUNCH, OR THE LONDON CHARIVARI.—November 15, 1911.

OVERDOING IT.

John Bull: "IS THAT THE LOT?"

33. *Punch* and Welsh Church disestablishment: the thin end of the wedge?

Churchmen wanted a system of self-governance to reflect the spiritual autonomy of the Church; Evangelicals wanted renewed and effective mission; Broad Churchmen wanted a truly national system to reflect aspirations for a comprehensive national Church.

The draft scheme that emerged in 1916 was the product of Archbishop Randall Davidson's careful negotiation and management in particular: full integration of the laity in the assembly; the universal establishment of Parochial Church Councils (PCCs); and devolved powers of self-government. But by now Britain had been at war for two years. Davidson was convinced – rightly – that there would be no appetite in Parliament for the enabling legislation until the war was over. But pressure for change was growing. The relative failure of Davidson's National Mission of Repentance and Hope in 1917 underlined the distance of the Church from ordinary people. This was the impetus for Life and Liberty, a group of enthusiasts for reform led by William

Temple, which, at a crowded London meeting, called for Parliament to declare its intentions on self-government for the Church.

Anglicans revere their prophets and mostly despise their statesmen and administrators. Temple has been given the credit for what was Davidson's plan. Temple led Life and Liberty magnificently: he gave up his day job at St James's, Piccadilly, and spent two years on the stump, arguing passionately up and down the land for 'liberty for the Church'. Undeniably he gave focus and impetus to the cause. He also changed the scheme in one important respect. Supporting the comprehensive national Church idea, and keen to encourage working people to participate, Temple argued successfully in the RCC for a baptismal franchise. Anglo-Catholics, led by Charles Gore, were disappointed. The electoral rolls which defined the electorate in each parish, when the universal creation of PCCs came into effect, rested on baptism, not confirmation, as the basis of church membership. Yet in all respects other than the franchise, this was Davidson's reform, not Temple's: the scheme mooted in 1916 came to fruition in the creation of the Church Assembly after the Enabling Act passed into law in 1919.

Political Anglicanism

Theologians and church leaders may have defended the Church's representative system time and again on theological and Patristic grounds, but the parallels with the emergent system of Parliamentary democracy were inescapable. The widening of the franchise (with legislation in 1867, 1884, and 1918), and the eventual achievement of universal franchise in 1928, was the single great fact in the changing landscape of British politics in the late nineteenth and early twentieth centuries. The Church could not afford to ignore it. It put pressure on political parties to mobilise and organise much more effectively than they had ever done before; it underlined the constitutional supremacy of the Commons; it enabled the eventual emergence of the Labour Party and the decline of the Liberal Party; and it underlay the emergence of systems of local and national social welfare that were eventually to evacuate the churches of much of their philanthropic significance. Perhaps its implications for the Church went further still: it was in the long run to marginalise the social, political and cultural influence of the churches in Britain, pushing elected political leaders ever more into the spotlight.

If that was the effect of the widening of democracy, it was not yet evident in the late nineteenth century. Nevertheless, Anglican clergy were often very wary of it. This was partly because they feared the effects of Nonconformist leverage on party policy. Few people at this stage genuinely feared the growing influence of atheism and secularism. The secularist Charles Bradlaugh fought an eight-year battle from 1880 to 1888 to substitute a non-religious affirmation in place of the usual religious oath on taking up a seat in Parliament, but in practice his victory was largely symbolic. Organised secularism was never very large.[5] Much the more common concern was rule by the mob. Even those naturally sympathetic to franchise reform were sceptical that the uneducated among the labouring poor should be able to exercise a vote. F. D. Maurice, for example, called the sovereignty of the people 'the silliest and most blasphemous of all contradictions'.[6] Anglicans supported popular education not merely as a good in itself, but because they assumed that a pious, God-fearing people would be the foundation of social stability. The inculcation of the principles of Anglican Christianity was, many believed, essential to the harmonious functioning of society. When Gladstone's first administration created the basis of the first truly national system of education in 1870, providing elementary schools to be built and supported by elected school boards, the ensuing politicisation of educational provision – with Anglicans and Nonconformists battling it out in elections for the school boards in order to protect or to reduce the role of Church schools – confirmed Anglican fears of the threat of popular politics.

It was actually in elections to the school boards as well as to some municipal authorities that women first exercised the vote in Britain from the 1870s on. Education arguably fell within the sphere of influence of the home and family – or at least, that is how it was conceived at the time – and women's right to a say there was not contested to the same extent that it was for national elections. But if many Anglican clergy and leading laymen often took some persuading of the merits of universal franchise among men, they were all the more sceptical about opening up political representation to women. The attitude of Hensley Henson, dean of Durham, speaking in 1914 at the height of the suffragette movement, was not untypical: he did not think that women 'generally were equipped with those powers judicial and political which qualified them for a seat on legislative assemblies'.[7]

So Anglican clergy were hardly free from the prejudices of their time. Yet there was a kind of 'political Anglicanism' that went beyond the articulation of commonly held values and opinions in the public arena. The old identification of historic Anglicanism with the Crown and with a constitutional position that had once shored up Anglican privilege had not completely faded. Probably a majority of Anglican clergy were Tory in sympathy. At local level, the strong association between Nonconformity and political Liberalism tended to fuel the opposite affiliation among Anglicans. There were clear identities of interest, for example, between the brewing industry, Toryism and Anglicanism, given how close the association of Nonconformity was with the temperance movement (and even though there were also strong Anglican supporters of temperance). But the constant threat of further constitutional reform, and the continuing local rivalries between Anglicans and Nonconformists over education, served simply to cement the alliance of Church and Crown. The clergy of the Church of England took an oath of allegiance to the Crown at ordination. They still do. It was very rare to find an Anglican clergyman expressing republican sentiments in the nineteenth century. Much more common was the kind of view expressed, somewhat excessively even in its time, by the diarist Francis Kilvert, after news of the recovery of the Prince of Wales from serious illness: 'How thankful we all are. I love that man now, and will always love him. I will never say a word against him. God bless him.'[8]

The greatest statesman of the age, William Gladstone, did not quite fit the common profile of an Anglican, combining as he did High Church religion with increasingly radical political Liberalism. But again a symptom of the divided reactions he engendered was that of Bishop Henry Phillpotts of Exeter:

> I am a very old man, Mr Liddon, and old men, you know, have not many words at their disposal; but when I think of Mr. Gladstone, there is only one word – only one word, Mr. Liddon – remember I am a very old man – that express what I feel; and that word is – Rascal![9]

It was Gladstone who had seen through the disestablishment of the Church of England's sister church, the Church of Ireland, in 1869, to the horror of many Anglicans on both sides of the Irish Sea. He did so as a convinced defender of the establishment in England, on the grounds that the Church of Ireland was a small minority church in a country dominated by Roman Catholicism, and as a concession to the Nonconformists who had voted for the Liberal Party in large numbers to put him in power in 1868. But those same Nonconformists were quick to point out the weakness of Anglicanism in Wales, too. In the form of the Liberation Society they had an organisation capable of continuing pressure for the separation of Church and State. Their cause was a principled defence of religious freedom: no church should be assisted, protected or favoured by the State; all religious institutions should be equally free to practise as they chose. Church schools should not be supported by local government. Bishops should be removed from the House of Lords. Church rates should end – that happened in 1868. Religious tests at the ancient universities should end – that happened in 1871. Nonconformists were not advocates of a secular society, however. They believed that creating a level playing field in organised religion would free and motivate churches to work as hard as they could for the evangelisation of society. They commonly shared much of the language of the old Puritan conscience.

But this 'political Nonconformity', as it was sometimes called, provoked organised opposition from Anglicans from 1871 in the form of a national body, the Church Defence Institution, and then a network of local Church Defence groups connected into what eventually became known as the Church Defence League. It was really only education, and particularly the regular elections for the school boards, that called out this kind of mobilisation across the country, and even then Anglicans never really got the hang of mass organisation. In a sense, they didn't need to. With their strength of support across the upper middle and upper classes, they still had what looked like an almost unassailable position at the heart of the constitution and of government.

Disestablishment in Wales

Yet the Welsh Church *was* vulnerable. The 1851 religious census had exposed the marginal position of the established Church there. Until the early eighteenth century, Wales had been almost solidly conformist.[10] But the relative poverty of many of its parishes and livings, and the difficulty of attracting and training a Welsh-speaking clergy, plus the tendency of bishops to spend a significant part of the year in the capital because of their political and courtly roles, had all taken their toll on the effectiveness of the Church.

The early Evangelical revival was particularly strong in parts of Wales, and although Methodism remained in the Church a little longer there than it did in England, when the breach did come, in 1811, the new connexion, the Calvinistic Methodists, rapidly became a dominant force in parts of Wales. Other Dissenting churches thrived, too, from the late eighteenth century. Methodists easily outnumbered active Anglicans in 1851. In rapidly expanding Merthyr there were three times more

Methodists than there were Anglicans, as well as Baptists and
Independents (Congregationalists).[11] It was widely believed
that there was a deliberate policy of 'anglicising' the Welsh. It
was not really true, at least not intentionally, but there was no
Welsh bishop in the four Welsh sees of St David's, Llandaff, St
Asaph and Bangor before 1870. The Church in Wales in the early
nineteenth century – at least in terms of the hierarchy – was
effectively 'a foreign institution'.[12] After the exposed position of
the Church of Ireland, Wales looked like the weakest link in the
case for a national Church.

There was an irony in this. The fact that there was no follow-
up census to 1851, plus the continuing impact of economic and
social change in the principality, meant that the impression of a
beleaguered, alien established Church lingered on into the early
twentieth century. But by then it was fast ceasing to be much
more than a myth. Already, long before 1851, determined efforts
were being made by the bishops to address the Welsh Church's
problems. The cumulative impact of the Ecclesiastical Commission's reforms benefitted the Welsh Church, bringing to an
end in due course non-residence and pluralism, augmenting the
poorest livings and tightening up clerical discipline.

Of local initiatives, probably the most significant, in the long
run, was the foundation of St David's College, Lampeter, as a
theological college for Wales in 1827. St David's faced difficulties of finance and recruitment for a long time, but eventually
it established itself as an effective training establishment. By
the 1880s it was training over a third of the Welsh Church's
ordinands, a large number of whom would have been Welsh-
speaking.[13] Gladstone's appointment of Joshua Hughes to St
Asaph in 1870 brought a St David's graduate to the bench of
bishops as the first Welsh-born, native Welsh-speaking bishop
for over a hundred and fifty years.[14] Hughes's appointment
signalled a fundamental shift in awareness on the part of politicians and senior clergy alike of the importance of the language
issue. Actually, increasingly English was outstripping Welsh in
the most populous part of Wales, the industrial south-east. No

matter: the Welsh language's symbolic importance as perhaps the most salient expression of national identity ensured it would remain a vital issue for Welsh Anglicans contemplating the revival of their Church. And this was the period when Welsh nationalism began to assume something like its modern form, influenced by Romantic conceptions of national, linguistic community, aiming for the foundation of national institutions, such as the University of Wales in 1893 ('the supreme achievement of nineteenth-century national consciousness') and the National Library of Wales and National Museum of Wales in 1907.[15] But, by then, so pervasive and overwhelming had proved the growth of Nonconformity that the association of the culture and values of the chapel with notions of Welsh identity and character was sealed in the public consciousness. It was a powerful combination. Its anti-Anglican animus was fuelled by the many inroads the High Church revival had made in the Welsh Church, with suspicion of Popery rife. Thus, even as Welsh Anglicanism was actually making gains in the principality, its reputation with political Nonconformity remained tainted.

The disestablishment of the Church in Wales became official Liberal Party policy in 1887. The coalition of 'Whig' gentry and aristocracy, middle-class Anglican Liberals and Nonconformist Liberals that made up Gladstone's party needed its constituent parts to be fed continuously with policy goals, and the case for disestablishment in Wales looked overwhelming. Gladstone himself accepted it personally in 1891. Bills were proposed in 1894 and 1895, but failed after meeting a wall of opposition from the Church and its supporters, especially over their plans for a policy of disendowment, removing all property and income from the four Welsh dioceses except anything acquired since 1703. By then Gladstone had retired anyway, and the Liberals were out of power in 1895.

Pressure for disestablishment continued to simmer away, however, and again was stirred up by the issue of education: Balfour's Education Act of 1902 offended Nonconformists by enabling voluntary schools – dominated by the Church of

England, but including Catholic schools as well – to receive financial support from local and national government. Its aim had been to bring the voluntary system into line with the national system of schools sponsored by the school boards: the boards were abolished, and all schools were made the responsibility of newly created local education authorities, under county and city councils. But it embodied a *bête noire* for Nonconformists – the public funding of denominational religious instruction, or, as it was called, 'Anglicanism on the rates', or, worse, 'Popery on the rates'. The Liberal landslide victory of 1906 set the scene for the final act in this particular drama. There was no question of immediate legislation. First, the new Liberal Government of Henry Campbell-Bannerman established a Royal Commission to investigate the state of religion in Wales.

The Commission's report, in 1910, confirmed the minority status of Anglicans in Wales. But it was far from discouraging. Although the Church could muster around a quarter of all worshippers across the principality, it was the largest denomination.[16] Moreover, although it had regional strengths and weaknesses, it had a presence in virtually every community. It might have not been in any realistic sense *the* national Church – Welsh Nonconformity was too closely identified at this point with Welsh national feeling and culture for that – but it was a truly national Church in its parish provision, and effectively the only Christian body to make that claim. The Church's gradual recovery from its mid-nineteenth-century low point was already evident. It had even benefitted somewhat from the great Welsh revival of 1904–5, on one view the last such revival in Britain, on another the first to exploit modern transport and print technology, though its long-term effects were probably modest.[17] The Welsh clergy, at first under the influence of Evangelicalism, later with a growing representation from Anglo-Catholics, were drawn increasingly from Welsh speakers, and with growing pastoral zeal and efficiency came a renewed sense of confidence about the prospects of the Church.[18] For this reason, Welsh Anglicans bitterly opposed disestablishment – why now, when things were on the mend? – but at the same time had less to fear from it than one might have thought.

The Liberal Government became bogged down for a time in its extensive programme of social reform and the ensuing constitutional battle, but by 1912 its planned measure for disestablishment was making its way through Parliament, finally going on the statute book in September 1914. The Welsh Church Act separated the four Welsh dioceses from the Church of England and made them into an autonomous body, removed the Welsh bishops from the House of Lords, ended the monarch's role as Supreme Governor of the Welsh Church, removed the legal, coercive powers of the Church courts, and appointed Welsh Church Commissioners to survey lands and property and transfer all endowments given before 1662 to local authorities or to the University of Wales. The point of that date? It was pushing the argument somewhat, but if you had to draw a line at which it could clearly be said that the Church of England could no longer realistically encompass all Christian believers within its scope, then the expulsion of many of the Puritan clergy in that year, treated by many Nonconformists as *de facto* the founding date of the Dissenting churches in England and Wales, was a better candidate than any other. Clearly property given to the Church before that date had been given for the whole community's benefit; it was perhaps harder to say the same afterwards. Disendowment, as in the case of the Irish Church, was the measure particularly feared by clergy, because it had the potential to impoverish the Church and to set back its pastoral ministry.

By the time the Act had been signed off, however, the First World War was under way, and implementation of the Government's legislative programme was effectively suspended for the duration of the war. The Welsh Church Commissioners none the less began the process of surveying and transferring endowment during the war. An Amending Act passed just after the war's end mitigated the financial impact, by granting a £1 million compensation payment to the Church and by allowing

the Church to make a charge on the value of transferred endowment. By then, the mechanisms of governance for the new
Church were already taking shape, with a governing body that
included bishops, clergy and laity, and provision for the election
of an archbishop for the new province from the Welsh bishops.

The nearly six-year delay from passage of the Act to its
formal implementation in March 1920 was a blessing in disguise.
It gave the Church time to adjust and plan for its new status,
and to begin a campaign of major fund-raising to make good
the losses from disendowment. The recovery of the Church in
Wales, as the new body was soon entitled, continued for much
of the twentieth century, even as Welsh Nonconformity began
a precipitous decline between the wars.[19] The old arguments
for a national Church in Wales may have gone forever, but the
new Church was free to develop its own, distinct Welsh identity
and culture in a way unavailable to it before. For Welsh Anglicanism, disestablishment was a paper tiger, or rather, to quote
one of its historians, 'the lion that failed to roar'.[20] But it was
a major change, and from then on Anglicanism in Wales and
in England went their separate ways – parallel, closely related,
warm in relations, but distinct in character.[21] The history of the
Church of England no longer encompassed Wales.

The Great Church Crisis

Welsh disestablishment, with its undertones of arguments
about religious liberty and its implicit cultural conflict between
a predominantly landed, rural Anglicanism and the Dissenting
culture of the chapels, epitomised the troubled situation of the
Church of England more broadly at the turn of the twentieth
century. On the one hand, the nineteenth-century reforms had
transformed the Church and rejuvenated its structures and ministry so that it was in a far stronger position than it had been
one hundred years before, despite its loss of constitutional privilege. On the other, the context in which it was operating seemed
ever more conflict-ridden, its internal politics laden with bitter

disputes over Ritualism and Liberalism. So the apparent success of the Church's practical reforms in the nineteenth and early twentieth centuries should not mislead us into thinking that it had arrived at its 'sunny uplands'. These were years that were to be called the 'great Church crisis'. The presenting issue was the growth of Ritualism within the Church, but the controversy over that symbolised in turn very different ideas about the constitution, the role of the Church and its relationship with the State, and national character.[22] All this played out against the unsettlement of the *fin de siècle*, with its sense of established certainties eroding, anxieties about the spread of Catholicism and threats to manhood, and the growth of a bohemian world which sat lightly with traditional morality.[23]

The failure of the 1874 Public Worship Regulation Act to curb Ritualism had disposed ardent Protestants, some within the Church, but others in the Free Churches, to much more direct forms of action. The leading spirit in this was John Kensit, founder of the Protestant Truth Society, who favoured interrupting Ritualist services, shouting criticism and condemnation. One of his most startling interventions was at St Cuthbert's, Philbeach Gardens, London, in 1898, when he interrupted a service of veneration of the cross by seizing the crucifix from the altar and shouting, 'In the name of God I denounce this idolatry in the Church of England; God help me!'[24] Kensit, ironically, died as he had lived, after being injured by an iron file flung at him in a protest on Merseyside. But however turbulent his actions, they helped to provoke an ultimately unsuccessful Parliamentary campaign in the late 1890s and early 1900s to put down Ritualism through strengthening Church discipline.

With the ultra-Protestant campaign growing both inside and outside Parliament, Church affairs were becoming once again an unwelcome political football. The Conservative Prime Minister Arthur Balfour took the heat out of the matter in 1904 by appointing a Royal Commission to examine the question of ritual and Church discipline. Reporting in 1906, the Commission's careful survey concluded that so widespread were many 'innovations' once regarded as rare and provocative, such as the wearing of colourful vestments for the celebration of communion, and the use of incense, that no purpose would be served by trying to suppress them. On the other hand, more extreme practices, such as some Marian festivals and the 'veneration of images and roods', were clearly incompatible with the Anglican formularies and ought to be prohibited. In a phrase that came to define the report's realism, it stated that the law governing public worship in church was 'too narrow for the religious life of the present generation'.[25]

As we saw in chapter 15, the theological latitude of the Church of England had already been pushed further and further apart in the nineteenth century. Liberals, Evangelicals and Anglo-Catholics had all claimed to find some support for their distinct positions in the formularies and traditions of the Church. Now the most toxic issue facing the late-nineteenth-century Church, the growth within it of 'Romish' ritual practice, had been accepted as a reality by a commission which included the archbishop of Canterbury, various bishops and politicians. This all but settled the matter in principle, though the commission's attempt to steer a middle way between the extremes of suppression and acceptance was bound to come under pressure from the more radical voices in Anglo-Catholicism, who would not abandon the practices condemned in the report.

Among the commission's recommendations was one fraught with serious implications for the Church's governance and identity. If discipline could no longer realistically be enforced to regulate acceptable ritual practices, then the law on public worship, and even the liturgy itself, needed revision. The Prayer Book simply could no longer serve on its own as an adequate, comprehensive liturgy for the Church of England. But how to revise it? Should it be replaced altogether with something more modern? Should alternatives be approved for use alongside it by parishes that chose to do so? Could there even be any sense in which the Church of England had a coherent theology embodied in its worship, if its liturgy was altered to accommodate different theological perspectives? And if Parliament retained the right to authorise, and therefore also veto, any proposed liturgical change, didn't that once again raise the prospect of a body of legislators who included non-Anglicans and non-believers exercising authority over the worship – and by implication belief – of a Christian Church? These questions were to play themselves out in a process of complex, internal wrangling over the next twenty years, only to be prolonged for a further fifty years when the Commons rejected the planned revision of the Prayer Book in 1927–8.

So the idea that peace had descended on the Church of England and on its critics in 1906 was, of course, completely illusory. Quite apart from the continuing arguments over Welsh disestablishment, the Church of England's extraordinary progress in reform, consolidation and even growth after the mid-nineteenth century was achieved despite (some would even argue *through*) continuing internal conflict. All of this gave Edwardian Anglicanism an air, not of confidence, but of insecurity and apprehension.

18

THE CHURCH IN A CENTURY OF CONFLICT

The War to End Wars

The Europe that went to war in August 1914 was a Christian Europe, divided by confessional difference, territorial and imperial ambition, historic grievance and political system. Religion played little role in the formation of the international alliances whose power play proved so disastrous, however. In 1913 the lower House of the Convocation of York had called for an all-out effort to avoid war, but by 1915 the Church was completely aligned with the national cause.[1] Once Germany had invaded Belgium and Britain's treaty guaranteeing Belgian neutrality had been invoked, and once stories of German atrocities – often, but not always, exaggerated – had begun to mount up, few could see any alternative to conflict. The Church of England's reputation in the First World War, at least in the last half century or so, has not been a happy one. Selective quotation of jingoistic and militaristic sentiment, a few stories of cowardly or ineffectual army chaplains and a broad, if unproven, assumption that the men in the trenches had no truck with organised religion have all combined to load the Church with the burden of a myth of failure.[2]

Closer examination of the evidence has produced a much more mixed verdict. The generation that went to war was overwhelmingly Christian in culture, and within that significantly identified with Anglicanism, even if with a sort of 'default' Church of England-ism. The 'diffusive Christianity' of non-churchgoers was naturally activated by the terror of war.[3] There was even talk of a religious revival among the troops in the early years of the war, though that had given way by 1917 to war-weariness and a growing cynicism.[4] The stories that grew up around angels near the battlefield, the apparent invincibility of some wayside shrines and calvaries, beliefs about the protective power of the Bible and various symbols and artefacts, the popularity of hymn singing, recourse to prayer for protection – these were all entirely understandable reactions by men who had had Christian values and beliefs inculcated in them by the Sunday Schools, the religious teaching in elementary schools and their own, family members' or acquaintances' experience of church or chapel. Army chaplains regularly reported very large numbers attending services, even those that were not compulsory. Church parades were a routine part of life at the front, with huge numbers present. On two successive days, for example, the Rt Revd Llewellyn Gwynne, Deputy Chaplain-General in France, preached to around 7,000 men at two services.[5]

The Church's official presence at the front was through its chaplains. The Army Chaplains' Department was interdenominational, but the Church of England dominated it. At the outset of war, 89 out of 117 chaplains were Anglican; by August 1918 the total had swollen to 3,416, of whom nearly 2,000 were 'C of E'.[6] Because of the Church's established status, before the war it was routine for all units recruited from England and Wales, as well as for some Irish units, to have Anglican chaplains, just as Presbyterian chaplains were appointed for Scottish regiments. In the first eighteen months of the war, however, Anglican chaplains were subject to different operational rules from the Free Church and Catholic chaplains and were required to remain in behind-the-lines bases and holding points during action, tending to the wounded and burying the dead, whereas their colleagues were free to move forward with the men in the front lines.

This rule was, understandably, deeply uncomfortable for many Anglican chaplains, and was often defied in practice, though it surely lay behind the belief of some soldiers that chaplains 'flunked it' and held back from danger. Once the rule was changed, Anglican chaplains proved themselves as brave as

34. The Church at war: a chaplain at the front

any others. Several won the Victoria Cross. Theodore Hardy, for example, a relatively elderly clergyman in his fifties who had had to press several times to be taken on as a chaplain after the outbreak of war, won the Distinguished Service Order in October 1917, the Military Cross in December 1917, and the Victoria Cross in October 1918, all for action to recover and tend wounded men under fire.[7] Quite apart from gallantry, some chaplains became famous simply as characters who went out of their way to look after men at the front. 'Tubby'. Clayton and Neville Talbot founded Talbot House ('TocH') at Poperinge, near Ypres, as a place of rest and recuperation for exhausted soldiers. The charismatic and immensely popular Geoffrey Studdert Kennedy, also a recipient of the Military Cross, acquired the nickname 'Woodbine Willie' for his habit of handing out cigarettes to soldiers at the front line.

But what of the home front? How did the Church fare there

during the war? Its reputation has been tarnished by association with the kind of enthusiastic jingoism particularly common in the early months of the war. Time and again the man quoted in this context is Arthur Winnington-Ingram, bishop of London for thirty-eight years, who is supposed to have preached a sermon in 1915 in Westminster Abbey in which he urged his congregation to 'Kill Germans ... to kill the good as well as the bad, to kill the young men as well as the old'.[8] Winnington-Ingram's language was often colourful, but in fact what he said was nothing near as bloodthirsty as this, and was rather a description of the indiscriminate nature of warfare. Yet the myth stands as a sign of the late twentieth century's disillusionment with the sentiments and the religious values of an earlier age. Anglicans were drawn into the general enthusiasm for the war in the beginning and, like Christians of other churches, often encouraged volunteers for war service, but then found they had to minister to the families hearing news of loss and injury on an unprecedented scale. Like members of other churches, they raised money, food and equipment for the men at the front, and helped buoy up general morale.

Yet to look at parish magazines and other records of the time is to look at a local world in which surprisingly little changed, even with large numbers of young men away on service. Church attendance on the whole did not collapse, though there was a gradual downward trend overall.[9] In some places like Colchester it seems to have held up very well, but then that was a barracks town.[10] In Coventry, by contrast, one priest was sure congregations were declining, partly because of Sunday labour in the munitions and other factories.[11] However, there were peaks of attendance not only on the great festivals of Christmas and Easter, but also on those days nominated as special Days of National Prayer.

In autumn 1916, the Church launched a great evangelistic initiative, called the National Mission of Repentance and Hope, designed to seize on the challenges presented by the war to galvanise Christian work and witness across the nation. Retreats, conferences, special services and sermons and public prayers were organised up and down the country. There was even a matching initiative at the front: Studdert Kennedy was commissioned to address the troops over ten days, speaking three times a day to large crowds.[12] But there was no nationwide religious revival. The National Mission was the first instance of a recurrent pattern in the twentieth century – a great national evangelistic strategy announced and pursued vigorously, only to be found to have, at best, slowed decline a little. Yet even this lacklustre conclusion should not be exaggerated. At the local level, the Church emerged relatively unscathed from the war, its parochial machinery intact, its public reputation largely untarnished.

On the other hand, the war was indeed a terrible shattering of illusions. Of the many consequences for the Church of England, one stands out. A new cult of sacrificial death was folded into the culture and memory of the Church. Language formerly applied to Christian martyrs, and above all to Christ himself, was extended to encompass ordinary people, the dead in war. Like all such language, it was necessarily ambiguous, holding together seemingly antithetical values and emotions: loss was also glorious; death for King and Country was also a forced sacrifice (especially with conscription); war was pursued for peace; the ordinary was transfigured into the extraordinary. The restrained and sober piety that many people assumed was characteristically Anglican (though, as we have seen, it was difficult to hold to a single way of describing anything Anglican by this stage) had to expand to include new depths of pain and suffering. A growing demand for prayers for the dead was one outcome: something effectively cut out of the Church at the Reformation, the idea had begun to make headway in Anglo-Catholic churches; now, in response to the sheer scale of family loss, it began to be a feature of more mainstream parishes. Another outcome was memorialisation, and the way it refocused the attention of many communities on the parish church. The annual service of Remembrance, the very notion of communities gathering together to remember and to honour their losses, gave religion a new local prominence.[13] Even when acts of Remembrance were civic rather than specifically religious, it was rare for local clergy not to be invited to participate and lead prayer, and so even the civic culture of Remembrance was given a religious, not to say in many places *Anglican*, gloss.

Recovery and Apprehension

The war was a great national crisis, and its ramifications lasted well beyond the Armistice of 1918. We can trace its impact through almost every branch of foreign, economic and social policy in the ensuing decades. It accelerated the break-up of Ireland, signalled the beginning of the end for landed society and the great estates, brought votes for women and ultimately universal suffrage, facilitated the Parliamentary rise of the Labour Party and the collapse of the Liberal Party, weakened the British economy, fuelled calls for better national systems of housing and welfare, transformed international relations and marked the advent of mechanised warfare and a revolution in transport. The Church was affected by all this no less than any other sector of British society. Far from undermining the Church's sense of its national role and vocation, the war if anything strengthened it, and gave renewed impetus to the determination of many Anglicans to overhaul its organisation and governance, leading to passing of the Enabling Act, as we saw in the previous chapter.

The new structures, with their devolved powers, from Parochial Church Council to Church Assembly, briefly released a wave of optimism about the future among senior Anglican clergy and laity. William Temple had toured the country in 1917–18, speaking about the new possibilities of the Church as a democratic mass movement.[14] Alas, it was not to be. Three particular moments in the inter-war years exemplified the ceiling of change and the end of optimism. First, as the initial fillip that peace brought to social affairs in Britain in the early

1920s quickly subsided into prolonged hardship and industrial
tension, and eventually issued in the General Strike of 1926, the
practical inability of the Church to function as an influential
mediator was exposed. Davidson's attempt to adopt a concil-
iatory, worker-friendly tone was rebuffed by the government,
and the BBC declined to broadcast his proposals; and when,
some months later, Temple, who was by then bishop of Manchester, tried with other bishops and members of the Industrial
Christian Fellowship to mediate between the coal owners and
workers in the ongoing dispute that had led to the General
Strike, their efforts were roundly condemned by the owners
and largely ignored by the unions.[15] For the most part, however,
clergy lined up behind the government, which hardly endeared
them to trade unionists. Hensley Henson, bishop of Durham,
for example, called the strike 'criminal' and thought it could not
go on without ending in civil war, though he had an instinctive
sympathy for the poor.[16]

The second moment was the failure of Prayer Book reform.
This was a long and convoluted process that had begun before
the war, and pitched ardent Evangelical Protestants against
Anglo-Catholics and many 'Broad' or Liberal churchmen. Conflict was particularly intense over proposed revisions to the
Order for Holy Communion that would produce a eucharistic
rite much more in harmony with a High Church theology of
real presence and eucharistic sacrifice, and also over provision
for use of the reserved sacrament for taking communion to the
sick, which could be kept in an aumbry permanently installed
in the sanctuary or a side chapel. A compromise book was produced which satisfied neither Protestant Evangelicals nor more
zealous Anglo-Catholics.[17] Moreover, since introduction of a
revised Prayer Book required amendment to the Act of Uniformity, and therefore statutory authorisation, there was no
way round obtaining Parliamentary approval: the newly won
legislative independence of the Church was irrelevant. Moved
by a coterie of strongly Protestant MPs, and buoyed up by a
residual anti-Catholicism, opponents of the revision secured its

defeat in two successive Parliamentary sessions in 1927 and 1928. More than anything else, this debacle demonstrated the limits of autonomy. In practice, the defeat was perhaps not as catastrophic as seemed at first sight, as bishops were able to license the revised book for use as an alternative to the Prayer Book in their own dioceses, and that happened commonly. But it broke the liturgical uniformity of the Church of England.

The third matter to check Anglican optimism in the interwar period was the abdication crisis of 1936. This was, frankly, a disastrous episode for the Church's leadership, which could not support King Edward VIII's desire to marry the divorcee Wallis Simpson without being seen to jettison the Church's own teaching on marriage, and equally could not uphold that teaching without jeopardising a popular tide of good will strongly running in support of the king. But Archbishop Cosmo Gordon Lang, who manoeuvred behind the scenes to help make way for the duke of York, George VI, unfortunately made matters worse with a sincere but tactless broadcast in which he voiced his regret that the king's 'craving for private happiness' should have led him to abandon 'a trust so great'.[18] Lang was the first archbishop of Canterbury to make extensive use of the new medium of radio, and his hostile postbag anticipated the reception bishops would face later in the century for speaking out on a range of controversial issues.

Troubled times were reflected in the changing nature of theology. The characteristic optimism of Victorian theology, typified by an Anglican philosophical idealism which combined intellectual progessivism with an orthodox understanding of doctrine, received a colossal check.[19] The Great War did not destroy Anglican idealism altogether. The strongest challenge to it emerged later in the philosophical movement called 'Logical Positivism' in the 1930s and 1940s, with its suspicion of metaphysics and more or less explicit espousal of materialism. But the ease with which, on both sides of the conflict, churches had been drawn into explicit support for their national governments deepened the scepticism of a younger generation of theologians about the credibility of church leaders' advocacy. In Continental Protestantism and in the United States theologians returned to perspectives that emphasised revelation distinct from human reason and philosophy. No English, Anglican equivalents emerged to theologians of the stature of Karl Barth, Emil Brunner or Reinhold Niebuhr, but these theologians left their mark on Anglicans. Even Temple shifted away from the synthesis of philosophy and theology that had marked his earlier work.[20] The younger Anglican theologians – many of them Anglo-Catholic – included a future archbishop, Michael Ramsey, whose first book, *The Gospel and the Catholic Church* (1936), partly influenced by Barth, was an eloquent defence of the Anglican understanding of the Church which made, if anything, a virtue of incompleteness and provisionality: 'it is sent not to commend itself as "the best type of Christianity", but by its brokenness to point to the universal Church wherein all have died'.[21]

In Ramsey's work we see the influence of two of the most striking developments of Anglican theology in the twentieth century, both with deep roots but strengthened by the war's impact. One was a renewed commitment to Christian unity. The competitiveness and mutual suspicion between the Free Churches and the Church of England gave way to a spirit of cooperation and mutual appreciation after the war. The beginnings lay in growing cooperation in overseas mission in the late nineteenth century, its arrival heralded by the great World Missionary Conference at Edinburgh in 1910, an event often taken as the 'start' of the ecumenical movement.[22] That conference, for all its global ambition, was mostly a gathering of delegates from western European and North American Protestantism, but communication between the German and Anglo-Saxon churches was severely disrupted by the war. International relations had to be rebuilt carefully. The Lambeth Conference, the great gathering of bishops of the Anglican Communion, which has usually happened every ten years or so since 1867, in 1920 issued an 'Appeal to All Christian People' which called for renewed effort in the search for unity, seeing episcopal order as a basis on which churches from different confessions could unite.[23]

With that as a background, and with a growing international focus on ecumenism, some important steps were taken between the wars to transform the Church of England's relations with other churches. Conversations with the British Free Churches unfortunately led nowhere concrete, though personal relationships between church leaders benefitted enormously. A series of informal conversations in Belgium between Church of England Anglo-Catholic theologians and mostly Belgian Roman Catholics, known as the Malines Conversations, were brought to an abrupt end in 1927 by the Vatican.[24] In 1931 the Bonn Agreement was signed between the Church of England and the Old Catholic Churches of the Union of Utrecht, a collection of national Catholic churches mostly based in the Netherlands, Germany, Switzerland and Austria which had broken away from the Roman Catholic Church; the agreement to establish a relationship of 'intercommunion', in other words a full recognition of each other's ministries and sacraments. Further steps were taken in ecumenical relations with the Church of Sweden (Lutheran) and the Orthodox churches under the patriarchate of Constantinople.[25]

Also noticeable in Ramsey's work both as a theologian and later as a bishop was the continued evolution of Anglican social theology. Here the great figure of the interwar period was unquestionably William Temple. Temple had clear sympathies with the Labour movement, friendships with figures on the centre and left such as William Beveridge and R. H. Tawney, and roots in the Christian Social Union of Charles Gore. He was the natural chair and inspiration of the great international conference on Christian Politics, Economics and Citizenship (COPEC) in 1924, which studied social problems and their impact on the lives of people. This was before the General Strike and, with the benefit of hindsight, it is clear that the conference's high-profile and much-lauded principles for guiding Christian conduct in social life and citizenship were almost entirely without practical traction. Possibly more influential was the Malvern Conference, organised by the Industrial Christian Fellowship in late 1940, over which again Temple presided, this time as archbishop of York. With the prospect of post-war planning in view – an extremely optimistic outlook in that of all years – it was possible by this juncture to envisage a consensus of sorts on a Christian social outlook across the political spectrum.

It is hard to know how much these theological developments affected ordinary parishes, if at all. Reform, with the foundation of new dioceses, continued in the inter-war years. Building even started for a new cathedral at Guildford in 1936, although it was not finished until 1965. Some church building programmes were undertaken on a scale as impressive as that of the Victorian period, especially for the new estates being built in response to the urgent demand for housing to replace slums and dilapidated tenements. The largest of these was in Middlesex, where the growth of suburban north London was extraordinarily rapid. Given the financial constraints, a major fundraising effort was needed, and the Forty-five Churches Fund was launched in 1930. By 1941, some twenty-eight new churches had been built, as well as a further thirty-one halls which could also function as churches, though fund-raising was getting harder, even before the outbreak of war in 1939.[26]

So there was growth, at least in terms of structures and buildings, but in other ways the position of the local church was gradually being marginalised. Sundays were rapidly losing their religious character, as cinemas, pubs, public transport and even the beginnings of mass car ownership opened up other leisure prospects, although there was no dramatic collapse. Church life went on much as before. There was even a post-1918 recovery for some years. The highest recorded figure for Easter Day communicants was 1927, with some 2.39 million, although this had fallen back to 2.25 million by 1939.[27] Decline in the Free Churches was almost certainly faster, although it affected all denominations except Catholics. At the outbreak of war in 1939 probably around 2.5 million people were Anglican communicants, and another 3 million or so regular attenders in some form (including young people and children), making a total of around 15 per cent of the population in some sense 'active' or at least other than nominally Anglican.[28] This was, by present standards, a very high figure and, taking into account nominal Anglicans and the very small percentage of people still of definite 'no belief', it underlines how much England was still consciously and culturally Christian.

That common Christian identity was a powerful appeal for politicians and church leaders as the international situation deteriorated after the Nazis' advent to power in Germany in 1933. Despite Anglicanism's class weighting and its poor positioning in the new class politics, the Church continued to have a significant national voice. With the waning of active Nonconformist politics and the decline of the Liberal Party, if anything Anglican leaders were more influential publicly than they had been at the beginning of the century. Radio helped this. Temple's appeal transcended the Church of England – he was a genuinely national figure. But though few Anglican leaders showed much sympathy for Fascist politics, and many – including Lang and Temple – condemned the Nazis' racial policies from the beginning, many others were very reluctant to countenance another war. Dick Sheppard, who was from 1929 dean of Canterbury, helped to found the Peace Pledge Union the year before his death in 1937. This was probably the outstanding Anglican contribution to the peace movement between the wars, even though a later generation would come to see it as disastrously misjudged. Much less representative of the age was the commitment of George Bell, bishop of Chichester, to support those German churches that, as the self-proclaimed 'Confessing Church', resisted Hitler's attempt to recruit German Protestantism to the Nazi cause. Bell was outspoken in his criticism of Nazism. But even Bell was wary of 'war-mongering', and advocated a peaceful settlement well into 1940, when Temple and Lang had already committed themselves to the position that there could be no peace with Hitler in power.[29] The very hubris that had caught Christians unawares in 1914, overidentifying with patriotism and seemingly blind to the coming catastrophe of total war, made them all the more determined to do whatever they could to stop war a second time.

The Church of England in the Second World War

The experience of the Great War, then, tempered the Church's reaction in 1939. Like most of the political class, and much of the country, Church leaders initially welcomed the Munich Agreement with relief, but little long-term optimism. There was little of the language of 'holy crusade' often used in the Great War. In its archbishops, and with the support of others such as Bell, the Church had an effective and formidable leadership in a national crisis. When Lang retired from Canterbury in 1942, Temple was his natural and obvious successor. His sudden death just two years later robbed the Church of a man who seemed poised to lead it into a new era of social reconstruction. It was Temple who coined the phrase 'welfare state' which came to typify the legislative achievements of the post-war Attlee government. More so than in the First World War, the Church of England by then seemed more consistently in tune with popular feeling. In this, it was aided by the improved relationships with the Free Churches that were a product of the ecumenical movement, but also by active cooperation – unprecedented in modern British religious history – with the leaders of the Catholic Church in England, and especially Cardinal Hinsley of Westminster.

This was evident in the role played by chaplains to the forces. There was no repeat of the controversy over whether or not Anglican chaplains could move forward to the front line – that was simply now accepted. Once again, the relatively small peacetime army had to expand quickly, but this time conscription applied immediately. For that reason, and perhaps also because of a greater readiness to recognise the importance of psychological well-being to troops in the field, the armed forces paid much more attention to identifying the state of morale and remedying it if it was found to be deficient. In this, chaplains played a key role. On the whole, commanders were strongly supportive. Bernard Montgomery, for example, who was himself the son of a missionary bishop, was exceptionally ready to affirm the importance of army chaplains, asserting after El Alamein that 'I would as soon think of going into battle without my artillery as without my Chaplains'.[30]

Much more so than in the First World War, the home front was itself an arena of destruction and death, especially in London and the industrial cities and ports. Over 50,000 British civilians lost their lives as a result of bombing, the largest number by far in London. With the injured, the bereaved and the homeless to look after, clergy and other church workers found themselves fully stretched on what was in effect a new front line. As for their colleagues in the forces, their work became an important part of the effort to sustain civilian morale. But the war was much more disruptive, particularly in urban areas, than in 1914 –18. Schools were affected by the loss of teachers recruited into the forces or into the various auxiliary organisations, and by the evacuation of children from the cities. The extensive effects of bombing, combined with programmes of replacement housing further out in the countryside after the war, accelerated the long-term population decline of parts of London and other big cities. Churches lost lay workers and volunteers to the Home Guard, the Royal Observer Corps, the Land Army and other agencies. Given all this, it is hardly surprising that many clergy reported a decline in church attendance. The best available estimate is that the Church of England lost some 3 per cent of its regular attenders in the course of the war.[31] Sunday Schools were particularly hard hit by a falling birth rate, the evacuation of children and the loss of teachers, and never regained their pre-war strength.[32]

Almost unprecedented, too, was the physical damage churches faced. In London alone, over 700 churches were damaged by bombing, with ninety-one completely destroyed. At the start of the war, thirty-two of Wren's London churches still survived; only fifteen of these were relatively unaffected by

35. A symbol of defiance: St Paul's in the Blitz

bombing.[33] Many of those destroyed or severely damaged were not rebuilt, their congregations having shrunk or even disappeared altogether; others took years to rebuild, with the aid of funding from the War Damage Commission, as well as from diocesan initiatives. Two Anglican churches in different ways became synonymous with the experience of Britain at war. The destruction of Coventry cathedral in a firestorm in November 1940 came to stand eventually as testimony to the futility of war and the desire for peace and reconciliation, though that was largely a work of post-war reconstruction, especially under the leadership of its wartime provost, Richard Howard. By contrast, St Paul's in London became a symbol of defiance and resistance, its seemingly miraculous survival despite the devastation around it expressed iconically in a famous photograph showing the great dome emerging from clouds of smoke. Taken by the photographer Herbert Mason, the photograph was a craftily edited and manipulated image. No matter – it quickly became probably the most famous photograph of the cathedral, and of any Anglican church in the war, except perhaps Coventry.[34]

Peace in 1945 marked a new era, emphasised by the electoral success of the Labour Party and defeat of Churchill's Conservatives, blamed as they were for appeasement and the poverty of the inter-war years, despite Churchill's war leadership. Confirmation of the appalling crimes of the Nazi regime was a vindication of the hardship and sacrifices of war, and the Allies' decisive victory seemed briefly to hold out the prospect of a new and lasting settlement in Europe. The legislative achievements of Clement Attlee's post-war government created a consensus on social and economic policy for over a generation. It is difficult to demonstrate this clearly, for lack of evidence, but it seems likely that the 1945 election began to mark a gradual shift in the political allegiances of the Anglican clergy, if by no means necessarily those of their congregations. The strength of the ecumenical movement before the war assisted in the rebuilding of Christian internationalism, too, as the creation of the World Council of Churches, planned before the war, was finally given effect in 1948. Mutual ecumenical appreciation, against the background of the Nuremberg Trials, also assisted the rehabilitation of the German churches, enabling Christians in the West to hold on to a distinction between the German people and the Nazi leadership, however tenuous or suspect this was in practice.

The Church in the Era of the Cold War

The mood of relief in 1945 was short-lived, however, as the ideological polarisation of the democratic West and Soviet-aligned East, and the arrival of the atom bomb, threatened the possibility of an even more destructive conflict. Despite the impression of a gradual return to normality and familiarity at home, the international situation was changing rapidly, with ramifications for the Church's self-understanding.

In the 1930s, the idea that the Church of England was the

'mother' church of the Anglican Communion, considered controversial in the United States, rested on the continuing existence
of the British Empire. Most of the colonial episcopate were
British; and nearly all of them were white. Missionary societies
were headquartered in London, sending out trained missionaries into Africa and Asia. The Church was an intrinsic part of
an imperial establishment, its Supreme Governor also Emperor
of India. The granting of independence to India and Pakistan
in 1947 marked the beginning of the dismantling of most of
the formal, political structures of empire. Independence movements in Africa and Asia, and in the Middle East, frequently
criticised the colonial churches, calling for their reform and for
a fully indigenous leadership. The long and sometimes painful
transition to a Commonwealth of nations, and to an Anglican Communion no longer led and largely controlled from
Lambeth, began. In Geoffrey Fisher, at Canterbury from 1945 to
1961, the Church of England had a solid, practical, dependable if
somewhat autocratic leader whose posthumous reputation has
suffered a little from being sandwiched between the prophetic
figure of William Temple and the brilliant, eccentric theologian
Michael Ramsey. But Fisher did mostly march with the times
when it came to grasping the momentous changes going on in
the worldwide communion, and in ecumenical relations.[35]

Peace brought stability at home, and the opportunity to
rebuild or repair damaged buildings, and restore parish life. The
late 1940s and 1950s have even been called a period of religious
revival.[36] Some of the statistics bear this out. Total Easter Day
communicant figures for the Church of England in 1947 were
1.73 million; these rose to a post-war high of 2.17 million in 1956,
before plateauing until the early 1960s, when they began to
fall again.[37] On the other hand, they never achieved the levels
of the 1920s and 1930s. Anglican baptisms rose from 365,000 in
1940 to 525,835 in 1947 – as a result of a post-war baby boom –
but thereafter declined.[38] Local sources suggest modest gains
after the war in many places, and then a period of stability or
gradual contraction.[39] So the description 'revival' is probably an

exaggeration, but the Church broadly maintained its position. Much effort was poured into youth work, and into educational work.[40]

This was the period in which immigration from Britain's colonies and former colonies in significant numbers began – the *Empire Windrush* voyage carrying over 800 migrants from the Caribbean was in 1948 – but at first this had little direct impact on British society; Britain remained overwhelmingly white and Christian. Parish ministry was put on a firmer financial footing by the Church Commissioners – the name given in 1948 to the body that oversaw the Church's estates and finances when the Ecclesiastical Commissioners and Queen Anne's Bounty were merged – in the 1950s, as stipends were standardised and monthly payments introduced in place of quarterly payments.[41] But if this, in one sense, helped to stabilise the ministry, there were ominous signs of pressures in the opposite direction. Long term, a Church with a disproportionate number of its buildings in the countryside, where the population was often declining, was going to struggle to follow the principle of 'one parish, one church, one minister'. In 1949, in Lincoln diocese, the first radical experiment was made in amalgamating parishes to create a large group, the South Ormsby benefice, with fifteen ancient parishes covering just a thousand people between them.[42]

The mood of optimism, post war, was reflected in an Indian summer of Anglican literary, theological and artistic creativity. Writers such as T. S. Eliot, Charles Williams, Rose Macaulay and Barbara Pym cannot be pigeonholed simply as 'Anglican' writers, but all were or became actively involved in Anglican churches and were unembarrassed about that. C. S. Lewis, who came from a Church of Ireland background, was more detached, but it was in this period that he began to publish his most famous works of apologetics. Even the poet W. H. Auden returned to the High Church influence of his childhood, though it would be hard to call him a specifically Anglican writer. A poet of whom it could be said more firmly was John Betjeman. Ambivalence about identification as 'Anglican' would yet be true, too, of a number of other writers, composers and artists who none the less had close links with Anglican churches and contributed to the broad culture of the Church of England, one way or another, in these years, such as Benjamin Britten, and Herbert Howells. Nor did Anglican theology lack vital force. These were the years of much of the best work of Michael Ramsey, but also of Austin Farrer, friend of Charles Williams and C. S. Lewis. Born a Baptist but converting to Anglo-Catholicism, Farrer was arguably the finest Anglican philosopher of religion of the century. More of a dogmatic theologian was his great friend Eric Mascall, also an Anglo-Catholic. These years probably provided the high water mark of Anglo-Catholicism as a literary and intellectual force.

But it is neither the cultural creativity of Anglicans nor the steady work in parishes that perhaps can best sum up the experience of the Church of England in the 1950s. It is a little arbitrary to pick out two events to stand for the tension the period encapsulated between establishment prominence and future threat, but the complex situation of the Church can be seen in the coronation of Queen Elizabeth II and the first Aldermaston march. The coronation in Westminster Abbey, on 2 June 1953, televised and broadcast to a vast international audience, appeared to epitomise the magnificence, permanence and stability of the constitutional settlement between Church and State, with ancient liturgical text and ritual, and yet it placed the Church's ministry at the heart of the modern State. Yet probably nothing from the era could better illustrate the ambiguities of the Church's position than the involvement of various clergy, including most prominently Canon John Collins, one of the founders of War on Want and of the Campaign for Nuclear Disarmament, and a tireless campaigner against apartheid in South Africa, in the annual Easter protests against nuclear weapons from 1958 that centred on the nuclear research establishment at Aldermarston, Berkshire.

19

DECLINE? THE RELIGIOUS 'CRISIS' OF THE 1960S AND LATER

Pluralism and Decline

Church leaders on the cusp of the 1960s had some reason for optimism, given the relative stability of congregations since 1945. Sunday Schools were struggling, there were difficulties holding on to young people, and various evangelistic initiatives had had mixed success, including Billy Graham's non-denominational crusade to London in 1954. But the position of the Church of England looked secure, its self-perception as the national Church buoyed up by its strong association with the monarchy and other traditional institutions. But its confidence was about to be shaken. Retrospectively, a series of defining moments have projected an image of cultural revolution which marked off the 'Swinging Sixties' from the stuffy and inert 1950s – the Lady Chatterley trial of 1960, the Profumo scandal, the rise of pop music and, especially for Church people, the controversy over John Robinson's book *Honest to God* (1963). Despite the increasing fragmentation of English Christianity over 400 years, England had remained overwhelmingly Christian. That was about to be blown apart.

The most unforeseen aspect of all this was the growth of other faith communities, as a consequence of mass immigration from former colonies and dependencies. From around 50,000 in 1961, the Muslim community, for example, rose to over two and a half million half a century later.[1] The growth of a multi-faith society in Britain may not be a direct concern of this book, but it was clearly a vital part of the context in which the Church of England increasingly had to operate. But the most pressing change was one that directly affected the Church itself. It was in the 1960s that the gradual decline in churchgoing turned into a sharp contraction. There were many causes. The arrival of the 'permissive society', with changing attitudes to sexuality, marriage and pleasure, contrasted with the traditional values espoused by the churches. Many people saw the churches as 'irrelevant survivals from a pre-technological age'.[2] One historian has argued that the withdrawal of women in particular from participation in church life, partly under the influence of feminism, was especially responsible for decline, but that has been disputed.[3]

What cannot be disputed is the scale of the fall after about 1963, and the inexorability of it, even though the sharpest period of contraction, beginning in the 1970s, eased somewhat towards the end of the century. Between 1960 and 1980, estimated communicant numbers fell by 26 per cent, from 2.34 million to 1.73 million.[4] Another twenty years on, they had fallen to nearer a million.[5] If the estimated figure for attendance, rather than communion, was probably around 3 million in 1960, by 2010 that was down by two-thirds also to around a million.[6] The number of confirmands fell by almost a half from a mean of around 177,000 a year in 1956–60 to around 96,000 in 1976–80.[7] By 2010–11 that number had fallen catastrophically to around 22,000.[8] There are some less alarming numbers. The number of Christmas communicants has not fallen as sharply as those at Easter, and there is evidence that a decline in the frequency of attendance has somewhat cushioned the fall.[9]

Changes in churchgoing habits were not spread uniformly. Broadly, Anglican practice and participation held up somewhat better in parts of the countryside, in affluent suburbs, in market towns and in historic cathedral cities than in many industrial or post-industrial towns and cities, in the south and west than in the north-west and north-east, and in traditional institutions such as the ancient universities, public schools and armed forces. It is worth mentioning two dimensions of marginalisation and exclusion that increasingly preoccupied Anglicans in England in this period. The first is perhaps the most commonly ignored or neglected, yet the most obvious – social class. We have seen in earlier chapters that, though it is a myth that the working class were completely lost to the Church of England by the nineteenth century, there was a pronounced class bias in the statistics of Anglican practice. The Church was present but not equally strong in all communities, its greatest weakness numerically lying mostly in the working-class neighbourhoods of the great cities, and in the dispersed post-war, out-of-town housing estates created after slum clearance and bomb damage.

David Sheppard, a socially minded bishop in Woolwich in south London, laid out the contrasts starkly from his time there in the late 1960s and early 1970s: in the parishes of leafy, suburban Surrey, around 9 per cent of the adult population were registered on parish electoral rolls (about as close to a definition of active Anglican 'membership' as we can get); but in working-class, inner south London, the figure was less than 1 per cent.[10] And that was in the early 1970s, with decades of contraction ahead. These areas were particularly vulnerable to institutional decline, losing attenders, financial support and professional lay volunteers, and the closing, demolishing or selling on of church buildings. The real impact may have been masked until the 1980s, but the massive contraction of British industry in that decade, leading to social dislocation and unemployment, simply highlighted how intertwined the Church was, given its commitment to the parish system, with the economic and social vicissitudes of these areas. There was a final flourish for the great tradition of Anglican social theology, with interest in alternative forms of ministry, including industrial chaplaincy, in an attempt to articulate more clearly the Church's mission to the marginalised, and the publication of the *Faith in the City* report in 1985, which attempted to clarify and strengthen that mission against a background of deepening concern for urban deprivation.

But another dimension of marginalisation was race. The Church of England has, from its history, much to regret about

its treatment of people from other parts of the world. Its record
of speaking out against slavery and other forms of oppression in
the British Empire is mixed, its clergy and laity often in collusion
with governing elites in the colonies, as well as at home. Many
of the plantation owners in the Caribbean, the merchants who
benefitted from the slave trade and the traders themselves were
seemingly God-fearing Anglicans. Even John Moore, archbishop
of Canterbury at the time when Wilberforce launched his Parliamentary campaign, opposed the abolition of the trade.[11]
Later, some Anglicans, such as George Selwyn, bishop of New
Zealand, and John Colenso, bishop of Natal, were unusual in
the support they gave to indigenous peoples and were a thorn in
the flesh of colonial administrators, but more commonly clergy
and missionaries reinforced the imperial mission.[12] Anglicans
were no freer than anyone else of prejudices about race and
cultural difference.

There were black Christians, particularly in urban parishes,
from roughly the seventeenth century on, but not many, and it
was migration from the Caribbean in the 1940s and 1950s that
profoundly changed the make-up of Christian congregations in
urban Britain. By 1965 net migration from the Caribbean in the
previous seventeen years stood at over 300,000, though it is difficult to argue this was a total figure for settlement, as many would
have returned, or perhaps made multiple trips.[13] Many of these
migrants were from churchgoing families, but their experience
of church in Britain was often discouraging. One commenta-
tor reckoned that 94 per cent of Caribbean migrants ceased to
attend church when they came to Britain.[14] Not all migrants'
experience of English churches was negative, however, and
some churches were alert to the needs of migrants from a relatively early date.[15]

In the long run, migrants from the Caribbean and, later,
Africa helped to sustain churchgoing in the inner cities. A survey
of London ethnicity and religious practice in 2003 reckoned that
twice as many UK-born Afro-Caribbean Londoners attended
church regularly as UK-born 'whites'.[16] London's burgeoning

multi-cultural and multi-ethnic demography was a significant factor in its standing out, by the end of the century, against declining attendance elsewhere, though much church growth there – as in other large cities – was in Pentecostal or independent churches, not Anglican. Even so, many black Anglicans had an abiding sense their voice was not being heard, and that their presence barely registered in the Church hierarchy. Wilfred Wood, the first black bishop in the Church of England and a powerful advocate of better race relations, was appointed to Croydon in 1985; others followed later, including John Sentamu to York in 2005, but the numbers of minority ethnic senior clergy overall were still very small.

Institutional Continuity and Change

Decline placed enormous strain on the Church, for the simple reason that it remained a curious fusion of centralised, hierarchical and radically local and semi-autonomous authorities. Ancient rights of patronage often gave laity and corporations, not the bishop, a decisive say in appointments. Incumbents, once appointed to a parish, were virtually irremovable. Theological colleges were almost all run by independent trusts with their own property. Dioceses themselves were also semi-autonomous, varying in their approach to many things. Imposing a central plan or programme on the Church of England was – and still is – almost impossible. This was not without repeated efforts to standardise and improve efficiency. Anglicans frequently complained about a burgeoning central bureaucracy, but from the centre the process looked anything but smooth and streamlined.[17]

Adaptation to social change – and especially declining numbers – was apparent in the sheer variety of experiments in forms of ministry from the 1960s on. In 1964 a comprehensive report, drawn up by the sociologist Leslie Paul, predicted an increase in numbers of candidates for the ministry, and recommended far-reaching changes to deploy clergy more effectively, including abandonment of the parson's freehold.[18] But many of these recommendations came to nothing, and recruitment almost immediately began to fall, not rise.

Instead, experiment came piecemeal. It included a steady increase in the number of combined benefices in the country-side. Some of these new ministry teams were very large indeed, such as the 'Golden Cap' team on the Dorset coast, which combined twelve parishes. Rural ministry was increasingly a matter of driving from one church to the next, trying to hold together disparate communities. Another stratagem was the growth of non-stipendiary ministry, which was cheaper for the Church – no stipend, as the minister remained in secular employment and probably had their own house – but complicated issues of deployment and length of service, since candidates for this ministry were generally older and more experienced. A further development, not universally adopted, was a specifically local, ordained ministry, usually with a greater focus on the specific community from which the candidate came. By the late 1990s numbers training for full-time or stipendiary ministry and for non-stipendiary ministry were almost equal. In turn, that had serious implications for theological education. Small colleges proved unsustainable: a series of closures in the 1970s was followed by more in the 1990s. Instead, new courses for part-time study were opened up, beginning with the Southwark Ordination Course in 1960.

Centrally, major changes also took place in this period. Perhaps the most significant development was the final achievement – within the remaining constraints of establishment – of the legislative autonomy that had been triumphantly proclaimed in 1919 and found wanting in 1927–8. This was the product of a long period of discussion and planning that finally came to fruition in a 1969 measure which led to the creation of the General Synod. It strengthened and consolidated legislative powers for the Church, better integrated the three houses of bishops, clergy and laity (though they retained separate identities and electorates and continued to vote separately), and made General Synod the final authority in matters of doctrine.

Once again, there was huge expectation from the change, and much eventual disillusionment. One of the earliest disappointments, at least for many, was the failure (in 1970) of a scheme for unity between the Church of England and the Methodist Church in England, which did not get the required two-thirds majorities in the houses of clergy and laity. At the end of a decade which saw significantly raised hopes of major progress in Church unity, against the background of the extraordinary changes in the Catholic Church's attitudes to other Christian traditions in the wake of the Second Vatican Council, the failure of the scheme was an early check to the new ecumenical optimism. It also illuminated what would become the ecumenical dilemma for the Church of England: seeking progress on all fronts, which meant not doing anything in the pursuit of unity with one tradition that would set back relations with others. The Church harboured both Anglo-Catholics unhappy with concessions on doctrine and church order designed to secure unity with fellow Protestant churches and Evangelicals unhappy with concessions aimed at unity with Catholics. That these and other such issues were now to be played out on the floor of Synod stimulated the mobilisation of Church 'party' opinion there. The increasingly fraught and divisive debates over women's ordination and human sexuality only fuelled this development, producing the unpalatable prospect of Church people behaving like machinating politicians.

A centralising move, greeted with alarm by many, was the creation of the Archbishops' Council in 1998. This came on the back of poor investment decisions by the Church Commissioners, and the ensuing financial turmoil in the early 1990s. The council assumed the role of a central standing committee, to which all the various, subordinate boards and councils reported. Its purpose was to 'provide a focus for leadership and executive responsibility'.[19]

For the ordinary churchgoer, the most obvious change was not organisational, however, but revision of the one thing that

36. Hail Jesus: the charismatic movement

hitherto had seemed to bind members of the Church together – the liturgy. Although some diversity had crept in with use of the 1928 Prayer Book as an unofficial alternative, 1662 remained the standard for most parishes. But those who felt it was a poor vehicle for contemporary worship were growing in number. One particularly powerful influence for change was the charismatic movement, which began to affect some parishes from the early 1960s and demanded much greater informality and flexibility in worship, especially non-eucharistic worship. Another was the 'Liturgical Movement', a Europe-wide movement of liturgical reform which traced its origins back to the nineteenth century but had a specifically English dimension in the 'Parish and People' movement advocated by the Anglican liturgical scholar Gabriel Hebert. It aimed at making the eucharist or 'parish communion' – not morning and evening prayer – the central act of worship for a community and supported nave altars and the clergy facing westward, towards the people, for the eucharist.[20] These influences pointed in different directions, and implied that the search for a common liturgical text was ultimately doomed to failure.

Work on a revised liturgy began in earnest under Michael

Ramsey. Three successive experimental texts were produced – Series One, Two and Three – for parishes to trial, combining the conclusions of up-to-date liturgical and historical scholarship with practicality and contemporary theological understanding. Not until 1980 was a complete book, the *Alternative Service Book* (*ASB*), produced, with the full authorisation of Synod.[21] Why *Alternative*? Because the 1662 Prayer Book still had statutory authority and could not be suppressed without a fresh Act of Parliament – something for which no one had any appetite. In most parishes, however, the *ASB* became the norm. At nearly 1300 pages, including psalms, it was nearly twice the length of 1662. That was partly because it recognised the internal doctrinal pluralism of the Church by offering various alternatives, especially for communion. But it was an unsatisfactory solution, not least because linguistic and liturgical fashion was in flux: the *ASB* adopted a radical approach to the rewriting of familiar texts that satisfied neither those who wanted something closer to the rhythms and language of 1662 nor those who wanted the language to reflect contemporary concerns, such as gender inclusivity.

With a permanent Liturgical Commission in place, it was perhaps inevitable that the *ASB* would be superseded in 2000 by *Common Worship*. The commission frankly gave up on the Reformers' idea of having all services in one book. *Common Worship* was a library of resources in several volumes, giving far more variety than its predecessor, and yet, in key texts such as the marriage service, returning to something of the cadence, if not the actual theology, of 1662. In theory, uniformity was to be achieved by a common shape, rather than a common text; but in practice *Common Worship* marked the end of the idea that the theological identity of the Church of England could be known in its worship, for its worship was multiple.

The Ministry of Women

After liturgical revision, probably the most obvious change

the Church experienced in this period was the full inclusion of women in the ordained ministry. For some, this was an alarming innovation, which fundamentally changed the character of the Church. For others, it was simply an extension of eligibility for the existing provision for the ordained ministry to include women, and did not alter the theology and organisation of the Church, though it certainly changed its experience.

There were some nineteenth-century precursors, including the creation of deaconesses to assist parish clergy.[22] Arguments ran on for decades about what a deaconess really was – was she a female equivalent to a male deacon, ordained into her role? Generally the answer was no. Though the question of women's ordination was raised more frequently as the century wore on, and as the professions and universities opened up to women, until quite recently most Church leaders considered the clerical role to be exclusively for men. Quite a lot of assumptions about physiological and psychological gender difference latent in these arguments began to fade, especially after the First World War.[23] Also potent were arguments about 'separate spheres': women were thought to be naturally suited to home duties and domestic management, but not to public roles. Again, views such as this were losing popularity by the 1920s and 1930s, though they remained powerful.[24]

There are quite a few influential Anglican women who are remembered for their powerful advocacy of particular causes – women like Florence Nightingale, Josephine Butler, social reformer and opponent of licensed prostitution, and Octavia Hill, housing reformer and co-founder of the National Trust – and who contradicted the common prejudices, but who none the less appeared themselves to accept some of the underlying assumptions about maleness and ordination. But these were opinions and roles in transition. It does not seem all that much of a leap from their advocacy of various causes including women's suffrage to the remarkable figure of Maude Royden, a real pioneer of women's ordination, who helped found the Church League for Women's Suffrage in 1909, and seems, around that time, to have come also to the conviction that women should not be excluded from the orders of deacon, priest and bishop. A powerful, charismatic preacher, Royden had to fulfil her calling in unofficial or extra-Anglican contexts, such as the City Temple, a Congregational church in Holborn, though she did not abandon her Anglicanism.[25] The first Anglican ordination of a woman to the priesthood happened not in England but in China, in 1944, when the Hong Kong deaconess Florence Li Tim-Oi was ordained as an emergency measure to provide for congregations without any clergy during the Japanese occupation. It was many years before there could be acceptance of this move even within the wider Anglican Communion, though it was there, especially in North America, that pressure really built from the 1960s and 1970s for the ordination of women as priests.

Why did it take so long? Once women had the vote, and could be MPs, doctors, civil servants and government ministers, pressure for change in the Church was probably inevitable. Again the 1960s and 1970s were the decisive decades, with the emergent feminist movement registering the real implications of full gender equality, even if the actual achievement often proved elusive. But there were also serious theological arguments to be had, and it was always a mistake simply to dismiss opponents as prejudiced or ignorant. Of the three wings of Anglicanism, it was generally the Liberal wing that first and most comprehensively accepted women should be ordained (though in practice male Liberal clergy were sometimes rather queasy about speaking out on the matter), not because – as their opponents alleged – they were captive to the spirit of the age, but because for them neither Scripture nor tradition inhibited development in the Church. For many Evangelicals, Scripture was problematic here, especially St Paul's teachings on women's subordination ('I suffer not a woman ... to usurp authority over the man', 1 Timothy 2.12), because the absolute authority of Scripture appeared to deny to women the opportunity to lead congregations and worship in which men were present. Women could have active roles, provided there was always a male lead, or 'head'. For many Anglo-Catholics, on the other hand, Catholic tradition – by which they meant the tradition of the entire Church of Christ over the centuries – provided no precedent for the change, and required the consent of the whole Church (therefore including the Catholic and Orthodox churches) to alter what had been practised from time immemorial. If this sounds a rather bizarre argument, given the Church's break from Rome in the sixteenth century, it should be borne in mind that for many Anglicans the whole point about the Anglican reception of tradition was that it had not innovated in faith, but simply held the common faith of the whole Church. But was women's ministry a question of faith, or doctrine, or was it rather the consequence of an inbuilt, long-held and now rapidly receding set of culturally conditioned assumptions about women's suitability for ministry? Some Anglicans, particularly Anglo-Catholic Traditionalists, took the further step of arguing that the eucharistic role of the priest precluded women, because the priest stood at the altar as representative of the incarnate Christ, a man, and was, then, an *icon Christi*, an icon of Christ.

The problem for Church leaders – especially bishops, with a special responsibility to 'maintain and further the unity of the Church', as the 1980 Ordinal put it – in favour of ordaining women was how to build sufficient consensus not to impair seriously the internal unity of the Church of England when powerful alignments were taking place among those strongly opposed. The Movement for the Ordination of Women (MOW) provided an increasingly effective voice advocating change in the 1980s and early 1990s, but opposing groups on both the Evangelical and Anglo-Catholic wings also mobilised, under the banners of Reform (Evangelical) and Cost of Conscience and then Forward in Faith (Anglo-Catholic).

The ordination of women as deacons was achieved by synodical process in 1987. Supporters of women's ministry saw this as only the first step, but for both Evangelical and Anglo-Catholic opponents much more serious was the ordination of women as priests, because it raised objections of 'headship' and eucharistic presidency. The debate and campaigning running up to the passing of the measure for ordaining women as priests in 1992 was all the more vociferous. It achieved the necessary two-thirds majorities in all three houses of Synod, but narrowly, and there was a price – compensation for male clergy who felt unable to continue to exercise their ministry, and an 'Act of Synod' which made pastoral provision for parishes which could not accept the ordination of women as priests, giving the power to refuse female appointments and to request oversight by a bishop who would not ordain women.[26]

Perhaps these measures were necessary to get the vote through, but to supporters it looked as if too much sensitivity was being shown to those unable to accept the will of the majority of the Church through its elected representatives, and discrimination was being permanently embedded within the very structures of the Church, while others were convinced this was a principled attempt to balance different 'integrities' in the Church. The divisions aroused by the vote and the ensuing Act of Synod almost certainly delayed the further step of ordaining women as bishops. Much fruitless energy was consumed on the matter in the 2000s, before a serious attempt fell just short of the required majority in the House of Laity in 2012, towards the end of Rowan Williams's archiepiscopate. A hastily assembled, renewed proposal was pushed through vigorously by the new archbishop, Justin Welby, in July 2014. Later that year, the first woman bishop, Libby Lane, was appointed to Stockport, and others rapidly followed.

There were many reasons for the eventual success of the movement, including generational change, a wider secular shift in perceptions of discrimination, the changing composition of Synod, inspirational female role models, the growing experience of parishes with women clergy, and the declining numeric strength of opponents (particularly on the Anglo-Catholic wing).[27] It was not lost on many people that growing numbers of women clergy could help to offset the patent decline in male candidates for the ministry. By 2011 almost a third of the clergy were female.[28] There was still a clear gender imbalance at the level of senior appointment, but that too began to shift after the women bishops measure went through in 2014. For two centuries or more, women had provided the majority of active congregation members; now their full participation was increasingly reflected at all levels of the Church's hierarchy. What, by the early 2000s, was becoming ever clearer was that if, in one sense, the ordination of women was a sea change in the composition of the clergy, in another sense it changed very little of the traditional culture and organisation of the Church – it was neither the catastrophe feared by some nor the revolution wanted by some others. It was business as usual.

Issues in Human Sexuality

The Church also found itself increasingly divided in the late twentieth century on how to react to rapid changes in popular sexual morality, and in legislation affecting such matters. The most divisive issue was homosexuality but, in order to see how complex and challenging this shifting context was for the Church, it is only necessary to list other relevant issues: abortion, contraception, divorce, sex education, extra-marital sex. Much of this story, time and again, was about pastoral adjustment to changing legal and social expectations. Again, there was a long back story.

In 1907 Parliament permitted a man to marry his deceased wife's sister, in direct contravention of the Prayer Book's 'Table of Kindred and Affinity'. But this was just the beginning of a growing gap between what might be permitted by law and what was enjoined by the Church. It seems extraordinary now that such a seemingly obscure or minor change should transfix Church leaders, but for them it was an ominous marker of the way the secular state could abandon a common Christian morality. One wonders how the bishops of 1907 would have regarded their successors of the 1950s, who accepted the recommendation of the Wolfenden Report of 1957 that consenting homosexual acts ought to be decriminalised, marking an acknowledgement that the law could not rightly legislate for morality in the 'private sphere'.[29] But these were all concessions to necessity, rather than a fundamental change in Church doctrine and Christian morality. Similar arguments were put forward in the 1960s in support of reform of divorce and legalisation of abortion.

Disagreements over sexuality polarised views about Scripture more sharply than those over women's ministry. Marriage was not the most sensitive issue, simply because the human institution of marriage evidently had a complex history and was partly defined by civil requirements that could not easily be mapped on to Jesus's teaching, though there was broad agreement across the Church about what *Christian* marriage actually was, at least until recently. But homosexuality was another matter altogether.

Here the teaching of Paul in particular seemed clear enough, at least to many Christians, rooted as it was in the Judaeo-Christian understanding of creation, and counterposed to the practice of the pagan ancient world.[30] For those who were resolutely opposed to any concession on the part of the Church to accepting or approving same-sex relations, the teaching of Scripture therefore seemed to stand foursquare with traditional Christian morality: same-sex relations were not only unbiblical, but also sinful and corrupt. Some Church people accepted that, notwithstanding that view, same-sex relations were an evident fact for some people who wanted to lead good and faithful lives, and the Church should therefore make pastoral adjustment to take account of that fact. This was to become a common position among many senior clergy in the 1970s and 1980s. For others, there was an emergent, new moral theology of human sexuality which took account of changing trends in Biblical scholarship and of the modern revolution in knowledge of human biology, and which assumed the Christian understanding of love and fidelity could be applied beyond the traditional scope of heterosexual marriage. Against the background of the movement of 'gay liberation', some Anglicans joined the Lesbian and Gay Christian Movement, a non-denominational organisation founded in 1976 at St Botolph's, Aldgate. The growing movement for changing the Church's public position energised opponents. Report followed report as debate continued unabated throughout the 1980s. Heated discussion in General Synod in 1987 led eventually, in 1991, to the House of Bishops' statement *Issues in Human Sexuality*, which tried to follow a careful line between pastoral sensitivity and defence of a traditional Christian view of sexuality.

The statement was plainly a fudge. It accepted the Church should welcome those 'homophiles' who were 'conscientiously convinced that a faithful, sexually active relationship with one other person ... is the way of life God intends for them'.[31] But what the statement gave with one hand it took away with another, for it effectively forbad this same pastoral extension to the clergy themselves, who were called, so it said, to a higher standard. It was clerical sexual relationships that were, in consequence, to bedevil the debate in the years to come. Even though the Church of England's position was a relatively conservative one, at least in comparison with developments in some other provinces of the Anglican Communion, including the US, Canada and New Zealand, it was enough to draw the ire of many other Anglicans.

Controversy in the Communion broke out into open conflict at the Lambeth Conference in 1998, when a motion asserting that 'homosexual practice' was incompatible with Scripture was passed by an overwhelming majority. The subsequent fallout across the Communion and within the Church of England itself – where bishops were strongly divided over the motion – formed the backdrop to the controversy that broke out in 2003 when Jeffrey John, a priest in the diocese of Southwark, was nominated to be suffragan bishop of Reading in the diocese of Oxford. John was a gay man living in a partnership, who had made no secret of his orientation and had published a defence of gay relationships.[32] This would have been the first open acknowledgement of gay clerical partnerships at senior level in the Church of England. It was not to be. The sheer

37. Internal conflict and inclusion: LGBTI protest at Church House, 2017

weight of opposition from some quarters, especially powerful Evangelical parishes, seemed unstoppable, and the nomination was withdrawn.[33]

All these arguments made it seem as if the Church was more preoccupied with sex than it was with spreading the Gospel and caring for God's people. But a gulf had opened up between popular culture in Britain and the values and traditions of the churches. Nowhere was that more obvious than in the realm of sexual ethics. Homosexuality was but the standout case; similar, though less intense, arguments ranged over other forms of non- or extra-marital sexual expression. Here, then, was the sharp edge of strategic disagreement over how the Church should respond to social change. One view was that it was called to stand against change, to reject the ways of the world, to affirm truths that transcended human convention, and to accept if need be the marginalisation and mockery that would follow. Quite a different view suggested that the Church's mission was precisely to minister to human beings in all their diversity and difference, and to follow the promptings of the Holy Spirit into situations which were remote from anything hitherto the Church had had to consider, with new knowledge and understanding. You could find sincere, intelligent Anglicans on both sides of that line.

A New Evangelical Revival?

The basic theological character of the Church of England was really established in the mid-nineteenth century, when it became clear that within the one church structure co-existed three distinct approaches to Christian truth. The positions adopted by the groups following each of these approaches in the 1960s would have been recognisable to their predecessors in the 1850s, though there had by this stage been a greater acceptance of modern critical approaches across Anglo-Catholicism, Liberalism and Evangelicalism. But Anglo-Catholicism was in retreat as a force within the Church, even before it was riven by disagreements over women's ministry and human sexuality. Even as, like all sectors of the Church, it was facing increasing difficulty retaining young people, it found itself at odds with the informality of popular culture. It remained influential as a theological tradition, with many notably theologians and historians, including Michael Ramsey and, latterly, Rowan Williams, and its affinity with the choral tradition provided an important institutional base. But numbers of candidates for ministry were beginning to fall, and the Anglican religious orders were also in decline.

By contrast, Anglican Liberalism, or, as some would have it, the 'centre ground', at first seemed to be strengthening. Some argued the years of Ramsey's archiepiscopate had seen the triumph of Liberalism and a capitulation to the spirit of the age.[34] Yet the reality was not so straightforward. In the 1960s, a more radical strand of Anglican theology looked back beyond the middle years of the century to a spirit more akin to the Modernism of the early twentieth century. John Robinson was the exemplar. He was bishop of Woolwich in the diocese of Southwark at the time of 'South Bank' theology, a movement of theological opinion not confined to London, but having roots in industrial mission and in the growing dissatisfaction many younger clergy felt with the Church's traditional ministry in northern industrial dioceses: it looked for inspiration outside the formal structures of the Church, embracing the language of secularism and immanence that appeared to be in tune with popular culture.[35] An academic Liberal theology calling for the reinterpretation or adjustment of traditional doctrine was exemplified by leading Anglican theologians such as Geoffrey Lampe, Maurice Wiles and Don Cupitt. But by the early 1980s this particular form of doctrinal Liberalism was beginning to wear thin. David Jenkins, bishop of Durham from 1984 to 1994, was commonly assumed to be a representative of this extreme Liberalism, particularly as he appeared to cast doubt on the literal truth of the resurrection, but in fact he was relatively conservative. His notoriety rested as much on his outspoken opposition to the policies of the Thatcher government as it did on anything he wrote or spoke about theology. Therein lies a sign of the paradox of modern Anglican Liberalism. Its theological radicalism in the past coincided with a moral conservatism that was almost at one with the rest of the Church, but as the former faded, the latter was upended, leaving Liberalism by the 1990s mostly orthodox doctrinally but liberal or progressive ethically.

The internal divisions and relative decline of these two wings of the Church were set against a new period of Anglican Evangelical resurgence. It is hard to date this precisely, but three events can be taken as symptomatic. The first was the emergence of the charismatic movement. Sometimes called 'neo-Pentecostalism', this was marked by an informal approach to worship, renewed emphasis on the action of the Holy Spirit in the Church, and charismatic gifts such as healing and speaking in tongues. The theology was largely conservative, but the informality and highly personal and familiar language, as well as the readiness to work through small, informal meetings such as house groups, chimed in very well with changes in popular culture.[36] For example, Michael Harper left the staff of All Souls,

Langham Place, in 1964 after he experienced baptism in the Spirit and spoke in tongues, putting him at odds with the rector, John Stott, and went on to found the Fountain Trust, an ecumenical Charismatic organisation. The charismatic movement became a lively, vibrant part of Anglican Evangelicalism, with thriving churches in most major towns and cities.

The second event featured Stott himself. Often seen as the *eminence grise* of modern Anglican Evangelicalism, at the Evangelical Alliance Conference in 1966 Stott resisted the appeal of Martyn Lloyd-Jones, a leading non-Anglican Welsh Protestant, to combine Evangelicals from all denominations into one body, and at the Keele Conference of Anglican Evangelicals a year later urged them to stay loyal to the Church of England. Stott's stance 'steadied wavering Anglican consciences' on the Evangelical wing, and many Anglican Evangelicals were to date their determination to defend their distinct position within the Church from that point.[37]

The third event was the appointment of Donald Coggan as archbishop of Canterbury in 1974. The first Evangelical archbishop for over a century, Coggan enthusiastically used his short tenure of the see (he was in post for only five years before retiring) to attempt a major national mission, Call to the Nation. But growing Evangelical strength was reflected in the further appointment of George Carey to Canterbury in 1991, and then Justin Welby in 2013.

The new Evangelical revival, if such it was, took place at a time when congregations were contracting sharply. Evangelicals were not the only Church people concerned about mission, but they were the most unabashed and energetic. Carey committed the Church to yet another national mission – the Decade of Evangelism. Again, much effort was spent, but to little avail. Some Evangelical parishes and organisations declined, like other parts of the Church, but many of the churches which continued to be large and flourishing and – crucially – to attract young people in significant numbers were Evangelical. Holy Trinity, Brompton was a standout example in London, 'planting' new congregations around London, and sponsoring the popular 'Alpha' course, a highly adaptable tool of Evangelism. Most university towns had at least one city centre Evangelical Anglican church with a strong connection to student Christianity, such as St Mary's, Wollaton, in Nottingham, or St Aldate's and St Ebbe's in Oxford.

By the late 1990s senior appointments in the Church were increasingly drawn from the Evangelical wing. Evangelicals themselves were divided over the ordination of women, and to a lesser extent over human sexuality. It was possible to trace three distinct subgroups by then – charismatics, conservative Evangelicals and moderate or even Liberal Evangelicals. These were fluid categories, and people could move between them or hold multiple positions that to outsiders looked in tension or incompatible. But what was not in doubt by the end of the twentieth century was the relative health of Evangelicalism in a Church increasingly beleaguered by the indifference or hostility of society around it.

20

POSTSCRIPT

There are few clean lines in the Church of England's history. It is all messy. It has no core confessional document, and no centralised authority able to impose discipline and order on a sometimes fractious organisation. No one can be 'thrown out'. That sometimes leads to the accusation that it lacks clarity and identity. What is the theology of the Church of England? Where would you find it? Not in a comprehensive catechism. It has authoritative documents, a representative structure, disciplinary processes, ordered worship, commissions and councils able to receive and write reports and reflect on issues. But what the Church 'thinks' on any one issue often has to be worked out in a dizzyingly complex vortex of relationships, and is subject to change.

At its best, the Church is like a well-rooted tree in a storm, bending to survive, but with roots which go down deep into Christian revelation, history and tradition. At its worst, it is a tangle or knot of incommensurate claims and counter-claims, like an overrun garden gone to ruin. It is no longer clearly a national Church, and yet it has held on to the symbols and some of the institutions of one. It subsists as the strange paradox of an established Church in a secular State. It continues to offer its ministry and pastoral care to everyone and imposes almost nothing by way of formal requirement, and yet it is unquestionably a church every bit as structured and shaped by social class as any other, and with a demonstrable bias towards the wealthy and powerful.

There is, then, no single unifying principle holding together the history of the Church. Theologians and Church leaders have often claimed to find one, but on closer scrutiny these claims usually turn out to be exaggerated. You cannot simply say the Church of England has always regarded its fidelity to Catholic order, the historic three-fold ministry of the Church, as its anchor, because that was not how most people saw things in the sixteenth century, and nor how significant numbers of Anglicans have continued to see things up to the present. Likewise, its identity does not simply lie in its Biblical witness, for what does that say about other churches? And anyway, how – mostly – we receive and interpret Scripture now is not identical to what was done in the past. But nor is there consistency and continuity for the Church of England in the claim often made that it is a moderate, reasonable 'centre way', however attractive that might sometimes seem, because again that cannot finally do justice to the conflicts in the early modern origins of the Church as an autonomous, independent national body.

To say as much is not to undermine the idea that a proper theological case has to be made for Anglicanism – it does. The late Stephen Sykes made a strong, provocative case for Anglicans to cut the fudge and take their theology seriously, and my own sympathies lie entirely in that direction.[1] But I doubt that the history of any church can be squeezed into a theological straitjacket; certainly this one cannot be. If this all seems confusing and chaotic – which is not necessarily the case, at least on a long view – it is the consequence of the overarching narrative I have been describing. It is where we have ended up, at the end – well, the current viewpoint – of this story. What we have seen in the previous chapters is a trajectory of development for the Church of England from Bede's church of the English people, an idea that not only survived at the Reformation but was expressly embedded in the union of monarch, realm and Church, to a church which essentially is one religious option among many, and a minority one at that. All sorts of features of the contemporary Church of England admittedly deflect the eye from this cold reality – the great churches and cathedrals, the royal connection, continuing presence in educational, military and caring institutions, and so on.

Into the twenty-first century, the Church of England has experienced simply a continuation of that long trend. It is arguable that the statistics of decline are not so panic-inducing as was the case thirty years ago, but they are bracing none the less. And they continue to fuel – how could they not? – the process of internal soul-searching, experiment and reform that characterised the last century. A great deal of hope rode on the back of the Church's commitment to alternative forms of worship and ecclesial belonging, the 'fresh expressions of church', as they have been called, in the wake of a report, *Mission-shaped Church* (2004), encouraged by Rowan Williams. There were hundreds of these by the end of the decade, spread across the dioceses – groups meeting in pubs or cafés, special interest groups, groups affiliated to local churches or almost separate altogether – and they certainly enriched the range of provision made by the Church. But they were not without controversy, to some seeming to cancel out the work of parish churches, and eighteen years on they have not fundamentally altered the religious landscape. In 2020, serious disruption of local parish life came with the Covid-19 pandemic and the measures taken to counter it, which included the (much criticised) complete closure of churches during lockdown. Online worship partially compensated for this, but the long-term effects of the pandemic in church life are still, as I write, unclear.

New forms of monasticism have been developed, and effort has been put into developing church 'plants' (this really began in earnest in the 1980s) in order to rejuvenate ministry in particular areas. Institutional reform continues apace. The success of new forms of theological education and training, pioneered especially in London with the creation of St Mellitus College in 2007, has helped the Church to continue to recruit and train ordinands, though the average age of ordinands continues to creep up. Under Justin Welby, an ambitious programme of investment and reform, entitled 'Renewal and Reform', was set in motion to try to shift resources and energy to initiatives that would drive forward the mission of the Church and seek to rebuild congregations. A favoured mission strategy of the Victorians, the expansion of the number of dioceses and the creation of more episcopal sees, was put into reverse in 2014 when the diocese of Leeds was formed from the amalgamation of Bradford, Ripon and Leeds, and Wakefield.

Alongside the continuing institutional struggle to adapt, survive and even grow, the Church of England has had to reckon on the seeping away of a common Christian culture around it. It is that loss of a recognisable Christian identity in the community at large that ultimately constrains all the work of the parishes and national Church institutions. By 2018, one survey reckoned that 52 per cent of British people were 'nones', that is, identified with no religious tradition.[2] The less knowledge and sense of familiarity with Christianity out there, the harder it is for churches to persuade people to have a go at attending services. Church of England clergy retain a certain recognisability in popular culture – in soaps, comedies, films – but there is much less understanding of what they actually stand for and do than there once was.

It is hard to know whether this broader process of secularisation is set to continue or not, though the age profile of Anglican congregations is not encouraging, with over 30 per cent of attenders over seventy-five, and only 4 per cent under thirty-four in 2018.[3] I am, of course, simply speculating about the continuation of a historic trend here, not necessarily supporting it. Whatever else you think about Anglicanism and the Church of England, it seems to me – stepping aside momentarily from looking at the trend – that there is a serious loss of cultural memory and resonance bound up in this wider shift, a kind of aphasia that risks distorting our ability to understand our own past, and its literature, art and music, because of a lack of familiarity with the Bible, the Prayer Book and basic Christian doctrine and history.

The growing dissonance between the Church and wider society has been intensified by the woeful stories of sexual abuse by clergy and others which have emerged over the last quarter of a century. No one could claim that the Church has generally handled these matters well, and their effect has been to highlight acute institutional failings as much as the actual crimes committed by particular individuals. The Church has not been alone in this – it joins a doleful list of professions and institutions which have had to acknowledge their shortcomings, and develop more thorough and effective mechanisms for dealing with allegations of abuse, and for safeguarding. There is as yet little serious academic research into rates of abuse, the chronology of abuse, effects on wider perceptions of the Church, and so on.[4] We are still in the middle of all this as I write, and it is an issue being played out intensively in the fast-moving context of digital media. There are notorious standout cases such as those involving Peter Ball, a former bishop jailed for indecent assault, and Robert Waddington, a former dean of Manchester, who died before multiple allegations against him could be brought to trial. But more revealing than the media coverage of those and other instances are the transcripts of evidence presented by Church leaders and survivors of abuse themselves to the government-established Independent Inquiry into Child Sexual Abuse (IICSA), started in 2014, which provide an extraordinary insight into the culture and processes of the Church over the last thirty years or so.[5]

It is a bad idea for a historian to try to peer into the future, but it may be helpful to think of the Church of England now in two contrasting ways, 'big' and 'small'. The 'big' Church is the extended Church of the imagined national English community. It includes all the existing parish churches, chapels and chaplaincies, but it also includes things which continue to reflect the history of the Church and its engagement with the nation at large – the presence of bishops in the House of Lords, the role of the monarch as Supreme Governor of the Church of England, the ceremonial and ritual role associated with the monarchy and with the armed forces, the residual role of parish custom and law which underpins a declining proportion of weddings, baptisms and funerals. It is, to me at any rate, impossible to think that the 'big' Church of England will survive in its current form into the twenty-second century. There must surely be a tipping point when the congregational base has become so thin, and the readiness to accept the Church's role so attenuated in the population at large, that some form of further reform and constitutional adjustment is inevitable. That in itself might not be such a problem for the Church, were it not for the enormous legacy of the medieval and Victorian churches that litter the landscape. Their survival, if the 'big' Church is to shrink, must surely depend in the end on some new relationship with the State, some new acceptance of the compatibility of supporting heritage with effectively subsidising local congregations by taking the costs of maintenance away from them.

But then there's the 'small' Church', by which I mean precisely the parishes, chapels and chaplaincies shorn of the other features of the 'big' Church. For these purposes, cathedrals are part of the 'small' Church, because they have congregations of their own, though their maintenance costs are immense and they already receive some government assistance. I can foresee the survival of the 'small' Church, provided the maintenance of buildings is taken care of as part of an eventual shrinking of the 'big' Church. The 'small' Church will eventually have to evolve into something more mobile and freer of its local moorings, perhaps even more structured around the associational model of churches simply attracting whoever wants to come to their services than is the case at the moment. There is no reason to suppose the large, powerful churches – particularly urban churches, and mostly but not exclusively Evangelical churches – will disappear. But there will need to be, eventually, a shrinking of the 'big' to map more closely on to the 'small'. Again, though, something would eventually be lost here: a breadth of Christian experience and expression, perhaps; the breadth and scale of the English choral tradition; the compelling curiosity of a Catholic tradition and culture contained within a Protestant ecclesial framework.

This is not an optimistic conclusion, but just a hunch, looking at the long trajectory of history. An enormous amount of work will need to be done even to achieve this modest position in the future. Turning the question round, and assuming (as I do) that Christian faith and discipleship will last into the future, is there a case far into the future for a way of being the Church in this country that tries to hold together radically different perspectives on the history of the Church and the nature of Church order? A Church that aims to reach out to the whole community and to serve and be present in every community? A Church that values its historic heritage but also tries to adapt constructively to new contexts and situations, that resists the easy temptation of a powerful centralised polity, and that encourages local debate ('Anglicanism is a trial-and-error form of Christianity', says one scholar), but above all in its actual, local life bears witness to the truth of the Gospel?[6] If the answer is yes, to all of these points, there remains a clear vocation for the Church of England. It cannot any more pretend to be the people's Church – but it can continue to be a Church for the people.

NOTES

Preface: The Real History of the Church of England

1. A. Powell, *Temporary Kings, A Dance to the Music of Time* 11 (1973; new edn, 2005), 27.

Prelude: Catholic Centuries

1. J. R. Tanner, *Tudor Constitutional Documents A.D. 1485–1603: With an Historical Commentary* (1940), 47.
2. The quotations are from Romans 12.4–5 and 1 Corinthians 12.27.
3. Bede, 'Ecclesiastical History of the English Nation', in Baedae, *Opera Historica*, I (J. E. King (ed.), 1971), III.
4. Ibid., II, 61.
5. Ibid., I, 163.
6. P. Hunter Blair, *An Introduction to Anglo-Saxon England* (2nd edn, 1977), 167.
7. Cf. A. Wessels, *Europe: Was It Ever Really Christian? The Interaction between Gospel and Culture* (1994).
8. H. Mayr-Harting, *The Coming of Christianity to Anglo-Saxon England* (1972), 104.
9. Bede, I, 205–11.
10. Mayr-Harting, 105–6.
11. N. Orme, *English Church Dedications: With a Survey of Devon and Cornwall* (1996), 13–15.
12. Ibid., 26.
13. Ibid., 31.
14. Ibid., 41.
15. D. Petts, 'Landscapes of Belief: Non-Conformist Mission in the North Pennines', *International Journal of Historical Archaeology*, 15 (2011), 467.
16. W. Shakespeare, *Richard II*, II, 1.

17. Quoted in H. Bettenson & C. Maunder (eds.), *Documents of the Christian Church* (3rd edn, 1999), 127.

18. Cf. C. M. D. Crowder, *Unity, Heresy, and Reform, 1378–1460: The Conciliar Response to the Great Schism* (1977); F. Oakley, *The Conciliarist Tradition: Constitutionalism in the Catholic Church, 1300–1870* (2003).

19. The Canons of the Church of England, at: https://www.churchofengland.org/more/policy-and-thinking/canons-church-england/section-c

20. Cf. N. G. Pounds, *A History of the English Parish: The Culture of Religion from Augustine to Victoria* (2000).

21. Pounds, *A History of the English Parish*, 17–25.

22. J. Morris (ed.), *Domesday Book: Surrey* (1975 edn), 5,9.

23. J. Betjeman, *Collins Pocket Guide to English Parish Churches: The South* (1968), 321; J. Ede & N. Virgoe (eds.), *Religious Worship in Norfolk: The 1851 Census of Accommodation and Attendance at Worship* (1998), 362–3.

2. Reformation and Turmoil

1. C. Dickens, *A Child's History of England* (1851–3; new edn, 1905), 306; cf., William Cobbett, *A History of the Protestant Reformation in England and Wales* (1824; new edn, 1899), 32–7.

2. The mural itself was destroyed in a fire in the 1690s, but several copies survive: cf. http://www.liverpoolmuseums.org.uk/walker/exhibitions/henry/whitehall.aspx

3. For example A. G. Dickens, *The English Reformation* (1964).

4. R. Rex, *The Lollards* (2002).

5. Cf. E. Duffy, *Marking the Hours: English People and Their Prayers* (2006).

6. C. Haigh, 'Anticlericalism in the English Reformation', *History*, 68 (1983), 391.

7. E. Duffy, *The Stripping of the Altars: Traditional Religion in England 1400–1580* (1992).

8. Haigh, 403–6.

9. P. Marshall, *Heretics and Believers. A History of the English Reformation* (2017), 192.

10. J. R. Tanner, *Tudor Constitutional Documents A.D. 1485–1603: With an Historical Commentary* (1940), 41.

11. D. MacCulloch, *Thomas Cromwell: A Life* (2018), 307–10.

12. G. W. Bernard, 'The Dissolution of the Monasteries', *History*, 96 (2011), 390.

13. R. Rex, 'The Religion of Henry VIII', *Historical Journal*, 57 (2014), 1–32; Rex takes issue with G. W. Bernard, *The King's Reformation: Henry VIII and the Remaking of the English Church* (2007).

14. 'The Second Royal Injunctions of Henry VIII', in C. H. Williams (ed.), *English Historical Documents*, V (1967), online edition at http://englishhistoricaldocuments.com/document/view. html?id=1780

15. D. MacCulloch, *Thomas Cranmer: A Life* (1996), 181–2.

16. This is such a common claim that it would be fruitless to reference it; it was central to the late Stephen Sykes's influential critique of arguments about Anglican identity: see S. Sykes, *The Integrity of Anglicanism* (1978).

17. There is a full text at http://justus.anglican.org/resources/bcp/ Litany1544/Litany_1544.htm; I have modernised spelling here and elsewhere.

18. A text can be found at http://justus.anglican.org/resources/bcp/ Communion_1548.htm.

19. A new edition of this and the second version produced by Cranmer was published by the Prayer Book Society in 1999; a fully annotated edition of the 1549, 1559 and 1662 books was edited by Brian Cummings and published in 2011.

20. The original text of Bucer's *Censura* is in the Parker Library at Corpus Christi College, Cambridge; see also E. C. Whitaker, *Martin Bucer and the Book of Common Prayer* (1974).

21. Of the extensive literature on Cranmer's liturgical work, see especially G. J. Cuming, *A History of Anglican Liturgy* (new edn, 1982), and G. J. Cuming, *The Godly Order: Texts and Studies Relating to the Book of Common Prayer* (1983); also B. D. Spinks, *The Rise and Fall of the Incomparable Liturgy: The Book of Common Prayer, 1559–1906* (2017).

22. J. Torrance Kirby, 'Lay Supremacy: Reform of the Canon Law from Henry VIII to Elizabeth I (1529–1571), *Reformation and Renaissance Review*, 8 (2006), 349–70.

23. J. H. Newman & J. Keble (eds.), *Remains of the Late Reverend Richard Hurrell Froude*, I (1838), 433.

3. Reaction and Settlement

1. P. Marshall, *Heretics and Believers: A History of the English Reformation* (2017), 402.
2. E. Duffy, *Fires of Faith. Catholic England under Mary Tudor* (2009), 126–8.
3. J. N. King (ed.,) *Foxe's Book of Martyrs: Select Narratives* (new edn, 2009), 167.
4. Duffy, *Fires of Faith*.
5. Marshall, 392.
6. The four editions of Foxe's work that appeared in his lifetime are available online at: https://www.johnfoxe.org/index.php?realm=text&gototype=&edition=1563&pageid=17
7. King (ed.), 154; the editors of the John Foxe website suggest there are grounds for doubting the veracity of these words: https://www.johnfoxe.org/index.php?realm=text&gototype=&edition=1570&pageid=1976&anchor=good%20comfort#C115F4f
8. P. Collinson, *Elizabethan Essays* (1994), 114.
9. R. Bowers, 'The Chapel Royal, the First Edwardian Prayer Book, and Elizabeth's Settlement of Religion, 1559', *Historical Journal*, 43 (2000), 317–44.
10. A. Walsham, *Church Papists: Catholicism, Conformity and Confessional Polemic in Early Modern England* (1993).
11. Pius V, *Regnans in excelsis*, full text at: https://www.papalencyclicals.net/pius05/p5regnans.htm
12. P. Collinson, *English Puritanism* (1983), 8–10; and also P. Collinson, *The Elizabethan Puritan Movement* (new edn, 1990), 22–8.
13. This shift is built above all on the work of Patrick Collinson, beginning with *The Elizabethan Puritan Movement*; for a useful summary, see D. D. Wallace, 'Via Media? A Paradigm Shift', *Anglican and Episcopal History*, 72 (2003), 2–21.
14. Collinson, *The Elizabeth Puritan Movement*, 76–83.
15. Ibid., 17.
16. R. Oates, 'Puritans and the "Monarchical Republic": Conformity and Conflict in the Elizabethan Church', *English Historical Review*, 127 (2012), 822; italics original.
17. Collinson, *Elizabethan Essays*, 31–57.

4. Revolution in the Parishes

1. P. Marshall, *Heretics and Believers: A History of the English Reformation* (2017), 25.
2. Cf. M. Tavinor, *Shrines of the Saints in England and Wales* (2016).
3. Cf. R. Rosewell, *Medieval Wall Paintings in English and Welsh Churches* (2008).
4. W. Parker, *The History of Long Melford* (1873), 72–3.
5. Cf. R. Whiting, *The Reformation of the English Parish Church* (2010), the best general introduction.
6. H. Gee & W. J. Hardy, *Documents Illustrative of English Church History* (1896), 270.
7. Ibid., 275–6.
8. Ibid., 277.
9. Ibid., 278.
10. D. MacCulloch, *Thomas Cranmer: A Life* (1996), 510.
11. Cf. R. Gough, D. Hey (ed.), *The History of Myddle* (1981).
12. Gee & Hardy, 428.
13. Cf. J. Rattue, *The Living Stream: Holy Wells in Historical Context* (1995).
14. M. Lapidge, *The Cult of St Swithun* (2003).
15. S. Roud & J. Bishop, *The New Penguin Book of English Folk Songs* (2012), 366–7 & 510.
16. On this, A. Ryrie, *Being Protestant in Reformation Britain* (2013) is indispensable.
17. Ryrie, 3; italics original.

5. A Middle Way? The Invention of Anglicanism

1. *Sermons, or Homilies, Appointed to be Read in Churches* (new edn, 1833), 27.
2. S. Wabuda, 'Hugh Latimer, (*c.*1485–1555)', *Oxford Dictionary of National Biography* (2009).
3. C. R. Trueman, 'Barnes, Robert (*c.*1495–1540)', *Oxford Dictionary of National Biography* (2010); cf. C. R. Trueman, '"The Saxons be Sore on the Affirmative": Robert Barnes on the Lord's Supper', in W. P. Stephens (ed.), *The Bible, the Reformation and the Church: Essays in Honour of James Atkinson* (1995), 290–307.
4. D. MacCulloch, 'Putting the English Reformation on the Map: The Prothero Lecture', *Transactions of the Royal Historical Society*, 15 (2005), 80.

5. Cf. B. Kaye, *The Rise and Fall of the English Christendom: Theocracy, Christology, Order and Power* (2018).
6. Cf. F. Senn, 'Church Orders and Liturgies, German', in M. A. Lamport (ed.), *Encyclopaedia of Martin Luther and the Reformation*, II (2017), 139–40.
7. The best introduction is O. O'Donovan, *On the Thirty-nine Articles: A Conversation with Tudor Christianity* (2nd edn, 2011).
8. J. Jewel, *Works*, I (1845), 20.
9. W. M. Southgate, *John Jewel and the Problem of Doctrinal Authority* (1962), 49.
10. J. Jewel, *The Apology of the Church of England* (1562; new edn, 1888), 7.
11. Ibid., 63.
12. Ibid., 12; italics mine.
13. Ibid., 15.
14. Ibid., 16–17.
15. J. Craig, 'Jewel, John (1522–1571)', *Oxford Dictionary of National Biography* (2008).
16. Cf. G. W. Jenkins, *John Jewel and the English National Church: The Dilemmas of an Erastian Reformer* (2006).
17. A. S. McGrade, 'Hooker, Richard (1554–1600)', *Oxford Dictionary of National Biography* (2004).
18. R. Hooker, *The Laws of Ecclesiastical Polity*, I (1597; new edn,1907), 228.
19. Ibid., 331.
20. R. Williams, *Anglican Identities* (2004), 49.
21. Hooker, *The Laws of Ecclesiastical Polity*, II, 423.
22. D. MacCulloch, 'Richard Hooker's Reputation', in D. MacCulloch, *All Things Made New: Writings on the Reformation* (2016), 284.
23. The former view is presented by N. Atkinson, *Richard Hooker and the Authority of Scripture, Tradition and Reason: Reformed Theologian of the Church of England* (1997); the latter by N. Voak, *Richard Hooker and Reformed Theology: A Study of Reason, Will, and Grace* (2003).

6. The Road to Civil War

1. K. Fincham & P. Lake, 'The Ecclesiastical Policy of King James I', *Journal of British Studies*, 24 (1985), 169.
2. Cf. K. Fincham, *Prelate as Pastor: The Episcopate of James I* (1990); also, K. Fincham (ed.), *The Early Stuart Church, 1603–1642* (1993).

3. Fincham & Lake, 174.

4. Cf. D Daniell, *The Bible in English* (2003); also, L. A. Ferrell, 'The Bible in Early Modern England', in A. Milton (ed.), *The Oxford History of Anglicanism, I: Reformation and Identity,* c.1520–1662 (2017).

5. Ferrell, 428.

6. K. Fincham & P. Lake, 'The Ecclesiastical Policies of James I and Charles I', in Fincham (ed.), *The Early Stuart Church,* 26.

7. Cf. R. G. Usher, *The Reconstruction of the English Church* (1910).

8. R. Baxter, *Autobiography ... being the Reliquiae Baxterianae* (1696; new edn,1931), 3–4.

9. Cf. E. Duffy, 'The Reformed Pastor in English Puritanism', in E. Duffy, *Reformation Divided: Catholics, Protestants and the Conversion of England* (2017), 327–46.

10. Calvinist bishops continued to be appointed under James, and even occasionally under Charles; for example, Barnaby Potter to Carlisle in 1629: Fincham & Lake, 'The Ecclesiastical Policies of James I and Charles I', 37.

11. P. Lake, 'Lancelot Andrewes, John Buckeridge, and Avant-garde Conformity at the Court of James I', in L. Levy Peck (ed.), *The Mental World of the Jacobean Court* (1990), 113–33.

12. T. S. Eliot famously praised Andrewes's literary style in an essay published in 1926, republished in T. S. Eliot, *For Lancelot Andrewes: Essays on Style and Order* (1928).

13. P. McCullough, 'Andrewes, Lancelot (1555–1626)', *Oxford Dictionary of National Biography* (2008).

14. P. E. More & F. L. Cross, *Anglicanism: The Thought and Practice of the Church of England, Illustrated from the Religious Literature of the Seventeenth Century* (1951), 465–6.

15. J. Tobin (ed.), *George Herbert: The Complete English Poems* (1991), 101–2.

16. R. Williams, *Anglican Identities,* 70; this is an interpretation affirmed by J. Drury, *Music at Midnight: The Life and Poetry of George Herbert* (2013), 168.

17. Cf. More & Cross; also, H. R. McAdoo, *The Spirit of Anglicanism: A Survey of Anglican Theological Method in the Seventeenth Century* (1965).

18. J. Davies, *The Caroline Captivity of the Church: Charles I and the Remoulding of Anglicanism* (1992); a similar viewpoint is shared by K. Sharpe, *The Personal Rule of Charles I* (1992).

19. N. Tyacke & K. Fincham, *Altars Restored: The Changing Face of English Religious Worship, 1547–c.1700* (2007), 177; also. S. Thurley, 'The Stuart Kings, Oliver Cromwell and the Chapel Royal 1618–1685', *Architectural History*, 45 (2002), 238–74.
20. Tyacke & Fincham, 178–80 & 184.
21. Ibid., 191.
22. Ibid., 213.
23. W. Bray (ed.), *The Diary of John Evelyn*, I (1952), 11.
24. G. Bray, *The Anglican Canons, 1529–1947* (1998), 532–52.
25. The phrase is used explicitly in J. Morrill, *The Nature of the English Revolution* (1993), 33.
26. J. Maltby, 'Petitions for Episcopacy and the Book of Common Prayer on the Eve of the Civil War 1641–1642', in S. Taylor (ed.), *From Cranmer to Davidson: A Church of England Miscellany* (1999), 148; see also J. Maltby, *Prayer Book and People in Elizabethan and Early Stuart England* (1998), 237–49.
27. J. Maltby, 'Suffering and Surviving: The Civil Wars, the Commonwealth and the Formation of "Anglicanism", 1642–60', in C. Durston & J. Maltby (eds.), *Religion in Revolutionary England* (2006), 167.
28. The complete text of Dowsing's journal, which records in detail his activity, can be found in T. Cooper (ed.), *The Journal of William Dowsing: Iconoclasm in East Anglia during the English Civil War* (2001).
29. G. Fox, *Journal of George Fox* (1694; abridged edn, 1924).
30. The existence of Ranters as a self-conscious, organised movement was denied in J. C. Davis, *Fear, Myth and History: The Ranters and the Historians* (1986).
31. Cf. C. Hill, *The World Turned Upside Down: Radical Ideas during the English Revolution* (1975); the title is from a ballad of the 1640s.
32. Maltby, 'Suffering and Surviving', 160.
33. K. Fincham & S. Taylor, 'Vital Statistics: Episcopal Ordinations and Ordinands in England, 1646–60', *English Historical Review*, 126 (2011), 320.

7. Restoration and Rebellion

1. W. Bray (ed.), *The Diary of John Evelyn*, I (1952), 341.
2. Ibid., 343.
3. Ibid., 355–6.

4. R. Latham & W. Matthews (eds.), *The Diary of Samuel Pepys*, II (1970), 85.

5. T. Harris, *Restoration. Charles II and His Kingdoms, 1660–1685* (2005), 43.

6. J. Spurr, *The Restoration Church of England, 1646–1689* (1991), 35.

7. Ibid., 34.

8. R. Baxter, *Autobiography … being the Reliquiae Baxterianae* (1696; new edn, 1931), 165.

9. Spurr, 44; cf. also G. Tapsell (ed.), *The Later Stuart Church, 1660–1714* (2012), 10.

10. W. B. Patterson, 'Thorndike, Herbert (bap. 1597?, d. 1672)', *Oxford Dictionary of National Biography* (2004); J. Rose, 'By Law Established: The Church of England and the Royal Supremacy', in Tapsell (ed.), 27; see also, J. R. Collins, 'The Restoration Bishops and the Royal Supremacy', *Church History*, 68 (1999), 567–9.

11. Spurr, 43.

12. S. Hampton, *Anti-Arminians: The Anglican Reformed Tradition from Charles II to George I* (2008).

13. Spurr, 46.

14. Harris, 63–4.

15. Spurr, 59.

16. Ibid., 83.

17. W. Gibson, 'The Limits of the Confessional State: Electoral Religion in the Reign of Charles II', *Historical Journal*, 51 (2008), 27–47.

18. B. D. Spinks, *The Rise and Fall of the Incomparable Liturgy: The Book of Common Prayer, 1559–1906* (2017), 85.

19. A. Thomson, 'Church Discipline: The Operation of the Winchester Consistory Court in the Seventeenth Century', *Journal of British Studies*, 91 (2006), 337–59.

20. Spurr, 73–4.

21. D. A. Spaeth, *The Church in an Age of Danger: Parson and Parishioners, 1660–1740* (2000), 10–29.

22. D. Olusoga, *Black and British: A Forgotten History* (2016), 73–6.

23. T. Harris, 'What's New about the Restoration?', *Albion*, 29 (1997), 192.

24. Spurr, *Restoration Church of England*, 90.

25. J. Childs, '1688', *History*, 73 (1988), 413–14.

26. G. Burnet, *History of His Own Times* (1906), 268.

27. Spurr, 94–5.
28. T. Harris, *Revolution. The Great Crisis of the British Monarchy 1685–1720* (2006), 274.

8. The Great Churches

1. For a detailed account of the destruction, which questions whether the bones were actually burnt, see J. Butler, *The Quest for Becket's Bones: The Mystery of the Relics of St Thomas Becket of Canterbury* (1995).
2. D. Keene, A. Burns & A. Saint (eds.), *St Paul's: The Cathedral Church of London 604–2004* (2004), 173.
3. S. E. Lehmberg, *English Cathedrals: A History* (2005), 122.
4. Ibid., 164.
5. Ibid., 165.
6. H. Gee & W. J. Hardy, *Documents Illustrative of English Church History* (1896), 435.
7. *Heritage and Renewal: The Report of the Archbishops' Commission on Cathedrals* (1994), 191.
8. Keene, Burns & Saint (eds.), 175.
9. Lehmberg, 179–80.
10. Ibid., 171.
11. Ibid., 176.
12. Ibid., 188, citing Bruno Ryves's *Mercurius Rusticus: or The Countries Complaint of the Barbarous Outrages Committee by the Sectaries* (1646).
13. Lehmberg, 190.
14. W. Bray (ed.), *The Diary of John Evelyn*, I (1952), 39.
15. Lehmberg, 196.
16. Ibid., 200.
17. I. Atherton, 'Dean and Chapter Restored, 1660–1836', in P. Meadows & N. Ramsay (eds.), *A History of Ely Cathedral* (2003), 199.
18. S. E. Lehmberg, *Cathedrals under Siege: Cathedrals in English Society, 1600–1700* (1996), 83.
19. Lehmberg, 273.
20. D. Verey (ed.), *The Diary of a Cotswold Parson: Reverend F. E. Witts, 1783–1854* (1979), 69.
21. G. F. A. Best, *Temporal Pillars: Queen Anne's Bounty, the Ecclesiastical Commissioners and the Church of England* (1964), 317–45.
22. H. B. J. Armstrong (ed.), *A Norfolk Diary: Passages from the Diary of the Rev. Benjamin J. Armstrong* (1949), 64.

23. P. Barrett, *Barchester: English Cathedral Life in the Nineteenth Century* (1993), 231–44.
24. Cf. W. O. Chadwick, *The Victorian Church*, II (new edn, 1987), 370 & 391.
25. Barrett, 238.
26. Keene, Burns & Saint (eds.), 89–91; also, G. L. Prestige, *St Paul's in its Glory* (1955).
27. D. H. Lawrence, *The Rainbow* (1915; new edn, 1981), 243.
28. Cf. J. Kennedy, 'Conservation and Renewal', in S. Platten & C. Lewis, *Dreaming Spires? Cathedrals in a New Age* (2006), 115–28.
29. See *Heritage and Renewal*.

9. Consolidation and Conformity: The Long Eighteenth Century

1. G. Tapsell, 'The Church of England, 1662–1714', in J. Gregory (ed.), *The Oxford History of Anglicanism, II: Establishment and Empire, 1662–1829* (2017), 27.
2. Voltaire, *Letters on England* (1733; new edn, 1980), 37.
3. S. Mandelbrote, 'Religious Belief and the Politics of Toleration in the Late Seventeenth Century', *Nederlands archief voor kerkgeschiedenis/Dutch Review of Church History*, 81 (2001), 101.
4. Cf. L. Colley, *Britons: Forging the Nation, 1707–1837* (1992); A. Claydon & I. McBride (eds.), *Protestantism and National Identity: Britain and Ireland, c.1650–c.1850* (1998).
5. N. Ravitch, 'The Social Origins of French and English Bishops in the Eighteenth Century', *Historical Journal*, 8 (1965), 319.
6. J. S. Chamberlain, *Accommodating High Churchmen: The Clergy of Sussex, 1700–1745* (1997).
7. Cf. R. Mackley, 'The Bishops and the Church of England in the Reign of George II: High Churchmanship and Orthodoxy', University of Cambridge PhD thesis, 2016.
8. Quoted in R. Ingram, 'The Church of England 1714–1783', in J. Gregory (ed.), *The Oxford History of Anglicanism, II: Establishment and Empire, 1662–1829* (2017), 55.
9. D. W. Hayton, 'Atterbury, Francis (1663–1732)', *Oxford Dictionary of National Biography* (2004).
10. H. Sacheverell, *The Perils of False Brethren* (1709), 13.
11. Cf. M. Goldie, 'Voluntary Anglicans', *Historical Journal*, 46 (2003), 977–90; also, J. Gregory, *Restoration, Reformation, and Reform, 1660–1828: Archbishops of Canterbury and Their Diocese* (2000), 90–101.

12. R. W. Church, *The Oxford Movement: Twelve Years, 1833–1845* ((1890; new edn, 1970), 11.

13. W. Gibson, *The Church of England 1688–1832: Unity and Accord* (2001).

14. P. Virgin, *The Church in an Age of Negligence: Ecclesiastical Structure and Problems of Church Reform, 1700–1840* (1989).

15. D. A. Spaeth, *The Church in an Age of Danger: Parson and Parishioners, 1660–1740* (2000).

16. J. Spurr, *The Restoration Church of England, 1646–1689* (1991), 199.

17. C. D. Field, 'Counting Religion in England and Wales: The Long Eighteenth Century, c.1680–c.1840', *Journal of Ecclesiastical History*, 63 (2012), 693–720.

18. Cf. A. Whiteman & M. Clapinson (eds.), *The Compton Census of 1676: A Critical Edition* (1986), xxiii–lxxxii; there is an online edition at: https://www.oxfordscholarlyeditions.com/view/10.1093/actrade/9780197260418.book.1/actrade-9780197260418-book-1

19. J. S. Chamberlain, '"A Regular and Well-affected" Diocese: Chichester in the Eighteenth Century', in J. Gregory & J. S. Chamberlain (eds.), *The National Church in Regional Perspective: The Church of England and the Regions, 1660–1800* (2003), 88.

20. J. Gregory, 'Archbishops of Canterbury, Their Diocese, and the Shaping of the National Church', in Gregory & Chamberlain (eds.), *The National Church in Regional Perspective*, 44.

21. S. Taylor, 'Archbishop Potter and the Dissenters', *Yale University Library Gazette*, 67 (1993), 124.

22. D. Petts, 'Landscapes of Belief: Non-Conformist Mission in the North Pennines', *International Journal of Historical Archaeology*, 15 (2011), 466.

23. J. Gregory, '"For All Sorts and Conditions of Men": The Social Life of the Book of Common Prayer during the Long Eighteenth Century: or, Bringing the History of Religion and Social History Together', *Social History*, 34 (2009), 38.

24. W. M. Jacob, *The Clerical Profession in the Long Eighteenth Century, 1680–1840* (2007), 115.

25. J. Walsh, C. Haydon & S. Taylor (eds.), *The Church of England, c.1689–c.1833: From Toleration to Tractarianism* (1993), 9.

26. Jacob, 114.

27. Gregory, '"For All Sorts and Conditions of Men"', 38–9.

28. J. G. Taylor, *Our Lady of Batersey: The Story of Battersea Church and Parish Told from Original Sources* (1925), 101.

29. Goldie, 990.

30. Mandelbrote, 108–9.

31. D. Hume, *A Treatise of Human Nature* (1739–40; new edn, 1962), 173.

32. B. Mitchell, 'Butler as Christian Apologist', in C. Cunliffe (ed.), *Joseph Butler's Moral and Religious Thought: Tercentenary Essays* (1992), 97–116.

33. E. Gibbon, *Autobiography* (1796; new edn, 1907), 180.

34. C. Middleton, *A Free Inquiry into the Miraculous Powers Which are Supposed to Have Subsisted in the Christian Church* (1749), 21.

35. H. G. Reventlow, *The Authority of the Bible and the Rise of the Modern World* (1984).

36. Cf. J. G. A. Pocock, *Barbarism and Religion: The Enlightenments of Edward Gibbon, 1737–1764* (1999); and also B. W. Young, *Religion and Enlightenment in Eighteenth-Century England: Theological Debate from Locke to Burke* (1998).

37. A. Starkie, *The Church of England and the Bangorian Controversy, 1716–1721* (2007).

38. G. M. Ditchfield (ed.), *The Letters of Theophilus Lindsey (1723–1808)*, I (2007), 125.

39. E. Burke, *Works*, III (1906), 301.

40. J. F. C. Harrison, *The Second Coming: Popular Millenarianism 1780–1850* (1979), 32.

41. Ibid., 86–124; see also J. Hopkins, *A Woman to Deliver Her People: Joanna Southcott and English Millenarianism in an Era of Revolution* (1982).

42. E. H. Davidson & W. J. Scheick, *Paine, Scripture and Authority: The Age of Reason as Religious and Political Idea* (1994); J. Fruchtman, *Thomas Paine and the Religion of Nature* (1993).

10. The Evangelical Revival

1. John Kent talks of 'primary religion' in *Wesley and the Wesleyans: Religion in Eighteenth-Century Britain* (2002), 1–30; cf. also P. Mack, *Heart Religion in the British Enlightenment: Gender and Emotionalism in Early Methodism* (2008).

2. B. Hindmarsh, *The Evangelical Conversion Narrative: Spiritual Autobiography in Early Modern England* (2007).

3. D. Bebbington, *Evangelicalism in Modern Britain: A History from the 1730s to the 1980s* (new edn, 2005), 5–19.

4. Cf. articles in *Fides et Historia*, 47 (2015), especially M. A. Noll,

'Noun or Adjective? The Ravings of a Fanatical Nominalist', 73–82. There is a wide-ranging consideration of the definition in relation to modern Evangelicalism in R. Warner, *Reinventing English Evangelicalism, 1966–2001: A Theological and Sociological Study* (2007).

5. Bebbington, 12.
6. I am mindful of Bebbington's caution that 'Characteristics need to have existed over time if they are to be treated as valid characteristics of the whole movement': D. Bebbington, 'The Evangelical Quadrilateral: A Response', *Fides et Historia*, 47 (2015), 89.
7. Cf. J. Coffey (ed.), *Heart Religion: Evangelical Piety in England and Ireland, 1690–1850* (2016).
8. M. Henry, *An Account of the Life and Death of Lieutenant Illidge* (2nd edn, London, 1720), quoted in M. A. L. Smith, 'Translating Feeling: The Bible, Affections and Protestantism in England c.1660–c.1750', in S. Ditchfield, C. Methuen & A. Spicer (eds.), *Translating Christianity: Studies in Church History*, 53 (2017), 321; italics original.
9. J. Walsh, 'The Origins of the Evangelical Revival', in G. V. Bennett & J. D. Walsh (eds.), *Essays in Modern English Church History* (1966), 140–53.
10. For the pan-European context of the Evangelical revival, see W. R. Ward, *The Protestant Evangelical Awakening* (1992); also W. R. Ward, *Early Evangelicalism: A Global Intellectual History, 1670–1789* (2006).
11. Cf. C. Podmore, *The Moravian Church in England, 1728–1760* (1998).
12. J. Wesley, 'The Marks of the New Birth', in *Sermons on Several Occasions* [The 'Forty-Four Sermons'] (1787–8; new edn, 1944), 172.
13. J. Newton, B. Hindmarsh (ed.), *The Life and Spirituality of John Newton* (2003), 64.
14. https://worldmethodistcouncil.org/about/member-churches/statistical-information
15. P. Jenkins, 'Church, Nation and Language: The Welsh Church, 1660–1800', in J. Gregory & J. S. Chamberlain (eds.), *The National Church in Local Perspective: The Church of England and the Regions, 1660–1800* (2003), 275.
16. H. D. Rack, *Reasonable Enthusiast: John Wesley and the Rise of Methodism* (1989), 164.
17. D. L. Morgan, 'Harris, Howel (1714–1773)', *Oxford Dictionary of National Biography* (2004).
18. Rack, 144.

19. H. S. Stout, *The Divine Dramatist: George Whitefield and the Rise of Modern Evangelicalism* (1991); but see also B. S. Schlenther, 'Whitefield, George (1714–1779)', *Oxford Dictionary of National Biography* (2004).

20. G. Whitefield, *Works*, cited in Schlenther.

21. S. J. Stein, 'George Whitefield on Slavery: Some New Evidence', *Church History*, 42 (1973), 243–56; see also W. A. Sloat II, 'George Whitefield, Afro-Americans and Slavery', *Methodist History*, 33 (1994), 3–13.

22. G. Whitefield, *A Letter to the Reverend Mr John Wesley: In Answer to His Sermon, Entituled, Free-grace* (1741).

23. Cf. B. S. Schlenther, *Queen of the Methodists: The Countess of Huntingdon and the Eighteenth-Century Crisis of Faith and Society* (1997).

24. D. Hempton, *The Church in the Long Eighteenth Century* (2011), 155.

25. D. Hempton, *Methodism: Empire of the Spirit* (2005), 54.

26. Ibid., 68–74.

27. R. Currie, A. D. Gilbert & L. Horsley, *Churches and Churchgoers: Patterns of Church Growth in the British Isles since 1700* (1977), 139.

28. See the county tables in B. I. Coleman, *The Church of England in the Mid-Nineteenth Century: A Social Geography* (1980), 40–41; see also the fuller discussion in K. D. M. Snell & P. S. Ell, *Rival Jerusalems: The Geography of Victorian Religion* (2000), 121–32.

29. D. Luker, 'Revivalism in Theory and Practice: The Case of Cornish Methodism', *Journal of Ecclesiastical History*, 37 (1986), 605.

30. S. Hampton, *Anti-Arminians: The Anglican Reformed Tradition from Charles II to George I* (2008); Hampton's work builds on R. Muller, *After Calvin: Studies in the Development of a Theological Tradition* (2003).

31. J. Griesel, 'John Edwards of Cambridge (1637–1716): A Reassessment of His Position within the Later Stuart Church of England', PhD thesis, University of Cambridge, 2019.

32. G. Carter, 'Romaine, William (1714–1795)', *Oxford Dictionary of National Biography* (2014) .

33. B. Hindmarsh, *John Newton and the English Evangelical Tradition: Between the Conversions of Wesley and Wilberforce* (new edn, 2001).

34. Cf. G. Atkins, *Converting Britannia: Evangelicals and Public Life, 1770–1840* (2019).

35. N. G. Annan, 'The Intellectual Aristocracy', in J. H. Plumb (ed.),

Studies in Social History (1955), 241–87; see also W. Whyte, 'The Intellectual Aristocracy Revisited', *Journal of Victorian Culture*, 10 (2005), 15–45, and Ford K. Brown, *Fathers of the Victorians: The Age of Wilberforce* (1961).

36. A. Stott, *Hannah More: The First Victorian* (2003).

37. Atkins, 57.

38. Cf. Atkins, chapter 2, 'Business, Banking and Bibles in Late Hanoverian London', 63–104.

39. D. Olusoga, *Black and British: A Forgotten History* (2016), 219.

40. E. Williams, *Capitalism and Slavery* (1944); for a more nuanced view, see R. Anstey, *The Atlantic Slave Trade and British Abolition, 1760–1810* (1975). An emphasis on the wider role of popular mobilisation can be found in S. Drescher, 'Whose Abolition? Popular Pressure and the Ending of the British Slave Trade', *Past & Present*, 143 (1994), 136–66; see also C. L. Brown, *Moral Capital: The Foundations of British Abolitionism* (2006) and J. Coffey, '"Tremble, Britannia!": Fear, Providence and the Abolition of the Slave Trade, 1758–1807', *English Historical Review*, 127 (2012), 844–81.

41. This echoes the conclusion of W. Palmer, 'How Ideology Works: Historians and the Case of British Abolitionism', *Historical Journal*, 52 (2009), 1039–51.

42. N. Scotland, *John Bird Sumner: Evangelical Archbishop* (1995).

43. J. C. S. Nias, *Gorham and the Bishop of Exeter* (1951); see also J. Wolffe, 'Gorham, George Cornelius (1787–1857)', *Oxford Dictionary of National Biography* (2004).

44. J. L. Altholz, 'Alexander Haldane, the *Record* and Religious Journalism', *Victorian Periodicals Review*, 20 (1987), 23.

11. The Fortunes of Clergy: From Patronage to Piety

1. This is an estimate, based on the figure of around 10,500 benefices, and taking into account curates or assistant clergy; precision in these matters is very difficult before the nineteenth century.

2. P. Virgin, *The Church in an Age of Negligence: Ecclesiastical Structure and Problems of Church Reform, 1700–1840* (1989), 60–1.

3. S. Slinn, *The Education of the Anglican Clergy, 1780–1839* (2017), 54.

4. J. Gregory, *Restoration, Reformation, and Reform, 1660–1828: Archbishops of Canterbury and Their Diocese* (2000), 73.

5. N. Virgoe & S. Yaxley (eds.), *The Banville Diaries: Journals of a Norfolk Gamekeeper 1822–44* (1986), 105.

6. W. Plomer, *Kilvert's Diary*, I: 1 *January 1870–19 August 1871* (new edn, 1960), 213–14.

7. R. E. Prothero, H. C. G. Matthew (rev.), 'Stanley, Edward (1779–1849)', *Oxford Dictionary of National Biography* (2004); W. O. Chadwick, *Victorian Miniature* (1991), 55.

8. W. N. Yates, 'An Opportunity Missed? The Provision of Education and Training for a Non-graduate Clergy: Comparative Case Studies of the Dioceses of St David's and Sodor and Man in the Eighteenth and Nineteenth Centuries', *Dutch Review of Social History*, 83 (2003), 321.

9. N. Surry (ed.), *'Your Affectionate and Loving Sister': The Correspondence of Barbara Kerrich and Elizabeth Postlethwaite 1733 to 1751* (2000), 94.

10. D. Hughes (ed.), *The Diary of a Country Parson: The Revd James Woodforde* (1992), 44.

11. Ibid., 95.

12. Ibid., 95.

13. Ibid., 102.

14. Ibid., 118.

15. Ibid., 229.

16. D. Verey (ed.), *The Diary of a Cotswold Parson: Reverend F. E. Witts, 1783–1854* (1979), 39.

17. W. M. Jacob, *The Clerical Profession in the Long Eighteenth Century, 1680–1840* (2007), 80.

18. Ibid., 84.

19. D. B. Haycock, 'Stukeley, William (1687–1765)', *Oxford Dictionary of National Biography* (2004).

20. Jacob, 167.

21. Hughes, 216.

22. Verey, 87.

23. P. Tovey, *Anglican Confirmation 1662–1820* (2014).

24. K. D. M. Snell, 'The Sunday-School Movement in England and Wales: Child Labour, Denominational Control and Working-Class Culture', *Past & Present*, 164 (1999), 126, 166.

25. Jacob, 252.

26. J. Arch, *From Ploughtail to Parliament: An Autobiography* (1986), 21.

27. J. Ayres (ed.), *Paupers and Pig Killers: The Diary of William Holland, a Somerset Parson, 1799–1818* (1986), 272.

28. S. J. Brown, *The National Churches of England, Ireland and Scotland 1801–1846* (2001), 10–11.

29. N. Patterson, *Ecclesiastical Law, Clergy and Laity: A History of Legal Discipline and the Anglican Church* (2019), 16.

30. Ibid., 82–4.

31. Ayres, 276–7.

32. C. Armstrong (ed.), *Under the Parson's Nose: Further Extracts from the Diary of the Revd Benjamin Armstrong* (2012), 17.

33. Ibid., 55.

34. Ibid., 93.

12. The Crisis and Reform of the Confessional State

1. R. Currie, A. D. Gilbert & L. Horsley, *Churches and Churchgoers: Patterns of Church Growth in the British Isles since 1700* (1977), 139–40.

2. S. J. Brown, *The National Churches of England, Ireland and Scotland 1801–46* (2001), 50.

3. M. Austin, *A Stage or Two beyond Christendom: A Social History of the Church of England in Derbyshire* (2001), 131.

4. Brown, 91.

5. S. Slinn, *The Education of the Anglican Clergy, 1780–1839* (2017), 30.

6. Cf. N. Dixon, 'The Church of England and the Legislative Reforms of 1828–32: Revolution or Adjustment?', in R. McKitterick, C. Methuen & A. Spicer (eds.), *The Church and the Law* (2020), 401–18.

7. G. B. Smith, V. Markham Lester (rev.), 'Henley, Robert, second Baron Henley (1789–1841)', *Oxford Dictionary of National Biography* (2004).

8. A. P. Stanley, *The Life and Correspondence of Thomas Arnold*, II (1844), 16.

9. A. Burns, 'Blomfield, Charles James (1786–1857)', *Oxford Dictionary of National Biography* (2004); see also M. Johnson, *Bustling Intermeddler? The Life and Work of Charles James Blomfield* (2001).

10. G. F. A. Best, *Temporal Pillars: Queen Anne's Bounty, the Ecclesiastical Commissioners and the Church of England* (1964), 296–347.

11. F. Knight, *The Nineteenth-Century Church and English Society* (1995), 121.

12. On the importance of High Church support for Church reform, see R. A. Burns, *The Diocesan Revival in the Church of England* c. 1800–1870 (1999).

13. J. Mill, 'The Church and Its Reform', *The London Review*, 1 (1835), 288.

14. E. Miall, cited in D. M. Thompson (ed.), *Nonconformity in the Nineteenth Century* (1972), 107.

15. E. B. Pusey, 'The Royal and Parliamentary Ecclesiastical Commissions', *British Critic* 46 (April 1838), 460.

16. P. Virgin, 'Smith, Sydney (1771–1845)', *Oxford Dictionary of National Biography* (2004).

17. S. Smith, 'First Letter to Archdeacon Singleton on the Ecclesiastical Commission', in S. Smith, *Works* (1869), 712–13.

18. W. H. Mackintosh, *Disestablishment and Liberation: The Movement for Separation of the Anglican Church from State Control* (1972), 64–5.

19. J. N. Morris, *Religion and Urban Change: Croydon 1840–1914* (1992), 114–17.

20. G. Williams, W. Jacob, N. Yates & F. Knight, *The Welsh Church from Reformation to Disestablishment 1603–1920* (2007), 246–9.

21. J. Breay, *A Fell-Side Parson: Joseph Brunskill and His Diaries 1826–1903* (1995), 91.

13. The High Church Revival

1. Cf. P. B. Nockles, *The Oxford Movement in Context: Anglican High Churchmanship 1760–1857* (1994); R. A. Burns, *The Diocesan Revival in the Church of England* c. *1800–1870* (1999).

2. Cf. A. B. Webster, *Joshua Watson: The Story of a Layman, 1771–1855* (1954).

3. J. Garrard, *Archbishop Howley, 1828–1848* (2015), 25.

4. M. Chandler, for example, describes the first Evangelical archbishop of Canterbury, J. B. Sumner, as Erastian, in *Queen Victoria's Archbishops of Canterbury* (2019), 77–126.

5. D. MacCulloch, *Thomas Cranmer: A Life* (1996), 606–32.

6. R. W. Church, *The Oxford Movement: Twelve Years* (1891; new edn, 1970), 258.

7. P. B. Nockles, '"Lost Causes and … Impossible Loyalties": The Oxford Movement and the University', in M. G. Brock and M. C. Curthoys (eds.), *The History of the University of Oxford, VI: Nineteenth-Century Oxford, Part I* (1997), 202.

8. Garrard, 69; cf. also W. Palmer, *A Narrative of Events Connected with the Publication of the Tracts for the Times* (1843; new edn, 1883), 48–53.

9. G. M. Murphy, 'Burgon, John William (1813–1888)', *Oxford*

Dictionary of National Biography (2004); J. W. Burgon, *Lives of Twelve Good Men* (1888), 319.

10. J. H. Newman, *Lectures on the Prophetical Office of the Church* (2nd edn, 1838), 19.

11. J. Keble & J. H. Newman (eds.), *Remains of the Late Reverend Richard Hurrell Froude M.A.* (1838).

12. A. Atherstone, *Oxford's Protestant Spy: The Controversial Career of Charles Golightly* (2007).

13. J. H. Newman, 'Tract XC: Remarks on Certain Passages in the Thirty-nine Articles', in W. G. Hutchinson (ed.), *The Oxford Movement: Being a Selection from Tracts for the Times* (1906), 212.

14. J. H. Newman, *Apologia Pro Vita Sua* (1864; new edn, 1905), 197–8.

15. B. Douglas, *The Eucharistic Theology of Edward Bouverie Pusey* (2015), 97.

16. Newman, 'Tract I: Thoughts on the Ministerial Commission', in Hutchinson (ed.), 8.

17. S. A. Skinner, '"The Duty of the State": Keble, the Tractarians and Establishment', in K. Blair (ed.), *John Keble in Context* (2004), 33–46.

18. Cf. Nockles, 146–83.

19. N. Sykes, *Old Priest and New Presbyter: The Anglican Attitude to Episcopacy, Presbyterianism and Papacy since the Reformation* (1956), 212.

20. J. Keble, *Sermons for Lent to Passiontide* (1878), 63–4.

21. Cf. D. Janes, *Victorian Reformation: The Fight over Idolatry in the Church of England, 1840–1860* (2009).

22. Cf. J. N. Morris, *The High Church Revival in the Church of England: Arguments and Identities* (2016), 46–9; for a different view, see G. Herring, *The Oxford Movement in Practice: The Tractarian Parochial Worlds from the 1830s to the 1870s* (2016), 191–6.

23. K. Leech, 'Stewart Headlam, 1847–1924, and the Guild of St Matthew', in M. Reckitt (ed.), *For Christ and the People* (1968), 61–88; R. Woodfield, 'Conrad Noel, 1869–1942, Catholic Crusader', in Reckitt (ed.), 135–80.

24. Morris, 81–9.

25. F. Oakeley, *Historical Notes on the Tractarian Movement* (1865), 62–3.

26. On St Paul's, Knightsbridge, F. Bennett, *The Story of W. J. E. Bennett and of His Part in the Oxford Movement of the Nineteenth Century* (1909), 28–45, and on St George's-in-the-East, D. Kent, 'High

Church Rituals and Rituals of Protest: The "Riots" at St George-in-the-East, 1859–1860', *London Journal*, 24 (2007), 145–66.

27. For discussion of the sensitivity over idolatry, see Janes, above.

28. Cf. B. Kilcrease, *The Great Church Crisis and the End of English Erastianism, 1898–1906* (2017).

29. Cf. P. F. Anson, *The Call of the Cloister: Religious Communities and Kindred Bodies in the Anglican Communion* (1955); A. M. Allchin, *The Silent Rebellion: Anglican Religious Communities, 1845–1900* (1958).

30. Anson, 244–8.

31. Ibid., 337–45.

32. Cf. R. Chapman, *Faith and Revolt: Studies in the Literary Influence of the Oxford Movement* (1970); K. Blair, *Form and Faith in Victorian Poetry and Religion* (2012).

33. Cf. M. Lewis, *The Gothic Revival* (2002).

34. Cf. W. N. Yates, *Buildings, Faith and Worship: The Liturgical Arrangement of Anglican Churches, 1600–1900* (new edn, 2000), 127–49.

35. J. F. White, *The Cambridge Movement: The Ecclesiologists and the Gothic Ideal* (1962).

14. Where Choirs Sing: Anglicanism's Cultural Experiment

1. M. Bent, 'The Old Hall Manuscript', *Early Music*, 2 (1974), 2–14; M. Williamson, 'The Early Tudor Court, the Provinces and the Eton Choirbook', *Early Music*, 25 (1997), 229–43.

2. The quotation is from the prefatory text 'Concerning the Service of the Church' from the 1549 Prayer Book, repeated in subsequent editions.

3. Cf. K. Carleton, 'John Marbeck and the Booke of Common Praier Noted', in D. Wood (ed.), *The Church and the Arts: Studies in Church History*, 28 (1992), 255–65.

4. R. Bowers, 'The Chapel Royal, the First Edwardian Prayer Book, and Elizabeth's Settlement of Religion, 1559', *Historical Journal*, 43 (2000), 341–2.

5. S. Cole, 'Who is the Father? Changing Perceptions of Tallis and Byrd in Late Nineteenth-Century England', *Music & Letters*, 89 (2008), 212–26.

6. Quoted in A. Gant, *O Sing unto the Lord: A History of English Church Music* (2015), 186.

7. S. J. Weston, 'Choir–Band Instrumentation: Two County Surveys', *The Galpin Society Journal*, 52 (1999), 305–13.

8. V. Gammon, 'The Performance Style of West Gallery Music', in C. Turner (ed.), *The Gallery Tradition: Aspects of Georgian Psalmody* (1997), 46.

9. V. Gammon, 'Singing and Popular Funeral Practices in the Eighteenth and Nineteenth Centuries', *Folk Music Journal*, 5 (1988), 412–47.

10. B. Rainbow, *The Choral Revival in the Anglican Church 1839–1872* (1970).

11. W. J. E. Bennett, in the first issue of the *Parish Choir*, 1846, quoted in Rainbow, 98–9.

12. Quoted in Rainbow, 166.

13. T. Day, *I Saw Eternity the Other Night: King's College Choir, the Nine Lessons and Carols, and an English Singing Style* (2018), 54–7.

14. Cf. Rainbow, 58–73 & 115–39; W. Shaw (ed.), *Sir Frederick Ouseley and St Michael's Tenbury: A Chapter in the History of English Church Music and Ecclesiology* (1988); P. Horton, 'Samuel Sebastian Wesley at Leeds: A Victorian Church Musician Reflects on His Craft', *Victorian Studies*, 30 (1986), 99–111; P. Charlton, *John Stainer and the Musical Life of Victorian Britain* (1984).

15. Cf. J. Dibble, *Charles Villiers Stanford: Man and Musician* (2002).

16. T. Storey, 'Music, 1800–2002', in D. Keene, A. Burns & A. Saint (eds.), *St Paul's: The Cathedral Church of London 604–2004* (2004), 405–7.

17. Cf. E. Routley, *Twentieth-Century Church Music* (1964).

18. Cf. D. Gray, *Earth and Altar: The Evolution of the Parish Communion in the Church of England to 1945* (1986).

19. E. R. Norman, *Anglican Difficulties: A New Syllabus of Errors* (2004), 22–5.

15. Liberalism

1. W. Conybeare, R. A. Burns (ed.), 'Church Parties', in S. Taylor (ed.), *From Cranmer to Davidson: A Church of England Miscellany* (1999), 340.

2. J. N. Morris, F. D. Maurice and the Crisis of Christian Authority (2005), 70.

3. F. D. Maurice, *The Religions of the World and Their Relations to Christianity* (1847).

4. Morris, 77–8.

5. B. Colloms, *Charles Kingsley: The Lion of Eversley* (1975), 226–7; S. S. Walker, '"Backwards and Backwards Ever": Charles Kingsley's

Racial-Historical Allegory and the Liberal Anglican Revisioning of Britain', *Nineteenth-Century Literature*, 62 (2007), 339–79.

6. Cf. G. Rowell, *Hell and the Victorians: A Study of the Nineteenth-Century Theological Controversies concerning Eternal Punishment and the Future Life* (1974).

7. Cf. F. D. Maurice, 'Concluding Essay – on Eternal Life and Eternal Death', *Theological Essays* (1853).

8. F. Maurice, *The Life of Frederick Denison Maurice, Chiefly Told in His Own Letters* (1884), 163–209.

9. M. V. Hughes, *A London Girl of the 1870s* (1934; new edn, 1977), 81.

10. B. Jowett (ed.), 'To the Reader', in *Essays and Reviews* (1860).

11. H. B. Wilson, 'The National Church', in Jowett (ed.), *Essays and Reviews*, 179.

12. H. B. J. Armstrong (ed.), *A Norfolk Diary: Passages from the Diary of the Rev. Benjamin J. Armstrong* (1949), 78.

13. P. B. Hinchliff, *John William Colenso, Bishop of Natal* (1964).

14. Cf. R. T. Shannon, 'Sir John Seeley and the Idea of a National Church', in R. Robson (ed.), *Ideas and Institutions of Victorian England* (1967), 236–67.

15. A. Symondson (ed.), *The Victorian Crisis of Faith* (1970).

16. Cf. R. Morgan (ed.), *The Religion of the Incarnation: Anglican Essays in Commemoration of Lux Mundi* (1989).

17. P. T. Phillips, 'The Concept of a National Church in Late Nineteenth-Century England and America', *Journal of Religious History*, 14 (1986), 26–37.

18. L. E. Nettleship, 'William Fremantle, Samuel Barnett, and the Broad Church Origins of Toynbee Hall', *Journal of Ecclesiastical History*, 33 (1982), 564–79.

19. See A. M. G. Stephenson, *The Rise and Decline of English Modernism* (1984).

20. C. W. Emmet, 'The Modernist Movement in the Church of England', *Journal of Religion*, 2 (1922), 561–76.

21. A. E. J. Rawlinson, M. Grimley (rev.), 'Barnes, Ernest William (1874–1953)', *Oxford Dictionary of National Biography* (2015).

22. E. Carpenter, *Archbishop Fisher – His Life and Times* (1991), 295–302.

23. M. Grimley, *Citizenship, Community and the Church of England: Liberal Anglican Theories of the State between the Wars* (2004).

24. A. Hastings, *A History of English Christianity 1920–1985* (1987), 261.

25. T. W. Jones, *Sexual Politics in the Church of England, 1857–1957* (2013), 131–61.

16. The Church in Industrial Society

1. For an excellent introduction, see E. Griffin, *A Short History of the British Industrial Revolution* (2010).
2. Griffin, 31.
3. G. Clark, 'The Condition of the Working Class in England, 1209–2004', *Journal of Political Economy*, 113 (2005), 1307–40; R .C. Allen, 'The Great Divergence in European Wages and Prices from the Middle Ages to the First World War', *Explorations in Economic History*, 38 (2001), 411–47.
4. W. Binns, 'The Religious Heresies of the Working Classes', *Westminster Review* (January 1862), cited in G. Parsons (ed.), *Religion in Victorian Britain, 3: Sources* (1988), 371.
5. The phrase is used in S. Evans, *The Church in the Back Streets* (1962), 5–8.
6. The statistics in R. Currie, A. D. Gilbert & L. Horsley, *Churches and Churchgoers: Patterns of Church Growth in the British Isles since 1700* (1977) remain an important source, but their collection has been partly overtaken by more detailed research at local level, and particularly by the work of Clive Field, for which see, for example, C. Field, 'A Shilling for Queen Elizabeth: The Era of State Regulation of Church Attendance in England, 1552–1969', *Journal, of Church and State*, 59 (2008), 213–53; and 'Counting Religion in England and Wales: The Long Eighteenth Century, c.1680–c. 1840', *Journal of Ecclesiastical History*, 63 (2012), 693–720.
7. They have been published at various times by Peter Brierley, working through MARC Europe; Clive Field gathers a vast range of data on the website http://www.brin.ac.uk/
8. Summary figures in H. Mann, *The Census of Great Britain, 1851: Religious Worship in England and Wales* (1854).
9. B. I. Coleman, *The Church of England in the Mid-Nineteenth Century: A Social Geography* (1980), 7.
10. Ibid., 40.
11. Ibid., 41.
12. J. N. Morris, 'Religion', in C. Williams & A. Croll (eds.), *The Gwent County History, 5: The Twentieth Century* (2013), 241–2 & 248–51.

13. M. A. Smith, *Religion in Industrial Society: Oldham and Saddleworth 1740–1865* (1994), 251.

14. B. Rainbow, *The Choral Revival in the Anglican Church 1839–1872* (1970), 118.

15. D. H. McLeod, *Class and Religion in the Late Victorian City* (1974), 301.

16. Coleman, 41.

17. P. Midgley, *The Churches and the Working Classes: Leeds, 1870–1920* (2012), 273.

18. R. Beaken, *The Church of England and the Home Front 1914–1918: Civilians, Soldiers and Religion in Wartime Colchester* (2015), 92.

19. Evans, 4.

20. R. Mudie-Smith, *The Religious Life of London* (1904), 257.

21. Ibid., 446.

22. D. H. McLeod, *Religion and Society in England, 1850–1914* (1996), 156–68.

23. E. R. Wickham, *Church and People in an Industrial City* (1957).

24. S. Brewitt-Taylor, *Christian Radicalism in the Church of England and the Invention of the British Sixties, 1957–1970* (2018), 134–8; cf. also J. N. Morris, '"Church and People" Thirty-three Years On: A Historical Critique', *Theology*, 94 (1991), 92–101.

25. Smith, 35.

26. M. F. Snape, *The Church of England in Industrialising Society: The Lancashire Parish of Whalley in the Eighteenth Century* (2003), 36–8.

27. S. J. Brown, *The National Churches of England, Ireland and Scotland 1801–1846* (2001), 69–71.

28. A. D. Gilbert, *Religion and Society in Industrial England: Church, Chapel and Social Change 1740–1914* (1976), 130.

29. W. R. W. Stephens, *The Life and Letters of Walter Farquhar Hook* (6th edn, 1881), 376–85.

30. R. Gill, *Competing Convictions* (1989).

31. F. Prochaska, *Christianity and Social Service in Modern Britain: The Disinherited Spirit* (2006).

32. J. C. Bennett, 'And One for My Friend the Barmaid: Pew-renting and Social Class in English Anglican Churches in the Nineteenth and Twentieth Centuries', *Anglican and Episcopal History*, 86 (2017), 167–85.

33. C. E. Osborne, *The Life of Father Dolling* (1903), 245.

34. J. N. Morris, *F. D. Maurice and the Crisis of Christian Authority* (2005), 130–60; P. D'A. Jones, *The Christian Socialist Revival 1877–1914:*

Religion, Class and Social Conscience in Late Victorian England (1968); A. Wilkinson, *Christian Socialism: Scott Holland to Tony Blair* (1998).

35. N. Scotland, *Squires in the Slums: Settlements and Missions in Late Victorian Britain* (2007).

36. L. Davidoff & C. Hall, *Family Fortunes: Men and Women of the English Middle Class 1780–1850* (1987), 74.

37. M. V. Hughes, *A London Girl of the 1870s* (1934; new edn, 1977), 41.

38. Ibid., 71 & 75.

39. P. Matthias, *The First Industrial Nation: An Economic History of Britain 1700–1914* (1969), 260.

40. J. Burnett (ed.), *Useful Toil: Autobiographies of Working People from the 1820s to the 1920s* (1974), 180.

41. Ibid., 184.

42. Ibid., 60,

43. E. Griffin, *Liberty's Dawn: A People's History of the Industrial Revolution* (2013), 186–211.

44. D. Hempton, *Religion and Political Culture in Britain and Ireland: From the Glorious Revolution to the Decline of Empire* (199), 136–9.

45. Cf. J. Cox, *English Churches in a Secular Society: Lambeth 1870–1930* (1982).

46. D. H. McLeod, *Religion and Society in England, 1850–1914* (1996); S. C. Williams, *Religious Belief and Popular Culture in Southwark, c.1880–1939* (1999).

17. The Reshaping of the Victorian and Edwardian Church: Bureaucracy and Tradition

1. J. N. Morris, 'Episcopal Leadership in Anglicanism, 1800 to the Present: Changing Form, Function and Collegiality', in P. Avis & B. Guyer (eds.), *The Lambeth Conference: Theology, History, Polity and Purpose* (2017).

2. A. Haig, *The Victorian Clergy* (1984); D. A. Dowland, *Nineteenth-Century Anglican Theological Training: The Redbrick Challenge* (1997).

3. D. M. Thompson, *Cambridge Theology in the Nineteenth Century: Enquiry, Controversy and Truth* (2008); D. Inman, *The Making of Modern English Theology: God and the Academy at Oxford, 1833–1945* (2014).

4. J. Hoppit, 'The Nation, the State, and the First Industrial Revolution', *Journal of British Studies*, 50 (2011), 307–31.

5. E. Royle, *Radicals, Secularists and Republicans: Popular Freethought in Britain, 1866–1915* (1980).

6. F. Maurice, *The Life of Frederick Denison Maurice, Chiefly Told in His Own Letters* (1884), I, 485–6.

7. Quoted in T. W. Jones, *Sexual Politics in the Church of England 1857–1957* (2013), 85.

8. W. Plomer, *Kilvert's Diary*, II: 1871–4 (new edn, 1960), 99.

9. J. O. Johnston, *Life and Letters of Henry Parry Liddon* (1905), 257.

10. G. Williams, W. M. Jacob, N. Yates & F. Knight, *The Welsh Church from Reformation to Disestablishment 1603–1920* (2007), 72–3.

11. B. I. Coleman, *The Church of England in the Mid-Nineteenth Century: A Social Geography* (1980), 40–41.

12. K. D. M. Snell & P. S. Ell, *Rival Jerusalems: The Geography of Victorian Religion* (2000), 92.

13. D. A. Dowland, *Nineteenth-Century Anglican Theological Training: The Redbrick Challenge* (1997), 34.

14. G. Williams, W. Jacob, N. Yates & F. Knight, *The Welsh Church from Reformation to Disestablishment 1603–1920* (2007), 337.

15. K. O. Morgan, 'Welsh Nationalism: The Historical Background', *Journal of Contemporary History*, 6 (1971), 162.

16. Williams, Jacob, Yates & Knight, 320.

17. Cf. E. J. Gitre, 'The 1904–5 Welsh Revival: Modernization, Technologies, and Techniques of the Self', *Church History*, 73 (2004), 792–827.

18. D. D. Morgan, *The Span of the Cross: Christian Religion and Society in Wales 1914–2000* (1999), 27–9.

19. K. Robbins, *England, Ireland, Scotland, Wales: The Christian Church 1900–2000* (2008), 189–98.

20. Williams, Jacob, Yates & Knight, 384.

21. Cf. C. Harris & R. Startup, *The Church in Wales: The Sociology of a Traditional Institution* (1999).

22. Cf. B. Kilcrease, *The Great Church Crisis and the End of English Erastianism, 1898–1906* (2017); also M. Wellings, *Evangelicals Embattled: Responses of Evangelicals in the Church of England to Ritualism, Darwinism and Theological Liberalism 1890–1930* (2003).

23. Cf. F. Knight, *Victorian Christianity at the Fin de Siècle: The Culture of English Religion in a Decadent Age* (2016).

24. M. Wellings, 'Kensit, John (1853–1902)', *Oxford Dictionary of National Biography* (2004).

25. Cited in N. Yates, *Anglican Ritualism in Victorian Britain 1830–1910* (1999), 330.

18. The Church in a Century of Conflict

1. D. Cruickshank, '"Remember That in This Land There [are] Two Kingdoms": The Church of England's Theology of Church and State in the First World War', *Kirchliche Zeitgeschichte*, 31 (2018), 138–9.

2. M. Snape, 'Church of England Army Chaplains in the First World War: Goodbye to "Goodbye to All That"', *Journal of Ecclesiastical History*, 62 (2011), 318–45.

3. M. Snape, *God and the British Soldier: Religion and the British Army in the First and Second World Wars* (2005), 19–58.

4. Ibid., 165–8.

5. P. Howson (ed.), *The First World War Diaries of the Rt Rev. Llewellyn Gwynne July 1915–July 1916* (2019), 28.

6. Snape, 89.

7. N. T. A. Cave, 'Hardy, Theodore Bayley (1863–1918)', *Oxford Dictionary of National Biography* (2007).

8. S. Bell, 'Malign or Maligned? – Arthur Winnington-Ingram, Bishop of London, in the First World War', *Journal for the History of Modern Theology*, 20 (2013), 127.

9. C. D. Field, *Periodizing Secularization: Religious Allegiance and Attendance in Britain, 1880–1945* (2019), 159–66.

10. R. Beaken, *The Church of England and the Home Front 1914–1918: Civilians, Soldiers and Religion in Wartime Colchester* (2015), 140–41.

11. Field, 161.

12. A. Wilkinson, *The Church of England and the First World War* (1978), 74.

13. Cf. J. Winter, *Sites of Memory, Sites of Mourning: The Great War in European Cultural History* (1996).

14. F. A. Iremonger, *William Temple, Archbishop of Canterbury: His Life and Letters* (1948), 252–65.

15. G. K. A. Bell, *Randall Davidson, Archbishop of Canterbury* (3rd edn, 1952), 1307–11; Iremonger, 337–42.

16. H. H. Henson, *Retrospect of an Unimportant Life*, 2 (1943), 119; cf. M. Grimley, *Citizenship, Community and the Church of England: Liberal Anglican Theories of the State between the Wars* (2004), 103–39.

17. J. Maiden, *National Religion and the Prayer Book Controversy, 1927–1928* (2009), 44–74.

18. J. G. Lockhart, *Cosmo Gordon Lang* (1949), 405; on the real role Lang played, see R. Beaken, *Cosmo Lang: Archbishop in War and Crisis* (2012), 133–210.

19. A. P. F. Sell, *Philosophical Idealism and Christian Belief* (1995); T. M. Gouldstone, *The Rise and Decline of Anglican Idealism in the Nineteenth Century* (2005).

20. A. M. Ramsey, *From Gore to Temple: The Development of Anglican Theology between Lux Mundi and the Second World War,1889–1939* (1960), 146–61.

21. A. M. Ramsey, *The Gospel and the Catholic Church* (1936), 220.

22. K. Cracknell, *Justice, Courtesy and Love: Theologians and Missionaries Encountering World Religions, 1846–1914* (1995); B. Stanley (ed.), *The World Missionary Conference, Edinburgh 1910* (2009).

23. C. Methuen, 'The Making of "An Appeal to All Christian People" at the 1920 Lambeth Conference', in P. Avis & B. Guyer (eds.), *The Lambeth Conference: Theology, History, Polity and Purpose* (2017),107–131.

24. J. A. Dick, *The Malines Conversations Revisited* (1989).

25. Cf. P. Avis, 'Anglicanism and Christian Unity in the Twentieth Century', in J. N. Morris (ed.), *The Oxford History of Anglicanism, 4: Global Western Anglicanism, c.1910–present* (2017), 186–213.

26. R. A. Walford, *The Growth of 'New London' in Suburban Middlesex (1918–1945) and the Response of the Church of England* (2007), 107–42.

27. R. Currie, A. D. Gilbert & L. Horsley, *Churches and Churchgoers: Patterns of Church Growth in the British Isles since 1700* (1977),129.

28. C. D. Field, 'Gradualist or Revolutionary Secularization? A Case Study of Religious Belonging in Inter-War Britain, 1918–1939', *Church History and Religious Culture*, 93 (2013), 91.

29. A. Chandler, *George Bell, Bishop of Chichester: Church, State, and Resistance in the Age of Dictatorship* (2016), 76–82.

30. Snape, 125.

31. Field, 242.

32. Ibid., 243.

33. P. Larkham & J. Nasr, 'Decision-making under Duress: The Treatment of Churches in the City of London during and after World War II', *Urban History*, 39 (2012), 288.

34. A. Saint, 'The Reputation of St Paul's', in D. Keene, A. Burns &

A. Saint (eds.), *St Paul's: The Cathedral Church of London 604–2004* (2004), 461.

35. S. Stockwell, 'Anglicanism in the Era of Decolonization', in Morris, *Oxford History of Anglicanism*, 4, 160–87.

36. Cf. C. D. Field, *Britain's Last Religious Revival? Quantifying Belonging, Behaving and Believing in the Long 1950s* (2015); also, C. G. Brown, *The Death of Christian Britain: Understanding Secularisation 1800–2000* (new edn, 2009), 170–75.

37. Currie, Gilbert & Horsley,129.

38. Ibid., 167.

39. Field, 52–4.

40. I. Jones, *The Local Church and Generational Change in Birmingham 1945–2000* (2012), 73–96.

41. A. Chandler, *The Church of England in the Twentieth Century: The Church Commissioners and the Politics of Reform, 1948–1998* (2006), 67–79.

42. A. Hastings, *A History of English Christianity 1920–1985* (1987), 439.

19. Decline? The Religious 'Crisis' of the 1960s and Later

1. https://www.ons.gov.uk/aboutus/transparencyandgovernance/freedomofinformationfoi/muslimpopulationintheuk/

2. P. A. Welsby, *A History of the Church of England 1945–1980* (1984), 103.

3. C. G. Brown, *The Death of Christian Britain: Understanding Secularisation 1800–2000* (new edn, 2009), 191–2; C. Field, *Secularization in the Long 1960s. Numerating Religion in Britain* (2017), 55.

4. Field, 51.

5. Church of England, *Statistics for Mission 2011* (comparative table), 17, at https://www.churchofengland.org/sites/default/files/2017–11/Statistics%20for%20Mission%202011.pdf

6. Ibid., 6.

7. Field, 54.

8. Church of England, 14.

9. P. Brierley, *'Christian' England: What the English Church Census Reveals* (1991), 48–50.

10. D. Sheppard, *Built as a City: God and the Urban World Today* (1974), 39.

11. N. Aston, 'Moore, John (bap. 1730, d.1805)', *Oxford Dictionary of National Biography* (2008).

12. Cf. R. Strong, *Anglicanism and the British Empire, c.1700–1850* (2007); N. Etherington, *Missions and Empire* (2005).

13. C. Peach, *The Caribbean in Europe* (1991), cited in C. Taylor, 'British Churches and Jamaican Migration – A Study of Religion and Identities, 1948 to 1965', Anglia Ruskin University PhD thesis, 2002, 126.

14. C. Hill, *West Indian Migrants and the London Churches* (1963), cited in Taylor, 140.

15. Taylor, 190.

16. E. Kaufmann, 'The Demography of Religion in London since 1980', in D. Goodhew & A.-P. Cooper (eds.), *The Desecularisation of the City: London's Churches, 1980 to the Present* (2019), 51.

17. Cf. K. A. Thompson, *Bureaucracy and Church Reform: The Organizational Response of the Church of England to Social Change 1800–1965* (1970); also, G. R. Evans & M. Percy (eds.), *Managing the Church? Order and Organization in a Secular Age* (2000).

18. L. Paul, *The Deployment and Payment of the Clergy* (1964), 210–14.

19. Archbishops' Commission on the Organisation of the Church of England, *Working as One Body* (1995), 39.

20. A. G. Hebert, *Liturgy and Society: The Function of the Church in the Modern World* (1935); A. G. Hebert (ed.), *The Parish Communion* (1937); C. Irvine, *Worship, Church and Society: An Exposition of the Work of Arthur Gabriel Hebert* (1993); D. Gray, *Earth and Altar: The Evolution of the Parish Communion in the Church of England to 1945* (1986).

21. Cf. R. C. D. Jasper, *The Development of the Anglican Liturgy, 1662–1980* (1989).

22. Cf. B. Heeney, *The Women's Movement in the Church of England, 1850–1930* (1988); S. Gill, *Women and the Church of England: From the Eighteenth Century to the Present* (1994); T. W. Jones, *Sexual Politics in the Church of England, 1857–1957* (2013), 93–130.

23. Cf. L. Delap, 'Conservative Values, Anglicans and the Gender Order in Inter-war Britain', in L. Beers & G. Thomas (eds.), *Brave New World: Imperial and Democratic Nation-building in Britain between the Wars* (2011), 149–68.

24. On implications for mission and empire, see E. E. Prevost, *The Communion of Women: Missions and Gender in Colonial Africa and the British Metropole* (2010).

25. S. Fletcher, *Maude Royden: A Life* (1989); S. Morgan, '"Sex and

Common-Sense": Maude Royden, Religion, and Modern Sexuality', *Journal of British Studies*, 52 (2013), 153–78.

26. Anon., *The Ordination of Women to the Priesthood: The Synod Debate* (1993).

27. Cf. I. Jones, *Women and Priesthood in the Church of England: Ten Years On* (2004); also, on role models, T. Beeson, *The Church's Other Half: Women's Ministry* (2011).

28. https://www.churchofengland.org/sites/default/files/2017–11/Ministry%20Statistics%202011_2.pdf, accessed July 2020

29. Cf. M. Grimley, 'Law, Morality and Secularisation: The Church of England and the Wolfenden Report, 1954–1967', *Journal of Ecclesiastical History*, 60 (2009), 725–41.

30. W. L. Sachs, *Homosexuality and the Crisis of Anglicanism* (2009).

31. House of Bishops, *Issues in Human Sexuality* (1991), para. 5.23.

32. J. John, *Permanent, Faithful, Stable: Christian Same-Sex Partnerships* (1993).

33. Cf. S. Bates, *A Church at War: Anglicans and Homosexuality* (2004).

34. Cf. E. R. Norman, *Anglican Difficulties: A New Syllabus of Errors* (2004); A. Nichols, *The Panther and the Hind: A Theological History of Anglicanism* (1993).

35. S. Brewitt-Taylor, *Christian Radicalism in the Church of England and the Invention of the British Sixties, 1957–1970* (2018).

36. Cf. Anon., *The Charismatic Movement in the Church of England* (1981).

37. A. Chapman, *Godly Ambition: John Stott and the Evangelical Movement* (2012), 95.

20. Postscript

1. Cf. S. W. Sykes, *The Integrity of Anglicanism* (1978); S. W. Sykes, *Unashamed Anglicanism* (1995).

2. https://www.bsa.natcen.ac.uk/media/39293/1_bsa36_religion.pdf

3. Ibid.

4. One helpful contribution is J. Fife & Gilo (eds.), *Letters to a Broken Church* (2019).

5. Verbatim transcripts are at: https://www.iicsa.org.uk/

6. D. MacCulloch, *All Things Made New: Writings on the Reformation* (2016), 361–2.

RECOMMENDED READING

Preface: The Real History of the Church of England
There are few modern one-volume surveys of the history of the Church of England – hence this book. Gerald Bray, *The History of Christianity in Britain and Ireland: From the First Century to the Twenty-First* (2021) is broader in scope and chronology than this book; so, too, is K. Hylson-Smith, *The Churches in England from Elizabeth I to Elizabeth II* (3 vols., 1997–9), in scope and in scale; and to a lesser extent D. Rosman, *The Evolution of the English Churches 1500–2000* (2003). The five-volume *Oxford History of Anglicanism* (2017–18), edited by Rowan Strong, is by far the best reference series introducing the history of the Church of England as well as that of the Anglican Communion at large. Individual volumes are referenced as appropriate in the footnotes here.

There is much useful material in various reference books on Anglicanism, including: S. Sykes, J. Booty and J. Knight (eds.), *The Study of Anglicanism* (3rd edn, 1998); I. S. Markham, J. B. Hawkins IV, J. Terry and L. N. Steffensen (eds.), *The Wiley-Blackwell Companion to the Anglican Communion* (2013); and M. D. Chapman, S. Clarke and M. Percy (eds.), *The Oxford Handbook of Anglican Studies* (2015). M. D. Chapman, *Anglican Theology* (2012) is the best short introduction to its subject, but useful, too, is B. Kaye, *An Introduction to World Anglicanism* (2008), and also the slightly older W. M. Jacob, *The Making of the Anglican Church Worldwide* (1997). The writings of Paul Avis on Anglicanism draw a great deal on history and are a vital overview of theological themes: see P. Avis, *Anglicanism and the Christian Church: Theological Resources in Historical Perspective* (new edn, 2002), and *The Identity of Anglicanism: Essentials of Anglican Ecclesiology* (2007). See also R. Williams, *Anglican Identities* (2004).

It is also important to mention here the *Oxford Dictionary of National Biography*, the growing number of original sources edited and published by the Church of England Record Society from 1994, and the published conference papers of the Ecclesiastical History Society, *Studies in Church History*, which have appeared regularly since 1964; all of these are immensely useful for anyone studying the history of the Church of England, and have been used for the present book.

1. Prelude: Catholic Centuries

N. G. Pounds, *A History of the English Parish: The Culture of Religion from Augustine to Victoria* (2000) is a solid overview. An indispensable source is the Venerable Bede, 'Ecclesiastical History of the English Nation', in Baedae, J. E. King (ed.), *Opera Historica*, I (1971), also available in various translations. A provocative thesis about Christianisation is A. Wessels, *Europe: Was It Ever Really Christian? The Interaction between Gospel and Culture* (1994). For the conversion of England and the Saxon Church, see: H. Mayr-Harting, *The Coming of Christianity to Anglo-Saxon England* (1972); P. Hunter Blair, *An Introduction to Anglo-Saxon England* (2nd edn, 1977); and J. Blair, *The Church in Anglo-Saxon Society* (2005). On the history and impact of the religious orders, see: J. E. Burton, *Monastic and Religious Orders in Britain, 1000–1300* (1994); S. Foot, *Monastic Life in Anglo-Saxon England, c. 600–900* (2006); but also the classic D. Knowles, *The Religious Orders in England* (2 vols., 1948–55). There is much on the Church and religion in standard medieval history text books, such as D. Carpenter, *The Penguin History of Britain: The Struggle for Mastery: Britain, 1066–1284* (2004), and M. Rubin, *The Hollow Crown: A History of Britain in the Late Middle Ages* (2006).

2. Reformation and Turmoil

For a massive but immensely readable survey helping to put the English Reformation in perspective, see D. MacCulloch, *Reformation: Europe's House Divided 1490–1700* (2003); shorter is P. Collinson, *The Reformation* (2003). There is a vast literature on the English Reformation. A. G. Dickens, *The English Reformation* (1964) was for long regarded as a standard account, but although still useful it has been overtaken by E. Duffy, *The Stripping of the Altars: Traditional Religion in England 1400–1580* (1992); and by P. Marshall, *Heretics and Believers: A History of the English Reformation* (2017). Outstanding as a short introduction is A. Ryrie, *The English Reformation: A Very Brief History* (2020).

Important perspectives on elements of the religious background are: P. Marshall, *Beliefs and the Dead in the Reformation England* (2002); R. Rex, *The Lollards* (2002); and E. Duffy, *Marking the Hours: English People and*

Their Prayers (2006). Accounts of the Henrician policy include R. Rex, *Henry VIII and the English Reformation* (new edn, 2006), and G.W. Bernard, *The King's Reformation: Henry VIII and the Remaking of the English Church* (2007). Edward VI's reign is covered in D. MacCulloch, *Tudor Church Militant: Edward VI and the Protestant Reformation* (1999). Biographies include D. MacCulloch, *Thomas Cranmer* (1996); J. J. Scarisbrick, *Henry VIII* (new edn, 1997); and D. MacCulloch, *Thomas Cromwell: A Life* (2018). There is a wealth of scholarship on the English liturgy, including: G. J. Cuming, *A History of Anglican Liturgy* (new edn, 1982) and *The Godly Order: Texts and Studies Relating to the Book of Common Prayer* (1983); and B. D. Spinks, *The Rise and Fall of the Incomparable Liturgy: The Book of Common Prayer, 1559–1906* (2017).

3. Reaction and Settlement

On Mary and her reign, see D. Loades, *Mary Tudor: A Life* (1989), and *The Reign of Mary Tudor: Politics, Government and Religion in England, 1553–8* (new edn, 1991); also, J. Loach, *Parliament and the Crown in the Reign of Mary Tudor* (1986); and E. Duffy, *Fires of Faith: Catholic England under Mary Tudor* (2009). Duffy provides the most up-to-date reassessment of the impact of the burnings, but to appreciate their propaganda value for Protestantism, it is important to read Foxe's Book of Martyrs; there are many selections, such as J. N. King (ed.,) *Foxe's Book of Martyrs: Select Narratives* (new edn, 2009), but the full text of various editions can be found at: https://www.johnfoxe.org/index.php?realm=textandgototyp e=andedition=1563andpageid=17.   On Elizabeth and her reign, see: W.T. MacCaffrey, *The Shaping of the Elizabethan Regime: Elizabethan Politics, 1558–1572* (1969); C. Haigh, *Elizabeth I* (1988); P. Collinson, *Elizabethan Essays* (1994); S. Alford, *The Early Elizabethan Polity: William Cecil and the British Succession Crisis, 1558–1569* (1998); D. Starkey, *Elizabeth: Apprenticeship* (2000); P. Collinson, *Elizabeth I* (2007).

On Puritanism, the work of Patrick Collinson remains authoritative; see P. Collinson, *English Puritanism* (1983), and *The Elizabethan Puritan Movement* (new edn, 1990). An essential study of the process of conforming is A. Walsham, *Church Papists: Catholicism, Conformity and Confessional Polemic in Early Modern England* (1993). On recusancy, see J. Bossy, *The English Catholic Community 1570–1850* (1975).

4. Revolution in the Parishes

E. Duffy, *The Stripping of the Altars: Traditional Religion in England 1400–1580*

(1992) is still the place to start in appreciating the impact of the Reformation on ordinary parishioners' religion, but see also, for a vivid local study, E. Duffy, *The Voices of Morebath: Reformation and Rebellion in an English Village* (2001). A good summary of the changes is R. Whiting, *The Reformation of the English Parish Church* (2010). A fascinating study that goes beyond the walls of the church to look at its geographical context is A. Walsham, *The Reformation of the Landscape: Religion, Identity, and Memory in Early Modern Britain and Ireland* (2011). Three books which are essential for understanding the new Protestant piety are: J. Maltby, *Prayer Book and People in Elizabethan and Early Stuart England* (1998); A. Hunt, *The Art of Hearing: English Preachers and their Audiences, 1590–1640* (2010); and A. Ryrie, *Being Protestant in Reformation Britain* (2013).

5. A Middle Way? The Invention of Anglicanism

For the *Book of Common Prayer*, see suggestions above for chapter 3; but also, A. Jacobs, *The Book of Common Prayer: A Biography* (2019). On the Thirty-nine Articles, see: O. O'Donovan, *On the Thirty-nine Articles: A Conversation with Tudor Christianity* (2nd edn, 2011); and the more recent M. Davie, *Our Inheritance of Faith: A Commentary on the Thirty-nine Articles* (2019).

There is relatively little recent scholarship on John Jewel, but see: W. M. Southgate, *John Jewel and the Problem of Doctrinal Authority* (1962); J. E. Booty, *John Jewel as Apologist of the Church of England* (1963); and the more sceptical G. W. Jenkins, *John Jewel and the English National Church: The Dilemmas of an Erastian Reformer* (2006). It is a quite different situation with Richard Hooker. For a modern biography, see P. Secor, *Richard Hooker: Prophet of Anglicanism* (1999). For an essential survey of the roots of Anglican moral theology up to and including Hooker, see P. Sedgwick, *The Origin of Anglican Moral Theology* (2019), and for an illuminating discussion of the changing reception of Hooker's ideas, D. MacCulloch, 'Richard Hooker's Reputation', in *All Things Made New: Writings on the Reformation* (2016), 279–320. Different interpretations are explored in: N. Atkinson, *Richard Hooker and the Authority of Scripture, Tradition and Reason: Reformed Theologian of the Church of England* (1997); N. Voak, *Richard Hooker and Reformed Theology: A Study of Reason, Will, and Grace* (2003); A. J. Joyce, *Richard Hooker and Anglican Moral Theology* (2012); and W. B. Littlejohn, *The Peril and Promise of Christian Liberty: Richard Hooker, the Puritans, and Protestant Political Theology* (2017).

6. The Road to Civil War

For the civil wars and Commonwealth there is a huge scholarly literature, in which religion features commonly as a main theme. Here are a few suggestions. Overviews include: J. Morrill, *The Nature of the English Revolution* (1993); R. Ashton, *Counter-Revolution: The Second Civil War and Its Origins, 1646–8* (1994); M. Kishlansky, *A Monarchy Transformed 1603–1714* (1997); A. Hughes, *The Causes of the English Civil War* (2nd edn, 1998); and N. Tyacke, *The English Revolution c.1590–1720: Politics, Religion and Communities* (2007). Specifically on the Church of England, see K. Fincham, *Prelate as Pastor: The Episcopate of James I* (1990); also, K. Fincham (ed.), *The Early Stuart Church, 1603–1642* (1993); A. Milton, *Catholic and Reformed: The Roman and Protestant Churches in English Protestant Thought, 1600–1640* (1995); C. Durston and J. Maltby, *Religion in Revolutionary England* (2006); and N. Tyacke and K. Fincham, *Altars Restored: The Changing Face of English Religious Worship, 1547–c.1700* (2007).

The significance of the 'Caroline' divines is emphasised in E. More and F. L. Cross, *Anglicanism: The Thought and Practice of the Church of England, Illustrated from the Religious Literature of the Seventeenth Century* (1951); and H. R. McAdoo, *The Spirit of Anglicanism: A Survey of Anglican Theological Method in the Seventeenth Century* (1965). A quite different perspective, highlighting the unrepresentative character of that version of Anglicanism is in J. Davies, *The Caroline Captivity of the Church: Charles I and the Remoulding of Anglicanism* (1992); and in K. Sharpe, *The Personal Rule of Charles I* (1992). An excellent essay on the religious ideals of Puritan or 'Godly' ministers in the civil war is E. Duffy, 'The Reformed Pastor in English Puritanism', in *Reformation Divided: Catholics, Protestants and the Conversion of England* (2017), 327–46. On the upsurge in radical and dissenting religion in the civil war and Commonwealth, see: C. Hill, *The World Turned Upside Down: Radical Ideas during the English Revolution* (1975); J. C. Davis, *Fear, Myth and History: The Ranters and the Historians* (1986); and A. Bradstock, *Radical Religion in Cromwell's England: A Concise History from the English Civil War to the End of the Commonwealth* (2011).

7. Restoration and Rebellion

A readable narrative is presented in T. Harris, *Restoration: Charles II and His Kingdoms, 1660–1685* (2005), and *Revolution: The Great Crisis of the British Monarchy, 1685–1720* (2006). For the events leading up to and including the 'Glorious Revolution', see P. Dillon, *The Last Revolution: 1688 and the Creation of the Modern World* (2006); and Tony Claydon, *William III and the*

Godly Revolution (1996). Tony Claydon's *Europe and the Making of England, 1660–1760* (2007) gives the important, broader context. The outstanding study of the Church under Charles II is J. Spurr, *The Restoration Church of England, 1646–1689* (1991); also G. Tapsell (ed.), *The Later Stuart Church, 1660–1714* (2012). S. Hampton, *Anti-Arminians: The Anglican Reformed Tradition from Charles II to George I* (2008) makes a strong case for the endurance of the 'Calvinist' tradition in the Church; but see also W. M. Spellman, *The Latitudinarians and the Church of England, 1660–1700* (1993), and A. Lacey, *The Cult of King Charles the Martyr* (2003). D. A. Spaeth, *The Church in an Age of Danger: Parson and Parishioners, 1660–1740* (2000) is a detailed and illuminating study of local church life. For a readable contemporary perspective from a Latitudinarian bishop, see G. Burnet, *History of His Own Times* (new edn, 1906).

8. The Great Churches

N. Orme, *The History of England's Cathedrals* (2017) is probably the best short, modern survey. More detail is presented in S. E. Lehmberg, *Cathedrals under Siege: Cathedrals in English Society, 1600–1700* (1996) and *English Cathedrals: A History* (2005). Mostly, however, these book are strongest on the early modern period; the modern history of English cathedrals and 'great' churches is still an under-researched area. One exception is P. Barrett, *Barchester: English Cathedral Life in the Nineteenth Century* (1993). Two books of essays edited by S. Platten and C. Lewis on the role of cathedrals in modern society are full of insight: *Flagships of the Spirit: Cathedrals in Society* (1998), and *Dreaming Spires? Cathedrals in a New Age* (2006). There is a brilliant historical chapter by Edward Norman in *Heritage and Renewal: The Report of the Archbishops' Commission on Cathedrals* (1994). Best of all, however, are the modern, scholarly individual cathedral and church histories. Some examples are: I. Atherton, E. Fernie, C. Harper-Bill, and H. Smith (eds.), *Norwich Cathedral: Church, City and Diocese, 1096–1996* (1996); P. Meadows and N. Ramsay (eds.), *A History of Ely Cathedral* (2003); D. Keene, A. Burns and A. Saint (eds.), *St Paul's: The Cathedral Church of London 604–2004* (2004); P. Linehan (ed.), *St John's College: A History* (2011); J. M. Massing and N. Zeeman (eds.), *King's College Chapel 1515–2015: Art, Music and Religion in Cambridge* (2014); and J. Gregory (ed.), *Manchester Cathedral; A History of the Collegiate Church and Cathedral, 1421 to the Present* (2022).

9. Consolidation and Conformity: The Long Eighteenth Century

There has been a revolution in our understanding of the eighteenth-century Church in the last three decades. P. Virgin, *The Church in an Age of Negligence: Ecclesiastical Structure and Problems of Church Reform, 1700 –1840* (1989) presented much new data, although it retained an overall pessimistic reading. But quite different were: J. Walsh, C. Haydon and S. Taylor (eds.), *The Church of England, c.1689–c.1833: From Toleration to Tractarianism* (1993); W. Jacob, *Lay People and Religion in the Early Eighteenth Century* (1996); and W. Gibson, *The Church of England 1688–1832: Unity and Accord* (2001).

The controversy over nationalism and religion is captured in: L. Colley, *Britons: Forging the Nation, 1707–1837* (1992); D. Hempton, *Religion and Political Culture in Britain and Ireland: From the Glorious Revolution to the Decline of Empire* (1996); and A. Claydon and I. McBride (eds.), *Protestantism and National Identity: Britain and Ireland, c.1650–c.1850* (1998). A. Starkie, *The Church of England and the Bangorian Controversy, 1716–1721* (2007) is an excellent study of one of the greatest internal church conflicts of the period. A. Whiteman and M. Clapinson (eds.), *The Compton Census of 1676: A Critical Edition* (1986) gives a picture of Church strength at the outset of the period. Local studies include J. S. Chamberlain, *Accommodating High Churchmen: The Clergy of Sussex, 1700–1745* (1997); J. Gregory, *Restoration, Reformation and Reform, 1660–1828: Archbishops of Canterbury and Their Diocese* (2000); and J. Gregory and J. S. Chamberlain (eds.), *The National Church in Regional Perspective: The Church of England and the Regions, 1660–1800* (2003).

Religious thought is well served by an extensive literature. A Europe-wide overview of the Enlightenment is J. Byrne, *Glory, Jest and Riddle: Religious Thought in the Enlightenment* (1996). See also the groundbreaking work in: B. W. Young, *Religion and Enlightenment in Eighteenth-century England: Theological Debate from Locke to Burke* (1998); J. G. A. Pocock, *Barbarism and Religion, I: The Enlightenments of Edward Gibbon, 1737–1764* (1999); and J. Shaw, *Miracles in Enlightenment England* (2006). An antidote, looking at popular religion, is J. F. C. Harrison, *The Second Coming: Popular Millenarianism 1780–1850* (1979).

10. The Evangelical Revival

English Evangelicalism has been exceptionally well served by outstanding historians in the last thirty years or so. An influential early essay was J. Walsh, 'The Origins of the Evangelical Revival', in G. V. Bennett and

J. D. Walsh (eds.), *Essays in Modern English Church History* (1966), 140–53.
W. R. Ward placed Evangelicalism in its wider European context in *The Protestant Evangelical Awakening* (1992) and *Early Evangelicalism: A Global Intellectual History, 1670–1789* (2006). The most influential general account remains D. Bebbington, *Evangelicalism in Modern Britain: A History from the 1730s to the 1980s* (new edn, 2005). But two volumes in the IVP History of Evangelicalism series are also excellent: M. Noll, *The Rise of Evangelicalism: The Age of Edwards, Whitefield and the Wesleys* (2003), and J. Wolffe, *The Expansion of Evangelicalism: The Age of Wilberforce, More, Chalmers and Finney* (2006). Other excellent studies are: B. Hindmarsh, *The Evangelical Conversion Narrative: Spiritual Autobiography in Early Modern England* (2007); J. Coffey (ed.), *Heart religion: Evangelical Piety in England and Ireland, 1690–1850* (2016).

On Methodism, the best overall account is D. Hempton, *Methodism: Empire of the Spirit* (2005), and the best biography of Wesley remains H. D. Rack, *Reasonable Enthusiast: John Wesley and the Rise of Methodism* (1989). On Whitefield, see H. S. Stout, *The Divine Dramatist: George Whitefield and the Rise of Modern Evangelicalism* (1991). A somewhat iconoclastic view is J. Kent, *Wesley and the Wesleyans: Religion in Eighteenth-Century Britain* (2002). S. Hampton, *Anti-Arminians: The Anglican Reformed Tradition from Charles II to George I* (2008) is an important corrective to common ideas about the disappearance of the 'Puritan' tradition from the Church of England. On Anglican Evangelicalism after the Methodist schism, see: B. Hindmarsh, *John Newton and the English Evangelical Tradition: Between the Conversions of Wesley and Wilberforce* (new edn, 2001); A. Stott, *Hannah More: The First Victorian* (2003); and G. Atkins, *Converting Britannia: Evangelicals and Public Life, 1770–1840* (2019). On Evangelicalism and abolitionism, see R. Anstey, *The Atlantic Slave Trade and British Abolition, 1760–1810* (1975).

11. The Fortunes of Clergy: From Patronage to Piety

The best introduction to the lives of the clergy in the past are the diaries and letters some of them produced, including those by James Woodforde, William Holland, Benjamin Armstrong and Francis Kilvert: publication details are in the end notes. There is no one, overarching modern interpretation or survey. An early and still valuable study is D. McClatchey, *Oxfordshire Clergy, 1777–1869: A Study of the Established Church and of the Role of Its Clergy in Local Society* (1960). B. Heeney, *A Different Kind of Gentleman: Parish Clergy as Professional Men in Early and*

Mid-Victorian England (1976), and A. Russell, *The Clerical Profession* (1980) are two influential studies deploying the idea of 'professionalisation'. But for three key modern research monographs, see: A. Haig, *The Victorian Clergy* (1984); W. M. Jacob, *The Clerical Profession in the Long Eighteenth Century, 1680–1840* (2007); and S. Slinn, *The Education of the Anglican Clergy, 1780–1839* (2017). A longitudinal study of a specialised clerical position is W. Gibson, *A Social History of the Domestic Chaplain, 1530–1840* (1997).

12. The Crisis and Reform of the Confessional State
S. J. Brown, *The National Churches of England, Ireland and Scotland 1801–46* (2001) is a brilliant overall assessment. For Anglican political theology on the eve of reform, see J. C. D. Clark, *English Society 1688–1832: Religion, Ideology and Politics during the Ancien Regime* (new edn, 2000). Biographies of two of the leading clerics in the period of reform are M. Johnson, *Bustling Intermeddler? The Life and Work of Charles James Blomfield* (2001), and J. Garrard, *Archbishop Howley, 1828–1848* (2015). See also R. Brent, *Liberal Anglican Politics: Whiggery, Religion, and Reform, 1830–1841* (1987). The mechanics and impact of reform are extensively covered in: G. F. A. Best, *Temporal Pillars: Queen Anne's Bounty, the Ecclesiastical Commissioners and the Church of England* (1964); F. Knight, *The Nineteenth-century Church and English Society* (1995); and R. A. Burns, *The Diocesan Revival in the Church of England c.1800–1870* (1999). W. H. Mackintosh, *Disestablishment and Liberation: The Movement for Separation of the Anglican Church from State Control* (1972) is important for the arguments against establishment. Local studies looking at church reform include J. N. Morris, *Religion and Urban Change: Croydon 1840–1914* (1992), M. Austin, *A Stage or Two beyond Christendom: A Social History of the Church of England in Derbyshire* (2001), and G. Williams, W. Jacob, N. Yates and F. Knight, *The Welsh Church from Reformation to Disestablishment, 1603–1920* (2007).

13. The High Church Revival
Two important, near-contemporary accounts of the Oxford Movement are J. H. Newman, *Apologia Pro Vita Sua* (1864; new edn, 1905), and R. W. Church, *The Oxford Movement: Twelve Years: 1833–1845* ((1890; new edn, 1970). Modern scholarship is at its best in: G. Rowell, *The Vision Glorious: Themes and Personalities of the Catholic Revival in Anglicanism* (1983); P. B. Nockles, *The Oxford Movement in Context: Anglican High Churchmanship 1760–1857* (1994); S. Skinner, *Tractarians and the 'Condition of England': The Social and Political Thought of the Oxford Movement* (2004); and G. Herring,

The Oxford Movement in Practice: The Tractarian Parochial Worlds from the 1830s to the 1870s (2016).

A readable survey which goes into Ritualism is J. S. Reed, *Glorious Battle: The Cultural Politics of Victorian Anglo-Catholicism* (1998); see also N. Yates, *Anglican Ritualism in Victorian Britain 1830–1910* (1999), and J. N. Morris, *The High Church Revival in the Church of England: Arguments and Identities* (2016). On the revived monasticism, see A. M. Allchin, *The Silent Rebellion: Anglican Religious Communities, 1845–1900* (1958). Liturgy and architecture are covered in J. F. White, *The Cambridge Movement: The Ecclesiologists and the Gothic Ideal* (1962), and W. N. Yates, *Buildings, Faith and Worship: The Liturgical Arrangement of Anglican Churches, 1600–1900* (new edn, 2000). On specific figures, see: I. Ker, *John Henry Newman* (1988); S. Gilley, *Newman and His Age* (1990); K. Blair (ed.), *John Keble in Context* (2004); and R. Strong and C. Engelhardt Herringer (eds.), *Edward Bouverie Pusey and the Oxford Movement* (2012).

14. Where Choirs Sing: Anglicanism's Cultural Experiment

Good introductions include: E. Routley, *A Short History of English Church Music* (1977); N. Temperley, *The Music of the English Parish Church* (2 vols., 1979); A. Gant, *O Sing unto the Lord: A History of English Church Music* (2015); and, more quirky, T. Day, *I Saw Eternity the Other Night: King's College Choir, the Nine Lessons and Carols, and an English Singing Style* (2018). On the post-Reformation situation, see C. Dearnley, *English Church Music, 1650–1750: In Royal Chapel, Cathedral and Parish Church* (1970). See C. Turner (ed.), *The Gallery Tradition: Aspects of Georgian Psalmody* (1997) for what was sung locally before the nineteenth century. Specifically on the Anglican choral revival, see: A. Hutchings, *Church Music in the Nineteenth Century* (1967); B. Rainbow, *The Choral Revival in the Anglican Church 1839–1872* (1970); and B. Zon, *The English Plainchant Revival* (1999). E. Routley, *Twentieth-Century Church Music* (1964) covers the first half of the twentieth century. Biographies include: P. Charlton, *John Stainer and the Musical Life of Victorian Britain* (1984); W. Shaw (ed.), *Sir Frederick Ouseley and St Michael's Tenbury: A Chapter in the History of English Church Music and Ecclesiology* (1988); and J. Dibble, *Charles Villiers Stanford: Man and Musician* (2002).

15. Liberalism

Three general surveys of Victorian religious thought have a great deal of material on Anglican Liberalism: B. Reardon, *Religious Thought in the Victorian Age: A Survey from Coleridge to Gore* (new edn, 1980); P. B. Hinchliff, *God and History: Aspects of British Theology 1875–1914* (1992); and J. C. Livingston, *Religious Thought in the Victorian Age* (2006). So does the more specialised T. E. Jones, *The Broad Church: A Biography of a Movement* (2003), and A. Symondson (ed.), *The Victorian Crisis of Faith* (1970); but see also T. Larsen, *Crisis of Doubt: Honest Faith in Nineteenth-Century England* (2006) for a refreshing corrective to conventional ideas of the journey from faith to doubt. Specific issues and perspectives are dealt with in D. G. Rowell, *Hell and the Victorians: A Study of the Nineteenth-Century Theological Controversies Concerning Eternal Punishment and the Future Life* (1974); A. M. G. Stephenson, *The Rise and Decline of English Modernism* (1984); I. Ellis, *Seven Against Christ: A Study of* Essays and Reviews (1980); M. D. Chapman, *The Coming Crisis: The Impact of Eschatology on Theology in Edwardian England* (2001); and D. M. Thompson, *Cambridge Theology in the Nineteenth Century: Enquiry, Controversy and Truth* (2008). See also the following studies of individual theologians: P. B. Hinchliff, *John William Colenso, Bishop of Natal* (1964); B. Colloms, *Charles Kingsley: The Lion of Eversley* (1975); P. B. Hinchliff, *Benjamin Jowett and the Christian Religion* (1987); J. Morris, *F. D. Maurice and the Crisis of Christian Authority* (2005); and J. Witheridge, *Excellent Dr Stanley: The Life of Dean Stanley of Westminster* (2013).

16. The Church in Industrial Society

Two early studies which saw the Church of England generally in the industrial era as a failure were E. R. Wickham, *Church and People in an Industrial City* (1957), and K. S. Inglis, *Churches and the Working Classes in Victorian England* (1963). Thereafter the growing trend was away from this pessimism. Key works on religious statistics are: R. Currie, A. D. Gilbert and L. Horsley, *Churches and Churchgoers: Patterns of Church Growth in the British Isles since 1700* (1977); B. I. Coleman, *The Church of England in the Mid-Nineteenth Century: A Social Geography* (1980); K. D. M. Snell and P. S. Ell, *Rival Jerusalems: The Geography of Victorian Religion* (2000); and C. D. Field, *Periodizing Secularization: Religious Allegiance and Attendance in Britain, 1880–1945* (2019).

Modern reassessment really began with D. H. McLeod, *Class and Religion in the Late Victorian City* (1974), followed by: A. D. Gilbert, *Religion and Society in Industrial England: Church, Chapel and Social Change 1740–1914* (1976); D. H. McLeod, *Religion and Society in England, 1850–1914* (1996); and C. G. Brown, *The Death of Christian Britain: Understanding Secularisation*

1800–2000 (new edn, 2009). Local studies have been important in this new understanding, including: J. Cox, *English Churches in a Secular Society: Lambeth 1870–1930* (1982); M. A. Smith, *Religion in Industrial Society: Oldham and Saddleworth 1740–1865* (1994); S. J. D. Green, *Religion in the Age of Decline: Organisation and Experience in Industrial Yorkshire 1870–1920* (1996); S. C. Williams, *Religious Belief and Popular Culture in Southwark, c. 1880–1939* (1999); and P. Midgley, *The Churches and the Working Classes: Leeds, 1870–1920* (2012). For a transnational view, see D. Hempton and D. H. McLeod (eds.), *Secularization and Religious Innovation in the North Atlantic World* (2017). A specific study of an innovative movement is N. Scotland, *Squires in the Slums: Settlements and Missions in Late Victorian Britain* (2007).

17. The Reshaping of the Victorian and Edwardian Church: Bureaucracy and Tradition

There is a significant lack of a thorough, critical survey of the Church reforms of the late nineteenth and twentieth centuries, with the exception of the sociological, schematic K. A. Thompson, *Bureaucracy and Church Reform: The Organizational Response of the Church of England to Social Change 1800–1965* (1970). But there is much useful material in G. F. A. Best, *Temporal Pillars: Queen Anne's Bounty, the Ecclesiastical Commissioners and the Church of England* (1964), and in W. O. Chadwick, *The Victorian Church* (2 vols., 1966–70). Two broader-than-Anglican surveys are also good: A. Hastings, *A History of English Christianity 1920–1985* (1987), and K. Robbins, *England, Ireland, Scotland, Wales: The Christian Church 1900–2000* (2008).

For an outstanding study of the complexities of the period, see F. Knight, *Victorian Christianity at the Fin de Siècle: The Culture of English Religion in a Decadent Age* (2016). See also B. Kilcrease, *The Great Church Crisis and the End of English Erastianism, 1898–1906* (2017), and M. Wellings, *Evangelicals Embattled: Responses of Evangelicals in the Church of England to Ritualism, Darwinism and Theological Liberalism 1890–1930* (2003). On the Church in Wales and disestablishment, see: C. Harris and R. Startup, *The Church in Wales: The Sociology of a Traditional Institution* (1999); D. D. Morgan, *The Span of the Cross: Christian Religion and Society in Wales 1914–2000* (1999); and G. Williams, W. M. Jacob, N. Yates and F. Knight, *The Welsh Church from Reformation to Disestablishment 1603–1920* (2007). The changing landscape of theological education is an important dimension: see D. Inman, *The Making of Modern English Theology: God and the*

Academy at Oxford 1833–1945 (2014); and D. A. Dowland, *Nineteenth-Century Anglican Theological Training: The Redbrick Challenge* (1997).

18. The Church in a Century of Conflict

Two readable and insightful books which take a largely negative view of the Church of England in the First World War are A. Marrin, *The Last Crusade: The Church of England in the First World War* (1974), and A. Wilkinson, *The Church of England and the First World War* (1978). A much more positive view has emerged in recent scholarship, epitomised by M. Snape, *God and the British Soldier: Religion and the British Army in the First and Second World Wars* (2005), and also *The Royal Army Chaplains' Department 1796–1953: Clergy Under Fire* (2008). An excellent local study is R. Beaken, *The Church of England and the Home Front 1914–1918: Civilians, Soldiers and Religion in Wartime Colchester* (2015). J. Winter, *Sites of Memory, Sites of Mourning: The Great War in European Cultural History* (1996) touches on long-term matters of memorialisation.

On the 1920s and 1930s, as well as books recommended for earlier chapters, see: R. Lloyd, *The Church of England in the Twentieth Century* (2 vols., 1946); J. Kent, *William Temple: Church, State and Society in Britain, 1880–1950* (1992); M. Grimley, *Citizenship, Community and the Church of England. Liberal Anglican Theories of the State between the Wars* (2004); J. Maiden, *National Religion and the Prayer Book Controversy, 1927–1928* (2009); and R. Beaken, *Cosmo Lang: Archbishop in War and Crisis* (2012).

Changing theological trends between the wars can be gleaned from: A. M. Ramsey, *From Gore to Temple. The Development of Anglican Theology between Lux Mundi and the Second World War 1889–1939* (1960); A. P. F. Sell, *Philosophical Idealism and Christian Belief* (1995); and T. M. Gouldstone, *The Rise and Decline of Anglican Idealism in the Nineteenth Century* (2005). The continuing vitality of the Church of England is stressed in R.A. Walford, *The Growth of 'New London' in Suburban Middlesex (1918–1945) and the Response of the Church of England* (2007).

The scholarship is thinner on the Church and the Second World War, but see essays in S. G. Parker and T. Lawson (eds.), *God and War: The Church of England and Armed Conflict in the Twentieth Century* (2013), and also, on the outstanding Anglican bishop of the war, A. Chandler, *George Bell, Bishop of Chichester: Church, State, and Resistance in the Age of Dictatorship* (2016). Post-war reorganisation and recovery can be studied in: A. Chandler, *The Church of England in the Twentieth Century: The Church Commissioners and the Politics of Reform, 1948–1998* (2006); I. Jones, *The*

Local Church and Generational Change in Birmingham 1945–2000 (2012); and
C. D. Field, *Britain's Last Religious Revival? Quantifying Belonging, Behaving
and Believing in the Long 1950s* (2015).

19. Decline? The Religious 'Crisis' of the 1960s and Later

In addition to Hastings and Robbins, mentioned above, chapter 17, P.
Welsby, *A History of the Church of England 1945–1980* (1984) is also useful.
On the 1960s and 1970s, the key books are: C. G. Brown, *The Death of
Christian Britain: Understanding Secularisation 1800–2000* (new edn, 2009);
D. H. McLeod, *The Religious Crisis of the 1960s* (2010); and C. Field,
Secularization in the Long 1960s: Numerating Religion in Britain (2017). S. Bre-
witt-Taylor, *Christian Radicalism in the Church of England and the Invention
of the British Sixties, 1957–1970* (2018) is an important corrective to some of
the more sweeping generalisations.

C. G. Brown, *Religion and Society in Twentieth-Century Britain* (2006)
and T. Rodger, P. Williamson and M. Grimley (eds.), *The Church of
England and British Politics since 1900* (2020) offer important broader perspectives. D. Goodhew and A-P. Cooper (eds.), *The Desecularisation of
the City: London's Churches, 1980 to the Present* (2019) represents a spirited
attempt to see a different side to recent claims of decline. R. C. D. Jasper,
The Development of the Anglican Liturgy 1662–1980 (1989) covers liturgical
change.

On the movement for the ordination of women, see: B. Heeney, *The
Women's Movement in the Church of England 1850–1930* (1988); S. Gill, *Women
and the Church of England: From the Eighteenth Century to the Present* (1994);
I. Jones, *Women and Priesthood in the Church of England: Ten Years On*
(2004); also, on role models, T. Beeson, *The Church's Other Half: Women's
Ministry* (2011). Strictly out of sequence here, but important as a recent
contribution on the earlier history is T. W. Jones, *Sexual Politics in the
Church of England 1857–1957* (2013). Two useful studies on the arguments
about human sexuality in Anglicanism are: S. Bates, *A Church at War:
Anglicans and Homosexuality* (2004); and W. L. Sachs, *Homosexuality and
the Crisis of Anglicanism* (2009). Politics and the Church are covered to
some extent in Liza Filby, *God and Mrs Thatcher: Religion and Politics in
1980s Britain* (2010), and M. D. Chapman, *Doing God: Religion and Public
Policy in Brown's Britain* (2008).

Some important biographies are: E. James, *A Life of Bishop John Robinson: Scholar, Pastor, Prophet* (1987); W. O. Chadwick, *Michael Ramsey: A
Life* (1990); R. Shortt, *Rowan's Rule: The Biography of the Archbishop* (2008);

and A. Chapman, *Godly Ambition: John Stott and the Evangelical Movement* (2012).

Finally, vastly different but stimulating contemporary outlooks are reflected in R. Scruton, *Our Church: A Personal History of the Church of England* (2012), and A. Brown and L. Woodhead, *That Was the Church That Was: How the Church of England Lost the English People* (2016).

LIST OF ILLUSTRATIONS

INDEX